ACKNOWLEDGMENTS

There are a number of people who made the completion of this book possible. We would like to thank them for their unique contributions.

Judy Semler, our agent, who understood our project and was tenacious in helping us bring it to fruition.

Jeff Krames, our editor, whose energy, vision, and sense of humor made doing business fun.

The many professionals who shared their experiences and knowledge about diversity so that others might learn and benefit.

Jeanne Hartley, Catherine Lawrence and Newton Margulies, Ph.D., valued colleagues whose feedback strengthened the book.

Donna Crawford-Smith, respected peer and editorial consultant who gently and meticulously combed over this manuscript and whose on-target comments helped us refine it.

Judy Rosener, Ph.D., friend, colleague, confidante and mentor, whose ideas and suggestions spark our mind and whose love and support touch our hearts.

Jorge Cherbosque, Ph.D., a magnanimous spirit and loving friend whose tricultural perspective and insightful comments were instructive.

Art Ojena, a respected and experienced human resource professional whose practical comments and resources so freely shared helped us tighten and clarify our manuscript.

Bill Johnston, Ph.D., and Francine Gray, Ph.D., kind friends whose generous hospitality gave us hideaways in which to write.

Ron Matheson, whose trustworthiness and competence exceed our already high expectations and whose computer expertise was invaluable.

Marco and Petra Sabovich, my parents, who gave me a foundation of love and strong values and who taught me to love, respect, and enjoy the richness of both my American and Serbian cultures.

Rosyne, my mother, and the memory of my father, Nathan, who raised me with pride in my heritage and a clear sense of my American Jewish identity. You continue to model an open mind and a loving heart.

My family—the "bloodline," the "platelets," and my diverse band of incredible nieces and nephews who continuously add spice, love, and meaning to my life.

Ann Petty, Ph.D., whose constant support and encouragement over 30 years make her one of our primary pillars.

Darrell, who through all his own difficulties, has been able to be there for me with love, support, and humor.

Lee Gardenswartz
Anita Rowe

v

CONTENTS IN BRIEF

CONTENTS

ACTIVITIES, WORKSHEETS, AND CHARTS

Section I

MAKING DIVERSITY WORK: THE WHAT AND HOW FOR MANAGERS AND TRAINERS

Chapter 1

Making This Book Work for You

This chapter will give you:
1. An overview of *Managing Diversity*.
   a. Who it is for.
   b. What is in it.
   c. How to use it.
2. A road map for using each of the sections.
3. A brief explanation of each of the chapters.

This generation of Americans has a rendezvous with destiny.

Franklin Delano Roosevelt

President Roosevelt's words, spoken to an earlier generation facing a different challenge, are just as true today as they were a half century ago. The fundamental demographic shifts that are changing the face and fabric of America are presenting American business leaders with choices that will set the course for our future well into the next century.

The startling and sobering statistics of the much discussed Hudson Institute report *Workforce 2000* stripped away the last vestiges of denial from corporate America in 1987. No longer can business leaders pretend not to see what is happening around them. On the shop floor and in office cubicles, in hospital wards and at drafting tables, at gas stations and in convenience stores, in fact everywhere but in the executive suite, things are changing. Women, people of color, individuals with physical limitations, and immigrants are becoming more the norm than the exception. No more can we think of ourselves as a predominantly white, Anglo-Saxon, Protestant nation. Our identity as a nation is changing, and Americanization itself is going through a transformation. The metaphorical melting pot is currently and more accurately described as a salad bowl. Individuals from diverse groups are less willing to shed their rich cultural identities as the price for belonging. Rather, they seek an America large hearted enough to accommodate the cultures of their disparate roots while they simultaneously adopt norms of mainstream culture.

This change from traditional assimilation to bicultural juggling has significantly impacted American business. Individuals who find value in their uniqueness are less willing to adapt to the dominant white male model of behavior in order to succeed. As workers from different racial, cultural, and ethnic backgrounds—as well as disabled, gay, and lesbian individuals—enter the workplace with increased strength, both in numbers and in feelings of worth, they are demanding that their realities be given credence, that their needs be addressed, and that their approaches be added to the pool of acceptable alternatives.

While this diversity brings stimulation, challenge, and energy, it does not always lead to harmony. The mix of cultures, genders, life-styles, and values often becomes a source of misunderstanding and conflict. Many enlightened managers, from CEOs in the executive suite to supervisors on the shop floor, want to create an environment where differences are valued and where people who look, talk, and think differently can work productively together. However, the knowledge and skills to do so are not part of most managers' experience. Like explorers in a new land, they are entering uncharted areas. Old methods fall short, and new ones have yet to be developed. Existing mind-sets are limiting, yet new paradigms have not come into focus. Long-held assumptions are no longer in sync with today's reality, and new truths are yet to be determined.

The task is daunting, the challenge formidable, the stakes enormous. Something new is being attempted in human history. Milton J. Bennett, a cross-cultural specialist, states,

> Intercultural sensitivity is not natural. It is not part of our primate past, nor has it characterized most of human history. Cross-cultural contact often has been accompanied by bloodshed, oppression, or genocide. Clearly this pattern cannot continue. Today, the failure to exercise intercultural sensitivity is not simply bad business or bad morality—it is self-destructive. So we face a choice: overcome the legacy of our history, or lose history itself for all time.[5]

Those who work in the diverse environment of American business today and readily accept Bennett's challenge are the new pioneers. This book is designed for those of you who spend much of your lives in organizations across this country and who are willing to overcome the legacy of human history by creating prosperous, positive, and productive organizations.

Whom This Book Is For

Managing Diversity can help you if you are one of the following:

A **manager** who sees the effects of diversity from the trenches. It has never been easy to deal with motivation, productivity, and morale, but the challenges facing the manager of today's diverse work force are monumental. The old tried-and-true techniques don't seem to work any longer. Dealing with work group issues and conflicts that are rooted in cultures, values, or languages different from those found in mainstream American business requires new skills, knowledge, and techniques. *Managing Diversity* can help you develop these skills and build a cohesive group when personal and cultural differences are getting in the way.

A **human resource (HR) professional** charged with the responsibility of managing the changing work force, recruiting staff to achieve a more diverse employee base, or opening up the promotional system to increase diversity at the top. Beyond managing change and attracting unique talent among the diverse population, this book is helpful to HR professionals concerned with systemwide strategies regarding career development, benefit packages, and accountability systems. It can also be an aid in discovering how diversity may be at the core of grievances, feelings of isolation, and repeated bouts of frustration that some employees experience because the organization seems unyielding, unwelcoming, inflexible, and exclusive.

A **trainer** who conducts seminars or workshops that offer knowledge, awareness, and skills regarding managing a diverse work force. This book presents content information for lecturettes about changing demographics and different cultural norms, as well as guidelines for dealing with specific issues. In addition, training activities, worksheets, and inventories are given in a ready-to-use format, along with directions for their use. Finally, the book offers information that can help the trainer design sessions that are effective with trainees from different backgrounds. Old training tools may not work as well in classes of diverse staff who have been reared on different teaching methods, often more pedantic and less participatory, more rote and less experiential. Training participants with limited English language skills poses new challenges, and suggestions are given for designing materials that are appropriate for all participants with multiple languages and various levels of educational sophistication.

An **internal** or **external consultant** leading an organization, division, or work group through the change process from monocultural to multicultural. Conducting a diversity audit may help determine where the problem areas might be. However, all the work might not be diagnostic. If a survey indicates a need for training to increase awareness, information, or skill building, this book offers the consultant that information as well. Whether the consultant teaches managers how to build more cohesive work teams or run better meetings, the necessary information and tools are there for immediate use.

A **facilitator** who works with groups to help them identify and solve diversity-related problems and build individual and group skills. A facilitator can make use of the tools offered in any chapter but would benefit greatly from the material on running effective meetings. There are clear guidelines for designing processes that involve participants from diverse backgrounds as well.

An **affirmative action officer** looking for tools and information to help managers create, one on one, a more open and diversity-friendly climate.

A **CEO** or **president** who understands that effectively utilizing the changing work force is part of the equation in being a profitable, successful organization. This is for the organizational leader who sees himself or herself as the person setting strategy, leading the change process, and determining both how to utilize the work force effectively and what policies and practices pose barriers to creating a more inclusive organization. It is also for a CEO or president who knows the importance of clearly communicating the message that managers will be held accountable for implementing changes that open up the organization. Finally, this book is for the CEO who knows the value of winning in the marketplace by attracting the best and the brightest, and by creating an organizational culture that is welcoming to both employees and consumers. The leadership of the CEO in capitalizing on diversity is all-important and will impact employee productivity, creativity, commitment, and ultimately, profitability. This book serves as a tool that these leaders can provide to staff members who have the responsibility of implementing a CEO's vision.

How to Use This Book

This book can be useful in a number of ways. It gives both a macro and a micro view of diversity. Which view you choose to focus on at a given time depends on the objectives and needs you have in your organization. In either case, by scanning the three sections and becoming familiar with the distinct contributions each makes before you actually read the whole book, you will get a sense of the scope of *Managing Diversity*'s content.

Section I is intended for practitioners who are dealing with the nitty-gritty issues that emerge when diverse people come together in the workplace. This section is full of ready-to-use tools that can be used as is or adapted by managers and trainers for use with individuals, work groups, or training session participants. Each tool is easily reproducible and ready for distribution to participants/employees. All training tools and inventories are accompanied by a guide with directions for how to use them. In addition to finding hands-on materials, you will also find suggestions for dealing with specific diversity-related problems you may be encountering, such as when to use an interpreter, how to solve culture-related conflicts, or what techniques to use in building cohesive work teams amid group members with different cultural practices and values.

The information in Section I will be most helpful if you start with Chapter 2, on culture, and then continue to read the remaining chapters in Section I in sequence. For example, while you may want to find out how to get more employee participation in performance reviews, it is important to first understand cultural variables and communication techniques that impact working with diverse employees. If you have a fragmented work team, we suggest you understand the cultural influences on those team members and possible explanations for their reactions to one another before trying to build a more cohesive team. Again, reading Chapters

2 and 3 before you dive into team-building activities would provide that important background. This section is designed to be used often, and we hope you will make repeated visits to the specific information you seek on an as-needed basis.

Section II provides the macro view for change agents and those in charge of strategic planning. The information in this section can help you modify existing organizational systems to remove the barriers that prevent your organization from capitalizing on diversity. Chapter 8 presents audit tools that can pinpoint the organizational Achilles' heels, while other chapters can offer suggestions about redesigning systems to be more inclusive. For example, if your recruiting efforts for women and people of color are good but your retention isn't, the information on mentoring and career development in Chapter 10 will be useful. While you're looking at retention issues, you may also decide that the organizational climate needs a little scrutiny. Chapter 7, on corporate culture, will give you tools to assess how inviting and responsive your organization's climate is to someone who is neither white nor male. Examples of organizations that are successfully adapting to change offer both food for thought and hope. If you're not the major power wielder in your company and you lack the clout to be the major catalyst in changing the systems, Section II can give you information to make your case and build support among those who do have the influence to make the necessary changes.

Section III offers reference material that explains the demographics in the changing work force and clarifies the difference between managing diversity and previous antidiscriminatory policies. It also gives you a host of other resources that can provide more information for further research. In Chapter 13, books, videos, newsletters, associations, and training materials in the form of games, simulations, and questionnaires are annotated and listed with information that tells you how to get hold of the material you are seeking. Beyond this reference material, the background information that helps trainers become quickly knowledgeable and conversant in diversity-related topics is easily accessible. If you need to make a 30-minute presentation to upper management about the differences between EEO, affirmative action, and managing diversity, Chapter 12 contains a succinct chart offering comparisons between the three to make your task easy. If an HR professional wants to suggest that an organization invest already tight resources on diversity-related issues, Chapter 11 contains data to help build the case. If a manager wants to find out more about a specific culture from which many of his or her employees come, resources indicating where you can get such information are also suggested in Section III.

What's in This Book

The following information will give you a chapter-by-chapter overview. Additionally, specific objectives are listed at the beginning of each chapter.

Section I—Making Diversity Work: The What and How for Managers and Trainers

Chapter 1, Making This Book Work for You, functions as a guide that tells you how to use *Managing Diversity*. It explains the three-part structure of the book, details the content you can expect to find in each chapter, and in general tells you how to maximize the learning while finding easy access to the specific material you need or want.

Chapter 2, Understanding the Range of Cultural Behaviors and Expectations, explains the 10 specific ways in which culture programs behavior and impacts workplace relationships and performance. You will see, for example, how such programming shapes everything from perceptions about the role of women in the workplace to how directly or indirectly to communicate or resolve conflicts. You will also get suggestions about how to deal with cultural differences that are obstacles to work-group harmony and productivity.

Chapter 3, Learning the Cultural Etiquette of Communication, gives critical information about communication across cultural barriers. From understanding the different nonverbal aspects of interactions and communicating with limited-English-speaking individuals to giving feedback and resolving conflicts, it offers techniques and strategies for effective interactions in a multicultural environment. Language issues such as using interpreters and translators, dealing with accents, and teaching English are also discussed.

Chapter 4, Building Multicultural Work Teams, identifies cross-cultural factors that impact team building among groups of individuals whose norms, practices, and values are different. While the dimensions of cross-cultural team building that show differences are highlighted, so are areas of common ground. Strategies are given for helping a team meet universal human needs such as self-esteem, belonging, and trust.

Chapter 5, Making Meetings Work in a Culturally Diverse Environment, presents essential factors in running effective meetings. Beyond general information about structuring productive meetings, Chapter 5 discusses concrete diversity-related factors that impact meeting productivity. Specific cultural values and practices that influence meeting participation and involvement are identified, along with a list of suggestions for boosting productivity amid cultural variables.

Chapter 6, Performance Evaluation in a Diverse Organization, explains aspects of diversity affecting the performance evaluation process and gives methods and techniques for making effective use of performance appraisal with a diverse staff. Specific how-tos, guidelines, and skills are shared.

Section II—Integrating Diversity into Your Organization: Modifying the Systems to Capitalize on the Benefits of a Pluralistic Work Force

Chapter 7, Creating a Corporate Culture that Embraces Diversity, deals with the issue of creating an inclusive organizational culture. It provides assessment tools for measuring how open the climate is and explains the resistance to change that is so often a factor in an organization's cultural rigidity. This chapter also details the steps involved in moving from a monocultural to a multicultural organization and offers two different organizations as examples of positive change.

Chapter 8, Conducting a Diversity Audit: Taking an Organizational Snapshot, compares three fundamental assessment methods: questionnaires, interviews, and focus groups. Suggestions are given for using each appropriately. The chapter also offers a myriad of assessment tools that measure individual attitudes, awareness, and knowledge; management skill; and organizational progress in managing diversity.

Chapter 9, Recruiting for a Diverse Workplace, presents numerous tools for an organization to assess how diversity-friendly the application and hiring process is. Suggestions of places to look for recruits are given, both inside and outside the organization, and cross-cultural networking tips are presented as a way to increase contact with a diverse employee base. Beyond hiring and recruiting, techniques for neutralizing the interview itself are given. Suggestions for asking questions and gathering information in culturally sensitive ways are provided to make the entire recruiting process more friendly to a pluralistic population.

Chapter 10, Making Room at the Top (and in the Middle, Too), focuses on what qualities and characteristics are rewarded and promoted in your organization. The chapter looks at what have been considered traditional male and female traits and discusses the value of each. The most effective leaders and organizations will find a way to value and promote both male and female traits equally. Beyond looking at what qualities are rewarded, Chapter 10 gives suggestions for using coaching and mentoring techniques to develop high-potential employees. Finally, this chapter advocates a top-down, bottom-up career development system.

Section III—Rounding Out Your Knowledge Base: Realities and Resources

Chapter 11, Diversity: Today's Demographic Reality, discusses the work-force demographic trends and their impact on organizations. It also dispels the myths about some of these changes and defines the various dimensions of diversity.

Chapter 12, Valuing Diversity Means More than Equal Employment Opportunity, helps place managing diversity in a historical context as part of a long evolution within American society and business. Specific differences between affirmative action, valuing differences, and managing diversity are delineated, and a tool for assessing your organization's progress in its evolution is presented.

Chapter 13, Resources for Managing Diversity, provides annotated lists of resources for reading, research, and training about various aspects of diversity. Relevant books, periodicals, newsletters, audiovisual materials, and associations are included, along with a short description of each.

Chapter 14, Making Diversity Work: Summing It Up, wraps up the book by looking at essential attitudes that need to be fostered in a diversity-friendly organization and identifies the organizational imperatives that must be in place if diversity is to work and become a corporate asset.

What Makes This Book Different

Managing Diversity is in the second generation of books on the topic of diversity. Books in the first generation were conceptual and explored the changes inherent in the *Workforce 2000* report. This book takes the important next step of providing tactics for responding to this changing work force. It provides hands-on activities for any member of the organization accountable to the CEO and organizational mission for making the diverse work force a corporate asset.

This book's most unique and valuable contribution is the plethora of learning tools and activities it offers managers, trainers, consultants, and facilitators. The inventories and worksheets are relevant, easily reproducible, and ready to use. Each learning activity comes complete with objectives, a description of the activity, processing questions, and notes about special caveats or considerations. The training materials, audits, instruments, questionnaires, and tools are user-friendly and provide variety in purpose and complexity. All will enable individuals and work groups first to look inside themselves, then to look outside the personal domain to the organizational arena, and finally, to move beyond insight and awareness toward change.

Managing Diversity is a blend of conceptual information and useful tools. The conceptual areas offer knowledge and insights, while the tools lead to practical application for individuals, work groups, and organizations. The combination of individual assessments, management training tools, systems audits, and clear models make this a one-stop shopping reference. Separate lists of charts, models, and training tools are given with page numbers to make them easily accessible. The comprehensive resource guide at the end, which delineates training materials, simulations, books, videos, and other resources, gives you a road map for future learning.

Visionary organizations that want to be leaders in their respective fields will take the reality of diversity and make it a corporate asset. Where diversity is in place, the results are already speaking for themselves. Increased creativity, the capacity to attract top talent, the ability to more readily capitalize on diverse markets, and the increased return on human capital that results from creating a more inclusive climate are a few of the bottom-line factors that indicate the following: *Creating an organization in which differences are truly valued is more than just a good idea. It is good business.* It can be your strategic advantage. A new day has clearly dawned in American business of every venue—in both corporate and entrepreneurial environments, in the public and the private sectors, and in small- and medium-size companies. Once organizational leaders accept this new reality and their responsibility to lead in these exciting times, *Managing Diversity* can help them achieve their visions.

Chapter 2

Understanding the Range of Cultural Behaviors and Expectations

This chapter will give you:
1. An explanation of culture and how it programs behavior.
2. Information about different cultural norms underlying behaviors you see.
3. Suggestions for managers in dealing with cultural differences on the job.
4. Exercises to increase cultural sensitivity and knowledge.
5. Activities that raise awareness about stereotyping and prejudice.
6. Tips for learning about other cultures and helping diverse employees learn your organization's culture.

- A manager promotes a top-performing Latino employee to a supervisory position and is perplexed when the employee refuses to accept the promotion.
- An African-American female accountant is shocked and upset by her performance review. Her boss tells her she did not get the highest rating because she's not perceived to be a "team player" by the rest of the staff, especially during the stress of tax season.
- A physician gives directions to a Filipino nurse. When he asks if she understands the procedure, she nods her head and says yes. Later, the physician notices her doing the procedure incorrectly. In exasperation he asks, "Why didn't you tell me if you didn't understand?"
- A manager is frustrated by mistakes made by one of her best employees, an immigrant from Indonesia. At the end of the shift, she asks the employee to stop by her office. She points out the mistakes that were made and tries to explain what needs to be done to avoid these errors in the future. The employee never returns to work.
- A supervisor is angry because one of his Latino employees takes the day off each time his wife needs to go to a doctor's appointment. The boss cannot understand the need for the employee to do this, as the wife drives and takes care of shopping and other errands on her own.

Traditionally, these kinds of difficulties have been called performance or motivation problems; however, they are not that simple. The cultural differences at the heart of each of these situations will become clear to you as you read this chapter. If you have had experiences such as these, you have probably already become aware of the differences among us due to our cultural backgrounds.

Culture: Behavioral "Software" that Programs Us All

All of us are programmed by cultural "software" that determines our behavior and attitudes, from whom to make eye contact with and when to smile, to how to deal with conflict or talk to a boss. Cultural programming guides our behavior. Without this programming we would be as useless as a computer without software. Culture teaches us how to interact with one another, how to solve life's daily problems, and, in effect, how to control our world. No society exists without these rules, and no individual is culture-free. Culture is more than manners. It directs the most subtle aspects of behavior, such as how long to wait between sentences, when it is okay to interrupt someone, and how to interpret the look on someone's face. Though most cultural rules are never written, they are all the more powerful because they are absorbed unconsciously as we watch others and their reactions to us.

It is easy for us to accept and understand that while we may eat cereal and juice for breakfast, someone else is having tortillas, rice, grits, or black coffee and cigarettes. However, when it comes to interpreting each other's behavior, cultural differences make understanding more difficult. To make matters worse, when we interpret another person's behavior through our own cultural software, we make mistakes. We take the nodding head to mean "I understand," rather than "Yes, I heard you," as in the case of the Filipino nurse. We think the quick smile means the person is friendly and affable, rather than that he is uncomfortable and perhaps embarrassed by our behavior or his own confusion. Or we assume that the employee who does not speak out in staff meetings is not a go-getter, not assertive, or worse yet stupid when in fact she may be showing you respect by keeping her ideas to herself.

How does this misinterpretation happen? According to Adler and Kiggunder,[2] when we encounter another's behavior we need to make sense of it, so we follow a three-step process. First, we describe what we see, as in the case of the Latino employee: "This employee has refused a promotion to a management position." Second, we interpret the behavior: "He is not interested in getting ahead and is missing a wonderful opportunity." Third, we make an evaluation: "He is lacking in initiative, ungrateful for this opportunity, underconfident, or any combination of these." Steps two and three are the ones that get us into trouble in our intercultural interactions. A critical step in bridging the gap is learning more about other cultures' programming so that we can avoid making incorrect assumptions about someone's behavior. For example, if you knew that the individual in the previous scenario was a young Mexican immigrant, you would consider that he might be avoiding the promotion because in his culture, being part of a group is more important than advancement or because it would put him in a supervisory position over friends and/or an older man from his same culture. Since by his norms, elders are respected and promotions are made by age, he would be very uncomfortable being forced to embarrass himself and his older compatriot by giving the older worker orders.

We Are All "Captives of Culture"

In dealing with a culturally diverse work force, one of the myths is that an individual needs to speak with an accent, have different color of skin, or wear exotic clothes to have a culture. Even those who can trace their ancestors back to the *Mayflower* are culturally programmed. Just as a fish doesn't know it is in water until it is taken out, we only begin to become aware of our own programming when we come in contact with different cultural norms.

Edward Hall, a famous anthropologist who writes about culture, tells us we are all "captives of culture." Try this activity to see by how much your behavior is culturally directed. Imagine you wake up tomorrow morning as a member of a different cultural group in this society. On page 14, check which aspects of your life would be the same and which would be different.

It may come as a surprise to those of us raised in America and schooled in the doctrines of individual freedom, personal choice, and free will to find that our choices and life paths are culturally influenced. An African-American man in this society would undoubtedly have much different life experiences from an American-born daughter of immigrants from Mexico or a recently resettled Southeast Asian refugee family. What is your reaction? Are you surprised at how many checks you have in the "different" column? Were you stumped because you didn't know enough about the other culture to know if aspects of your life would be different? Perhaps you were irritated because this activity forces you to make assumptions about that other culture. Yet that is how we make sense of our world when there is an information gap. When we don't know or understand, we fill in the void with assumptions, that is, our own explanations for the events or situations that perplex us. And often, our assumptions are incorrect.

Culture and You

If you woke up tomorrow morning and found that you belonged to another culture or ethnic group, how would your life be the same and how would it be different?

	Same	Different
1. The friends you associate with		
2. The social activities you enjoy		
3. The foods you prefer		
4. The religion you practice		
5. The way you dress		
6. The community where you live		
7. The home you live in		
8. The job/position you hold		
9. The car you drive		
10. The music you enjoy listening to		
11. The language(s) you speak		
12. The political party you belong to		

Suggestions for Using *Culture and You*

Objectives:

- To help individuals see the pervasiveness of cultural programming.
- To increase awareness about the interplay between culture and individual personality in influencing life situations.
- To empathize with individuals of other cultural backgrounds.

Intended Audience:

- Individuals seeking to increase their own awareness about cultural differences.
- Participants in diversity training sessions.
- Work group members coping with diversity-related issues.
- Staff dealing with customers/clients of other cultural backgrounds.

Processing the Activity:

- Individuals are asked to imagine themselves suddenly becoming members of another cultural or ethnic group in this society. Stress that they are to imagine being born into and socialized by that other culture. As a variation, individuals may be asked also to imagine themselves of a different gender, sexual preference, or physical ability level.
- Individuals discuss reactions and insights in pairs, triads, or small groups.
- Smaller groupings share discussion highlights with a total group in a wrap-up discussion.

Questions for Discussion:

- Which parts of your life would remain the same? Which would be different?
- On what did you base your decisions about where to place your checks?
- What surprises did you have? What reactions?
- What questions or issues does this raise for you?
- What did you learn from this activity?

Caveats and Considerations:

- Some individuals may balk at being asked to make choices based on assumptions or stereotypes. This activity can lead to a discussion of such issues.
- When giving directions, be sure to emphasize that the purpose of the activity is not to reinforce stereotypes, but to see how culture influences our lives.
- Issues beyond culture, such as income or education level, will undoubtedly be brought up as influences. This serves to broaden the scope of the discussion to other dimensions of diversity.

Why Treating Everyone as You Want to Be Treated Doesn't Work

It is said that the Golden Rule is a universal principle underlying the foundations of most religions and moral codes. While "Do unto others as you would have them do unto you" is in spirit a wonderful rule, in practice it may create problems. As Sondra Thiederman, intercultural communication expert, says, "We all have the same basic needs for dignity, survival and social contact. What is different between groups is the way in which these needs are satisfied."[39] Stop for a moment to consider how you like being treated.

How I Like to Be Treated

Check off any of these statements that are true for you. Feel free to add more of your own as well.

_____ "I want to be told when I make a mistake so I don't make it again."

_____ "I want you to tell me if you disagree with me."

_____ "I like being told when I'm doing well so I know I'm on the right track."

_____ "I want the boss to ask for my input and to listen to my concerns."

_____ "I want the freedom to do things my own way."

_____ "I want my boss to roll up his/her sleeves and help out when we're busy."

_____ "I don't want to have to ask for directions and approval every step of the way."

_____ "I like it when others tell me what's on their minds."

_____ "I like it when people call me by my first name."

_____ "I want my staff to see me as their partner rather than as their boss."

_____ "It feels good when I am noticed and singled out for praise."

_____ "I like to be seen as an individual, not just considered one of the group."

_____ "I like being treated as an equal."

_____ "I like people to look at me in the eye when they talk to me."

_____ "I like _____."

_____ "It feels good when _____."

Suggestions for Using *How I Like to Be Treated*

Objectives:

- To identify one's own behavioral preferences and expectations of others.
- To increase awareness of the cultural influences on those preferences.
- To empathize with those who hold different expectations.

Intended Audience:

- Individuals wanting to increase their own sensitivity to cultural differences.
- Trainees in diversity seminars.
- Managers desiring better communication and relationships with diverse employees.
- Work-group members attempting to overcome cultural obstacles in work relationships.

Processing the Activity:

- Ask individuals to check their own preferences, adding others if desired.
- Have individuals jot down their typical reactions to not being treated as desired.
- Discuss, in small groups or together as a whole group, how culture influences these preferences.
- Ask individuals to share "war stories" about examples of differences in preferences.
- Lead group discussion of the consequences for individuals and work relationships when individuals do not give or get the desired treatment.

Questions for Discussion:

- Which did you check? Which did you not check?
- How/where did you acquire these preferences?
- Which are part of the mainstream culture of your organization?
- What happens if you don't get the behavior you want? How do you feel? How do you react?
- What does this tell you about dealing with and managing diverse individuals?

Caveats and Considerations:

- To avoid arguments and polarization over which of these behaviors are *right* or *better,* explain that they are individual preferences. It is important to recognize them so we can clearly communicate expectations and so we can avoid judging others who act otherwise and have different expectations.

How many of these statements did you check off? Did you realize they were typically American cultural preferences that are not shared by many other groups? In each case, if you treated individuals from other cultures like you wanted to be treated, you would *not* be treating them as they would want. In fact, you would be embarrassing them and/or treating them rudely by their cultural standards. For example, the dominant American preference for directness ("Tell it like it is," "Don't beat around the bush," and "Put your cards on the table") is not universally shared. In many other cultures, such as those in Asia and the Middle East, communication is much more indirect and subtle. Our direct, no-frills approach is seen as harsh or rude and may lead to loss of face. Another cultural difference can be seen in the expectations employees have of bosses. In most other places in the world, there is a more hierarchical structure and workers feel more security when they are told rather than asked what to do. Pay attention to your staff, colleagues, and customers and to their reactions. If they seem uncomfortable, incommunicative, or evasive, it may be because they are confronted by behavior that breaks their cultural rules. Once you are aware of this barrier, you are in a position to do something different to change the interaction.

A friend of ours spent a number of years working in Vietnam when her husband, a newsman, was assigned to cover stories there during the war. She recounted an incident that demonstrates how differently people want to be treated. Patti had worked at her new office job in Saigon for about a month. Being new to the country and not having family or friends around, she felt the need to get to know her Vietnamese colleagues better, so she invited the whole office staff over for dinner the following Sunday. She spent all weekend cleaning, shopping, and preparing an elaborate dinner for her co-workers. Then she waited. She was devastated when she realized no one was going to show up. The next morning at the office when she asked why no one came, she was at first given a polite runaround. No one wanted to discuss it. Finally, they began to explain that after only a month, they did not know her well enough to go to her home for dinner. In exasperation she asked, "Why didn't you tell me?" They told her they could not hurt or embarrass her by saying no and refusing the invitation. In Patti's culture, not showing up was the biggest sin; in theirs, it was saying no to an invitation. So much for the Golden Rule. Treating others with consideration and respect for who they are may be a more insightful mind-set.

Sources of Cultural Programming: Where We Learn the Rules

We learn the rules of our culture from the first sounds and sights we experience as babies. The smiles and frowns of our parents are usually our first teachers. When we behave in socially accepted ways, we are praised, smiled at, and rewarded. When we don't, we are scolded, punished, or ignored. We soon learn the rules, from table and bathroom etiquette to how to talk to adults to get what we want. When we venture beyond our family of origin, to preschool and kindergarten, we continue the process. In his gem of a book *Everything I Ever Needed to Know I Learned in Kindergarten,* Robert Fulgham talks about how the instruction one receives at age 5 has implications for all of life. We go on to learn from the larger culture in our neighborhoods and cities, and from radio, television, movies, and records. Additional rules come from the religions we practice or are taught. We continue to be enculturated by the colleges and universities we attend and the professions, industries, and organizations in which we work.

Each individual is like the proverbial onion, with layer upon layer of cultural teaching. Each of us has a unique culture of his or her own, which is an amalgam of what has been absorbed from these various influences. An individual's cultural identity is shaped by the following:

1. Ethnicity—the ethnic group with which the individual identifies, including the native language the person speaks.
2. Race—the racial group(s) with which the individual identifies.
3. Religion—the organized religion, denomination, or sect to which the person adheres, has been taught, or rejects.
4. Education—the level and type of education the person has experienced.
5. Profession/field of work—the type of work the person is trained to do.
6. Organizations—groups, associations, and organizations to which the individual belongs or has belonged, for example, the military, the Girl or Boy Scouts, a labor union or a fraternal organization.
7. Parents—the messages, both verbal and nonverbal, given by our parents about ethnicity, religion, values, cultural identity, prejudices, and so on.

While the above are powerful cultural influences, one's gender, family, peers, and place of birth also significantly impact cultural identity.

Each Individual as a Culturally Diverse Entity

Because we get our cultural teachings from a variety of sources, none of us has exactly the same program. If you have been married or have lived with another adult, you've surely seen some culture clashes as you disagreed over the rules of conduct because you each got your rules from different places. The next activity gives you a chance to examine your own cultural influences so that you can better understand other people's programs. In each circle, write one of the sources of your programming. Parents or family of origin would undoubtedly go in one (although some individuals in our seminars put each parent in a different circle, saying they learned very different rules from each). Religion might go in another, for example, Catholicism, Islam, or Orthodox Judaism. The dominant national culture of the country in which you grew up, for example, the United States, Mexico, or Japan, might be in another circle. In another you might put the community in which you were reared—a small town or a big city; a rural, an urban, or a suburban setting. Continue filling in each circle, and add more circles if you need to. Then write down the most important things you learned from each of these sources of your programming. For example, if you grew up in the United States, you might have learned that individual freedom and independence are to be treasured, while you might have learned to respect and honor elders if your parents were of Asian or European ancestry. If your family emigrated from the Philippines, you might have learned to place importance on harmonious relationships, while if your parents came from Iran you might have learned to have a deep loyalty to extended family members.

You as a Culturally Diverse Entity

Directions: In each circle write one of the sources of your cultural programming. Then next to each circle write the most important rules, norms, and values you learned from that source.

1. What reactions to and/or surprises do you have regarding your own cultural diversity?

2. Do any of your cultural programs come in conflict with one another? If so, where?

Suggestions for Using *You as a Culturally Diverse Entity*

Objectives:

- To identify the sources of one's own cultural programming.
- To see oneself as a microcosm of the societal dynamic of intercultural contact.
- To increase awareness about the complexity of each individual's cultural programming, which in turn affects behavior.
- To raise awareness about the need to find out more about the backgrounds of others in the workplace.
- To understand that everyone has a culture.
- To learn more about others with whom one works in order to increase understanding.

Intended Audience:

- Individuals wanting to increase their understanding and awareness about cultural influences and intercultural interactions on the job.
- Trainees in diversity seminars.
- Members of work teams wanting to understand each other better.
- Managers wanting to learn more about employees.

Processing the Activity:

- Have the group brainstorm sources of cultural programming and chart responses on an easel or a board. You might get them going by asking them how they learned the rules of behavior they now live by.
- Individuals write one source of their own cultural programming in each circle on the diagram. Next to each, they write the most important rules, norms, and values they learned.
- Individuals, in pairs or small groups, share information from their circles. They then discuss their reactions and the implications of the information.
- Total group discussion of reactions, insights, and learning.

Questions for Discussion:

- Which were the most important sources of your programming?
- Where do they come in conflict?
- Under what circumstances does one take priority over another?
- How are these differences resolved?
- What similarities and differences did you find with your partner(s) in your discussion group?
- What do you know about the programming of your colleagues, staff members, bosses, and so on? How can you find out more?
- What insight did you get?
- What does this say about dealing with others who are different from you?

Caveats and Considerations:

- This activity causes participants to look back to childhood, which can be a painful or emotional experience for some. It is not surprising to see tear-filled eyes as individuals share their experiences and memories with others in the room.
- Tell people at the beginning of the activity that they will be sharing their diagram with another person or a small group. In this way individuals can control the degree of disclosure.

Are there any places where different parts of your programming come into conflict? For example, were you taught at home that women should be mothers and wives rather than professionals, while your education and your position at work have made you value being a career woman? Perhaps your upbringing has taught you to be modest and self-effacing about your accomplishments, yet the dominant culture has shown you that you don't get ahead unless you toot your own horn a bit.

In one training session, a young Filipina shared her conflicts. While her upbringing and religion had taught her to focus on being a full-time mother with many children, her education and training as a nurse had led her to a career she loved and from which she derived much fulfillment. She was dealing with both the internal conflicts between her different worlds and the external conflicts between herself and her family of origin, who wanted her to stay home and have more children. In her case, her husband supported her career desires and both were satisfied with the two children they had.

In another example, a new training professional recognized the source of her discomfort at being required to teach older men and call them by their first name. In her European-American upbringing, she had been taught to respect her elders, to see men as authority figures, and to address new acquaintances more formally.

Some important lessons can be learned. First, how do you resolve conflicts between aspects of your own programming when they come up? While these internal conflicts can cause some pain, most of the time you make your peace with them. In the same way, culture-related conflicts between individuals can be resolved if they are acknowledged and dealt with. In addition, working through this activity, you probably came to realize how complex we all are and that no one can be pigeonholed into a particular pattern ("All Filipinos do . . ." or "Mexicans never . . ."). Finally, ask yourself how much you know about the cultural programming of your staff. What influences are in their backgrounds, and what rules were they taught? Consider discussing these ideas or even doing this activity with them at a staff meeting. You might be surprised at what you learn about your staff, but there will probably also be a team-building spin-off, giving staff a greater understanding of one another, a greater appreciation of their common areas, and an increased cohesiveness.

Ten Aspects of Culture: Understanding Cultural Programming

How frequently you bathe, how close you stand to someone with whom you are talking, how you address a boss, how you solve a problem, and how you respond to stress are all determined by your cultural programming. For example, the African-American accountant mentioned at the beginning of this chapter was not regarded as a team player because she demonstrated and dealt with her stress differently from her colleagues. Under pressure, her response was to get very quiet, close her office door, and hunker down to work. Her Euro-American co-workers, on the other hand, went around complaining about being overworked and pressured, getting sympathy from one another. It was only when the accountant's boss uncovered the reasons for the conflict that he could correct his own and his staff's misinterpretation of her behavior. Then he could work with his whole team to help them understand one another's behavior and negotiate a mutually satisfying resolution.

To understand the aspects of cultural teachings, it is helpful to contrast different cultural rules within the 10 areas of cultural programming described by Harris and Moran.[19] However, the risk in doing so is that new stereotypes will develop. The cultural norms described in the following section are generalizations that do not take into account individual personalities or the degree of acculturation to the dominant American culture. For example, while the American culture teaches individuals to make direct eye contact and speak their minds, many Americans are shy, avert their eyes, and keep their opinions to themselves. In addition, there is much variation within any group. The term *Latino* can mean a second-generation Mexican-American, a recent immigrant from El Salvador, a Cuban exile, or a Puerto Rican businessman.

1. Sense of Self and Space

Have you ever felt uncomfortable because someone stood too close when talking with you? Have you ever felt put off when your warm hug was received with a stiff, statuelike response? Or have you reacted to what you consider the pretension of someone addressing others by their titles instead of their first names? Chances are these rubs have their roots in cultural norms.

"Too close for comfort" and "Get out of my space" are common expressions that deal with the issue of space. The dominant American culture teaches us to stay about 1½ to 3 feet, or an arm's length, from people with whom we are talking in a business or friendship relationship. Any closer is reserved for more intimate contact with family, romantic relationships, or very close friends. Maintaining greater distance signifies a desire to stay aloof or protect oneself. When someone steps into your space, you'll probably move back to maintain a comfortable distance. Other cultures have different norms. In the Middle East, people stand close enough to be able to feel your breath on their face and to be able to catch your scent.[18] On the other hand, people in Japan maintain an even greater distance than those in the United States. As for greeting, in Japan it's a bow; in North America a hearty handshake; in Mexico and South America a warmer, softer handshake sometimes accompanied by a hug; and in the Middle East a hug and a ritualistic kiss on each cheek.

These physical aspects of the way we respect an individual's sense of self and space also have a less tangible counterpart in the degree of formality we expect in relationships. Many languages (Spanish, German, Tagalog, etc.) have two forms of the word *you*—the formal and the familiar. In these cultures, the familiar form is reserved for children, family members, close friends, and those below you in the social hierarchy, such as servants. English long ago dropped the familiar *thee* and *thou*, so we are left with one pronoun, *you*, for all relationships, whether we are talking with the president, a boss, or a spouse.

"Let's not stand on ceremony" is the dominant American culture's response to what most Americans consider stuffy formality. New acquaintances, bosses, and older individuals are commonly called by their first names. In other cultures, formal introductions using Mr., Mrs., and titles are expected as a sign of respect for both parties.

Since most other cultures are more formal than the dominant American culture, you are safest if you err on the side of formality. Trying to be buddy-buddy with a staff of people from other cultures that expect more formal behavior from a boss is apt to make workers uncomfortable and embarrassed. In business relationships and discussions, keeping a more reserved tone also tends to send the message that you respect the individuals with whom you are meeting. An American employee of a Japanese company doing business in the United States learned the hard way. Well schooled in both the Japanese language and culture, she made a presentation at a meeting. Because the company had succeeded in achieving its goal, she couldn't contain her excitement and she ended her recounting of the success statistics with a "Yeah!" Her Japanese boss told her later that her show of emotion was inappropriate for a formal business presentation.

Suggestions for Managers:

- Make sure you say good morning and good-bye to each employee every day.
- Introduce new employees to their co-workers formally, taking the individual around to meet each new colleague.
- Be careful in using first names, especially with older workers.
- Ask people what they prefer being called.
- Guard against being overly familiar with workers.
- Learn to listen and create an atmosphere of trust where you can learn about each other's needs.

2. Communication and Language

It is clear that language differences often accompany cultural differences. However, more is involved than just the specific language an individual speaks. It is estimated that over half of our communication is nonverbal, indicating the significance of gestures, facial expression, tone of voice, and intonation patterns.

The most obvious of the nonverbal signals is eye contact. All cultures use it to send signals. The difficulty comes when the signals are misinterpreted. "Look at me when I'm talking to you!" we were told by our parents when being reprimanded as children. We break eye contact when we want to end the conversation with the bore who has cornered us at a party. We catch the eye of the waiter to let him know we want the check in a restaurant. Not making eye contact in our culture is taken as a sign of deceitfulness, nonassertion, or disinterest. However, in Asian and Latin cultures, averting one's eyes is a sign of respect and the proper behavior when in the presence of an older person or authority figure.

Gestures are another nonverbal communicator, one we often depend on when there is a language barrier. Yet gestures can get us into trouble in multicultural groups. The okay sign, for example, made with the thumb and forefinger, is an obscene gesture in Greece and some parts of South America. Smiling, often considered an international gesture, is another nonverbal cue that can be misinterpreted. The following examples are cases in point:

- A bank's customer service representative assists a limited-English-speaking customer in filling out a form. In an attempt to put the customer at ease, he smiles and speaks in a lighthearted manner. He is shocked when the customer calls from home a few minutes later to complain about being laughed at and treated disrespectfully.
- An engineering manager asks why the Asian engineers whom he supervises smile so much. "I feel like they are snickering and laughing at me," he says.
- A visiting professional from Germany being taken around by his host, an outgoing Texan, is quite impressed. He notices that each time they pass through a tollbooth on the Texas highways, they are greeted by a smiling toll taker who

says, "Hi. How y'all doin' today?" At the end of the day, the German says, "I'm amazed at how many friends you have."

A smile is seen as a welcoming, friendly gesture in this culture. In Asian cultures, it may be a sign of embarrassment, confusion, or discomfort. In the Middle East, a smile from a woman to a man can be construed as a sexual come-on. In Germany, smiling is reserved for friends and family.

Nodding the head is yet another nonverbal cue that causes problems. Saying no is considered rude, impudent behavior in many cultures because it upsets the harmony of relationships. A nod often means "Yes, I heard you," not "Yes, I understand" or "Yes, I agree."

Perhaps the difference that causes the most difficulty in communication is the subtlest. It has to do with the degree of directness or indirectness, or the amount of information that is stated rather than implied. In Japanese culture, for example, communication is very indirect, depending on subtle contextual cues. An individual would not tell someone to turn the heat on but would instead hug herself. If that did not get a response, she might mention that it was a bit chilly. The other party would immediately pick up the cue and turn the heat on. Japanese employees are not told they must stay at work until the boss leaves, yet only after he has gone through the office saying good night do workers, in order of rank, begin to leave. A manager wanting to tell an employee about some errors on a report might suggest the employee look it over again. If both manager and employee are Japanese, the employee would understand that this subtle suggestion meant something was wrong with the report. This implied direction would be missed by most American employees, who would probably be perplexed by the suggestion.

Contrast this approach with the "Don't beat around the bush" dictum of American culture, which favors a very explicitly stated message. When these two approaches collide, problems can result. The Japanese, for example, are often exasperated at what they see as Americans' "irresponsibility" when they interpret literally an offhand comment such as "I'll give you a call" or "I'll get on that right away." On the other hand, Americans are just as frustrated when they miss the unstated clues that their Japanese counterparts automatically pick up. "How was I supposed to know I had to wait until the boss left? Why don't they just tell me?"

Suggestions for Managers:

- When there is a language barrier, assume confusion. Don't take the nod or *yes* to mean the individual understands or agrees. Watch for tangible signs of understanding such as immediately beginning the task and doing it correctly.
- Consider that smiles and laughter may indicate discomfort or embarrassment. See if you can identify what is causing the difficulty.
- Avoid smiling when giving directions or when having serious work-related discussions with employees, especially when giving feedback or when conducting performance reviews.
- Be careful not to think out loud. Employees hearing you may take your off-the-cuff comments literally and may even act on them.
- Watch for subtle clues that may be speaking volumes. A comment about another worker's frustrations may be telling you about a work-group complaint. Hints about family members moving in might be couching a desire for a raise.

3. Dress and Appearance

Though we may be taught not to judge a book by its cover, in this culture we do. The problem is that each culture has different rules about what is appropriate. Not only does "dressing for success" mean different things in different cultures, but also within a society rules differ. Pinstripe-suited Wall Street executives dress very differently from their Honolulu counterparts, who wear Hawaiian shirts and muumuus on Fridays, known as Aloha Days in the islands.

A dashiki or a shirt and tie? A bright silk dress or a dark gabardine suit? Which is the best choice for a job interview? It depends on which group you ask. In some cultures clothing is a sign of social class; hence, much money and attention are spent on dressing expensively. In others, clothing offers a chance to express one's personality and creativity, so the brighter and more decorative, the better. In still others, clothing is just a necessity of life, neither a status symbol nor an individual statement.

Take a look at the different workplace implications of dress. One client almost discounted a qualified job applicant because of these differences. The selection committee was interviewing applicants for a community outreach position in which the individual would be developing business with minority-owned firms. When this interviewee arrived dressed in a bright silk dress, lots of jewelry, and long painted nails, the committee collectively gulped. However, they thought about what they had learned in cultural diversity training and realized she was dressing very appropriately for her culture. More important, her appearance might be right in sync with the community members with whom she would be working. In another example, one government agency dealing with the management of state vehicles found that the rift between male and female mechanics was made less of a problem when all wore unisex uniforms that minimized the differences between the sexes and became a badge of their profession.

In still another situation, a draftsman was transferred from the San Francisco office to the Los Angeles office of a large engineering consulting firm. As an immigrant from Europe, used to more formal dress, he had noticed that shirts and ties were the "uniform" for all engineers and draftsmen in this company. He continued to wear what he considered appropriate dress in this new location. It was only when the draftsman was teased about trying to look like an engineer that he realized the rules were different in Los Angeles, where only engineers wore ties while draftsmen wore sport shirts without ties.

Hair can also be an appearance hot spot. Turbans, dreadlocks, Afros, ponytails on men and mohawks are just a few of the different hairstyles that raise eyebrows cross-culturally. Since the days of Samson and Delilah, hair has been a bone of contention. While in many mainstream American companies and in the military hair for men must be above the collar, in other cultures the rules are different. Hindus believe that the hair should never be cut, and the men wrap their heads in turbans. Orthodox Jewish men wear forelocks, while their wives cover their hair in public. Sometimes, hair makes a statement, as in the 1960s when wearing an Afro sent the "Black is beautiful" message or, more recently, when Sinead O'Connor shaved her head to draw attention to her political protests. In many cultures, hair is a symbol of virility for men, femininity for women, and individual dignity for all. Prisoners, for example, are often shorn, thereby striping them of their individuality and humanness.

Probably one of the most uncomfortable areas to deal with regarding grooming is body odor. The dominant American culture has a near fetish on the topic. We have a deodorant for almost every part of the body. In polite society, we react negatively to the smell of another human being. Not so in other parts of the world. According to Edward T. Hall, in the Middle East, marriage go-betweens often ask to smell the girl before they recommend her as a prospective bride.[17] Also, as mentioned, it is considered a normal part of communication to be able to feel and smell another's breath when talking. In still another cultural norm, Iranians bathe after sexual intercourse so as to be clean and pure for prayers. Body odor, whether from a lack of deodorant use or from diet (as in the garlic-laden kimchi eaten by Koreans), can cause real problems in work teams when people find each other's odors offensive.

Suggestions for Managers:

- Before reacting to another's appearance, stop to consider the meaning attached to appearance by the individual.
- When making assessments about job applicants, consider their cultural norms regarding dress.
- Consider the job the individual will be doing and the people with whom he/ she will be interacting when determining appropriate dress.
- Teach individuals the cultural rules required in your organization regarding dress and grooming.
- Remember that body scent is not necessarily a sign of uncleanliness.
- Consider uniforms as a way to eliminate differences and build common ground.

4. Food and Eating Habits

While you may know that what we eat, when we eat, and how we eat it are culturally directed, you may ask what food and eating habits have to do with work. When asked about the benefits of living and working in a multicultural environment, food is almost always mentioned high on the list. Most of us enjoy the potlucks with exotic and enticing dishes that result from having a diverse staff. Yet in the workplace, differences can cause conflict, as in the following examples:

- At a catered lunch at a management meeting, the entrée is quiche lorraine made with ham. Two managers never touch their plates.
- Employees at a manufacturing plant complain about the smell of the fish lunches being heated and eaten by their Vietnamese co-workers.
- An elderly couple being cared for by a Filipino home health aide nearly starves to death. While their nurse cooks gourmet meals for them, they are unfamiliar with and do not like Filipino cuisine. It is finally discovered that because they really like their nurse they are throwing the food away after she leaves.

Understanding food restrictions and taboos is a starting point. Prohibitions against certain foods are often associated with religious rules. Among the Kosher food laws adhered to by some Jews is the prohibition against eating pork and shellfish. Devout Muslims also refuse pork and alcoholic beverages. Hindu religious beliefs prohibit the eating of meat of any kind. In addition, many individuals choose to eat a vegetarian diet because of ethical considerations, medical reasons, or personal preferences.

Beyond restrictions, cultural norms influence our food preferences. Animals that are pets in one culture may be a food source in another. The American repugnance and outrage at the eating of dog, horse, or cat meat are probably akin to a devout Hindu's feelings about Americans eating beef.

Do you eat with chopsticks or a fork and knife? In which hand do you hold your fork and knife? What do you think about eating with your hands? Chopsticks are the utensils of choice in most of Asia, while holding the knife in the right hand and the fork in the left is proper for Europeans. In parts of the Middle East, eating with the right hand from a communal bowl is the accepted practice.

Smacking one's lips, burping, and picking one's teeth at the table are considered breaches of etiquette in America, yet these behaviors may be entirely acceptable elsewhere. In fact, belching is seen as a compliment to the cook in Asia. Europeans eat with both hands on the table, while Americans are admonished to keep the left hand in the lap unless cutting food. Before you judge others' table manners, stop and think about what might be proper by their standards. Also consider that others may be just as appalled by your table manners.

Suggestions for Managers:

- When planning catered meals or snacks for meetings and group gatherings, include a variety of foods so there will be something edible and acceptable for all.
- Avoid serving food that might be offensive to some staff members.
- Have alternate dishes available (e.g., a vegetarian plate or fruit salad).
- When choosing restaurants for business meetings, keep individual dietary restrictions and preferences in mind.
- Provide well-ventilated or outdoor eating areas for staff where odors can be more easily dissipated.

5. Time and Time Consciousness

When asked about the hardest adjustments they've had to make, Americans who work abroad invariably talk about the differences in time consciousness. The so-called mañana attitude in Mexico and the *Inshallah* of the Arab world clash with the "Time is money" and "The early bird gets the worm" American views of time. In this culture, time is seen as a commodity to be used, divided, spent, and saved. It is linear and finite. However, in other parts of the world, such as Latin America and the Middle East, time is considered more elastic and more relative. Time is used not just to accomplish tasks but also to develop relationships and enjoy oneself. When things happen depends on not just a schedule, but also on other events, priorities, and the will of God. So, *mañana* does not necessarily mean "tomorrow," but sometime in the future. *Inshallah* may mean "whenever it comes to pass."

An American concerned with deadlines is understandably frustrated by what may appear to be a lack of motivation, efficiency, or honesty when encountering such a response. The American, on the other hand, may be seen as always in a hurry and more concerned with tasks than with people.

Suggestions for Managers:

- Recognize that differences in time consciousness are cultural and are not a sign of laziness.

- Allow time in your schedule for the development of relationships.
- Make it a point to spend some time each week with each employee.
- Explain the reasons for deadlines and schedules.
- Explain the part promptness plays in assessment of performance and work habits.

6. Relationships

In the dominant American culture, hiring relatives is considered nepotism and is, in fact, prohibited in many organizations. Yet in most other parts of the world, hiring kin is not only common but also expected. Not to do so would be considered abdicating one's responsibility to one's family. Furthermore, while *family* in America usually means the nuclear group of one's parents and siblings, in other cultures it involves a large network of extended family members—cousins, aunts, uncles, nieces, nephews, and in-laws. Loyalty is expected toward one's kin, and obedience and respect are paid to older family members. Organizational rules or directions that require employees to go against these norms will be circumvented or disobeyed. You might experience an employee who hides the fact that his "friend" is really a relative, for example, or an employee who takes extended leaves to go back to his home village during the holidays.

In most other cultures, families are not egalitarian democracies. There is a definite hierarchy of status, with age being the determiner of power and respect. A definite pecking order exists, for example, with an older brother having authority over a younger one or a grandmother having matriarch status. An employee from such a family would not think of making a work-related decision such as seeking a promotion or accepting a transfer without talking it over with the "head of the family." This same sense of respect may transfer to the work unit, where employees apply a similar hierarchy within the group.

A seminar participant related how she learned about this kinship hierarchy on the job. As a nursing manager, she was in charge of running her unit, which included dealing with patients' family members and visitors. A problem arose one evening when one of her patients, a Gypsy, had the entire extended family, of more than 20 people, visiting. There were complaints from staff and other patients, so the manager went in to deal with the problem. Luckily, a security guard accompanied her. Before she could say anything, the guard formally introduced her to the head of the family, explaining that she was the manager in charge. She then explained the situation to the head of the family and asked for his cooperation. She got it. However, she was certain that without the cultural sensitivity and savvy of the security guard, she would not have paid attention to the family hierarchy and probably would not have gotten the quick cooperation she did by respecting the group's cultural norms.

Suggestions for Managers:

- Recognize that family responsibility and loyalty to kin will be a prime value of many workers. Take this into consideration when identifying rewards and motivators for staff (e.g., hiring relatives and giving time off for vacations and holidays).
- Allow employees time to discuss important decisions with family members before they give you a final answer.

- Recognize the informal leadership older members may hold in the work unit. Consult with them and seek their cooperation.
- Show respect to older employees by addressing them first and giving them formal authority when appropriate.
- Recognize that, as the boss, you may be seen as the "head of the work family." Employees may come to seek your advice and counsel about problems in and out of work.

7. Values and Norms

One of the cornerstones of American society is the doctrine of individual freedom. We fought a revolution to attain independence and the inalienable rights of life, liberty, and the pursuit of happiness. The Bill of Rights goes further in specifying the extent of our individual freedoms. The promise of freedom has attracted immigrants to these shores for centuries. In recent times, the idea of personal entitlement has pushed the ideas of individual freedom even further. Not so in most other cultures, where conformity to the group, family, and larger society is the norm. To most Americans, the need to conform—to subjugate one's individual needs to the those of the group—would feel confining and stifling. To many Asians, on the other hand, the dominance of the group over the individual assures harmony and order, and brings a feeling of stability to life. In an interesting experiment, a group of bilingual Japanese women were given a series of open-ended statements to complete in both Japanese and English.[14] When asked in English to complete the statement "When my wishes conflict with my family's, . . . ," one woman responded, "I do what I want." When asked to complete the same statement in Japanese, the response was "It is a time of great unhappiness." In the workplace this difference may show itself in employees' discomfort with individual praise, especially in public; with staff members' reluctance to break rank and blow the whistle; or with workers' difficulty in openly seeking advancement.

Related to this group orientation is another difference: the competition versus cooperation dichotomy. The competitive spirit is an underpinning of American life and the capitalist economic system. However, competition upsets the balance and harmony valued by cultures that prefer cooperation and collaboration. A Japanese high-tech firm doing business in America discovered this difference in attempting to correct a problem. Dismayed to learn of the theft of some expensive equipment, top management assembled a group of middle managers to come up with a solution. The American managers concluded that offering a reward to the individual who reported the thief was the best solution. The lone dissenting voice came from a Japanese manager, whose suggestion that the team that did not whistle-blow and that did not have any theft problem be rewarded was laughed at. Each solution, however, was culturally appropriate.

Another cultural difference that emerges in the workplace regards privacy. To many newcomers, Americans seem naïvely open. Discussing personal matters outside the family is seen as embarrassing, and opening up to someone outside of one's own cultural group is rare. Thoughts, feelings, and problems are kept to oneself in most groups outside the dominant American culture. Off-the-cuff thinking, shooting from the hip, and giving an immediate response to a question from the boss would be difficult for someone raised with this cultural norm.

On the other hand, when it comes to privacy in space as opposed to thoughts and feelings, Americans are not so open. Perhaps because the United States has had the luxury of vast open spaces, we have a culture that fences off each person's area—children have their own rooms (sometimes with a Keep Out or Knock First sign on the door), backyards are fenced, and office spaces are partitioned into cubicles. In much of the rest of the world, such fencing off is not the case. Families may sleep in the same room, and on the job the work spaces are communal. In Japanese offices, the boss generally does not have a separate office but rather shares a portion of the work space with employees. Likewise, in public areas, a new passenger on a bus or train would generally take a seat next to someone rather than sit in an unoccupied section. That would be considered odd behavior at best, and dangerously threatening at worst, in this country.

Loyalty is still another value that is differently displayed from culture to culture. Most Americans are taught loyalty to such abstract principles as "truth, justice, and the American way" and believe no one is above the law. Mexicans, Filipinos, and Middle Easterners, on the other hand, are loyal to individuals rather than to abstractions. That personal allegiance might mean breaking a rule to help a friend or covering up for a relative's infraction. Employees feeling this personal attachment also tend to give their allegiance to the boss rather than to the organization.

Finally, we get to an issue critical to all human beings—respect. While all of us want to be treated with dignity and respect, we define and demonstrate respect differently. Loss of face is important to avoid in all cultures. In Asia, in the Middle East, and to some extent in Latin America, one's face is to be preserved at all costs. In fact, death is preferred to loss of face in traditional Japanese culture, hence the ritualized suicide, hara-kiri, as a final way to restore honor. Any embarrassment can lead to loss of face, even in the dominant American culture. To be criticized in front of others, to be publicly snubbed, or to be fired would be hard to swallow in any culture. However, inadvertent slights or unconscious faux pas can cause serious repercussions in intercultural relationships.

In Mexico, the Middle East, and parts of Asia, for example, the separation of the individual from the behavior is not so clear. "I am my behavior and my behavior is me" might be the motto. Criticism of performance may be taken as a personal insult, hence the case of the Indonesian worker who quit because of the loss of face he experienced in being corrected by his boss. In another example, the owner of a large travel agency had decided to reorganize her company, streamlining in the face of an economic slump during the Persian Gulf crisis. In doing her assessing, she noticed that one supervisor's group had slowly dwindled so that there was no one left for the supervisor to manage. The owner, an immigrant from the Philippines herself, called in her Chinese-born supervisor to discuss reorganization plans. While the employee understood the need for the changes, she begged the boss not to take away her title of supervisor and demote her. "I would lose face in my community if I lost my title," she said. The boss, understanding that "face" in this case took priority over a logical organization chart, complied. "What difference does it make to me what her title is? I just care that she is a satisfied and committed employee. If letting her be called supervisor accomplishes that, why not?" she thought.

Suggestions for Managers:

- Consider giving rewards and feedback to the whole work group rather than to individuals.
- Structure tasks to require teamwork rather than individual action.
- Give workers time to think about and formulate responses to input requests.

- Consider the face-losing potential of any actions you are planning. Seek out ways to achieve your objectives while avoiding diminishing employees.

8. Beliefs and Attitudes

Religion probably comes to mind when you think of beliefs and attitudes with regard to cultural programming. Whether we practice them or not, religions are powerful influencers of our beliefs and attitudes. While the doctrine of separation of church and state is set down in the U.S. Constitution, there is a strong Judeo-Christian foundation in this country, with an emphasis on the Christian part. If you don't think so, look at legal holidays and school vacations.

Given today's pluralistic work force, it is important to realize that everyone does not practice the same religions, celebrate the same holidays, or want the same days off. An observant Orthodox Jew, for example, cannot work during the Sabbath, from sundown Friday to sundown Saturday, so holding important staff meetings on Friday afternoons or scheduling a team-building retreat on a Saturday would exclude this person, as it would a Seventh-Day Adventist. Among Muslim religious observances is the month of Ramadan, during which devout Muslims can have nothing to eat or drink each day from sunup to sundown. This might be a month to avoid holding heavy-duty negotiations or employee recognition luncheons if you have Muslims on your staff. One manager reported that since one of his employees reserved the noon hour for midday prayers, the manager made sure he never scheduled meetings during lunch.

Holiday celebrations are often times when religious differences are inadvertently ignored. In one client organization, management was surprised to find that not all employees appreciated the red poinsettia plants that were purchased to decorate all office cubicles at Christmastime. Many of the staff were not Christians and so did not celebrate Christmas.

In addition to religious views, beliefs about the position of women in society differ among cultures. In some groups, it is accepted that women work outside the home. In other groups, it is seen as a deficiency on the part of the male head of the house if any of the women from his family work. In other cases, while women may work outside the home, they cannot be in a position of authority over men. For a man to take orders from a woman would cause loss of face. This difference may cause problems between bosses and subordinates or between female staff and male clients/customers. In one local city with a large group of residents newly arrived from the Middle East, this problem became acute. Many of the Armenian immigrant men who came to do business with the city utility department were unaccustomed to dealing with women in business and demanded to talk with a man. However, there were no male employees in the customer service department. This culture clash caused much stress for the female city employees. Another situation that highlights the differences in attitudes about the role of women arose in a manufacturing company. The supervisor of one of the shifts was a Latina. Many of the male assembly-line workers refused to work for a woman. The only way the owner could keep her employees was to have segregated male and female work teams. Beyond ethical principles, with today's laws regarding equal employment opportunity (EEO) and affirmative action, organizations need to educate employees about the legal risks involved in discriminating because of gender.

Still another area of cultural programming regards attitudes about social order and authority. In Asia, students don't question teachers, employees don't confront bosses, and children don't talk back to parents. Not so in America, where the culture tends to be more egalitarian than in cultures that have more traditional and hierarchical attitudes about authority. While no society is truly classless, there is a wide range in views about social class, from the social mobility suggested in the "It's not who you are but what you are that counts" motto and Horatio Alger stories popular in America to India's more rigid caste system. Once you understand this difference, you can interpret others' behavior more accurately. You will see differently the housekeeper who calls you Miss/Mr./Mrs. before your first name, the employee who will not participate in group decision making at meetings, or the staff member who will not take direction from a countryman who is younger or on a lower social scale than he.

Suggestions for Managers:

- Find out what religious holidays staff members celebrate. Keep those in mind when planning work-group activities, holiday celebrations, and individual schedules.
- Avoid scheduling meetings and training programs on any religious holidays.
- Take advantage of the fact that employees want different holidays, days off, and vacation times (e.g., some people would be willing to work on Sundays or on Christmas day).
- Help newcomers understand the reasons for shared decision making and the need for suggestions and input from employees.
- Educate employees about EEO and discrimination. Explain the legal liabilities as well as the principles of equality that, though not always adhered to, are foundations of this country.

9. Mental Processes and Learning

Do you prefer getting directions in words or with a map? Do you learn best by listening and taking notes; by being involved in experiential activities; by seeing models, diagrams, and graphs; or by taking part in lively discussions? Do you attribute your successes to your hard work and tenacity, or to luck and fate?

We all have preferences in learning and thinking styles, and some of these preferences are cultural. A few years ago, George Will quipped, in contrasting the United States and the then USSR, that the game that represents the thinking style of the United States is poker, while that of the USSR is chess. These two games represent very different styles of problem solving and thinking. Such different approaches may show up on your staff.

Perhaps the most obvious difference in problem solving has to do with the perception of human control. The dominant American culture professes a "fix-it" approach to problems, one that assumes that we have the power to control our world. Problems are seen as obstacles to be overcome, and success in doing so depends on our actions. Progress and change are often seen as ends in themselves. In most of the rest of the world, the view is different. Problems are viewed as situations to which one must adapt and the changes required by problem solving are seen as a threat to order and harmony. In addition, fate and luck play a great part in determining the outcome of ventures. Cause-and-effect relationships are less emphasized in this kind of thinking. American culture also has a preference for logical analysis, while other cultures may bring more intuition and holistic thinking to a problem.

Another difference is in learning style. Teaching and learning are generally much more didactic, formal, and one-way, from teacher to student, in most of the rest of the world. There is also more dependence on written information. Therefore, staff from other cultures might feel lost in a typical American training seminar that emphasizes experiential activities and role playing, which require the learner to draw his/her own conclusions. Participants might also want copies of all information charted at the board or easel, or they may ask for lecture notes or outlines.

Suggestions for Managers:

- Explain cause-and-effect relationships when getting staff members involved in problem solving.
- Ask staff members what they suggest be done about the problems and complaints they express.
- Use nonlinear problem-solving methods such as brainstorming that capitalize on lateral thinking and intuition rather than logical analysis.
- Ask troubleshooting questions such as "What would happen if . . . ?" in order to get staff to think about possible consequences.

10. Work Habits and Practices

"The devil makes work for idle hands" exemplifies the Protestant work ethic, a cornerstone of American society. In this view, work is seen as more than a means to survival. It is a divine calling, a "vocation." In today's vernacular we talk about job satisfaction, finding one's magnificent obsession, and creating a career that brings joy, esteem, and achievement. Work is not always held in such high regard in other cultures. In fact, it may be seen as a necessary evil.

The type of work one does may also be seen as a sign of status. In this culture, we make distinctions between blue-collar and white-collar work, manual labor and professional work, and exempt and nonexempt employees. In other cultures, such as in India and the Arab world, for example, working with one's hands has lower status than doing professional work. This may explain why workers balk at certain tasks or prefer one kind of work over another. A physicist who manages an international staff at a premier space and technology research organization related the differences he has seen among members of his multinational staff. From his observation, the Swedish and German scientists love to tinker, work with their hands, and build models. The Indian scientist, on the other hand, disdains working with his hands and finds it beneath his dignity to have to input his own data into the computer.

An area critical to understanding if you are trying to get motivation and commitment from staff is the reward structure. What an employee considers rewarding is in the eye of the beholder, and that eye is cultural. A promotion to management might be considered a reward to one individual and a punishment to another; a bonus for a job well done might feel like a pat on the back to one employee and an insult to another. Paying attention to what individuals consider rewarding is important in any work group, but in a diverse group it may be more difficult to figure out. If you know that an employee has family responsibilities outside of work, allowing a more flexible schedule with staggered hours might be more of a motivator than a promotion would be. If an employee is trying to save money to bring other family members to this country, giving overtime assignments as tangible reinforcers might be appreciated.

Taking initiative and being self-directed are other work habits not universally taught. In most other cultures, workers are not expected to exercise independent judgment, make decisions, or initiate tasks without being directed to do so. When you notice employees waiting for direction, do not immediately assume these employees are unmotivated or lazy. They may be waiting for you to exercise your leadership role.

Suggestions for Managers:

• Get to know your employees and find out what place work plays in their lives. Find out what gives them satisfaction on the job.
• Be sensitive to employees' perceptions about the status of certain kinds of work. Explain the reasons for each assignment and its importance in the whole scheme of things.
• Talk to employees and find out what is rewarding to them.
• Understand that taking initiative and making independent decisions may be difficult for some employees. Take time to coach them in this direction.

The chart *Comparing Cultural Norms and Values* gives a brief recap of the major differences between mainstream American and other cultures relative to the 10 aspects of culture discussed. The three tools that follow offer activities that can help individuals learn about cultural differences and apply that knowledge to their own real-life situations. *Dimensions of Culture* gives you a format to record information about different cultural norms. *Analyzing Cultural Differences* helps you apply that knowledge to specific work relationships. Finally, *Cross-Cultural Hooks* enables you to gain a better understanding of your own intercultural button-pushers.

Comparing Cultural Norms and Values

Aspects of Culture	Mainstream American Culture	Other Cultures
1. Sense of self and space	Informal Handshake	Formal Hugs, bows, handshakes

2. Communication and language	Explicit, direct communication
	Emphasis on content—
	   meaning found in words
		Implicit, indirect
		   communication
		Emphasis on context—
		   meaning found around words

3. Dress and appearance	"Dress for success" ideal Wide range in accepted dress	Dress seen as a sign of position, wealth, prestige Religious rules
4. Food and eating habits	Eating as a necessity—fast food	Dining as a social experience Religious rules

5. Time and time consciousness	Linear and exact time
	   consciousness
	Value on promptness—
	   time = money
		Elastic and relative time
		   consciousness
		Time spent on enjoyment of
		   relationships

6. Relationships, family, friends	Focus on nuclear family
	Responsibility for self
	Value on youth, age seen as
	   handicap
		Focus on extended family
		Loyalty and responsibility to
		   family
		Age given status and respect

7. Values and norms	Individual orientation Independence Preference for direct confrontation of conflict	Group orientation Conformity Preference for harmony

8. Beliefs and attitudes	Egalitarian
	Challenging of authority
	Individuals control their destiny
	Gender equity
		Hierarchical
		Respect for authority and
		   social order
		Individuals accept their destiny
		Different roles for men and
		   women

9. Mental processes and learning style	Linear, logical, sequential Problem-solving focus	Lateral, holistic, simultaneous Accepting of life's difficulties

10. Work habits and practices	Emphasis on task
	Reward based on individual
	   achievement
	Work has intrinsic value
		Emphasis on relationships
		Rewards based on seniority,
		   relationships
		Work is a necessity of life

Dimensions of Culture

The following chart gives you an opportunity to make some notes about cultural differences you have encountered in each of the 10 areas of cultural programming.

Dimensions of Culture	Examples of Differences
1. Sense of self and space • Distance • Touch • Formal/informal • Open/closed	
2. Communication and language • Language/dialect • Gestures/expressions/tone • Direct/indirect	
3. Dress and appearance • Clothing • Hair • Grooming	
4. Food and eating habits • Food restrictions/taboos • Utensils/hands • Manners	
5. Time and time consciousness • Promptness • Age/status • Pace	
6. Relationships • Family • Age/gender/kindred • Status	
7. Values and norms • Group vs. individual • Independence vs. conformity • Privacy • Respect • Competition vs. cooperation	
8. Beliefs and attitudes • Religion • Position of women • Social order/authority	
9. Mental processes and learning • Left/right brain emphasis • Logic/illogic	
10. Work habits and practices • Work ethic • Rewards/promotions • Status of type of work • Division of labor/organization	

Source: Adapted from Philip R. Harris and Robert T. Moran, *Managing Cultural Differences*, 2nd ed. (Houston: Gulf Publishing, 1987).

Suggestions for Using *Dimensions of Culture*

Objectives:

- Identify both mainstream and other cultural norms.
- Recognize the cultural roots of behaviors encountered at work.
- Expand understanding and knowledge of different cultural norms.

Intended Audience:

- Individuals wanting to increase their knowledge about different cultural norms.
- Trainees in a diversity seminar.
- Employees wanting to understand and deal more effectively with individuals (staff, customers, or clients) from other cultures.

Processing the Activity:

- During a lecturette on the information on the preceding pages regarding different cultural norms in the 10 areas of programming, individuals make notes on the chart.
- Group is divided into smaller groups, with each discussing one or two of the areas of programming and sharing differences and their impact in the workplace. Information is charted on a flip chart or board.
- Small groups report to the larger group, giving a recap of the points made in their discussion.

Questions for Discussion:

- What are mainstream norms in each area? Norms of other cultures?
- What are the norms in your organization?
- Which differences cause problems or misunderstanding?

Caveats and Considerations:

- It may be difficult for individuals to see the cultural influence beneath the behaviors. You may need to help by giving additional examples or asking participants from other cultures to share examples.
- It is important to avoid giving the impression that people from other cultures are so different, and that other norms are so strange, that we cannot understand them. One way is to present sets of differences as a continuum, for example, conformity ↔ individualism. Peer pressure and group solidarity are powerful shapers of behaviors in mainstream America, and in cultures that value conformity, individuals do have their own opinions and may want the freedom to do things their own way.
- It is also important to avoid creating new stereotypes about different cultural groups. It can be insightful to have individuals from the same culture discuss how differently they interpret their own culture's norms. The group then sees that all those of a particular group (African-Americans, Cambodians, Russians, Israelis, etc.) are not the same and that there are as many differences within a group as from group to group.
- This activity can also be expanded by having the group identify mainstream norms using popular sayings and aphorisms, for example:

    Better late than never, but better never late.

    A penny saved is a penny earned.

    You are your brother's keeper.

    —which express cultural values.

Analyzing Cultural Differences

Apply what you just read about different cultural programming to your own situation. Choose one of your employees whose cultural programming is different from yours. (You'll get more from this analysis if you choose an individual with whom you are experiencing difficulties.) Analyze your own programming first, in each of the 10 areas; then analyze what you think your employee's programming has been.

   See if you can identify any of the areas where differences in programming and expectations may be causing some rubs. How can you use this information to help you overcome some of these cultural barriers? Perhaps you will see and interpret this employee's behavior differently now, so it will not irritate you quite as much. Or maybe you can explain your own behavior to the employee to clear up misunderstandings and erroneous assumptions. Better still, can you negotiate a resolution by each of you giving a little and creating a new norm you both can live with?

Aspects of Culture	Employee	You
1. Sense of self and space		
2. Communication and language		
3. Dress and appearance		
4. Food and eating habits		
5. Time and time consciousness		
6. Relationships, family, friends		
7. Values and norms		
8. Beliefs and attitudes		
9. Mental processes and learning style		
10. Work habits and practices		

Suggestions for Using *Analyzing Cultural Differences*

Objectives:

- Apply information about cultural programming to specific work relationships.
- Identify cultural differences that may be at the root of performance problems or communication barriers.
- Gain more information and a new perspective that can help in resolving interpersonal issues on the job.

Intended Audience:

- Managers wanting to improve their relationship with, resolve a conflict with, or increase commitment from a specific employee or a group of employees from a similar background.
- Managers participating in a managing diversity seminar.
- Employees needing to increase effectiveness with customers/clients from other cultures.
- Employees wanting to resolve a conflict with someone from another cultural background.

Processing the Activity:

- Individuals jot down information about their own cultural programming in each of the 10 areas, then about the programming of one of their employees (or customers/clients, or co-workers).
- Individuals analyze differences at the heart of the problem.
- Individuals share their analyses in pairs or small groups, getting input from their partner(s) and responding to the discussion questions.
- Total group shares insights gained.

Questions for Discussion:

- What are the most irritating differences?
- What are the advantages and disadvantages of your norms, rules, and values? The other individuals'?
- What does this analysis tell you that can help you resolve this problem?
- What are you willing to do or expect differently in order to resolve this? What do you need to ask the other individual to do or expect differently?

Caveats and Considerations:

- Occasionally, individuals are so emotionally involved in an interpersonal impasse that it is difficult for them to stand back and analyze it more objectively. You can help them by offering some examples of differences that may be operating.

Cross-Cultural Hooks

Another way to help get beyond irritations you may feel when encountering cultural differences is to identify the specific behaviors that bother you and then look deeper to understand the cultural programming that underlies them. Using the following cross-cultural hook list will help you do that.

Put a check by any of the cross-cultural hooks that could result in frustration or negative interactions between you and another individual. Then, next to any you've checked, jot down your reaction when you encounter this hook.

☐ Discounting or refusing to deal with women.

☐ Speaking in a language other than English.

☐ Bringing whole family/children to appointments.

☐ Refusal to shake hands with women.

☐ No nonverbal feedback (lack of facial expression).

☐ No eye contact.

☐ Soft, "dead fish" handshake.

☐ Standing too close when talking.

☐ Heavy accent or limited English facility.

☐ Coming late to appointments.

☐ Withholding or not volunteering necessary information.

☐ Not taking initiative to ask questions.

☐ Calling/not calling you by your first name.

☐ Emphasizing formal titles in addressing people.

☐ Other: _____ .

What aspects of cultural programming are at the root of this behavior?

Suggestions for Using *Cross-Cultural Hooks*

Objectives:

- Identify personal cross-cultural button pushers.
- Recognize the cultural sources of irritating behaviors.
- Take a first step in getting beyond culturally connected blocks to productive relationships.

Intended Audience:

- Individuals seeking to increase cross-cultural understanding.
- Trainees in a diversity seminar.
- Managers who are finding difficulties in dealing with their diverse staff members.
- Employees who are experiencing negative interactions with other employees and/or customers/clients of other cultures.

Processing the Activity:

- Individuals check those behaviors they find irritating. Then they jot down their typical reaction to each behavior checked.
- After a lecturette or explanation of the 10 dimensions of culture, individuals discuss in small groups or total group the dimensions of culture that may be at the source of each behavior checked.
- Individuals discuss insights or new perspectives gained.

Questions for Discussion:

- What are your typical reactions when you get hooked?
- How does this affect how you deal with the situation?
- Which areas of cultural programming come into play?
- What are you willing to do to adapt to a particular norm?
- What are you willing to do to teach others to adapt to a particular norm?

Ten Ways to Learn More about Other Cultures

If this analysis shows you what you don't know and leaves you with a desire to learn more, here are some ways.

1. Ask the Employee

Sometimes the best way to find out about another culture's norms is to ask employees from that culture to teach you about it. You'll get a better response if you make your request a real search for information, not an accusation. Also, choose someone who has some degree of acculturation and ask specific questions such as the following:

- What are the biggest differences between Philippine and American cultures?
- What are some of the most difficult adjustments you have made in living in the United States?
- What do you wish Americans understood about your culture?
- What does it mean in your culture when a person . . . ?

2. Ask Colleagues from Other Cultures

If you don't get enough information from your employees themselves, ask fellow managers who are from the cultures you are trying to learn about. These colleagues can be invaluable *cultural informants* who can teach you about subtle but often powerful cultural norms that may be causing misunderstandings. From their management perspective, they're apt to be able to see things biculturally and so give you some interesting insights into the areas of friction you may be trying to resolve.

3. Tap Community Resources

Another rich source of information about cultures is community organizations such as the Anti-Defamation League that have been dealing with these differences for a long time. Ethnic associations (e.g., the Korean Businessmen's Association), social service agencies, and refugee resettlement agencies are good sources of information about the cultures they represent or serve. They may provide publications with concrete answers to your questions, as well as speakers. In addition, school districts both through their English as a Second Language (ESL) departments and their staff development units have long been teaching about multiculturalism. A call to your local school district headquarters could give you some of the information you are looking for. Finally, community relations groups make it their business to help various segments of society understand one another. The Los Angeles County Commission on Human Relations, for example, has published a booklet entitled ''How to Communicate Better with Clients, Customers and Workers Whose English Is Limited.''

4. Read about Different Cultures

Reading nonfiction books such as *Communicating with the Mexicans* or *Considering Filipinos* is one way to get information directly. Another is to read fiction that is set in other cultures, for example, *Love in the Time of Cholera* or *Shōgun*. A list of resources is provided in Chapter 13.

5. Observe without Judgment

Pay attention to how people behave without judging the behavior (e.g., avoid thinking "Oh, that's poor taste," "It's low class," or "How ignorant"). One of the most enlightening learning experiences in our doctoral program was an assignment to observe parent-child interactions in two cultures—American and Mexican. Watching parents and their children communicate in Los Angeles and Tecate, Mexico, was an instructive way to see culture in action. Among the many differences, one stood out. American parents were much more verbal, giving directions by telling their children what they wanted them to do. Mexican parents, on the other hand, were less verbal and more physical, walking over, taking the child's hand, and leading him/her. This kind of detached observation may help you understand your work group.

6. Share in Staff Meetings What You Have Each Found Out and Learned

Talk about cultural differences at staff meetings and at management meetings. Share insights about cultural norms and how to deal with them. Dr. Jorge Cherbosque suggests that you can even form a peer support group with a multicultural configuration. You can then be resources to one another, giving and getting consultation and advice.

7. Conduct Focus Groups

If you still want to find out more, you might want to organize some culture-specific focus groups to get information through group discussions. Questions such as those mentioned in tip 1 above might be used. Additional information about using focus groups is given in Chapter 8.

8. Use Employee or Customer Survey Information

Pick up the clues from what people tell you or complain about. If they make comments that people always seem in a hurry or that they feel rushed, they may be talking about differences in time consciousness. If they complain about the performance review process, they may be surfacing issues related to loss of face. If they feel the boss doesn't take an interest in them, they may be alluding to an emphasis on task at the expense of relationship.

9. Experiment with New Methods

When we interview managers who are dealing effectively with their diverse staffs and ask how they learned what to do, they invariably say, "Trial and error." If you are experiencing a culture-related block, try a new behavior or a different approach. Then watch to see how it works.

10. Spend Time in Other Cultures

Immersion in other cultures is a less traditional but very effective way to learn about different norms. This doesn't mean you need to take a leave of absence and live in Mexico, the Philippines, or Korea, though that experience would undoubtedly be enlightening for anyone. You can immerse yourself by watching foreign films, tuning in to the Spanish-language channels on TV, reading literature from and about another culture, and spending time in ethnic communities such as Little Saigon, Chinatown, or Koreatown, for example.

Helping Others Acculturate to American Norms

Learning about cultures is a two-way street. There is also a need for you to help others learn the norms of their adopted land.

1. Explain the Reasons

Telling employees the reasons for the preferred behavior helps them understand and accept it. For example, you could say, "It is important to let people know when you don't understand so they can explain it another way. That way they can help you."

2. Show Employees the Benefits

You might position the desire for more open requests by saying, "Americans have a saying that the squeaky wheel gets the grease. This means that you won't get any help unless you let people know you need it. That help makes the whole team's performance better." In teaching employees to take more responsibility for their careers, you could say, "You might be overlooked for a project or promotion if you don't let people know you are seeking it."

3. Suggest Resources

Books and movies are great cultural resources. Considering the interests and education level of the individual, you might suggest appropriate material. A book such as *American Ways: A Guide for Foreigners in the United States,* by Gary Althen, hits the issues head on. Valuable insights into American values can also be gained by reading such classics as *To Kill a Mockingbird, Tom Sawyer,* and *The Old Man and the Sea.* Movies such as *Mr. Smith Goes to Washington* and *All the President's Men* serve the same purpose.

4. Spend Nonwork Time Together

While the example of our friend working in Vietnam demonstrates that you must take time in building a relationship foundation first, eating lunch together, going bowling after work, or inviting an employee over to your home gives them a chance to experience American culture outside of work. We often complain that immigrant workers are clannish, yet we seldom invite them into our homes. One friend of ours, who is a teacher, invited an Armenian immigrant colleague and her family over for Sunday dinner. Both host and hostess were taken aback when the colleague's husband thanked them as they sat down to eat. "You know, we have been in this country for 12 years and this is the first American home we have been invited to." It's difficult to learn all the cultural rules on the shop floor, in the office, or at the supermarket.

5. Talk about Differences Openly

When you see surprise, confusion, or hesitancy, stop and discuss the cultural differences at play. "I'll bet this is different from the way this is done in your country. How do bosses let you know how you're doing in your culture?" Or, "This may be awkward at first because I believe people are a little more direct here. They don't mean to be rude. It is considered helpful to tell someone when they make a mistake."

How Ethnocentrism Sabotages Valuing and Managing Diversity

When we look at other cultural norms, it is easy and human to make judgments about rules different from our own. The feeling that one's own cultural rules are superior or more right than the rules of other cultures is the essence of ethnocentrism. Cultural comparisons are natural. The problem isn't the comparison, but rather the universal tendency to see those other norms in a less favorable light. Those who have a different time consciousness are judged lazy and undependable. People from cultures that respect authority and stress harmony are considered unassertive and lacking in initiative. Those from cultures with an exacting dependence on promptness and an irritation at wasting time are seen as cold and robotlike. Those whose cultures depend on less direct communication are seen as devious and sneaky. We are both targets and perpetrators of such ethnocentric judgments, which create some of the biggest barriers to intercultural harmony.

One way to overcome this "Our way is the best way" attitude and to see things in a more neutral light is to recognize that each cultural norm has advantages and disadvantages. See if you can recognize the two sides of the following American cultural norms. Then see if you can find both the upside and the downside of the foreign cultural norms.

Decreasing Ethnocentrism

	Disadvantages	Advantages
American Cultural Norms		
1. Emphasis on promptness and time	_____	_____
2. Direct explicit communication	_____	_____
3. Competitive spirit	_____	_____
4. Rugged individualism	_____	_____
5. Informality in relationships	_____	_____

	Advantages	Disadvantages
Other Cultural Norms		
1. Emphasis on harmony and order	_____	_____
2. Respect for authority	_____	_____
3. Precedence of group over the individual	_____	_____
4. Focus on relationship building	_____	_____
5. Emphasis on saving face	_____	_____

Suggestions for Using *Decreasing Ethnocentrism*

Objectives:

- To see cultural norms in a less ethnocentric, more neutral light.
- To increase open-mindedness in encountering different norms.

Intended Audience:

- Individuals seeking increased cultural sensitivity.
- Managers frustrated with behaviors arising from different cultural norms.
- Employees frustrated with behaviors of co-workers or clients/customers that arise from different cultural norms.
- Trainees in diversity seminars.

Processing the Activity:

- Individually or in groups, list the advantages of both mainstream American and other cultures' norms.
- Discuss reactions, surprises, and insights gained.
- As a personal application, individuals identify a particular norm they find difficult. They follow the same process, listing advantages and disadvantages of that norm.

Questions for Discussion:

- Which norms were hard to find either advantages or disadvantages for?
- Which norms do you feel strongest about?
- What surprises did you have? What insights?
- How can this help you in dealing with differences on the job?

Caveats and Considerations:

- Individuals may want to get into discussions about the *rightness* and/or *wrongness* of particular norms. Avoid polarization by reminding them that while they may have preferences, all cultural norms cut two ways and that working with others who have different norms is made much easier when we approach them without the judgments that their ways are wrong or inferior.
- As a variation, groups may make their own lists of favorite American norms and irritating foreign norms.

How did you do? Was it hard for you to see the downside of American norms and the upside of foreign cultural norms? Seeing that all cultural norms cut two ways makes it easier to be patient with and less judgmental of others.

Since ethnocentrism is a normal, predictable human response, you might wonder what's wrong with it. When we approach others from different cultures with this "My way is better than yours" attitude, we trigger a defensive, protective, ethnocentric response from them in return. On the other hand, when we approach different norms less judgmentally, with an understanding that all cultural rules have advantages and disadvantages, we have a better chance of making everyone feel valued and wanted. What's more, when people feel accepted, they are more open to learning your way, too.

Prejudice: Recognizing the Archie Bunker in All of Us

Archie Bunker became an American antihero in the 1960s, an Everyman whose exaggerated bigotry we could all laugh at. Perhaps the reason we laughed so hard at him was that there is a bit of Archie in all of us. Prejudice, holding preconceived and often erroneous views about other groups, is a common, human response to a complex world. Stereotypes, generalizations that are at the base of prejudice, help us organize our thinking and manage massive amounts of information. Since none of us can know every individual in every group, we make categories to simplify our worlds and then slot people into those pigeonholes. Our world then becomes more ordered and more stable. Generalizations sometimes serve a useful purpose, as in the case of lifeguards who know to watch certain groups at the beach more carefully because more individuals from these groups are involved in near drownings. However, more often stereotypes serve to limit perceptions about individuals and their capabilities. Gordon Allport, the foremost writer and thinker on the topic of prejudice, illustrates this resistance of stereotypes to facts in the following dialogue in *The Nature of Prejudice*.[3]

> **Mr. X:** The trouble with the Jews is that they only take care of their own group.
> **Mr. Y:** But the record of the Community Chest campaign shows that they give more generously, in proportion to their numbers, to the general charities of the community, than do non-Jews.
> **Mr. X:** That shows they are always trying to buy favor and intrude into Christian affairs. They think of nothing but money; that is why there are so many Jewish bankers.
> **Mr. Y:** But a recent study shows that the percentage of Jews in the banking business is negligible, far smaller than the percentage of non-Jews.
> **Mr. X:** That's just it; they don't go in for respectable business; they are only in the movie business or run night clubs.

In addition, stereotypes provoke strong emotional reactions both in the victims and the perpetrators. Those who hold them often do so with a vehemence that literally and figuratively defies reason. Those who are the objects of the overgeneralized belief can find themselves hurt, angry, resentful, or depressed by the inaccurate and impersonal assumption and its inherent insult.

Stereotypes do not develop out of thin air. They are built on some experience that produced information about a group. That information may be due to misinterpretation of other cultural norms (it may be they are not lazy, but place a higher priority on relationships than time), or it may indeed be based on accurate information ("Three people I've hired from this group have left without giving me advance warning"). Even when based on "facts," stereotypes are overgeneralizations that do not fit everyone in that group. Dr. Jorge Cherbosque, an intercultural psychologist and trainer, points out three characteristics that make stereotypes particularly harmful:

1. They are seldom neutral; they are often charged with negative assumptions.
2. They are rigid and unyielding to information that contradicts them.
3. Usually, when stereotyping and prejudice occur, the person is saying, "Don't bother me with the facts. My mind is already made up."

No one group has the corner on the market when it comes to prejudice, and no one is exempt from being the target of these preconceived notions. We hold them, not just about other groups, but about people from other parts of this country, those of the opposite sex, alumni of other schools, and members of other political parties or professions. What are your assumptions about used car salesmen? Lawyers? Harvard graduates? Politicians? New Yorkers? Californians?

What thoughts come to mind? What do you expect from people who fit these categories?

Assumptions Become Self-Fulfilling Prophecies

Like the hypochondriac who had "See, I told you so" carved on his tombstone, what we think often becomes reality. We look for behavior that validates our preconception and disregard what does not fit. We continue to collect evidence to prove our prejudices right and ignore that which shows us another picture. If, for example, you think a particular group sticks together and doesn't want to assimilate, you will notice every time employees from this group are together, talking on breaks, eating lunch, or exchanging information on the job. What you won't notice is when they are talking with people of different groups. You will probably operate according to your assumptions, ignoring people from this group, not including or inviting them to join your interactions because you believe they want to be separate. And so it goes, each time you get "proof" that your assumption is accurate, you add another brick in the barrier that separates you from them.

There is clear evidence from the many Pygmalion experiments that people perform to the level of expectation that is held for them. The expectations of those in power over us are the most influential and formative: parents over children, teachers over students, and managers over employees. If you see employees from another group as lazy, though you may never say it, your behavior will broadcast your feeling. You will continually hover or nag and prod. You might ignore them when more interesting work comes along or turn a deaf ear to their complaints. You will, in subtle ways, teach them to live down to your expectations.

One manufacturing organization refused to get hooked by these sabotaging assumptions. The managers noticed a problem on the assembly line that packaged restaurant condiments. Production was slow, and there were too many defective packets. The typical response in cases like these was to blame the immigrant workers: "They're slacking off, "They're not paying attention," or "They don't care." However, in this case, the managers went to the lead man and asked what was wrong. While not totally fluent in English, he explained that the new packaging film was the problem. They listened, but more important, they got others to listen. They set up a meeting with executives from both their own company and their film supplier. They invited the lead man to explain, with the help of an interpreter, the problem directly to the supplier. The supplier responded with a potential solution; however, the lead man explained why there would still be a problem. The good news is that he had management's support throughout. The even better news is that the meeting did not end until the supplier agreed to provide the quality of film necessary for proper packaging. By getting beyond the assumptions such as "They don't care about their work," "They're lazy and unmotivated," and "They're here to rip us off," this organization was able to get the best from this immigrant work force. They expected top-level performance, they believed these employees would give it, and they were right.

Admitting Stereotypes: The First Step

As painful as it may be, the first step in getting beyond our preconceived notions about others is admitting that we hold these stereotypes. We all have them about some other groups. None of us is exempt. Stop for a moment and try this little brain teaser:

> Just before the nurse died of the effects of an attack, she said, "He did it, the villain!" referring to one of the three doctors in the room. She didn't glance or point in his direction. The doctors were named Green, Brown, and White. Why was Dr. Brown immediately suspected?

The answer is that Dr. Green and Dr. White were both women. Did you get hooked by your own stereotypes about the roles of women and men? If so, take heart. You're human.

Take a look at the 25 statements in the box labeled *Stereotypes,* and check off any you have thought or said about any other group. Then check off any you have heard around you, though you might not have thought it yourself. Like secondhand smoke, stereotypes that are part of the society around us do color us, even though we may actively disagree or not consciously hold that stereotype. Then identify the group about which you thought, said, or heard this stereotype.

Stereotypes

Check any of the following assumptions and beliefs you have held about other cultures or ethnic groups. Also check any you have heard, though not thought yourself. Then identify the group. Finally, write the name of an individual who disproves the stereotype.

			Group	**Disprove**
_____	1.	Are smart and work hard	_____	_____
_____	2.	Are very good at sports	_____	_____
_____	3.	Tend to keep to themselves	_____	_____
_____	4.	Are usually good dancers	_____	_____
_____	5.	Are lazy, don't work hard, and aren't reliable	_____	_____
_____	6.	Usually become rich by cheating others	_____	_____
_____	7.	Are sneaky and not trustworthy	_____	_____
_____	8.	Are uninsured and don't have driver's licenses	_____	_____
_____	9.	Are dirty and smell bad	_____	_____
_____	10.	Are uneducated and not very intelligent	_____	_____
_____	11.	Are associated with organized crime	_____	_____
_____	12.	Think they are better than others	_____	_____
_____	13.	Don't want to become American	_____	_____
_____	14.	Are aggressive and pushy	_____	_____
_____	15.	Talk and think only about making money	_____	_____
_____	16.	Are happy-go-lucky and easy-going	_____	_____
_____	17.	Laugh and smile a lot	_____	_____
_____	18.	Don't want to learn English	_____	_____
_____	19.	Have illegitimate children	_____	_____
_____	20.	Can't hold their liquor and drink too much	_____	_____
_____	21.	Do well in school and get advanced degrees	_____	_____
_____	22.	Make good gardeners	_____	_____
_____	23.	Make the neighborhood go downhill	_____	_____
_____	24.	Are bigoted, prejudiced, and biased	_____	_____
_____	25.	Are miserly and ungenerous	_____	_____

Suggestions for Using *Stereotypes*

Objectives:

- Becoming aware of and admitting one's own stereotypes.
- Recognizing the pervasiveness of these preconceived assumptions in society.
- Taking steps to overcome stereotypic and prejudicial thinking.

Intended Audience:

- Individuals who want to increase sensitivity in dealing with others different from them.
- Managers who work with diverse groups.
- Trainees at a diversity awareness and cultural sensitivity seminar.
- Employees needing to deal more sensitively with individuals from diverse groups.

Processing the Activity:

- Individuals check any stereotype they have held or heard. They then write the group about which each one checked is said. Then they write the name of an individual from their own experience who disproves this stereotype.
- Individuals discuss their responses in pairs or small groups, and their reactions and insights as well.
- Total group discusses reactions and insights.

Questions for Discussion:

- What was your reaction to doing this activity?
- What surprises did you have?
- Where do these assumptions come from?
- How do they impact your behavior at work?
- What can you do to overcome this kind of thinking?
- How can you respond when you hear stereotypic comments?

Caveats and Considerations:

- Tell participants before they begin that they will be sharing their response with others.
- Expect tension and nervous laughter, as this activity is uncomfortable for most people. Discuss these feelings when processing the activity.
- Individuals apply the activity by listing the diverse groups they work with, the assumptions they hold about these groups, and finally examples which disprove the assumptions.

It may be painful or embarrassing to see such blatantly bigoted comments and to realize we are all the perpetrators of these assumptions. Even when the stereotypes are positive ("smart," "good students," "go-getters") they force us to put people into boxes, which prevents us from knowing the real person beneath the label.

Stereotype Busting: Getting beyond Limiting Assumptions

One way to begin breaking free of your assumptions about others is to find new evidence, to look for information that disproves your stereotype. Go back to each statement you checked in the list above and see if you can name one person from your experience who can disprove each of these assumptions. How did you do? If you can't find someone who doesn't fit the stereotype, start looking. Make it your task to search out new information, that which doesn't validate your assumptions.

Now, do the same for the assumptions you hold about the groups that work for you. List the diverse groups, then the assumptions you hold, and finally the examples that disprove the assumption.

Culture is a powerful factor in all human behavior. Understanding its pervasiveness and its various rules is a critical step in managing your multicultural staff more effectively. There is a relevant Chinese saying that advises, "We see what is behind our eyes." You have just taken an important step in expanding your vision.

Chapter 3

Learning the Cultural Etiquette of Communication

This chapter will give you:

1. Information about cross-cultural communication barriers that go beyond language.
2. Tips for communicating with non- and limited-English-speaking individuals.
3. Ways to deal with other languages on the job.
4. Guidelines for when and how to use interpreters and translators.
5. Strategies for getting employees to improve and learn English skills.
6. Ways to deal with accents that block communication.
7. Appropriate terms for diverse groups in a pluralistic environment.
8. Exercises for improving feedback skills.
9. Ways to resolve culture-related conflict.

"If they'd just learn English, everything would be okay," is a commonly heard refrain in organizations with multicultural staffs or clientele. If it were only that simple. Effective communication requires a shared base of experience and a common set of rules about the meaning of not just words, but intonation patterns, word order, volume, pauses, facial expressions, and gestures.

How differently we say, "I'm going to get you," as we teasingly tickle a baby under the chin as opposed to the same sentence uttered threateningly in anger to someone who has wronged us. Someone may say, "Sure, I'm okay," but his rolling eyes and sarcastic tone tell you he's not really okay at all. In addition, the word we stress in any sentence can drastically alter its meaning. Try the following sentence, stressing a different word each time:

I am going to do this for you tomorrow.

I **am** going to do this for you tomorrow.

I am **going** to do this for you tomorrow.

I am going to do **this** for you tomorrow.

I am going to do this for **you** tomorrow.

I am going to do this for you **tomorrow**.

It's More than Language: Cultural Sources of Misunderstanding

Communication is definitely more than just words, and in addition to language differences, cultures have varied norms about the nonverbal aspects of getting the message across. Newcomers who learn English may still be operating according to the nonverbal rules of their native languages, and herein lies the confusion and chance for misinterpretations such as these:

- The Arab who speaks louder and stands closer is seen as pushy.
- The Latina who drops her eyes when speaking with a boss is seen as unassertive.
- The Japanese who has an impassive facial expression is seen as inscrutable and deceptive.
- The Filipina who confuses the pronouns *he* and *she* is thought to be uneducated.
- The Middle Easterner who takes time to chitchat before getting down to business is seen as inefficient.
- The African-American who makes direct eye contact is seen as challenging and aggressive.

Let's take a look at the differences in nonverbal rules that are at the source of miscommunications such as those above.

Degree of Directness

Even the purpose of communication is culturally defined. Americans and Northern Europeans see communication pragmatically, as a means of getting information across and accomplishing tasks. Much of the rest of the world sees it as a means of building relationships. In the Middle East, for example, business is not transacted until there has been a cup of tea and a period of chitchat, inconsequential conversation that eases both parties into the relationship. This ritual of small talk may seem like a time-wasting block to efficiency by American standards, yet it is an expected and necessary part of business for Middle Easterners. Americans' direct, "Let's get to the point" approach, on the other hand, may seem rude, cold, and offensive to a Latin American or an Arab expecting a more subtle approach.

Appropriate Subjects

Still another difference is apparent in the subjects that are considered appropriate. Many Asian groups regard feelings as too private to be shared. Latinos generally appreciate inquiries about family members, while Arabs and Asians find this topic far too personal to discuss with work associates. Filipinos and Arabs think nothing of asking the price you've paid for something, while Americans would usually see such behavior as rude.

Facial Expressions and Eye Contact

What makes facial expressions and eye contact such stumbling blocks in communication is that these behaviors are learned at an early age and are generally unconscious. The widened eyes that show an American's anger have their counterpart in a Chinese person's narrowed eyes. A smile may not signify affability and friendliness, but may be a sign of embarrassment on the part of your Asian employees. A direct stare by an African-American or Arab is not meant as a challenge to your authority, and dropped eyes may be a sign of respect from your Latino and Asian employees. A smile and nod from many Asians may mean they are trying to preserve harmony and save face. Differences in eye contact during listening have caused misunderstandings between African-Americans and Caucasian-Americans. According to communication expert Dr. Bob Mezoff, whites look away while speaking but make eye contact when listening. Because blacks do just the opposite, the impression is often made that they are not paying attention when listening or that they are challenging the white listener when they are speaking.[42]

Touch

One of the most powerful nonverbal communicators is human touch. Yet whom and how we touch is culturally prescribed. Devout Muslim and Orthodox Jewish men never touch a woman outside of their families, even to shake hands. A soft, warm handshake, which is seen as welcoming and friendly in Mexican culture, might be viewed as weak and wimpy by American standards. In addition, in some cultures people are sensitive to being touched in certain places. The Chinese, for example, never want to be touched on the head. Flip Wilson's "Don't you touch me" comedy routine poked fun at African-Americans' dislike at being touched when angry. It has been suggested that the recent culture clash between Koreans and African-Americans in both Los Angeles and New York may have its roots in different cultural rules about touch. Korean store owners, feeling it is rude to touch anyone they do not know, place change on the counter. Their African-American customers, on the other hand, expecting to have the change placed in their hands, are offended at what they perceive as the Koreans' repulsion at touching them.

Loudness and Pitch

Americans are often viewed as noisy and rude by the English and other Europeans who speak more softly, while Arabs and southern Europeans generally speak more loudly. Many Asian languages make use of higher pitch levels, which may be grating to the ears of those who are used to lower pitches.

Silence

Even not talking is culturally prescribed. While in the mainstream American culture there is a recognition of the "pregnant pause," silence is generally something to be avoided. Because of this discomfort with silence, someone will usually jump in and start talking. In Japanese culture, silence is considered an important part of communication, a chance for serious consideration of what has been said and a gesture of respect for the speaker. It is no wonder that the Japanese are often irritated by the American's constant barrage of words while the listener is trying to think. They also find the all-too-common American habit of finishing a person's sentences disconcerting, rude, and even arrogant. Even when individuals learn English, many of their native-language rules will stay with them, influencing both how they send and receive messages.

Dealing with the Frustration of Not Understanding or Being Understood

Whenever we ask seminar participants what they do when they are attempting to communicate with someone who does not speak English, they invariably reply, "Speak louder and slower." It is common for us to continue to repeat unsuccessful behavior, getting more and more frustrated all the time. A recent experience with a Korean store clerk showed us the pointlessness of this approach.

It was December 23, and Anita ran into her local minimarket to get a few lottery tickets as last-minute stocking stuffers. Because she was in a rush and harried by holiday season pressures, she blurted out in her usual rapid-fire speaking style to the unsuspecting Korean clerk behind the counter, "I'd like five rub-off lottery tickets." She couldn't understand what the clerk said, but she could read the confusion on the clerk's face, so she repeated her original request, only this time louder and slower: "I'd like five rub-off lottery tickets." Again the clerk said something unintelligible, this time looking even more bewildered. For the third time, louder and with even more exaggerated mouth movements, Anita repeated her request. In exasperation, the clerk went to the computerized ticket machine and punched out a ticket with five quick picks. By this time Anita's slow burn had turned to a boil, and she said between clenched teeth, "This is not what I asked for. I want five rub-off tickets!" At this point, another clerk came to the rescue, saying a few words in their native language. The no longer frantic clerk turned to Anita with a smile of relief on her face. "Scratch-off, scratch-off," the clerk kept repeating.

This incident points up some of the difficulties and frustrations experienced on both sides of the language barriers we face regularly in our multicultural society. It also clearly shows the mistakes we often make in communicating with people whose command of English is limited.

What Doesn't Help

The biggest stumbling block in situations like these is the anger that often comes from the frustration of not understanding or being understood. That anger becomes a powerful saboteur of communication in two ways. First, a message that comes out of anger threatens the receiver, making him/her less able to use the little English he or she may know. Anger also blocks the thinking of the sender, preventing that person from finding creative solutions to the impasse. So, the sender keeps repeating the same unsuccessful behavior, each time louder, slower, and with more irritation.

What Does Help

Understanding the source of your anger is a step in getting beyond it. Language is more than just a means of communicating. The language we speak gives us our identity and defines our nationality. Although the Pilgrims had found freedom from religious persecution in Holland, they felt compelled to leave to come to America because their children were growing up speaking Dutch. Closer to home, the battles about bilingual education rage on in school districts all over our country.

But language is more than identity. It also represents turf. My territory, my barrio, or my country is defined by the dominant language spoken there, hence the fights in many communities over English-only laws or the heated debates about bilingual ballots and driver's tests. The emotional content of these arguments signals much deeper issues than the rule or regulation being debated. Power and esteem are at stake.

Finally, being able to communicate gives us one of our most powerful means of control in the world. It is our prime vehicle for influencing events and people. We see its impact daily when we explain procedures to a subordinate, order food in a restaurant, or get directions when we're lost. When we can't communicate and find it difficult to get our message across, we feel our control slipping away. The less control we feel, the greater our frustration and our stress. And that frustration is generally directed toward those whom we don't understand.

Dealing with Other Languages on the Job

One of the most divisive issues in multicultural workplaces is that of the speaking of other languages on the job. Tempers flare, and employees polarize into warring camps, building resentment and animosity toward one another. Let's take a look at the issue from a little different perspective. Imagine that you've just been transferred to a division in one of your company's manufacturing plants in Brazil. Wow! Images of carnival, Ipanema, Sugar Loaf, and the Amazon flash through your mind. When reality sets in, you realize you don't speak Portuguese. But you think there must be people there who speak English—there are always people who speak English.

You take a crash course in Portuguese, enough to get the basics, though you're still far from comfortable. When you get there you find that there are many bilingual supervisors and a few U.S. transplants working at your new location. You breathe a sigh of relief. Ask yourself what language you would use when

- Talking with your bilingual supervisors?
- Having a meeting with other American managers?
- Eating lunch with another U.S.-born manager?
- Conferencing with British, Australian, or Canadian business associates?
- Phoning home to talk with your spouse and/or children?

Wouldn't it feel awkward *not* to use English in these situations? Yet we take offense when others speak their native languages around us, especially at work. A first place to start in dealing with the language issue is to examine and question the almost automatic assumptions we make when confronted with languages other than English.

Assumptions that Get Us into Trouble

1. They're Talking about Me

When you hear a group of staff members speaking a language other than English, you may jump to the conclusion that you are the topic of conversation. In fact, they may be talking about their families, a work problem, or the weather. If you knew that they were speaking English but couldn't overhear what they were saying, would you still assume that they were talking about you?

2. They Don't Want to Learn English

Huge enrollments and long waiting lists at adult education English classes in cities with large immigrant populations tell us that newcomers to this society do want to learn English. Evans Adult School in downtown Los Angeles, one of 27 adult schools in that city, offers English and amnesty classes from 5:30 A.M. to 2:30 A.M., and still has a waiting list of over 15,000 would-be students. In addition, the Los Angeles Community College district reports that the number of hours spent teaching ESL increased 178 percent from 1980 to 1988. However, making a living and taking care of family may take up all the waking hours some employees have. At a subsistence level, spending two to three hours in the evening at school may be a lower priority than taking a second job. It is clear to everyone in this society that English is the language of power and that to advance in this culture, one must learn English. How long that takes—a few months, a few years, or a generation— depends a great deal on economic circumstances.

3. They Know English; They Just Don't Want to Use It

Even when someone is learning a new language, he or she may be hesitant to use it until he or she feels more proficient. How easy is it for you to use your high school Spanish or French when traveling? Most of us feel self-conscious and unsure of ourselves when beginning to use a new language. In a "Managing a Diverse Work Force" seminar, one Filipino nurse manager expressed her feelings about the stress of having to speak a second language all day. While she does speak English on the job and requires her native-Tagalog-speaking nurses to do the same, she understands their stress level and the comfort they feel in lapsing into their native tongue. Imagine the pressure of having to think, speak, and perform in a second language all day.

Finally, there is another factor operating. Many newcomers to the United States come from cultures where social class distinctions make it difficult to initiate conversations or converse at all with someone whom they believe to be above them in society's pecking order. To do so in a language in which they are not confident is doubly difficult.

Rethinking your assumptions and walking in the other person's shoes help you come to a more neutral position about some of the language clashes you experience. Resolving this issue is a two-way street. Every nation needs a common language as a unifying element. Newcomers do need to make an attempt to learn English. On the other hand, those who are native-born Americans or longtime residents can help the process of acculturation by showing understanding and openness to those who haven't yet acquired proficiency in English.

One way to do this is to team-build around language differences. Use these differences as an opportunity to strengthen your work group's feeling of teamness. Have employees share perceptions as well as their needs in relation to language differences. Speakers of other languages need to hear the reactions of co-workers who may be feeling left out or talked about, while English-only speakers need to understand the comfort that others find in speaking their native tongues. Open-ended statements such as the following are often helpful in getting the discussion started and in keeping it focused:

When I hear employees speaking another language, I . . . .
When I don't understand someone who speaks with an accent, I . . . .
When someone doesn't understand me, I wish they would . . . .
I speak my native language to others at work because . . . .
When someone doesn't understand me, I . . . .
One thing that is frustrating for me is . . . .

These discussions can lessen tension by helping staff members understand each other's difficulties. Insights gained improve relationships and can lead to creative problem solving.

It is also important to clarify the language policy at work. Let people know the rules about language—what's permitted and what's off-limits. Some legal precedents have been set recently regarding this issue, so be careful about respecting the rights of employees when they are on their own time at breaks and lunch. When all is said (or not said) and done, remember, there is a form of communication that supersedes all tongues: the language of attitudes. As we approach one another in our multicultural world, our attitude speaks volumes. As someone once quipped, "Attitude is more important than aptitude."

Communicating with Limited-English-Speaking Staff

In the meantime, you still need to find a way to communicate effectively. Here are a few techniques that could work in your organization.

1. Make It Visual

As the saying goes, a picture is worth a thousand words. Using pictures, signs, diagrams, and symbols gives you another dimension beyond words with which to make yourself clear. In Anita's lottery-buying impasse, had she drawn a picture of a lottery ticket, pointed to one, or shown a sample, she could have quickly overcome her difficulty. A veteran army instructor who regularly taught courses to allied military personnel from many countries advised that diagrams, charts, and graphs were critical aids in teaching his classes where most students had limited command of English. International symbols on road signs have long been used in Europe, where there are many languages spoken in a relatively small area and where there is much travel between countries. Be wary, however, of overkill with visuals. One organization attempting to explain its new 401K plan to Spanish-speaking employees used an elaborate slide presentation full of graphics and diagrams. Most of the assembly-line workers in the audience had no experience reading bar graphs and pie charts and were totally confused by the presentation.

2.   Show-and-Tell

Kindergarten isn't the only place where show-and-tell is useful. Demonstrating what you are explaining can often get the message across faster than words in any language. Wouldn't you rather have someone show you how to do something than have to figure it out from written instructions in a manual? Anita could have taken a coin and made scratching motions to show the clerk what kind of lottery ticket she wanted. In on-the-job situations, this works best when you first show the person how to do a task, then do it together, and finally observe the individual in action so you can be sure she has understood.

3.   Use Their Language

If getting your message or information across is more important than showing your displeasure at someone's limited English, then using the other person's language may be your best bet. Don't panic. This doesn't mean you need to speak the other person's language. Emergency instructions, school district letters to parents, and signs in airports are common uses of bilingual or multilingual communication. However, there are more. A local nursing home was temporarily stumped when its elderly residents kept complaining about not being able to communicate their needs to the mainly Spanish-speaking aides. The solution? Bilingually printed sheets with the 20 or so most-used requests written in English in the left column and Spanish in the right. Now when residents need something, they just point to the request on the English column and the aide reads it on the corresponding line in the Spanish column. Another example of bilingualism in action is the Teatro Para Los Niños (Children's Theater), which performs Spanish/English musicals for elementary school children. A recent performance focused on changing role stereotypes, showing that it is okay for boys to cook and for girls to play basketball. Without the use of both languages, many students would not have understood the message.

4.   Take It Easy

When a language is not one's mother tongue, processing information in it takes longer. Not only is the vocabulary often unfamiliar, but grammar and intonation patterns are sometimes new. It is helpful to slow down and pause between sentences so the listener has time to let each segment of your message sink in. Then summarize at the end, pulling all the pieces together.

5.   Keep It Simple

"Take the ball and run with it," "go the extra mile," "a tough row to hoe," "a thumbnail sketch," and "beyond the call of duty" are examples of idiomatic expressions common in everyday speech. Most of us probably use many throughout the course of a day. Yet, for a non-native speaker who tries to translate them literally, they make no sense at all. In addition, jargon, that is, words that are specific to a particular business or industry, may also be confusing. In construction, for example, calling mortar "mud" or talking about "roughing in the plumbing" would be difficult for anyone outside the profession to understand, let alone someone struggling with English. Finally, it helps to use simple words that are commonly heard, for example, *problem* rather than *glitch* or *snafu*.

6.   Say It Again

When you're having difficulty making yourself understood, it does help to repeat if you use different words. One caution here, however. When looking for another way to say something, beware of cognates, words in other languages that look and sound similar to English words. The most common mistakes occur between Spanish and English. While *largo* in Spanish looks like *large*, it means "long." And if you're embarrassed, don't say you're *embarazada* because that means "pregnant."

7.   Assume Confusion

Whatever you do, don't ask people if they understand and then take their *yes* to mean they do. In many other cultures, saying no is the height of rudeness. Besides, even in the mainstream American culture, we often say we understand even when we're a little fuzzy because saying we don't understand makes us feel inadequate. Instead of asking, watch the person's face for nonverbal signs of confusion to see if they are following your directions correctly. Also watch behavior as the individual begins to act on what you've said. Often the look on the face of the person with whom you are communicating lets you know if you've gotten your message across.

8.   Get Help

When you've done steps 1 through 7 and you still are having trouble, get help. A bilingual friend or colleague can often get you out of a bind. In many organizations, staff who speak other languages are listed and called on a rotating basis to translate in interchanges between staff and customers or clients. Just make sure the person who is doing the interpreting is fluent enough in both languages to be able to make things clear to all parties. Also make sure the interpreter understands the concepts you are communicating

9.   Walk in Their Shoes

To help reduce your frustration and anger when you get blocked by a language barrier, try to put yourself in the other person's place. Have you ever been somewhere where no one spoke English? How did it feel? What would have helped you? Remembering these times gives you some empathy for the bewilderment that the individual might be feeling.

10. Smile, but Don't Laugh

A smile helps others relax, and the reduction of tension increases your chances for effective communication. However, be careful not to appear to be laughing at the individual. The Los Angeles County Commission on Human Relations reports that immigrants' most common request is that people not laugh at them when they try to speak English. When we're not confident of our ability in an area, we're particularly vulnerable and sensitive to slights. While you may not be laughing at the person's poor English, your joking manner or teasing banter may seem like ridicule. No matter what languages we do or don't speak, all of us need to be treated with dignity and respect. Communication that has these elements at the base will go a long way toward overcoming language and cultural differences.

Speaking of Accents

"I couldn't understand a thing they said!" is a common response to accented English. While we may think accents are charming, all too often, native English speakers tune out the minute they hear an accent. Instead of trying to understand the speaker, attention is focused on finding a pause to interject an irritated "What?"

All accents are not created equal in our perceptions. A British accent calls up images of an Oxford scholar or a Shakespearean actor, and a continental accent might be a prized qualification for a Maître d'. Not so with many other accents, though. There is often an assumption that the person speaking with the accent is less competent or knowledgeable.

The "Fax Solution"

A clever manager at American International Group, a large insurance company, found a unique solution to the accent barrier. Many of the company's claims takers in the San Francisco home office were Filipinas with strong accents. There were continual complaints from the French Creole employees in Louisiana who regularly phoned in claims to the home office that they couldn't understand the claims processors. To deal with this impasse, the boss designed a form that was sent via fax to the claims department. It contained all the information previously obtained through phone conversation and avoided the interpersonal rub. It worked to smooth out the procedure, reducing claims response time from 72 hours to 24–48 hours. But an even bigger miracle took place. The fax exchange brought these two groups of employees together. When the claims reporters saw how efficiently the claims were processed by people they had previously discounted, they gained new respect for their accented home-office colleagues. Employees from the two groups began talking with each other and developing more productive relationships. The frequency of phone conversations increased, problems were solved more quickly, and complaints about accents disappeared.

In communicating with people who speak with accents, it is helpful to remind yourself that an accent tells you an individual is attempting to learn and use English. Second, have a little empathy. How perfectly do you speak Spanish, French, or some other language? Third, recognize that no matter how well someone learns English, he or she will almost never be able to sound like a native speaker because of a number of language differences.

Sounds

It is believed that all human babies are capable of making all the sounds of every language in the world. By the age of 5, however, children are able to reproduce only the sounds of their native language. Hence, some sounds may be impossible for a non-native speaker of a language to learn to articulate as an adult. English has 26 letters, yet 44 sounds. Many of these sounds do not exist in other languages. The *sh* and *th* sounds are as difficult for many non-native speakers as the rolled *r* is for Americans. In Spanish, for example, there is no *sh* sound, hence the substitution of the *ch* as in *chave* for "shave" and *chure* for "sure." In addition, *b* and *v* have the same sound in Spanish and are used interchangeably, so there is generally a difficulty in distinguishing between the two in English. In Tagalog, there is no *sh* or *f* sound, so *s* is substituted for *sh* (*see* for "she") and *p* for *f* (*pun* for "fun"). Japanese people often confuse the *l* and *r* sounds. It helps to pay attention to the sound patterns of the accents you deal with most frequently and learn the most common substitutions people make.

Structure

Languages differ in more than just vocabulary. They have different systems of syntax (word order), grammar, and parts of speech. When someone attempts to translate into English vocabulary using another language's syntax and grammar, meanings may become distorted, resulting in confusion. In Spanish, as in many European languages, for example, adjectives follow the nouns they modify rather than preceding them as they do in English ("the house white" versus "the white house"). Some Slavic languages have no articles (the, a, an), so figuring out when and how to use these words in English may be difficult. A native speaker of Serbo-Croatian, for example, may leave out the article when needed, as in "I go to store," or add it when not appropriate, as in Czechoslovakian-born Ivana Trump's "the Donald." In Tagalog, there is no distinction between the masculine and feminine pronouns *he/she* and *him/her*, so it is common to hear Filipinos using the wrong pronoun when speaking English.

Accent Reduction Training for Presenters and Customer Contact Staff

While you may be open to taking the time to develop the extra patience and skill to get across the accent barrier, your customers and clients may not. Employees whose responsibilities involve customer/client contact or those who make presentations need to communicate as clearly as possible. In many cases that calls for accent reduction training. Not only does this improve relations with those using your organization's services or products, but it often serves as an aid in the employee's career mobility. Generally, this type of training is conducted by a communication consultant with expertise in accent reduction and focuses on the following:

- American pronunciation of vowels, especially the *schwa* sound (the *uh* sound of a vowel in any unaccented syllable) and consonants, especially *r, ch, sh, th, l, n, s,* and *d.*

- Intonation and stress patterns.
- Linking rules to create smoother-sounding statements.
- Presentation skills for staff involved with this responsibility.

Judith Weidman, a Los Angeles–based communications consultant who teaches ESL and American pronunciation classes, offers advice to organizations about this type of training. First, she cautions them to bill the course as effective communication rather than finger-pointing at the immigrant employee. She suggests advertising the training in company newsletters, on bulletin boards, and through managers and supervisors at staff meetings. Once the first course is completed, she says, graduates then become the best promoters.

Ms. Weidman goes on to say that the consultant needs to understand both the organization and the students in order to tailor the training appropriately. For example, simulations of meetings and presentations that give participants a chance to practice are important vehicles for learning, and they need to fit the organizational reality. Rewards such as certificates and newsletter mention are important as well. Finally, supervisors and managers need to be encouraged to reinforce the use of new learning by employees on the job.

Ms. Weidman, a former Peace Corps volunteer who taught English in the Philippines, coaches her students to become "pronunciation detectives" so they can continue learning on their own. She gives them tips such as the following:

- Find a mentor/model, such as a favorite television announcer, and tape that person speaking. Listen to the tape in the car or whenever there is time.
- Tape yourself speaking English on the phone at work or at home. Listen to your pronunciation. What do you need to work on?
- Make tapes of radio talk shows. Not only does this help with pronunciation but it also teaches the art of asking questions, something many non-native English speakers find difficult.

Teaching English: How to Set Up Classes and Recruit Students

Helping employees learn English benefits both the employee and the organization. Workers' confidence and career options increase when they have greater facility with English. Employees appreciative of the organization's investment in them result in lower turnover for the company. In addition, the greater ease of communication that English skills bring means higher productivity from fewer mistakes and higher morale from decreased frustration on the part of English-only speakers. One of the challenges is getting employees to participate in ESL programs. Older workers who are comfortable with their limited English-language skills may have a difficult time overcoming inertia. Other employees may be embarrassed about their poor English and may not want to call attention to themselves. Finally, workers who have not had much education or who have had bad experiences with school may not have the confidence in their own ability to succeed in a class.

Beyond the personal blocks, the most formidable obstacles to getting employees to learn English are the perennial time and money limits. Clever organizations have found some creative ways to deal with these obstacles.

1. On-Site Classes

Many organizations have brought English classes to employees by hiring instructors who teach classes after hours on site. Both the organization and employee invest. The organization pays for the instruction, while the employees give their time. Employers like Memorial Medical Center in Las Cruces, New Mexico, make use of U.S. Department of Education National Workplace Literacy Project grants to help fund on-site classes in their Step Ahead comprehensive literacy program. Employees attend during work hours, and classes are paid for by the employer.

Transamerica Occidental Life Insurance Company used a similar approach in providing ESL classes for its data processing department. Instruction was provided at the request of managers who wanted help for their non-native speakers of English. Complaints were registered from internal customers who reported having difficulties in communicating with the heavily accented speech of data processing staff members, most of whom were Asian, with the largest group being native Chinese speakers. The first ESL course was given to a group from a variety of native-language backgrounds. The second time around, the model was refined and the course was offered to native Chinese speakers only, enabling the course content to be tailored to the specific language acquisition and accent reduction needs of the group. Courses were arranged through UCLA's American Language Center and provided on site, with Transamerica paying tuition and workers giving the time, four one-hour sessions per week for eight weeks. Managers were included in planning and debriefing sessions. In planning future classes, Dr. Joan Klubnik, coordinator, says she would recommend more support for managers in helping them reinforce the learning on the job; more emphasis on the "buddy system" of reinforcement for participants; and the use of Visipitch, a device that helps language learners see pitch ranges and thereby modify their speech.

Care needs to be taken in how classes are set up, however. Another organization decided to provide ESL classes for its mainly Spanish-speaking housekeeping staff. Classes were held on site immediately after shift at 3:00 P.M. As the department had no budget for education, employees were asked to pay a nominal fee for the 10-week course, approximately $50–$60. Because they were happy with the convenience of the time and location, workers were willing to pay their own tuition. Once classes began, another group of limited-English-speaking employees joined. These, however, were researchers with Ph.D.s. Since they worked until 5:00 P.M., classes were held during their regular work hours. In addition, since their boss had sent them, they requested that their department pay for their tuition. Because this department had money in its education budget, the department head complied. Both groups were learning and enjoying the experience. However, when the housekeeping staff found out about the differences in arrangements, they felt they had been unfairly treated. Although they still wanted the class to continue, because of the discriminatory nature of the arrangement, the organization canceled the class.

2. Joining Forces with Community Colleges and Adult Schools

If your organization has a potential group of ESL students, you may be able to team up with a local community college or adult school. Since these schools are generally reimbursed by the state based on the number of students they have and the instructional hours they provide, they may be willing to hold classes for your employees on site if you provide the classroom space. Even if classes are held in school facilities, fees are minimal.

3. Paying for Students' Tuition

Some organizations pay the tuition for private English instruction for key employees or for accent reduction classes for those who need it. Generally, independent consultants who specialize in this area are contracted with to provide this tutoring.

4. Rewarding English Acquisition

In other organizations, employees are given pay increases as they pass into higher levels of English proficiency. Promotions and pay upgrades may depend on these skills.

5. Teaching Supervisors the Language of Employees

Teaching supervisors the language of employees may sound counterproductive. If you are attempting to teach employees English, why teach their language to supervisors? Pic N Save, a Southern California retail chain, found this approach very effective. Their initial objective in presenting Spanish-language classes for supervisors on company time was to enable them to communicate more easily with their Spanish-speaking workers. They got more than they bargained for. When workers saw their supervisors trying out their fledgling Spanish, they felt that the organization was trying to meet them halfway. This effort gave them the motivation to use the English they were learning. And as they heard supervisors make mistakes in Spanish, they were less self-conscious about doing so in English. What had been a language barrier now became a cooperative venture, with each asking the other for help: "How do you say *shelf* in Spanish?" "Como se dice *caja* en Inglés?" ("How do you say *box* in English?").

Using Computer-Assisted Instruction

One way to teach English to employees in a cost-effective way is to make use of computer-assisted instruction. Weber Metals, a Paramount, California, manufacturer of aluminum and titanium forgings for aerospace, had a problem. Most of its 200 employees are Latino workers whose native language is Spanish and who have a low level of formal education. In addition to communication difficulties, the company was concerned about employees' ability to deal with planned-for changes such as computer-assisted design and manufacturing (CAD/CAM) and an expanded management information system (MIS). Enter Sinclair Hugh, a personnel consultant who engineered a partnership with the Paramount Unified School District to deal with the challenge. Knowing how difficult it was to get workers to go to the school, Ed Quesada, director of the district's adult school and cocreator of this partnership, helped bring the school to the workers. With a $50,000 federal grant, the school district set up four computers at Weber Metals, which were hooked to the adult school's mainframe. The Computer Assisted Instruction Centers, in a pilot project with Computer Curriculum Corporation of Sunnyvale, California, now offer 24 courses in 1,800 hours of instruction to Weber employees. Programs feature self-paced learning and interactive instruction, with the computers asking the students questions and telling them if their answers are correct. The ESL program even has a digital speech system that gives the learner audio information through headphones so he can hear digitized pronunciation of English words and sentences. In addition to ESL, programs in reading, math, communication skills, and GED preparation have been added, and a Spanish-language program is in the works.

A school district coordinator spends three hours per day at the company helping students, and two Weber employees have been trained to assist learners and answer questions. Though employees are not given time off to spend at the learning center, over 50 percent of the factory work force have enrolled, and ESL is the most popular course. What motivates these hourly employees to come in before work, stay after their shifts, or eat lunch on a morning break so they can spend their half-hour lunch period on the computer? Weber entices employees with lottery tickets and a gift program in which they receive a $15 gift for each five hours of instruction. However, the greatest motivators seem to be the increased promotional opportunities and self-esteem gained by employees who take advantage of this opportunity. One ESL participant's increased bilingual skills, for example, helped him get promoted to supervisor. Another center student commented that what he gained in knowledge was worth the $20 a day he lost in overtime by coming to the center.[20]

Solving the Interpreter and Bilingual Dilemmas

If your organization makes the decision that communication in an additional language is necessary, there is a need for setting up a mechanism for doing so. One of the biggest complaints by bilingual staff who are asked to interpret is that this extra duty takes time away from their regular work and leaves them continuously backlogged. Another complaint is that they are sometimes asked to interpret when the message sender does not want to give bad news, for example, calling to collect on an overdue bill or telling a family member that a loved one has died in the emergency room. A third complaint is that the organization wants them to use their second language with clients and customers who speak that language, but punishes them for using it with co-workers. To avoid some of these problems and to assure that interpreters are available, organizations have devised the following methods.

1. Rotating Interpreter Bank

At one hospital, all bilingual staff members are listed by language on a master list. When an interpreter is needed, the next person on the list is called so that no one is unduly burdened.

2. Full-Time Interpreter

One organization with a large Spanish-speaking clientele employs a full-time interpreter who is on call at all times. Since she is a trained interpreter who understands the culture and language of the receivers of the information and a professional who understands the content of the messages she is relaying, the organization can be assured that the correct information is getting through. In another company, which has targeted a small but lucrative Japanese clientele, there is a Japanese interpreter on duty 24 hours a day.

3. Pay for Bilingual Skills

Many organizations pay additional bonuses to those who have and use their bilingual skills on the job. One such employer allows managers to make a request for this bonus by documenting the need for the use of the second language by one of their staff members. In others, employees applying for the bilingual pay differential must pass written and oral tests in the second language to be certified.

4. Hire or Train Bilingual Supervisors

Bilingual ability can be a job requirement when hiring supervisors, or existing supervisors can be taught a second language. A third option is to target bilingual employees with managerial potential and teach them supervisory skills.

5. Informal Interpreter Network

The informal interpreter network—or the "Call Maria or Juan" method—is probably the most common. This system works if your bilingual employees have a good command of both languages and if they understand the content of the information that needs to be communicated. Nguyen from the shop floor and Lupe from the cafeteria may be able to help in relaying directions in their own departments. However, these impromptu interpreters would probably have difficulty in quickly explaining and comprehensively providing specialized information about changes in, say, the organization's health insurance coverage.

Avoiding the Common Pitfalls in Translation

In communicating in a multilingual environment, you may find the need to put information in writing in other languages. Monica Moreno, intercultural communications expert and translator, explains that organizations may unknowingly subvert their goals by not making use of professional translators. She sees the mistakes and the problems caused when translations are not professionally done, such as the case of the poorly translated employee benefit program that led to workers' disgruntlement when they didn't get the "prize" (*premio*) they were mistakenly promised. To make her point, Monica asks executives if they would be comfortable having the receptionist make a presentation on a complex company policy or program. She then explains that is often what they do when they assign a translation to any employee who happens to speak the second language. What often results are the most common translation pitfalls:

- Poorly written translations due to incorrect grammar and misspelling, which insult readers.

- Inadequate translations due to lack of understanding on the part of the translator.
- Inaccurate translations due to lack of vocabulary and understanding on the part of the translator.
- Inappropriate translations due to the translator's inability to write to the level of the reader.

Monica, a native of Argentina, gives the following suggestions to assure accurate and appropriate translations that achieve the organization's objectives:

1. The translator should be a native speaker of the language he/she is writing. While Monica is fluent in English, Italian, and French, she writes only the Spanish translations because Spanish is her native language. A native speaker generally has the most complete grasp of a language.
2. A translation should be edited by a native speaker from a different country than the original translator's. This is especially important in the Spanish-speaking world, where regional and national differences in vocabulary and idiomatic expressions can cause confusion.
3. Use a professional translator. While interpreters in the United States are certified, there is no official U.S. certification for translators as there is in many other countries. A professional understands the nuances of communication and has the ability to grasp different levels of content from simple to complex. Information may be more credible coming from an objective outsider who has no vested interest in the communication nor previous relationship with staff. He/she is also able to adjust the translation to suit the target group. Checking references and having a native speaker read a sample might be ways to verify the translator's skill.
4. Augment the translated message with question/answer sessions in the language of staff. An employee newsletter is generally understandable to all who can read; however, if the document being translated has to do with policies, procedures, or programs, there is a need for employees to discuss implications, get clarification, and verify their understanding. This can best be done in an explanation session held in the employees' native language.
5. Think ahead, and budget for translation services. To have a document that is written by an executive vice president and checked by the legal department translated by a bilingual employee with a sixth-grade education is asking for trouble. Include the cost of translation in the budget when planning for any program that needs to be communicated to non-English-speaking employees.
6. If you use internal bilingual staff to translate, verify the translation. Having the document translated back into English by another bilingual employee is a way to check for accuracy.
7. Provide the option of translation in a nondiscriminatory way. If you ask employees if they want a translation of a document or a session in their native language, workers are apt to say no. Most don't want to be a burden to the organization nor expose their lack of English skills, so they would be reluctant to respond with a yes. It is more helpful to make the option available in a matter-of-fact-way, by providing two stacks of documents, one in each language, or two discussion groups, Spanish in room A and English in room B.

From the Organization's Point of View: Formal Communication that Everyone Understands

Getting information to employees is a critical link in any organization, one that is not easily accomplished anywhere. When employees don't understand English, the task is even more difficult. Witness the following:

- A group of Spanish-speaking new hires in a large metropolitan hospital sit through four hours of new employee orientation, not understanding a word of what's being said. Many take the written materials home and have their children explain it to them in Spanish.
- A manufacturing firm introduced a new employee stock option plan (ESOP) program to employees. Knowing that many production-line workers do not speak English, the firm had the program translated into Spanish. After the extensive Spanish-language presentation was made, the first question that was timidly asked was, "What is stock?"
- A firm that is attempting to reach its limited-English-speaking staff has its newsletter printed bilingually. The Spanish portion, however, is so poorly written, with grammatical and spelling errors, that the Spanish-speaking readers are insulted.

In working through these communication mazes, an important question needs to be answered. What is the objective of the communication and who is the end receiver? If the goal is to get information to a particular group of employees, all of whom do not understand English, then sending the message in English probably won't meet your objective.

English-Only versus Bilingual Communication

Many organizations have policies that proclaim English as the official language of the organization. Other companies routinely communicate in more than one language. Rather than polarize opinions between these two extremes, let's take a look at the advantages and disadvantages of each and the range of alternatives between them.

It is said that India, with its myriad of native languages, would not have become a nation without the English language as a unifying force. Using one language throughout the organization can be a common base for all staff. It also has the advantage of not showing preference for any one second-language group. In addition, having documents translated into many different languages or having a session in 10 different languages may be unwieldy and costly. Waving an "English Only" banner, on the other hand, can alienate workers who are non-English speaking, making them feel less valued. A policy of all-English communication may also keep you from getting your message across. It may lead to a distortion of the message because you do not control how the English is being informally translated. We've all played the game of telephone and seen how even in the same language, a message gets altered as it is passed from person to person. When employees are left to figure it out for themselves, the translations of their bilingual children or co-workers can produce the same misinterpretations. When misunderstandings can be dangerous, as in the case of labels on hazardous chemicals, you may be legally required to make sure you convey necessary information to workers.

Bilingual or multilingual communication is common among utility companies, school districts, and other agencies that need to get information to users of their services in the community. The main difficulty seems to be in determining when a group has enough people to warrant the use of its language. While you have 150 Spanish-speaking employees and only 10 Vietnamese workers, are the 10 any less important than the 150? Once begun, the practice sets a precedent that needs to be followed with each succeeding group.

There are some alternatives that have merit. One is to have all written communication in English but hold bilingual explanation sessions where employees can comfortably ask questions and get clarifications and additional explanations in their native languages. Another is to set up multilingual discussion groups where employees can discuss the information in their own languages and have the one employee in the group who is most proficient in English present the group's questions to the presenter or panel.

Suggestions for Managers and HR Professionals

In communicating formally with employees, considering the following points will be helpful:

1. Adjust the level of the communication to the education level of the employees to whom it is aimed. The legalese of a new 401K plan would be unintelligible to most employees regardless of language. New employee orientation materials written at the 12th-grade level may be over the heads of many entry-level new hires. Complicated graphs and charts may only confuse someone with little formal education.

2. Pictures that show in action what you are describing in words are helpful. Visual depictions are especially helpful in explaining safety procedures. For example, the international symbol

   is generally understood cross-culturally. The correct and incorrect ways to lift a box can be shown more clearly in pictures than in many pages of text.

3. Demonstrations that show right and wrong ways overcome language barriers. Showing the group the wrong, then the right, way to climb a ladder, for example, will get the message across faster and more effectively than pages of written explanations.

4. Using video presentations to augment written material gives the receiver more information. It also makes the material come alive. A welcome from the CEO, for example, becomes a little more human when it comes through video than from a short written statement at the front of the employee handbook. Using a few words of the native language of employees can work wonders, too. It

produced great results for President Kennedy in Berlin and for First Lady Jackie in South America.

5. Leave employees with written information they can take away to go over later. This gives them the option of asking for an explanation from a bilingual friend and rereading it slowly at home.

Giving Directions that Are Clear and Comprehensible

In a multilingual environment, frustration and confusion can result when directions are given. Employees who do not understand are often reluctant to ask questions or indicate they are confused. They may fear upsetting the boss or direction giver, not want to imply that the directions were not given clearly, or not want to call attention to their own lack of language facility. To preserve harmony, avoid hurt feelings, and not appear incompetent, they pretend to understand. It may become apparent only after mistakes are made that the directions were not understood. Many of the same points apply that were mentioned in communicating with limited-English-speaking staff members. A few more points can be added.

1. Hire or Train Bilingual Supervisors

The most frequent direction-giving interface is between the supervisor or lead person and the first-line worker. Communication consultant Monica Moreno advises that if the demographics of the labor market indicate that first-line workers are going to continue to be non-English or limited-English speakers, a very immediate solution is to have those who supervise them have bilingual ability. Taking this step not only helps in overcoming communication barriers but also helps workers feel more comfortable and accepted.

2. Print Basic Instructions Bilingually or Multilingually

When health and safety are concerned and when the priority is to get the message across as quickly as possible, print instructions in the necessary languages. Using a two-column approach, matching English and the other language(s) line for line, serves three purposes. It enables the non-English speaker to immediately grasp the information, it allows an English speaker to communicate by pointing to corresponding lines, and it helps the employee learn English.

3. Be Specific and Explicit

Misunderstandings occur even in monolingual situations because "that report," "the same room," or "a longer board" may mean different things to the speaker and the listener. Pointing to the report in question, identifying the room as the second-floor conference room, and specifying that the board needs to be 38 inches, not 36, would be clearer. Holding up an example; giving exact measurements, dates, or numbers; and using descriptive words and examples help clarify directions. See if you can make these directions more specific:

	Vague and Confusing	**Explicit and Clear**
a.	"Take this downstairs and get it fixed." (Where is downstairs and what needs to be done?)	_____ _____
b.	"All special requests must be turned in by morning." (Which requests are special, and when is morning?)	_____ _____
c.	"Drop these off down the hall on your way out." (Where down the hall and to whom?)	_____ _____

4. Give the Reason

When workers understand the reason for a direction, they are much more willing to accept it, figure it out, and make it work. Explain simply the reason why a certain process is followed, why a procedure should be done a certain way, and what happens if it is not.

5. Use as Many of the Learning Modalities as You Can—Visual, Auditory, and Kinesthetic

There is an old Chinese saying, "I hear and I forget, I see and I remember, I do and I understand." If you give directions both orally and visually, in writing, diagrams, or pictures, and then have the employee try it out him- or herself, you will have generally ensured success.

Calling People What They Want to Be Called: Preferred Diversity Language

Generally, people want to be dealt with as individuals, not categories or labels. Juan probably wants to be seen as an excellent mechanic, not the Mexican new hire, and Corazon wants to be regarded as a skilled nurse, not a Filipina recruited because of a nurse shortage. Nancy expects her colleagues to think of her as an excellent data processor, not the quadriplegic down in DP. However, there are times when we need to talk about a group by name. We have seen the labels shift over time, for example, from colored to Negro to black to African-American. Preferences among members of any group vary. It is not uncommon to hear people disagree over what they want to be called—Hispanic, Latino, Mexican-American, or Chicano; disabled, handicapped, or differently abled. Fortunately, today's society has evolved to a point where derogatory racial epithets are not acceptable. The focus now is on what *to* say rather than on what *not to* say. Judy B. Rosener,

Lexicon of Appropriate Terms

When Referring to	Use	Instead of
Women	Women	Girls, ladies, gals, females
Black people	African-Americans, Caribbean-Americans, black people, people of color	Negroes, minorities
Asian people	Asian-Americans, Japanese, Koreans, Pakistanis, etc.; differentiate between foreign nationals and American born; people of color	Minorities
Pacific Islanders	Pacific Islanders, Polynesians, Maoris, etc.; use island name, e.g., Cook Islanders, Hawaiians; people of color	Asians, minorities
American Indians	American Indians, Native Americans; name of tribe, e.g., Navajo, Iroquois; people of color	Minorities
People of Hispano-Latin-American origin	Latinas/Latinos, Chicanas/Chicanos; use country of national origin, e.g., Cubanos, Puerto Ricans, Chileans; people of color; Hispanics	Minorities, Spanish-surnamed
Gay men and lesbians	Gay men, lesbians	Homosexuals
Differently abled people	Differently abled, developmentally disabled, physically disabled, physically challenged	Handicapped, crippled
White people	European-Americans; use country of national origin, e.g., Irish-Americans, Polish-Americans; white people	Anglos, WASPs
Older/younger adults	Older adults, elderly, younger people, young adults	Geriatrics, kids, yuppies

Ph.D., and Marilyn Loden, in their book *Workforce America!*, present the following list of preferred terms.[27] To help determine the most appropriate label to use when identifying a particular group

- Ask the people involved about their preferred term: "Do you think of yourself as black or African-American?" Not only can they tell you about their preference, but they can teach you as well.
- Pay attention to how people identify their own group—a feminist organization, the Latino Employee Support Group, or the Asian Pacific League, for example.
- Remember that all group members will not necessarily have the same preference.
- Realize that just as fashions change, so do the terms used to describe groups.
- Understand that terms used within a group may not be acceptable when coming from an outsider. The epithets used in joking banter and teasing may be reserved for members only.

Finally, remember that people care more about how they are being treated than whether they are called by today's correct term. Anita's husband, Darrell, who walks on crutches due to a paralyzing spinal injury, tells us he has no problem with any of the terms, including crippled, handicapped, or disabled. What he does object to is people ignoring him or talking about him as though he were not there: "Can he walk down these stairs?" "Is this seat all right for him?"

Ten Ways to Provide Constructive Feedback without Loss of Face

Feedback is essential in any work environment. Employees need to know when they are on track and when they are not. However, feedback is difficult enough to take in mainstream American culture, which values directness, let alone in cultures that value more subtle communication, harmony, and the saving of face. Before giving feedback, it is important to examine your motives. What is your reason for giving it? Is it really a chance to help the employee learn, or is it a way to assert your authority or to get the person back for something? Feedback that comes out of benevolent motives is more apt to be accepted positively. Once you're clear that your feedback is truly constructive, the following are some tips that will help.

1. Position the Feedback as a Benefit to the Receiver

We think that feedback can be helpful, as in being told by a dinner partner that we've got spinach on a tooth. A few seconds of discomfort prevent long-term embarrassment when we find out once we get home that we've spent all evening talking and laughing with a green tooth. When an individual sees how the information can help improve performance or the chances for a raise, he/she might be more receptive. You may say, for example, "You know, I was thinking about your frustration the other day with the long wait for materials. There is a way it might be avoided . . . .'' Think about some feedback you want to give. See if you can find two or three benefits that will ''hook'' the receiver into being open to it.

2.   Build a Relationship First

Feedback is most effective when it occurs in the context of a supportive and caring relationship. You probably have noticed in your own life that you can accept some of the most difficult and painful feedback from people who you know have your best interests at heart. Spending time building relationships with employees will pay off when you need to give constructive criticism. When asked how feedback is given in his country, a Japanese manager explained that the employee and boss have a relationship developed over time by socializing after work and spending time together. When feedback is necessary, the boss has already built rapport with the staff member.

3.   Go from Subtle to More Direct Communication

The same Japanese manager mentioned above explained that if he were giving a subordinate feedback on a report that had an error, in order to save face he would never directly point this out. He would merely suggest that the employee look over the report again. This would be enough to alert the staff member that something was wrong. As long as both are Japanese, this works because both pick up the subtle cues. However, an American employee might be confused about the need to reread the report and would expect the boss to save time by pointing out problems.

   Along the same lines, in Arab cultures less direct, more circuitous communication is also used to save face. If, for example, a report had a problem area, the boss might praise one part of the report, emphasizing its excellence. The employee would then infer that the part not mentioned was weaker and needed work. The message is clear. If you are working with an employee who is particularly concerned with saving face, the subtler the better. You can always move toward more explicitness, but it is difficult to retreat once you have ''let the cat out of the bag.''

4.   Make Observations about Behaviors and Conditions, Not Judgments about the Person

In any culture, defensiveness is apt to be the reaction when judgments are made. You can prevent this response and help the employee understand more clearly what is expected when you comment on behaviors and conditions. For example, you can say, ''This carton had three defective units in it,'' rather than ''This is careless work.'' Try improving each of the following pieces of feedback by focusing on behaviors and conditions rather than judgments:

Judgment/Evaluation	Behavior/Situation
a. This report is incomplete.	*I'd like to see a table of contents and summary added.*
b. Your tardiness has become a problem.	_____ _____
c. Your work area is sloppy.	_____ _____
d. I'd like more professional behavior from office staff.	_____ _____
e. I've heard complaints about your attitude.	_____ _____

5. Use the Passive Rather Than the Active Voice

By saying "The switchboard was left uncovered for 15 minutes this morning," rather than "You were late," you avoid accusing the person and causing humiliation. The employee then can make the inference that it was his/her responsibility to be there and that the absence was noticed. In Spanish and Arabic, the passive and reflexive forms are very common so that actions are not attributed to individuals. In Spanish, for example, one does not say "I forgot my notebook," but rather "My notebook was forgotten to me" (*Se me olvidó el cuaderno*).

This may take practice since English favors the use of active verbs. Try transforming the following typical feedback statements from the active to the passive form:

Active	Passive
a. You forgot to turn off the air conditioner.	*The air conditioner was left on all night.*
b. You made some errors in these computations.	_____ _____
c. You are late from lunch again.	_____ _____
d. The night shift left these charts incomplete.	_____ _____
e. You department is slow in returning these forms.	_____ _____

6. Be Positive, Telling What You Do Want, Not What You Don't

"Stop that!" sounds like a reprimand whether you are 2 years old or 52. When you tell the employee how you do want something done, you avoid the wrist-slapping emphasis on the mistake. Try changing the following statements from negative to positive:

	Negative	Positive
a.	That's not the way to do that.	*Try it this way.*
b.	Don't be late to the meeting.	_____ _____
c.	Don't forget that your time cards are due on Thursdays now.	_____ _____
d.	There's not enough initiative on this staff.	_____ _____ _____
e.	You are not following procedures.	_____ _____

7. Give Feedback to the Group Rather Than to Individuals

Giving feedback to the whole group dilutes the sting and makes the information something the whole staff deals with rather than a personal affront to an individual. This may be difficult for you if it goes against your individualistic American reaction to making the whole group suffer for one person. However, if you have a group of employees from a culture that emphasizes the group over the individual, peer pressure may be able to influence the individual to get with the program. It also has the advantage of sending a more subtle, roundabout message that can get the point across without "nailing" the offender.

8. Make It Low-Key

Speak in a gentle, low tone of voice. While you may be using your normal tone of voice, to someone used to lower sounds you may sound like you are yelling or upset. The tension felt by the receiver of the feedback may make that person extra sensitive to the sound of your voice. Remind yourself to adjust your tone to a softer level that will not add to the already emotionally charged environment. Remember also to make it private, not public. That may mean going into your office; taking a walk; finding a conference room or a quiet, out of the way corner; waiting until you catch the person alone; or going out to lunch. Try to be unobtrusive in setting up the appointment as well. Announcing loudly that you want to talk with the person in your office has the same effect as giving the feedback in public.

9.   Use an Intermediary

Much embarrassment can be avoided and acceptance gained if you use a third person to act as a go-between. Making a comment to a trusted friend of the employee such as, "I wish Nino would consider taking that CAD course. I think it would help him improve his drawings," might be a way to communicate feedback without loss of face. Be careful, though, that you are not perceived as talking about the person behind his/her back. Another way use a go-between is to ask the intermediary for help. "I'd like to find a way to help Flora with her phone skills but I don't want to offend her. What would you suggest?" A third way is to ask the go-between to show the person what to do. "Oscar, could you help Hector in redesigning the work flow so it is more efficient?"

10.   Assure the Individual of Your Respect for Him/Her

Above all, let the employee know you value him/her as a person and that you appreciate what he/she brings to the work group. Telling is one way, but many times actions speak louder than words. Spending time with an individual can be one of the most powerful communicators of respect. Another is asking for advice or sending others to the person for help. Finally, including yourself as part of the solution shows respect for the employee by demonstrating that you are both on the same team. "Let's see how we can solve this" is an approach that reinforces mutual respect because it concedes that no one person has all the answers and that you value the employee's views.

Using the *Intercultural Feedback Skills* worksheet will give you a chance to practice the three verbal skills discussed earlier. In addition, the *Intercultural Feedback Checklist for Managers* can help you integrate these techniques into your repertoire and increase your effectiveness on giving feedback to your diverse employees.

Intercultural Feedback Skills

1. Make observations about behaviors and conditions, not judgments about the person.

Judgment/Evaluation	Behavior/Situation
a. This report is incomplete.	*I'd like to see a table of contents and summary added.*
b. Your tardiness has become a problem.	_____
c. Your work area is sloppy.	_____
d. I'd like more professional behavior from office staff.	_____
e. I've heard complaints about your attitude.	_____

2. Use the passive rather than the active voice.

Active	Passive
a. You forgot to turn off the air conditioner.	*The air conditioner was left on all night.*
b. You made some errors in these computations.	_____
c. You are late from lunch again.	_____
d. The night shift left these charts incomplete.	_____
e. Your department is slow in returning these forms.	_____

3. Be positive, telling what you do want, not what you don't.

Negative	Positive
a. That's not the way to do that.	*Try it this way.*
b. Don't be late to the meeting.	_____
c. Don't forget that your time cards are due on Thursdays now.	_____
d. There's not enough initiative on this staff.	_____
e. You're not following procedures.	_____

Suggestions for Using *Intercultural Feedback Skills*

Objectives:

- To practice three specific feedback techniques useful in intercultural communication.
- To develop additional feedback skills that can prevent loss of face.

Intended Audience:

- Managers wanting to gain additional skill in giving feedback to diverse employees.
- Trainees in a managing diversity seminar.
- Trainers wanting to gain additional skill in giving feedback to diverse trainees.

Processing the Activity:

- After reading the section *Ten Ways to Provide Feedback without Loss of Face* or hearing a lecturette on the topic, individuals write their own feedback statements for each of the three techniques.
- Then, if in a group, they can form smaller groups to share their statements, giving each other feedback on them. If working individually, compare statements to the suggestions at the end of the chapter.
- Total group then discusses difficulties encountered and learning from this activity.
- To apply the learning, individuals using situations from their own experience write three feedback statements, one for each technique, which they would give in their real-life situation.

Questions for Discussion:

- Which techniques were easiest? Most difficult?
- Where could you use these?

Caveats and Considerations:

- Some individuals may feel disgruntled because techniques 1 and 3 are standard feedback skills suggested in many supervisory and management development programs. Acknowledging their previous training in these areas up front may help circumvent this potential resistance. Stress that while it is an *old* technique, it has value with this *new* issue.
- Technique 2, using passive language, is apt to be difficult for native English speakers. There may be resistance from those who see it as vague, beating around the bush, and avoiding the issue. Help individuals see that it is an additional technique they may choose to use or not to use when and if appropriate.

Intercultural Feedback Checklist
for Managers

Think of a recent feedback situation in which you gave feedback to an employee from a different background. Check each of the techniques you used in that process.

_____ 1. I positioned the feedback as a benefit to the receiver.

_____ 2. I built a relationship first.

_____ 3. I went from subtle to more direct communication.

_____ 4. I made observations about behaviors and conditions, not judgments about the person.

_____ 5. I used the passive rather than the active voice.

_____ 6. I was positive, telling what I wanted, not what I didn't want.

_____ 7. I gave the feedback to the group rather than to individuals.

_____ 8. I gave feedback in a low-key and private way.

_____ 9. I used an intermediary.

_____ 10. I assured the individual of my respect for him/her.

Suggestions for Using the *Intercultural Feedback Checklist for Managers*

Objectives:

- To become aware of additional feedback techniques that could be employed.
- To identify feedback techniques utilized.
- To help managers plan more effective approaches for future feedback giving.

Intended Audience:

- Managers wanting to overcome cultural barriers in giving feedback to employees.
- Trainees in a managing diversity seminar.
- Trainers wanting to overcome cultural barriers in giving feedback to trainees.

Processing the Activity:

- Individuals analyze recent feedback-giving experience by checking which of the 10 techniques they used.
- In pairs or small groups they discuss their satisfaction with their feedback session, which techniques were used, and which could have been used to make the feedback even more effective. (If working alone, these same issues can be considered.)
- Large group discussion of insights, learning, and application.

Questions for Discussion:

- How satisfied were you with effectiveness of your feedback giving?
- Which techniques did you use? Which did you not use?
- Which might have helped make the feedback giving more effective?
- What would you do differently the next time you give feedback to diverse employees?

Caveats and Considerations:

- This activity can also be used as a planning guide for future feedback giving.

Reinforcing Positive Results: Rewards that Enhance Rather than Insult

Positive reinforcement, which can be a powerful modifier of behavior and can help you get the desired performance from your staff, is based on three premises. First, a behavior that is reinforced will continue. As long as I get what I want by performing in a particular way, I'll keep doing it. Second, a behavior that is not reinforced will be extinguished. When I don't get what I want by behaving in a certain way, I'll quit. Third, a behavior that is negatively reinforced will not be extinguished, but rather will be masked. If I get punished for a behavior, I will do it more covertly.

The key to using this method is to figure out what the reinforcers are for those you manage. What is considered rewarding depends first on individual preferences; for example, one person may want overtime while another may want time off. Culture influences the rewards as well. Time off for religious holidays or family celebrations may be important motivators. A reward that is not desired is no reward at all and will have no positive effect on behavior.

It has been said that we never really grow up—we just get older. Praise, whether it's the "good boy/girl" of childhood or the "great job" of adulthood, always feels good. As social creatures, human beings have basic needs for approval, belonging, and esteem. One of the most powerful reinforcers of behavior is sincere praise. Cultures differ, however, in their preferences about praise and how it should be given. Arabs tend to be pleased by praise, the more glowing and flowery the better. In cultures that prefer cooperation to competition, emphasize the importance of the group rather than the individual, and respect a social hierarchy, being singled out for praise is embarrassing, not rewarding. Giving a compliment at a staff meeting or publicly praising the accomplishments of one of your Asian or Native American employees might have the opposite effect of what you desire. In the case of employees from these groups, a private conversation where you pay a low-key compliment or a letter put in the person's file might be a more effective way to give praise. Traditional methods such as posting a picture of employee of the month or giving a preferred parking space might draw too much attention to the individual in his/her eyes, causing disruption in harmony, and hence would be counterproductive.

In cultures, such as that of Mexico, that value formality and outward symbols, the reward value of a spoken compliment would be greater if it were accompanied by an official certificate commending the individual. Business cards and titles have a similar effect among individuals from hierarchical cultures such as the Chinese and Mexican.

Reinforcement can be used with groups as well as with individuals, avoiding the singling out of particular workers. Paying the group a compliment is one way. "You guys did a great job on that rush order yesterday. Thanks." Another might be to host a group celebration to reward staff. Springing for pizza to thank a shift for coming through or having a staff picnic to show appreciation for a job well done might work more effectively than individual praise with group-oriented employees.

Suggestions for Managers

In rewarding employees appropriately and effectively, remember the following points:

1. Consider the individual's culture in choosing the reward. Watch the person's reactions. Do you get a beam or a frown? Does the reward seem to produce more effective behavior or not?

2. Reward effort and initiative, not just accomplishment. Let the person know you appreciate a try, a risk, an attempt, even if the result is less than perfect. Reinforcing small steps may be the best way to get employees to achieve your objectives.

3. Be careful not to overpraise. Heaping on compliments may backfire by making the individual feel patronized. This is especially true among some Asian groups. The Japanese, for example, do not expect to be complimented for doing a good job. That performance is taken for granted. Overenthusiastic praise may also send the subtle message that you are surprised at the person's accomplishment, that the level of performance was unexpected.

4. Consider the employee's life situation in choosing rewards to reinforce behavior. A single parent may appreciate a more flexible schedule so she can attend parent conferences at her child's school, while a recent immigrant may find the extra overtime a boon to his savings to bring his wife and children here.

5. Be clear and specific about what you are reinforcing. Make sure there is a clear connection in the mind of the employee between the reward and the behavior it is reinforcing. For example, you can say, "That was very smart of you to stop the production line when you saw the defects. I'm glad you called me." Or, "All of you who volunteered to work extra hours on that project will have first choice for future overtime assignments."

6. Practice what you preach. Employees will learn from what you do more than what you say. There is a wonderful scene in the movie *Starman* where the character from another galaxy shows what he has learned about Earth driving culture. Through a series of mishaps, he is forced to drive his Earth hostess's car for the first time. Riding with him, she is horrified when he approaches a yellow signal and accelerates. When she reprimands him for not following the rules, he assures her he knows the rules. Red means stop, green means go, and yellow means go faster! If you tell people you want them to take initiative, then punish them when they make their first mistake, they'll continue to avoid taking initiative. If you tell staff you want them to let you know when things go wrong, yet you blame them for the first problem they announce, they'll soon learn to hide mistakes.

Communicating Your Expectations: Letting Staff Know What You Want

Every employee spends part of his/her time figuring out what the boss wants. Job security, as well as satisfaction, depends in good measure on getting along with one's boss and doing what the boss expects. This is not always easy even when both boss and subordinate are from similar cultural backgrounds. Much of the communication about expectations is left unstated, with the we'll-figure-it-out-as-we-go-along mentality. When there are differences in cultures, employees may never clearly understand what is expected, and both boss and employees get increasingly frustrated. Even in monocultural groups, it is essential for a boss to let staff know what is expected, as each manager has a distinct style and preferences.

However, this is more critical when cultural barriers may make the figuring out of and coming through on expectations next to impossible.

As a first step, assess your expectations of subordinates. Using the *Expected Employee Behaviors* checklist, identify which of these behaviors you expect of your staff.

Expected Employee Behaviors

Place a check mark next to those behaviors you expect of your staff. Then go back and place an X next to those behaviors you have a difficult time getting.

I expect employees to . . .

Time

_____ Be on time for work, meetings, appointments.

_____ Be prompt in returning from breaks.

_____ Be responsible for their own time, taking breaks and lunch when needed.

_____ Give early notification of absences due to illness.

_____ Stick to assigned break and lunch times.

_____ Give requests for vacation time in advance.

_____ Meet deadlines on projects and tasks.

_____ Give advance notification of deadlines that can't be met.

_____ Other: _____.

Taking Initiative and Solving Problems

_____ Suggest improvements and solutions.

_____ Participate in staff meetings by discussing and sharing.

_____ Work together to find solutions to problems.

_____ Take independent action to deal with problems, then tell me about it.

_____ Use good judgment about when to ask me before they take independent action.

_____ When carrying out delegated tasks, check in with me as planned.

_____ Other: _____.

Announcing Problems and Giving ''Bad News''

_____ Let me know when there's a problem so we can fix it.

_____ Tell me when they disagree.

_____ Let me know when they are having difficulty.

_____ Tell me about complaints from clients/customers.

_____ Let me know when a mistake has been made.

_____ Other: _____.

Communication

_____ Let me know when something is unclear or confusing.

_____ Ask if they don't understand.

_____ Speak English on the job.

_____ Make no derogatory remarks about another group.

_____ Not speak another language around others who do not understand.

_____ Other: _____.

Suggestions for Using *Expected Employee Behaviors*

Objectives:

- Identify behaviors expected of employees.
- Pinpoint those that are forthcoming and those that are not.

Intended Audience:

- Managers wanting to increase productivity, follow-through, and commitment of staff.
- Trainees in a managing diversity seminar.

Processing the Activity:

- Individuals check those behaviors they expect of employees, then go back and place an X next to those they have difficulty getting.
- In groups, individuals share their checklists and discuss those behaviors that are most difficult to get from staff. They then discuss ways to get the desired behaviors from staff.
- Individuals make a commitment to take specific action to get the desired behavior(s).

Questions for Discussion:

- Which behaviors are hardest to get from employees?
- What might be the cultural norms influencing employees' behavior?
- How can you communicate these expectations to employees?
- What can you do to get more of the desired behaviors?

Caveats and Considerations:

- This tool can be used by HR professionals or employee relations specialists in coaching managers to more effective behavior.
- This tool can also be used in general supervisory/management training courses.

Once you have identified which behaviors you want, as well as those you are and are not getting, you need to figure out how you can teach these American cultural expectations to your staff. Explaining the reason for the behavior's desirability is important in this process. For example, you may say,

- "It may sound odd, but I like 'bad news.' I want to know when something goes wrong so we can fix it as soon as possible. If no one tells me, I'm not able to do my job, which is to solve problems that get in the way of productivity."
- "When you participate in staff meetings and make suggestions about improvements, that shows me you take your job seriously and are a committed employee."
- "Being on time for meetings shows you respect others' time."
- "Speaking a language that others do not understand makes them feel left out. It may also make them angry and resentful."

By simply clarifying expectations, conflicts can sometimes be avoided. However, even with the best of communication, when human beings work together, there will be times when there is friction, anger, and disagreement.

Resolving Conflict in Culturally Sensitive Ways

Disagreements, disruptions, and tension in relationships are not relished in any environment. Most of us would prefer not to have to deal with the out-of-control feelings and potential loss of approval we risk in conflict. Even in the dominant American culture, with its preference for direct confrontation, most people tend to play the ostrich, avoiding dealing with the situation until there is no other alternative. Hoping it will go away is generally wishful thinking, though. Conflicts that are not dealt with usually continue to fester, escalating into more serious situations. In addition, unresolved conflict is a significant source of stress, causing morale and productivity declines for the organization and illness for the individuals involved. Dealing with conflict is necessary, though often less than pleasant. Dealing with it in a diverse environment can be even more daunting.

Cultural Norms Affecting Conflict in a Diverse Environment

1. Conflict Is Seen as Disruptive to Harmony

In cultures such as the Thai, Vietnamese, and Filipino, which put a premium on harmony and smooth interpersonal relations, the disruption caused makes conflict something to be avoided at almost all costs. Employees may deny, ignore, and avoid talking about or confronting the differences.

2. Conflict Presents a Risk of Loss of Face

Because confrontation sometimes leads to accusations, blaming, and arguments, there is a great risk of embarrassment. Employees from cultures such as those mentioned above, as well as Latino and Middle Eastern groups, will be very reluctant to participate in any interactions that could lead to someone's losing face. When loss of face occurs, drastic measures may be required to restore lost honor. Reducing the potential of loss of face is critical.

3. Very Real Cultural Communication Style Differences Can Make Resolution More Difficult

Take a look at this case in point. In a disagreement between two employees, one African-American and the other Filipino, a few heated words were exchanged. Wanting to avoid further disruption, the Filipino employee walked away. The African-American employee, on the other hand, coming from a culture that values directly confronting conflict and wanting to settle the problem, followed her co-worker, trying to talk to her. This only caused more anxiety and panic for the Filipina, whose culture undoubtedly taught her to value harmony and smooth interpersonal relationships, so she continued to refuse to discuss it. When the African-American persisted, the Filipina turned and threatened her co-worker, telling her if she came any closer, she would hit her. What resulted was a grievance where both employees reported being physically threatened by the other.

While individual personalities vary, there are culture- and gender-based tendencies in conflict styles. Women sometimes cry, while men pound desks. African-Americans tend to confront verbally, while Filipinos get silent. Differences such as these can present barriers to resolution.

4. There Exists the Risk for Interpretation of the Conflict as Discrimination and Prejudice

Among groups with a history of discrimination—for example, African-Americans, Mexican-Americans in the Southwest, or Puerto Ricans in New York—there may be a heightened sensitivity to prejudice and a tendency to perceive unwanted feedback or confrontation as discriminatory: "They're only doing this because I'm. . . ."

Understanding the cultural dynamics influencing the conflict arena is an important first step. Next, you need to work to resolve the impasse. Nancy Adler suggests a three-step process in resolving conflicts that are rooted in cultural differences.[1]

Nancy Adler's Model of Cultural Synergy

1. Define the Problem from Both Points of View.   Let's take the case of the supervisor whose Latino employee takes the whole day off each time he takes his wife to the doctor, even though the wife can drive. The first step is to identify the points of view of each party. How does each view the conflict? What does each think is wrong? The boss in this situation is irritated and upset that the employee is not there when he needs him. In fact, the boss described the employee as "irresponsible" for taking time off work. The employee undoubtedly feels his boss is being insensitive and punitive.

2. Uncover the Cultural Interpretations.   The second step is to uncover the cultural interpretations. What assumptions is each making about the other, based on his own cultural programming? In doing this, the boss might realize that in the employee's culture, his role of head of the family required that he take his wife on such important appointments and that he was being very responsible within the context of his cultural values. The employee might realize that in his boss's programming, work commitments take precedence over nonemergency family matters and that family members take care of such responsibilities on their own. The issue is not who loves his family more, who is a better spouse, or who is a more committed worker, but how can this be worked out.

3. Create Cultural Synergy.   Now, devise a solution that works for both. They might, for example, decide that the employee can use his sick days for such family responsibilities or that he might only take a few hours off for the appointment. What is important in this process is the recognition and acceptance of others' cultural values and the working out of mutually acceptable alternatives.

Suggestions for Managers

1. **Use the Indirect Approach.**   Use a go-between, a third party who can give you suggestions for resolution and find out the other party's desires. This avoids direct confrontation, and, like the paper walls in Japanese homes which create the illusion of privacy, it allows both parties to save face by never having to confront the issue face-to-face.

2. **Emphasize Harmony.**   In attempting a resolution, talk about the cooperative spirit and harmony that would result if the disagreement were settled. You can say, "This problem is upsetting for all of us and is causing remarks from other departments."

3. **Clarify the Cultural Influences Operating.**   Help each party understand the cultural programming of the other. For example, talking privately with the African-American and Filipino employees about the differences in cultural styles of communicating could help each see the other's behavior less threateningly and less as a personal affront. It may also help to encourage each party to see the other in nonstereotypic ways. For example, you can ask, "What is one thing about [name] that does not fit the stereotype of [group]?"

4. **Work with Informal Leaders.**   Get help from the most respected member of each party's culture or group. Ask for their advice and assistance in bringing the two individuals or groups together. This is especially helpful in group-on-group conflict.

5. **Get Specific.**   Have each party spell out their rubs with one another and their needs in specific behaviors and situations. It helps to give people time to think these through first. Open-ended statements such as the following are a good way to get the individuals involved to think constructively about the situation:

> I get most irritated when . . . .
> When this happens, I feel . . . .
> What I'd like from you is . . . .
> I'd be willing to resolve this if . . . .
> If this conflict were resolved, I'd . . . .
> If this disagreement continues . . . .

6. **Get Honest with Yourself.**   Recognize you own reactions and preferences. You, too, are culturally programmed. You may have a preference for one person's style or one group's position over another. If you are a party to the conflict, you may find the behavior or values of the other party's culture distasteful. Dealing with your own reaction, feelings, and ethnocentrism before you get involved in attempting resolution will help you remain more objective and more helpful in the negotiation.

7. **Find Out How Conflicts Are Resolved in the Culture of the Other Party.** Knowing that a go-between is always used, for example, can help you choose an appropriate strategy. Seek help from a *cultural informant,* someone familiar with practices and norms in the other culture. Get that person's perceptions and explanations of the situation, as well as suggestions for resolution strategies.

8. Keep Out of Corners. In any conflict situation, avoid cornering someone in a losing position. Just as animals attack when cornered, human beings of any culture are apt to strike back in unpredictable and irrational ways when they feel they have no recourse. Always leave room for both parties to get something. Either/or ultimatums produce losers who can become powerful saboteurs of any resolution.

9. Capitalize on the Relationship. If you have developed a relationship with the individual, use it to help you in working out a solution. You can say, "We've always had a cooperative working relationship. I'd like for that to continue. Having this tension between us is bothering me, and I care enough about you to want to work it through."

10. Respect, Respect, Respect. If an individual is treated with dignity and respect, he/she will be much more likely to work with you. If this universal law of human relations is broken, you may have created an enemy for life. How does one show respect? By dealing with the other party (or parties) privately and as discreetly as possible. By listening and not discounting what they have to say. By owning your part of the problem and being willing to give as well as take in the negotiation. By apologizing. By showing sincere appreciation for this person's contribution to the work unit.

Sample Responses for Exercises

Giving Directions

- **Be specific and explicit (p. 77).**

    a.   *Take this to environmental engineering in B-36 and tell them to fix the broken switch.*

    b.   *Requests for vacations and time off during November and December must be turned in by 9:00 A.M. tomorrow.*

    c.   *Drop these off at the mailroom slot on your way out.*

Giving Feedback

- **Make observations about behaviors and conditions, not judgments about the person (p. 81).**

    b.   *You need to be at your work station by 8:00 A.M. each day.*

    c.   *I'd like the work area clear of food and coffee cups.*

    d.   *I'd like the phones answered by the third ring with "Good morning/afternoon, data processing, this is Teresa."*

    e.   *I'd like customers greeted with a smile and treated like a guest in your home.*

- **Use the passive rather than the active voice (p. 81).**

    b.   *There are a few errors in these computations.*

    c.   *The desk was uncovered for a half hour this afternoon.*

    d.   *These charts were found incomplete this morning.*

    e.   *These forms have been turned in late for the last three weeks.*

- **Be positive, telling what you do want, not what you don't (p. 82).**

    b.   *I'd like to start the meeting promptly at 9:00.*

    c.   *Please remember to turn in time cards on Thursdays now.*

    d.   *I'd like to see people offering to help each other when their own work is done.*

    e.   *I'd like you to follow the steps outlined in the personnel manual when calling in sick.*

Chapter 4

Building Multicultural Work Teams

This chapter will give you:
1. A look at cross-cultural values and norms and their impact on team functioning.
2. Ways to adapt traditional team building tools and theory to cross-cultural teams.
3. Ready-made assessments that indicate when team building is necessary.
4. Training materials and other assessment inventories that define team strengths and weaknesses.
5. 10 dimensions by which to gauge a cross-cultural team.
6. Suggestions for increasing a sense of belonging, esteem, and trust among team members.

*THE
BUILDING
MULTICULTURAL
WORK TEAMS*

"Team building," cross-cultural synergy," "work-group cohesion"—to paraphrase Shakespeare, a rose by any other name is still a rose, and team building in the 1990s, no matter what it's called, still requires that people who are fundamentally interdependent in a work group perform their tasks in some systematic, unifying way. However, this goal becomes more complicated when working in a culturally diverse environment where the norms, values, expectations, traditions, and priorities of team members from different backgrounds may seem foreign and out of sync with one another. In some cases, the best team building may be accomplished by design, not by osmosis. In others, it is important to consider informal, indirect team building by striving for strong relationships that enable a work group to persist through any obstacle. This chapter will help you understand the cultural influences that impact any cross-cultural team as you attempt to build harmonious and productive work units. By creating an environment where all employees are valued for their unique contributions, you can create a staff whose interconnectedness resembles a brilliantly colored kaleidoscope rather than a collection of shattered glass.

Team Building: Is the Whole Idea Culturally Biased?

When a colleague of ours was called to facilitate intergroup problem solving between an Anglo and a Latino group, the leader of the Latino group didn't want to participate. He saw team building as one more Western invention that he didn't want or need. Was he right? The answer to this question is both yes and no. His perception that team building is a culturally biased intervention is accurate in three significant ways:

1. It is a linear, American intervention, designed to "fix" dysfunctional work groups or teams. It is reflective of the mainstream American culture's need to problem-solve whatever ails it and, in so doing, make it better.
2. The directness of the team-building method reflects the directness of American mainstream culture. If the issues are interpersonal, we design processes that enable staff members to articulate what they need from one another to smooth out relationship glitches. Then, in productive one-on-one negotiations, participants clarify their expectations and resolve their differences. Other cultures, on the other hand, communicate in more contextual and less direct ways. John C. Condon, in his book *With Respect to the Japanese*, says that in Japan, "the shortest distance between two points is a curve."[8] People are expected to observe nonverbal cues or pay attention to facial expressions as a way to determine conflict in relationships. In most of the world, where harmony is a prime value, American team-building directness is difficult and counterproductive. In Asia, the Middle East, Mexico, or Central America, the traditional American team-building directness would cause discomfort.
3. Team-building priorities differ. Mainstream America values both task accomplishment and satisfying relationships, but good relationships are not viewed as an end in themselves. They help grease the wheels of business. In most of the world, relationships have intrinsic merit. How people are treated is often more important than how, or even whether, the job gets done.

Beyond these examples of cultural bias in team building, symptoms of teamwork are culturally demonstrated. Trust, for example, is prized and valued worldwide. Team members in any work group would say that for maximum productivity, they must be able to trust their co-workers, but how you demonstrate and build that trust is cultural. In mainstream America, trust is frequently enhanced by looking someone in the eye. The opposite is true in Asia. Also, in this culture, trust is built on someone's integrity and predictability. The thought goes something like this: If you are perceived to be honest or believable, and over time you validate that perception by coming through on your commitments, trust increases. However, in many cultures, to disappoint you is unthinkable. An employee who can't meet a deadline or complete a task would rather "lie" to protect you from hurt and disappointment than to speak the objective truth, which very well may be, "I didn't know how to do this job, and I was afraid to ask for directions, so I didn't get it done." In the United States, protecting someone from unpleasant information erodes trust; not so in other places.

In spite of these examples of team building, American-style, a part of the answer to the question "Is team building culturally biased?" is still no, in the sense that every culture wants work groups to function productively, profitably, collaboratively, and harmoniously. The goal of having productive work teams is universal. It is the process of how to achieve this goal that has many cultural variations.

Team Building: When Is the Effort Justified?

There are any number of good reasons to engage in the process of team building. The umbrella under which most reasons fall includes the belief that effective teams enable an organization to accomplish its goals and objectives in a timely and effective manner. The following five reasons are frequently cited as justifications for team building. As you read them, see if any seem appropriate for your group.

1. Form a New Team, Committee, or Task Force

Responsive, adaptive organizations frequently create groups or task forces for the purpose of accomplishing specific goals. These groups usually have a short "shelf life." Nevertheless, in order to function efficiently, members operate with an eye toward defining a clear purpose, creating group norms that foster productivity, establishing operating rules that get the job done, and building smooth working relationships so that work is conducted in a comfortable and creative environment. This becomes more difficult when a group is heterogeneous, though it is not necessarily a picnic on monocultural teams, either. Having different priorities can cause problems even with people who look and act alike. Cultural differences just complicate the issue. Look at the role of values, for example. Middle Eastern culture places extensive emphasis on hospitality and socializing before getting down to business. Reconciling this hospitality and socialization with the mainstream culture's strict time consciousness and get-down-to-business approach is a challenging task. If the need to focus on business and accomplish goals is not balanced against cross-cultural norms of groups other than the one that dominates in a given organization, the team will be less productive. In fact, its efforts could be sabotaged.

2. Improve the Functioning of the Existing Team

When dealing with permanent work groups, team building can act as a self-cleaning oven, an important ongoing process that helps a group look at itself and how it operates. As a team increases its diversity, such questions as "What makes us effective?" or "What norms and procedures do we need to change in order to be even more effective?" are timely and relevant. However, the way such questions are asked needs to make accommodations to the backgrounds of employees. For example, in a group with Middle Easterners, you'll get better answers to your questions if you avoid using the first or second person pronoun in a group discussion of that nature. But you could say something to this effect: "Our work group does a lot of things well. It meets its production goals and improves its performance every month. But if we were to operate differently for the betterment of all, what changes would we need to make? How might these changes be brought about?" The impersonality makes the subject approachable without causing offense.

Another tool that can improve the functioning of a team is brainstorming. However, this takes some cross-cultural adaptation. In the case of Latinas, initiating discussions and being free to brainstorm is contradictory to what is expected from a loyal employee. It takes time and education to invite employees to offer their suggestions. You may increase a group's willingness to do so if you help its members understand that loyalty, a prime value in Latino culture, is partially defined by extending one's ideas. To improve your group's functioning, look at its composition. Then see what accommodations need to be made in how you team-build and how you operate.

3. Develop a Strategic Plan

Effective teams plan carefully. In fact, strategic planning can be a very effective team-building tool, directly and indirectly. But long-term strategic thinking is something American business has not done very well. Its planning has been more immediate and short term. However, the light is starting to dawn that American business needs to look beyond the next quarter when it measures profitability. Think about your group. Is this a time for your cross-cultural team to define its values, mission, goals, and objectives? Should it spend time considering where it wants to be three or five years down the road? By defining some measurable goals in the process of achieving this diversity, your group is indirectly team building while it plans.

4. Conduct Valuing Diversity Training and Skill Development Sessions

Training and skill development on a variety of topics are legitimate uses of team-building sessions. Having employees look at their reactions to change, or having them face their fears and prejudices, can be eye-opening, clarifying, and relationship building. Some training may center on skills such as how managers conduct performance appraisals in culturally sensitive ways, while others may help solve intercultural conflict or design career paths that enable all employees to achieve career satisfaction.

5. Solve Group Problems or Make Decisions

In American organizations, one of the most frequent reasons for team building is to engage in shoulder-to-shoulder problem solving. Being in the trenches together can build strong bonds and take care of business at the same time. A work group can even use the problem-solving mechanism to deal with diversity-related issues such as what kind of language policy might work well on our team. The following are other sample questions that might be addressed: ''How do we get more women and people of color in the promotional pipeline?'' ''How do we keep them once we bring them on board?'' ''How do we create a diversity-friendly culture in our company or department?''

Though team building may not be directly cultivated through group problem solving and decision making, the process a team utilizes can enhance work-group cohesion. The mainstream American manager/facilitator/ consultant who conducts this kind of team building needs to do so in a way that is very comfortable for people who differ from the dominant power structure. For example, employees from cultures where harmonious relationships are primary would be reluctant to engage in the Western model of analyzing relationships, then straightforwardly prescribing solutions to make them better. On the other hand, problem solving related to a task can be a very appropriate intervention. The method is purposeful in dealing with impersonal systems issues and can indirectly shape and improve relationships. To see if your team is in need of a tune-up, use the *Team Effectiveness Checklist*.

Team Effectiveness Checklist

There are 15 questions, and all you need to do is respond by putting a check in the appropriate column.

Symptoms	Yes	No
1. Our team (or task force) has clearly defined objectives.	____	____
2. Expectations of how we are going to operate have been collectively determined.	____	____
3. An effective mechanism exists for dealing with interpersonal and/or intercultural conflict.	____	____
4. Group trust builds because people come through on their commitments.	____	____
5. Group members help each other out when needed.	____	____
6. Team members can talk easily about joys and frustrations on the job.	____	____
7. There is usually an absence of competition between members of our team.	____	____
8. Effective processes exist for solving both system and interpersonal problems.	____	____
9. Cultural differences such as time consciousness are acknowledged and dealt with.	____	____
10. Our mission statement has been discussed and jointly agreed upon.	____	____
11. The values we preach are the values we practice.	____	____
12. There is a strong belief in our mutual purpose and interdependence.	____	____
13. Each person on the team is clear about everyone's job.	____	____
14. *Nonjudgmental* is a word that accurately describes the attitude toward differentness on this team.	____	____
15. Official communication is more reliable than the grapevine.	____	____

Suggestions for Using the *Team Effectiveness Checklist*

Objectives:

- Enable team members to assess their collective effectiveness.
- Determine areas where the team needs strengthening.
- Gain awareness about how individual team members view the strength and weakness of the team.

Intended Audience:

- Managers to use with their own work groups.
- Internal and external training professionals who conduct team-building sessions.
- Human resource professionals who teach their managers how to use this tool.

Processing the Activity:

- Distribute questionnaire. Ask participants to focus on their own team as they put a check in the appropriate column.
- Put people in pairs or small groups so they can discuss their responses.
- Identify *no* answers on which there is consensus.
- Discuss results and perceptions among the whole group.
- Make two lists on the easel and flip chart. One label is *Greatest Strengths*. The other is *Need to Improve*. Get responses from the group about which items go where.
- Discuss where the biggest weaknesses lie and what you want to do about them.

Questions for Discussion:

- What are your/the team's greatest strengths? Areas ripe for improvement?
- What happens if we/you do nothing?
- If we/you decided to select one area for improvement right now, which one would have the largest impact on our performance?
- What would you do differently the next time you give feedback to diverse employees?

Caveats and Considerations:

- If you have many different cultures represented, some people who are less acculturated to the mainstream may have a hard time speaking up about the group's weaknesses.
- Put people in small groups with those they trust and with whom they feel comfortable. That will produce the most involvement and best data.
- Respect people's reluctance. Work with them quietly and slowly to build trust. Over time, you will get more participation and openness.
- Get the cooperation of informal group leaders and you will increase chances of getting the data and participation you want.

Directions for Scoring the *Team Effectiveness Checklist*

Count your *yes* checks first, then your *no* checks. The more *yes* checks you have, the less your group needs team building. However, even if you have one or two *no* answers, the content embedded in the questions should raise some interesting issues for your group's consideration. Look at item number 2, for example. If you have a group of newly arrived immigrants, there is a very good chance that their cultural programming indicates a preference for tight structure and rigid hierarchy. They would probably feel most comfortable with preset expectations determined by the boss. Someone who answers *no* to that question because expectations were not collectively determined may still be a highly satisfied team member when you consider the cultural programming. Consider your own team's cultural variations as you apply these questions to your particular group.

It is one thing to determine there is a benefit to formal team building. It is another thing to go about the task of conducting productive and constructive team-building sessions. Once you have determined that team building is necessary, it is important to consider the cultural lenses of team building.

Recognizing How Cultural Lenses Impact Teamsmanship

Cultural software influences how you and other people in your organization view team participation. The dominant American culture has traditionally focused on two areas in regard to team building: task and relationship. Depending on what ills happen to plague a team, one of the two might be more important than the other at a given time. However, in most other cultures, relationship building takes priority over task accomplishment. This does not mean that completing the task is not important. It does mean that work will get done better and more efficiently if relationships are attended to in culturally appropriate ways. The cross-cultural lens on team building shows that relationships nurtured lead to tasks accomplished. Said a little differently, taking care of people is the best way to take care of business. And that can best be done with an understanding of how other cultural values impact team building.

1. Desire for Harmony

Members of the mainstream American culture do not love conflict, but for the sake of getting the job done, North Americans will openly engage in it—though they sometimes have to be dragged to it kicking and screaming. For the dozen or more years that we have been conducting team-building sessions, we have seen literally hundreds of team members reluctant to surface differences. Conflict doesn't have to blow up or be difficult. Nevertheless, fear of conflict is common. We recently worked with a homogeneous group where several frightened people called us ahead of time to ask how volatile the sessions were going to be. Before our meeting, one was suffering from insomnia, the other, irritability and anxiety. In fact, at the end of the second meeting with the group, when Lee asked what was the best thing that came out of the session, one woman said, ''I lived through it.'' Even though

Americans dislike dealing with conflict, this culture handles it differently than most others do. Mainstream culture values dealing with differences and solving problems that arise from them more than it values harmony.

Part of the difference in the mainstream American culture and much of today's immigrant work force can be seen in what is called American pragmatism. There is the realization that limited resources balanced against different priorities and objectives will inevitably result in some level of conflict. American business sees team-building sessions as a legitimate place to deal with these different priorities and perceptions, particularly as they relate to productivity. The pragmatic American doesn't necessarily expect harmony. It's a bonus when it occurs, but life isn't structured around creating it. However, in the Middle East, the Orient, Central America, and Mexico, harmony is central. The value placed on smooth interpersonal relationships would make it very difficult and highly unlikely to surface conflicts and deal with them in a team-building session. Differences will get dealt with and problems will get solved through the informal network, which is powerful in maintaining harmony and dealing with conflict simultaneously. For example, the after-hours drinking for which Japan is so famous serves a legitimate business purpose. It is in these informal settings that many of the differences are dealt with and resolved. The same would be true, minus the drinking, in the Middle East.

2. Social Status Based on Family or Connections

The Horatio Alger myth lives on in mainstream America. Clarence Thomas is the latest example. Underlying that myth is a strong belief in a culture that advocates treating people equally. Merit and personal competence are what count, not your bloodline. In North America, Canada and Western Europe, team building is designed to forge a collaborative, egalitarian work unit where bosses and employees roll up their sleeves, pitch in, and collectively get the job done. Bosses are commonly greeted on a first-name basis, which contributes to the perception that we are in this together and little separates us. This is not so in most of the world, nor is it desired. The extreme version of social hierarchy is the caste system in India. But in Middle Eastern, Latino, and Asian culture, egalitarianism is neither valued nor desired. A person's identity comes from his or her social status and family background, and often the *her* part of the social status automatically means less equal. This view of the social order has a dramatic impact on a team that a manager or consultant is trying to bring together.

In addition to family status, other cultures also place a premium on age and seniority. There is deference to the elder worker and those on the job the longest. This presents another interesting wrinkle in the team-building challenge. Issues of family status, age, gender and seniority all impact expectations of team members who have been differently acculturated. For example, a manager who recognizes that men from some cultures are not used to working with women, or who learns that most employees are used to having bosses determine the rules, may be hard-pressed to get staff members to embrace egalitarian team building. We have worked with a client firm where men from Indonesia refused to work for a Latina. Reporting to a woman was too degrading. This example is not uncommon for those who are less acculturated. What's needed in situations like this are clear boundaries and expectations. While you want to be sensitive to different upbringings and norms, there are also places where you won't bend because it will create team norms that you can't support and don't want to reinforce.

3. Emphasis on the Group

Validating the importance of the group can create a values overlap that will enable you to speak the figurative language of your diverse team members. In fact, if some people are reluctant to go through a team-building process, positioning it as a chance to foster good relationships and build trust is one of the best ways to minimize resistance. A successful intercultural marriage takes place when you encourage individual growth and development as something that contributes to the overall team effort. Individual achievement can be channeled toward group accomplishment and rewarded accordingly. In that way, you support a mainstream value, build self-esteem, encourage the strengthening of the group, and cultivate collaboration rather than competition.

According to Dr. Jorge Cherbosque, another cultural difference relating to group affiliation is the issue of inclusion/exclusion. In some cultures, to exclude a member is an offensive act. When planning a team-building strategy, a typical American response might be to include only those directly involved. However, in other cultures, those excluded might be deeply offended. Think carefully about who belongs in the team-building sessions so that you don't create more problems than you solve.

4. Fatalism and External Locus of Control

Team-building sessions designed to solve problems will be impacted by cultural views of self-determination. Members of the dominant culture believe that their fate is in their hands. They try to control their environment by identifying and solving a particular problem with the help of a tried-and-true analytical technique or decision matrix. In cultures in which predestation is a strong force, problem solving may be inhibited. "God's will" may be invoked and can influence a person's willingness or desire to invest in problem solving. It is assumed that some issues are out of the domain of mortal human beings, no matter how sophisticated the problem solving systems. What impact does this have on your team building? A manager may determine that a person or a group of people is being difficult—resisting and sabotaging group efforts—when the person or group really is being responsive to cultural upbringing and belief. To understand how culture has influenced your own behavior as a team member, respond to the continuum *Understanding How Cultural Lenses Impact Teamsmanship*.

Understanding How Cultural Lenses Impact Teamsmanship

In order to understand how culture shapes these four values, and the impact of these value differences on the effectiveness of your team, look at the following continua. For each, mark an *X* at the point that appropriately expresses your values as seen through demonstrated behavior. Once you have marked all four, connect the *X*s to get a values profile.

1. ....

Value on harmony

Value on surfacing and resolving differences

2. ....

Status based on family or connections

Status based on merit or achievement

3. ....

Emphasis on the group

Emphasis on the individual

4. ....

External locus of control

Internal locus of control

Suggestions for Using *Understanding How Cultural Lenses Impact Teamsmanship*

Objectives:

- Illustrate the impact that culture has on values.
- Show graphically how culture and values impact team dynamics.
- Gain awareness about similarities and differences between self and team members in four key areas that influence team performance.

Intended Audience:

- Any work team facilitated by a manager, an HR professional, or an internal or external consultant or trainer.

Processing the Activity:

- Distribute the learning activity and a different color of marker or pen to each participant.
- Discuss four values and the opposite ends of the continuum regarding each. Then ask participants to put an *X* at the spot that most accurately reflects their values.
- Ask participants to draw a values profile by connecting dots. Put their name on the paper and, with masking tape, put their profile on the wall.
- Ask participants to get up, walk around the room, and see the different profiles. When finished, they come back to their seats.

Questions for Discussion:

- What surprised you, or what did you notice about yourself when marking your own responses?
- When you walked around and saw other team members' profiles, what struck you?
- What seem to be the areas of greatest similarity?
- Where do we seem to have the most difference?
- What can we do to minimize the conflict from differences?
- How can we make the differences work for us? Make us stronger?

Caveats and Considerations:

- If you have some people who seem reticent, process the discussion in small groups first.

All of these differences in values can be worked with. Help staff members, whatever their gender or from wherever they hail, understand where you're flexible and where you're not. Explain why the values that relate to team cohesion are important to you, while at the same time you extend that same understanding to them. The most important realization for you is that different cultural upbringing will create a different team-building reality and perception. Once you interpret behaviors through cross-cultural lenses, you will be less defensive, more understanding, and more open. You can also help all staff members increase their openness, the old-timers as well as the newcomers. The most effective team building is a hybrid—of East and West, old and new, task and relationship.

The Need for Esteem and Belonging: Ways to Build Common Ground

Sondra Thiederman, in her book *Bridging Cultural Barriers for Corporate Success,* mentions Abraham Maslow and the fact that his needs hierarchy crosses cultures.[39] All human beings, regardless of culture, need esteem and belonging. Those two needs are the dominant shapers of functional team behavior. For the manager or the facilitator, the skill comes in realizing that the way esteem and belonging needs are met may vary, depending on the culture. But treating people with dignity and respect never goes out of style and transcends national boundaries.

We recently had this belief reaffirmed. Lee visited Professor Joel Kotkin's M.B.A. class at Pepperdine University in Culver City, California. Professor Kotkin thought Lee might like to talk to his students about their thoughts on what constitutes effective management in a cross-cultural environment. There was not a single student among the eight who was native born. They came from England, Turkey, Japan, Taiwan, and Korea, and all said they plan to return to their respective countries once they have earned their degrees. Some of the questions we wanted answers to were:

- How do you want to be managed? What would your ideal boss be like?
- Describe the team or work environment that gets the best from you.
- How are problems solved, conflicts resolved, or feedback given in your culture? How would you suggest managers conduct these practices effectively in a cross-cultural setting?
- What is the most important piece of advice you would give to a manager trying to manage a diverse work force today?

The theme that came up repeatedly was the need to be treated with dignity and respect. The students talked about having a strong need for self-confidence and a feeling of competence. They said they believe a boss can help build and reinforce esteem by letting employees know what they're doing well. All the students agreed that they could even handle negative feedback without feeling a loss of face if a boss told them what they did well before he told them where they needed to improve. This classroom discussion reaffirmed our view that people are much more alike than different. The need for validation and connection provides ample common ground. There are several aspects central to team building that impact esteem and belonging needs. As you read, think about how these issues are, or might be, dealt with on your team. Then use the worksheet at the end of this section, *Increasing Esteem and Belonging on Your Team*, as a catalyst for your action plan.

1. Identify and Build on Shared Values

For any group to function well as a team, there must be a commonly shared set of assumptions, expectations, and priorities that arise out of organizational values. Some examples might be (1) We, at hospital X, offer the highest quality of health care; (2) At store Y, the customer is always right and no effort at customer satisfaction is too great; (3) In our company, we do whatever it takes to stand behind our product; and (4) In this organization, every human being is entitled to equal dignity and respect, no matter what the job. The values behind these four statements are excellence in quality and delivery of services, product accountability, and the intrinsic worth and value of each human being. These values are supported, at least in theory, by most cultures with whom we come in contact. Agreement on their merit is a starting point in building common ground, and making these values operative would increase the feelings of worth and belonging of employees.

2. Get Commitment to the Group's Goals and Objectives

While values may define a work group, it is the concrete goals and objectives that are its life's blood and vitality. Meaningful goals help create a sense of belonging because employees feel connected by participating in a worthwhile venture. Each job needs to be valued for its contribution, and those who do the work need to decide how it can be done better. Employees who clean tables and empty trash will know better what systems glitches might impede cleanliness than will a CEO far removed from the task. Creating an environment where employees want to offer suggestions is one factor that separates high-performing teams from those that muddle along. In the dominant American culture, it is savvy to speak up at meetings and "throw your two cents in." However, there are many cultures where this is not so—particularly if giving input could be construed as diminishing an authority figure who, by virtue of position, is considered to have the answers. Getting information from employees informally or one-on-one is an acceptable way to get feedback, refine goals, and ultimately, develop a more productive team. If you seek this information from your team members in a way that's comfortable for them, you will get not only the feedback you want but commitment, too. And there is a bonus. The process of getting commitment to team goals builds esteem and belonging in the process.

3. Reward Excellence

Reward excellence, but do so in a way that feels like a reward. Over the past dozen years, while working with organizations, many of which were fairly homogeneous, the theory held that highlighting someone's superior performance would validate that individual and motivate others besides. Calling attention to some people through awards, announcements, and pictures on bulletin boards works—in some cases. It can also embarrass and intimidate. In some cultures, this kind of attention would be an affront to the person, while in mainstream culture, being singled out usually makes employees feel validated and appreciated. It is important to acknowledge excellence as a way to reinforce and strive for continuing high performance. However, do so in a way the individual appreciates.

Our friend and colleague Dr. Cherbosque relayed two relevant and real examples. The first asks the question "When is a reward not a reward?" The answer is, when an employee who thrives on contact with others is rewarded by being given an office of his own that isolates him from his colleagues. No matter how good the intentions, his "reward" will turn to ashes and the result will be decreased motivation. Cherbosque's second example was interesting because it involved using money as a motivator in an industry that was having financial difficulty. Management's desire to show employees appropriate gratitude resulted in a 20-cent per hour raise for first-line workers. Some employees were insulted by the modest increase, and management was outraged by what they viewed as a lack of appreciation for their effort in this largely symbolic gesture. What to make of this example as it relates to your organization? Just this: One of the most significant team-building rewards is getting people involved in the decision-making process. Had management done so, this bombshell could have been averted. Focus on your company and think about some ways you can show your team members appreciation.

Maybe a very quiet "thank you," or a simple nod of the head and a smile when looking at a report or a product, would be a valued reward for some employees. Use this private moment as an opportunity to ask an employee if she would object to a public acknowledgment. Maslow undoubtedly would advise you to reward the performance to build esteem and belonging. We would add, reward it in a way that validates and enhances the individual.

4. Demonstrate an Appreciation for Each Person and Each Culture's Uniqueness

Paying lip service to valuing differences is easy. The hard part is making it come alive in the work group. We saw this with one of our clients last Christmas. Because America is a predominantly Christian country, it never dawned on one group we worked with that non-Christians such as Muslims, Buddhists, and Jews wouldn't necessarily want to partake in Christmas festivities at work. Poinsettia plants and Christmas decorations found their way to all cubicles. Through a series of casual conversations, it became clear that not only do all people not celebrate Christmas, but awkwardness or unnecessary discomfort results when the assumption is made that they do. We imagine that next year's holiday decorating will be done differently. Respect for these differences goes a long way toward building good will and extending cooperation. More important for long-term team effectiveness, acknowledging and making room for differences can, paradoxically, create a deep sense of unity and belonging.

5. Acknowledge Cultural Conflicts

Conflict is normal and natural in any work group, but seldom do we stop to realize that on a diverse team, conflict is often the result of cultural differences rather than personal ones. One executive team we worked with was primarily white, but there were a few people of color. An African-American woman who had previously worked at a very large organization had a hard time acculturating to a different industry and transplanting herself from the big city to a smaller suburban area.

Furthermore, her style of dealing with conflict was very different from her co-workers'. As an African-American woman, she had been reared to stand up for herself so she would not be taken advantage of. Her style of management on this executive team of 12 was abrasive by the others' perceptions. Her own staff loved her, but her colleagues questioned her willingness to be a team player.

There were many dynamics operating, but none of these differences were dealt with openly because everyone denied that race or culture had anything to do with the differences. Could this team have become cohesive had the conflicts been openly dealt with? We'll never know. The sad part, and the end result, is that the woman and five of the other vice presidents left the organization by choice. No one could stand the stress and disruption. Avoiding the reality of cultural influence creates conflict and builds neither esteem nor belonging.

6. Learn to Read the Group Accurately by Becoming More Culturally Sensitive

It is human nature to ascribe meaning to actions. The difficulty in doing this in a culturally diverse work group is that you may be wrong. Work groups can accommodate differences, but not until we know what the differences are and understand them. A manager from a foreign culture may think Americans are loud and aggressive. On the other hand, we may define speaking up as being industrious and a sign of a real go-getter. The natural inclination is to use one's own culture as the yardstick by which all other actions are judged—or esteemed. But the probable inaccuracy of the messages and stereotypes that result is almost always harmful and destructive. Learn the cultural norms of others, and team-build at the same time by pairing people from different backgrounds so they can help one another. Buddy systems can simultaneously build relationships and increase cultural sensitivity.

7. Engage in "Activity Team Building"

The essence of activity team building is doing something together and being active in a nonwork environment. By definition, it means that a work group in either a recreational setting or an atypical work environment finds ways to interact that build a sense of belonging. Recreational functions include company picnics, bowling leagues, or sporting and cultural events. Some organizations even form softball, volleyball, or basketball teams. The emphasis in recreational team building is fostering harmonious relationships through just plain fun. Work may be your initial connection, but in this circumstance it is not the emphasis.

There is another kind of activity team building where the activity is one part of the process and consciously applying the learning to work back at the office is the other. An example of this is the ropes course, famous for building trust, developing leadership skills, and enhancing cohesion amid natural surroundings. The intent is that participants have a good time in a beautiful environment. But the higher priority is that, in a surrounding far from the ritual and familiarity of the office, team members get to know one another in a different light. This course, while very safe, tests people in untraditional ways. Physical strength and skill are on the line, as is psychological mettle. The intent is that depending on one another in the natural wilds should transfer to counting on one another in the organizational wilds. Maria Rubly, vice president at Baxter, told us of her organization's trip for top execs. They went to Alaska to fish together and to get to know one another in a different setting. When we talked, she had just returned from the experience, so it's hard to calculate long-term effects. But it is clear that the experience was meaningful and provocative. It enabled her to build esteem because she overcame some of her own barriers, and it increased belonging because she enhanced her relationships with her co-workers.

There is one more suggestion to consider in activity team building that combines the structured with the informal. We use it with some of our clients as a finale in team-building sessions. The group is asked to answer a few critical questions, such as Who are you as a team? What do you stand for? What are your purposes and goals? Then their task is to create with Tinkertoys a structure that best represents their team. It is not only fun for them but also instructive. They get so involved in the process that they pay no attention to their team dynamics, but we function as observers who give them feedback about the roles everyone played in accomplishing the task. Inevitably, this example of activity team building, as well as the others, invokes group pride and a strong sense of cohesion. It also crosses cultural barriers. Activity team building may mean that there are some learning methods and bonding tools that are more effective and pertinent in some cultures than in others. The idea is to find the most culturally appropriate vehicle. Dr. Cherbosque, for instance, tells us that Latinas are storytellers. The use of myths and stories to illustrate points is very effective. Do a little investigating. Find out what would be most effective with your employee population.

8. Acknowledge Cultural Differences

A team-building session may be designed to educate employees about cultural differences. Use the *Cross-Cultural Team-Building Scale*, which measures sameness and difference, to help your group learn about one another's values and culture-based behaviors.

Cross-Cultural Team-Building Scale

Directions: All human beings have values preferences that significantly impact work group cohesion. To see your values profile, mark an X along the continuum for each item and then connect the Xs. The benefit of this exercise to your team is that you will all see where the similarities and differences are. From there, the next step is to discuss how you make your individual differences a collective advantage.

Value change	Value tradition
Specificity in communicating	Vagueness in communicating
Analytical, linear problem solving	Intuitive, lateral problem solving
Emphasis on individual performance	Emphasis on group performance
Communication primarily verbal	Communication primarily nonverbal
Emphasis on task and product	Emphasis on relationship and process
Surface different views	Harmony
More horizontal organization	More vertical organization
Informal tone	Formal tone
Competition	Collaboration
Rigid adherence to time	Flexible adherence to time

Suggestions for Using the *Cross-Cultural Team-Building Scale*

Objectives:

- Understand how different values impact work-group cohesion.
- Identify cultural differences that influence team functioning.

Intended Audience:

- Members of any functional work team.
- Any manager, facilitator, internal/external consultant, HR professional, or trainer charged with the task of creating a cohesive team.

Processing the Activity:

- Discuss and define each of the items on the continuum.
- Ask team members to mark an *X* where they see their own values. Then connect the dots to see the values profile.
- Divide members into small groups. Ask them to compare their individual profiles.
- Come back to the whole group for discussion.

Questions for Discussion:

- What values similarities and differences were most notable among group members?
- What surprises, if any, did you find in the responses of any of your team members?
- When you look more closely at the values differences, what impact do they or might they have on our team?
- How can we make those differences work in our favor?

Caveats and Considerations:

- Refer back to the worksheet in this chapter called *Understanding How Cultural Lenses Impact Teamsmanship* (p.109) The suggestions for processing that activity may be appropriate for the *Cross-Cultural Team-Building Scale* as well.
- After people fill out the scale, compare the various profiles and talk about the implications of the differences. Ask the group for their suggestions on how to use this information productively while honoring the various norms. Depending on the size of the team, you might break people into small groups, getting a good cross-cultural mix in each. But asking the group to come up with some suggestions for how to get maximum input, involvement, harmony, and support while respecting values differences will be helpful and enlightening. The responses will give you pertinent information, while the process will help you create a team where esteem and belonging needs are met.

Increasing Esteem and Belonging
on Your Team

Directions: In the space below, write down your suggestions for increasing esteem and belonging of all team members.

Suggestions for Increasing Esteem and Belonging	How to Do It
1. Identify and build on shared values	
2. Get commitment to the group's goals and objectives	
3. Reward excellence	
4. Demonstrate an appreciation for each person and each culture's uniqueness	
5. Acknowledge cultural conflicts	
6. Become more culturally sensitive	
7. Engage in activity team building	
8. Acknowledge cultural differences	

Suggestions for Using *Increasing Esteem and Belonging on Your Team*

Objectives:

- Explore ways to have all team members feel more valued and included.
- Gain commitment of all team members toward this goal.
- Create realization that all team members are responsible for the climate or atmosphere on a team.

Intended Audience:

- Members of any functional work team.
- Any manager, facilitator, internal/external consultant, HR professional, or trainer charged with the task of creating a more cohesive, high-performing team.

Processing the Activity:

- The manager, facilitator, or trainer discusses the importance of members' getting esteem and belonging needs met in order to have a highly productive unit.
- Discuss each of the eight items on the worksheet and what they contribute to increased esteem and belonging needs, and their collective impact on performance.
- Then divide the group into small groups of approximately four to seven participants in each, depending on the number of people.
- Give groups the task of coming up with suggestions for each of the eight areas. How many each group is responsible for depends on the number of groups you have.
- Each group will write their ideas on chart paper so the suggestions can eventually be typed up and distributed.
- When finished brainstorming ideas, each group will report their suggestions to the whole group. That will provide an opportunity to add suggestions, answer questions, or modify any comments.

Questions for Discussion:

- Where can we pat ourselves on the back for already creating a healthy climate and helping employees get esteem and belonging needs met?
- Were some of the eight items harder to come up with suggestions for than others? If so, which ones?
- How do we (you) hold one another accountable so these suggestions become our norm?
- Which ones might make the most and best difference in our (your) functioning?
- What is the one thing I (you/each of us) will begin doing tommorow to make this happen?

Caveats and Considerations:

- The questions will be asked with a *we* pronoun if the manager is working with his or her own team.
- The *you* emphasis will be used by any outsider to the group.
- Depending on the size of the group, you could even have people self-select groups. For example, any group size of 21 or more would enable you to put chart paper and markers at eight stations around the room, each labeled with one of the eight areas. You can tell people to select the area they want to work on, but also tell them the number of people at each station so that each of the eight stations is covered.
- The report from each group at the end and the subsequent discussion is time-consuming. Set clear parameters and give precise directions.

Ten Dimensions of Cross-Cultural Team Building

Building a cohesive work unit among people of diverse backgrounds is an exciting challenge and opportunity. To give you a yardstick by which to measure your team's progress, utilize the following 10 criteria that are essential to any successful cross-cultural team-building effort. As you read about each of these factors, we suggest that you conduct your own mental audit to see how your group stacks up so far. Then check out the accuracy of your perceptions by having the staff rate the team as well.

1. A Clearly Articulated Mission

In any effective and profitable company or group, the raison d'etre is clear. Why employees show up for work involves more than a paycheck. The job should be meaningful as well. For example, we can imagine that the mission of the Walt Disney Corporation involves bringing entertainment and joy to people's lives, whereas the mission of most hospitals is to save lives while providing quality care and service. Both of those purposes are meaningful, and employees involved in either venture could legitimately feel that they contribute to improving the lives of others in some way. In the retail field, we see Wal-Mart as an organization that wants to provide struggling consumers with an economical one-stop-shopping depot amid excellent and friendly service. A Wal-Mart employee who accomplishes that goal can also feel good about improving the lives of others. Similarly, we remember growing up on the General Electric commercial of years ago that boasted, "Progress is our most important product." GE's message told consumers and employees that innovation was critical—that advancing knowledge and putting it to use in practical ways for human beings was at the heart and soul of the organization.

At executive levels, a mainstream team-building process that articulates an organizational mission works well. The process of how to define a mission will differ with first-line staff. With them, it may be more appropriate to give your group a mission that supports the larger organization and, when appropriate, to seek their input regarding how they contribute to this mission. There are any number of ways to craft a mission statement. The following process is one we frequently use with groups of between 7 and 12 people. Lee recently used it with the public affairs division of a hospital in Los Angeles when she helped the group members define their purpose as it related to the overall organization. Begin by asking each team member to write down his or her version of the mission statement on a piece of paper. In the public affairs group there were seven people, so Lee went around the group getting each person to read his or her statement aloud. As each did so, Lee copied the statement onto a flip chart in front of the group.

With seven statements clearly visible, the group members immediately started discussing areas of agreement and disagreement. They discarded content areas when there was no agreement, especially when no one could make a strong case for including a particular idea in the statement. Over a four-hour period in two separate sessions held a week apart, the team came up with a collective statement that reflected the best thinking of the group. There was participation by all and more vitality than the group had seen in a while. They discussed semantic and real differences about purpose and scope of departmental duties. They felt a deep commitment to the newly articulated mission.

The sessions were electric with different viewpoints. Some members felt that public affairs was strictly an internal communication tool. Others felt it was external, functioning as the marketing arm of the hospital to the outside world. No one was bashful. You could see the evolution of long-held tenets as opposing ideas were expressed. After the two productive sessions, a statement was agreed to that became the foundation for the group's strategic planning and priorities. The process of defining this statement in a consensus fashion à la the formal meeting environment is very mainstream, yet it worked with this diverse staff (among the group are an older black male, two black females, an Armenian immigrant, a Polish American, and a Latino). In the group Lee worked with, the process was appropriate, and these employees did perform better and feel more committed once they were in the service of a clearly articulated purpose. But how you define that purpose can vary, depending on several factors. Before you decide how to involve your staff, answer some pertinent questions:

1. How acculturated have your team members become to the American ways of doing business? The more Westernized, or the more "Americanized," they are, the more the dominant culture team-building norm that seeks input will not only make sense but also feel comfortable and be expected.

2. At what level of the organization are your employees operating? The higher level the employees, the more they will expect to be involved in the process. But it is also important at lower levels because it increases the sense of identification among employees who might other wise feel isolated. That connection will bolster commitment. It will also keep the pipeline open between employees and consumers, where success is ultimately measured.

3. What cultural programming do your employees bring to the workplace that might influence their reaction to team building? For example, older employees or those from hierarchical cultures might be more reluctant to give input than younger employees who feel entitled to participate. The answer to this question will shape the process you use in defining a group purpose.

Once you answer these questions, what adaptations do you need to make? Dr. Jorge Cherbosque suggests that in Mexican and other cultures where a hierarchical structure is the norm, employees will be more comfortable if the mission statement is given to them rather than constructed participatively. Then as a group, employees can discuss its content and figure out how to accomplish the objectives that flow from the statement. In the Middle East or parts of Asia that favor consensus, utilize the informal structure to deal with differences. If people in your work group have been reared with different cultural programming, count on the fact that many of the differences can be more easily resolved informally.

Having the same cultural programming is no guarantee that employees won't see things differently. Individuals in every society can be polarized over any number of issues. For example, in our own backyard, some people are tolerant of those with different sexual preferences, and some aren't. Some people believe women belong at home raising children; others are adamant about women having an array of choices in their lives. There are always differences between people, inter- and intraculturally. But however challenging it may be to navigate your way through those differences regarding a statement of organizational purpose, it is critical to do so. It is your compass.

2. A Realization that Team Members Are Functionally Interdependent

Team building in any culture is irrelevant if group members are not tied together by the functions they perform. We recently interviewed a "team" of scientists who are doing research on independent projects. It is clear they are a team in name only. They do not need data, information, or much of anything else from one another in order to get their respective jobs done. However, imagine the astronauts on any shuttle mission trying to go it alone. Their success and effectiveness are contingent on coordination between astronauts and mission control in Houston, as well as close coordination and cooperation with one another in the space capsule. They could not conduct their experiments or successfully complete their missions if they operated alone. Before you invest any time in team building, regardless of cultural differences, determine whether or not you are functionally interdependent. Once a functional work link is established, team building is a legitimate priority.

3. Well-Defined Roles and Responsibilities

Another critical aspect of creating a hyperperforming work team involves having a clear sense of who does what. This area of team building requires delineating each person's role on the team and what his or her responsibilities are. At the top of the organizational hierarchy, that might mean a clear definition of roles so the duties of the vice president of strategic planning and marketing do not overlap with those of the vice president of communication or the vice president of human resources. No organization needs the costly turf battles, waste, and bruised egos that result from duplication of services.

Anita recently helped a team sort its way through the who-does-what issue when she was called in to work with an administrative staff. The chief financial officer was moving money in and out of fellow administrators' staff budgets without consultation or request. Since these administrators were held responsible for the fiscal health of their divisions, they didn't appreciate the CFO's mode of operating.

To deal with this issue, Anita used a process that is Western in its analytical and compartmentalized style. It utilizes the worksheet entitled *Goal Clarification Sheet,* which combines questions on mission statement, functional interdependence, and roles/responsibilities. The fact that Anita's participants were asked not only to define their own role but also to articulate what they needed or wanted from others was very clarifying. In our experience with this method, the negotiation and articulation of specific duties has worked well on teams of executives or professionals where language skills are not an issue. However, when working with new immigrant first line-staff, predefined roles work best, at least in the beginning, because they are the most comfortable for some staff members.

Goal Clarification Sheet

A team's mission determines its goals and direction. A team's reason for being is an essential step in developing team unity and is effective to the degree that the mission is both clear and agreed on. As a beginning step in goal clarification, define your team's mission as you perceive it.

Goal Clarification

My team's mission is:

_____

_____

_____

What goals logically follow from this mission?

_____

_____

Role Clarification

To implement these goals, my role/responsibilities are:

_____   _____

_____   _____

_____   _____

Other member's roles and responsibilities are:

Name   **Role**

_____   _____

_____   _____

_____   _____

To carry out my responsibility, I need from you:

Name   **Need to Get**   **Need to Give**

_____   _____   _____

_____   _____   _____

_____   _____   _____

Suggestions for Using the *Goal Clarification Sheet*

Objectives:

- Articulate and define the team's mission.
- Determine what goals follow from this mission.
- Clarify roles and responsibilities in order to accomplish these goals.

Intended Audience:

- Members of any functional work team.
- Any manager, facilitator, internal or external consultant, HR professional, or trainer who is helping the team define its purpose and clarify who does what.

Processing the Activity:

- Ask each team member to fill out the mission statement first. Suggest looking at an abstract rather than a concrete statement of purpose.
- Record each team member's statement on an easel in front of the group.
- Look for points of agreement and build on those. Reword till all agree with the statement.
- Then ask each person to list the top three objectives that logically follow from that mission statement.
- Go around the group and again, on an easel, list all suggestions. Indicate repeated suggestions with checks in a different color marker from that with which you are writing.
- Discuss all suggestions and through group discussion and reference back to mission statement, decide on the top three.
- Based on that outcome, have each person write down his or her responsibilities and those of other team members as the person sees them.
- Then in rotating one-on-one rounds that last about 15 minutes each, have people negotiate their roles and expectations with one another.

Questions for Discussion:

- Are there any semantic or language issues that are getting in the way of defining our mission? If so, how can we say things so all people support the statement?
- Of all the goals listed, which will help us get closest to accomplishing our mission?
- Is there any role or responsibility that is still not clear after negotiations?

Caveats and Considerations:

- This is a lengthy process. Rarely do groups have the luxury to do it all at once. But you can break it up into parts that break naturally. The mission statement definition may take one or two sessions. Defining goals can take one, and defining roles and responsibilities another. If you do this at a team-building retreat rather than on work time, it can be done in one session.
- Team members need to be acculturated to fully participate in this process.

4. Formal and Informal Mechanisms for Giving and Soliciting Feedback

In the dominant culture, a formal team-building setting is seen as a great opportunity to get and give feedback. Do you want to know how people view working on this particular team? Are you curious about what is going well and what isn't from each team member's perspective? Do you have an idea about what obstacles exist that inhibit staff from getting the job done in a timely and effective manner? And would you like to know how employees see the ideal work environment? Just ask. The norms in these sessions favor American directness. Again, the more acculturated the employees, the more comfortable they will feel in giving and getting feedback. Try the following technique, using the *Team-Building Response Sheet*, as a way to build trust and get feedback at the same time. Use small groups to provide safety for team members less comfortable with this directness. When discussing operational issues, if you are offering individual suggestions regarding performance, one-on-ones are best.

Team-Building Response Sheet
(A Tool to Increase Cohesion
through Feedback)

This series of open-ended statements is intended to help you discover and clarify your reactions, opinions, and thoughts about your job and organization. You will have a chance to share and learn from other group members' responses. Directions are as follows: (1) Take turns initiating the discussion, (2) complete responses orally, and (3) respond to statements in any order you choose.

1. Basically, my job is . . .

2. Usually, I am the kind of person who . . .

3. When things aren't going well, I . . .

4. When I'm confused or not sure what to do, I . . .

5. On the job, I'm best at . . .

6. One place where I could use some improvement is . . .

7. The best boss I ever had . . .

8. The strength of this group lies in . . .

9. One thing this group could do differently to be more of a team is . . .

10. A work group is positive and constructive for me when . . .

11. I am most involved and excited about my job when . . .

12. When I am approaching a deadline, I . . .

13. As a member of a team, I . . .

14. I prefer to work with people who . . .

15. I can help my team by . . .

Suggestions for Using the *Team-Building Response Sheet*

Objectives:

- Clarify and discover each team member's reactions, opinions, and thoughts about the team, job, and organization.
- Learn more about other team members' reactions, opinions, and thoughts.
- Build trust and openness on the team.

Intended Audience:

- Members of any functional work team.
- Any facilitator, manager, consultant, or HR professional leading a team through trust-building or feedback activities.

Processing the Activity:

- State purpose of activity. Tell participants not to write answers down. Just discuss responses orally.
- Divide into pairs or small groups. Have people discuss responses.
- Discuss some responses in whole group afterward.

Questions for Discussion:

- What information or responses were the most surprising or interesting to you?
- Which were easiest for you to answer? Which were most difficult?
- What's the biggest insight or learning you got about yourself? Your team members?
- What should we do with this learning?

Caveats and Considerations:

- The way you divide people (pairs or larger groups) and whether or not you ask them to group with those they know best or least has to do with trust level and your objective.
- Even with those who think they know each other best, there will be new information and surprises.
- Pairs are best when trying to provide safety and security; bigger groups are better when trying to show breadth of differences and perspectives.

This tool can be adapted depending on group size. In groups of 15 or more, have people pair up or discuss these questions in small groups. Doing so creates safety. It also helps people get to know one another and builds trust. Without being too personal or intrusive, the questions are legitimately important for employees who have to work together. The small groups will ensure discussion and participation from those who would be reluctant to speak up in a large group. Give them 10 or 15 minutes to discuss as many of these items as possible, and then select several items for discussion among the whole group. It can be instructive to see the variety of perceptions and responses, and can provide a good jumping-off point for discussion about what makes a good team.

In smaller groups with a long history of being together, you might have each person address one or two statements that provoke the most thought or discussion. You could still have people discuss as many of the items as they can in pairs first, but then you can process the information any number of ways. One suggestion is to ask the whole group to respond to a couple of statements. Tell participants ahead of time to listen to responses from their co-workers and make note of any answers that surprise them. You may also want to ask a question that everyone has to answer. Once you've heard from all involved, then you can discuss both similarities and differences and try to figure out what all this feedback means to you as a team.

Another variation on a theme is to take two or three statements from this list and put them on a chart. Depending on the size of the group, have people discuss the questions in small groups. Then you can either get random responses to all of the questions or go around the group and hear from every person present. Here's a sample of how this works:

1. The best thing about being a part of this team is . . . .
2. The diversity on this team strengthens us by . . . .
3. One thing that might improve out team functioning is . . . .

You could select one of those three statements to hear from everyone or get random responses on all. Keep the format of these statements in mind when you get to Chapter 5, on meetings. They are good examples of warm-up questions.

The process we have been describing works well in terms of asking for and getting feedback in mainstream culture because it is structured and direct. It can broaden everyone's picture of the group as a whole, as well as give specific information about and to individual team members. This process works well on any team where there is high trust. It can also be used to build trust by encouraging people to open up appropriately, a little at a time. Furthermore, it can help create an understanding of cross-cultural norms on teams that have people from different backgrounds, or even new staff members. On a culturally diverse team, this process works best when you let people talk in small groups and pick their own partner. They can even do so in their native languages if facility in English is still limited. Doing so will give employees security and privacy while you get the data you seek.

If you want to get or give individual feedback, do so privately as opposed to making it part of the team-building session. Make sure you give the good news first, and then suggest specific behaviors that you are looking for. You can go to the informal group leader for suggestions as to how feedback might be given to a particular person in an appropriate way so that it will be heard.

The key adaptation to make as you look at getting and giving feedback in a diverse environment is that much of it is done informally through the strength of your relationships. We have a colleague who was managing a plant in Puerto Rico. He held management staff meetings every Friday afternoon and could not understand why his normally motivated group turned glum and irritable at these meetings. Staff members did show up, but the manager's attempts at getting participation all fell flat. Finally, he went out for a beer with one of the fellows after a frustrating session and found out that the staff was irritated because they considered Friday afternoon the beginning of their weekend and meetings were infringing on their time. Once the manager got that piece of feedback, he changed the meetings to Thursday. The group's irritation was gone, and meetings were productive. This manager solicited feedback in the informal system, and he had good enough relationships to get an honest answer. No one would have told him in public, nor would anyone have volunteered the information. Good relationships and sensitivity are key to getting and giving feedback in any culture.

5. Mutual Support, Both Psychological and Task Focused

A colleague of ours, Dr. Natasha Josefowitz, states that we all need three kinds of support. In no particular order, they are, "a shoulder to cry on," "a brain to pick," and "a kick in the pants."[24] Dr. Josefowitz's definition of support is applicable to all persons, regardless of cultural programming. There are times we need the Band-Aids that are applied as salves when our feelings get bruised. We also need ideas and suggestions from others as we try to effectively make choices and decisions in our jobs or lives. Finally, the kick-in-the-pants aspect of support functions like a full-length mirror, giving us an honest, realistic snapshot of us or our lives at a given moment. All three kinds of support are essential to having an effective team. They can contribute to better problem solving, higher morale, and genuine commitment; but like any other aspects of team building, while universal in need, support is culture-bound in its manifestation.

For example, men in the mainstream American culture show support for one another differently from men in Europe, the Middle East, Mexico, or Central America. Men in the latter cultures are more demonstrative. They greet one another with hugs, or they walk down the street arm in arm. Men reared in the United States are pretty closed when it comes to showing physical affection for one another or even accepting emotional support. Prior to Robert Bly, demonstrations of friendship and male bonding were usually limited to the athletic field. There are also differences in how North Americans pick brains or give kicks in the pants. In the United States, it is common to use formal team-building and problem-solving sessions to pick brains, whereas other cultures do a lot of brain picking and problem solving after hours, on breaks, or during lunch.

Regarding the kick in the pants, North American honesty or directness flies in the face of all other cultures. You would have to know someone from another culture for a very long time, and this person would have to be very acculturated, to develop the trust that allows him or her to be nakedly honest, even if he thought it was for your own good. That level of honesty on your team won't happen in any culture overnight. Recall the memorable fable "The Emperor's New Clothes." No one in this fable wants to be honest with the emperor, who harbors the illusion that he is magnificently dressed when in reality he is stark naked. Finally, one person has the courage to tell the emperor the truth. How often are people in your own organization afraid to speak their version of the truth when they have perceptions that differ from those in power? Employees, even at high levels, are often afraid of retribution when they're honest. If you really want to reinforce kick-in-the-pants honesty on your team, you have to reward those who bring you bad news. Thank them for it. This is hard to do in mainstream American culture, and almost impossible to do in other cultures, but if you want to build a supportive culture on your team, you must.

Two strategies will help you give support regardless of acculturation or trust level. The first is observation. In cultures with more contextual communication, the things people can't or won't say are often the loudest. Pick up the nonverbal cues. Watch faces. Notice relationships. Be a real student of the interpersonal dynamics on your team. The second strategy to pursue is continued relationship building, because over time, as trust builds, honesty will increase. In that way, you will experience more of all three of the kinds of support identified by Dr. Josefowitz.

6. An Ability to Deal with Conflict in a Mutually Satisfying and Positive Manner

Conflict, viewed from a North American perspective, may not be pleasant, but it can be a useful catalyst for change. Of all the criteria on the list of cross-cultural team-building dimensions, how a work group resolves its differences is one of the most significant. Unsolved, differences remain an obstacle to commitment and productivity.

However, the pragmatic view of conflict held by the dominant culture is in stark contrast to that of most of the world. Elsewhere, conflict is seen as the evil that upsets balance or harmony. We gave you numerous tips on ways to deal with conflict in Chapter 3. Nevertheless, we want to reemphasize a few points regarding conflict as it relates to team building:

- The use of informal leaders, elders, or intermediaries is a very effective way to help deal with differences.
- As you build a cohesive team, focus on expanding everyone's repertoire of behaviors, helping newcomers learn to acculturate while assisting old-timers to be open, sensitive, and nonjudgmental.
- Create a climate where being genuine and maintaining integrity is the norm and where these differences can be discussed in a low-stakes, productive way, an inch at a time.

We recently saw all these factors at work in varying degrees on a team that was mostly Filipino. The manager was African-American. The group was not meeting some of its objectives, and when the manager convened a meeting to deal with various issues, the staff didn't have the experience of openly surfacing problems. The manager had developed good relationships and built trust with everyone, especially the group's informal leader. She asked each staff member to write down the problems as he or she saw them. At first, there was reluctance, but the leader got some help from a few of the team members, and after a time they all did it. She collected the data and compiled it on the spot so the group could use it. To everyone's surprise, she got full participation. Team members got more interested and involved than they intended. The manager was encouraged because she could see her staff's individual and collective growth. She realized that none of her staff members were native born, and none had been taught to deal with conflict openly. Nonetheless, they had done so with her. She felt the relationships and the process she used had moved the group noticeably closer as a team. Team members saw that no one was hurt by dealing with the conflicts caused by these problems, and in fact the group was helped.

7. Acknowledgment of the Impact of Cross-Cultural Values and Norms on the Team

Two important factors are critical in dealing with values and norms related to team building. The first is a realization by team members that values lead to different ways of seeing and of being a team member. Whether you were reared in Armenia or Australia; the depression era of the 1930s or the idyllic 1950s; the rebellious 1960s or the greedy 1980s; rural Mississippi or New York City will create a vast difference in how you see the world and the values by which you live. The connections between where you're reared, what you value, and how you behave are strong. Here's a case in point. A boy who grows up in the United States and serves on athletic teams for any length of time will probably be around the traditional locker room talk where women may be the subject of suggestive comments and innuendos about sexual conquest and where homosexuals may be the butt of degrading jokes. In this environment, what message will be transmitted to impressionable young men about women? Homosexuals? About their place in society and their value to his world? What message might the athlete pass on to his children about how women or gays should be treated? In his adult professional life, what difference might the messages sent years ago about women, for example, make on the corporate team, where some of his colleagues are women (or should be, by virtue of their talent and accomplishment)? Values and norms shape us all, but sometimes we aren't aware of their influence.

An effective team needs recognition that different norms and values lead to different behaviors and can cause team conflict. If you want to move your team forward in acknowledging and dealing with these differences, we offer a technique that's important because it honors the values of all cultures. It is direct enough to surface the issues but provides enough indirectness and safety not to hurt any one person's feelings. The directions are given in the *Norms/ Values Worksheet*.

Norms/Values Worksheet

1. Pass a sheet of paper out to each team member.

2. Ask participants to think about values or norms they currently see at work that are different from those found in their culture of birth. Once they identify several, have them make two lists as indicated below, with those values they like in one column and those that are difficult to deal with in the other.

3. The manager or facilitator collects the information from each person and then has someone read the data aloud while the manager/facilitator charts the information on the chart paper or on an overhead. If you prefer to have each team member involved in reading the data aloud, shuffle the lists, then redistribute them and have each person read the data aloud from a colleague's list.

4. Once the data are posted, you can ask the group to identify benefits of the values that are hard for people to deal with. Use the expertise of group members who have found a way to deal with different cultural values successfully. End with concrete suggestions for how to handle the ones that may get in the way. If this is facilitated well, it can be enormously helpful. (We will give you information about effective facilitation in Chapter 5.)

Norms/Values I Like and Enjoy	Norms/Values that Are Difficult for Me
Make people and relationships a high priority (example)	Lack of time consciousness and directness (example)

Suggestions for Using the *Norms/Values Worksheet*

Objectives:

- Identify any cross-cultural values and norms that may be difficult for individual team members to deal with.
- Identify ways to more effectively deal with those values and norms that are a problem.

Intended Audience:

- Members of any functional work team.
- Any facilitator, trainer, manager, internal or external consultant, or HR professional who will process the activity.

Processing the Activity:

- Pass the worksheet to each team member.
- Ask them to think about values or norms different from theirs.
- In one column list those they like and enjoy; in the other, list those that are difficult for them.
- Collect the information from everyone and have one member read all answers aloud. The facilitator charts them.
- Get suggestions from group members about how to deal effectively with those that may be hard for some while not so hard for others.

Questions for Discussion:

- What ways have some of you found to deal with these norms that no longer make them a problem?

Caveats and Considerations:

- Collecting everyone's paper and having the data remain anonymous as one person reads all the information will maximize the learning and get beyond cultural discomfort.
- You can collect and redistribute papers so no one has to be accountable for reading his or her own.

8. Effective Problem-Solving and Decision-Making Processes

The Chinese wish/curse, "May you live in interesting times" is a foregone conclusion on the culturally diverse work team of today. Remaining or becoming competitive, profitable, and productive means that group problems will need to be solved and decisions will need to be made. There are two cross-cultural norms that could impede your team's problem-solving capability. The first is that less acculturated employees or hourly workers from any culture may not feel it is their job to solve team problems. If you're the boss, in deference to your title, they may feel awkward and uncomfortable being treated as an equal whose input is valued and sought. It will take some time and patience on your part to create a new norm. It is doable, particularly if you work with informal leaders and position this involvement as loyalty to the boss.

The other cross-cultural norm that could work against effective problem solving and decision making is the external locus of control, which has already been mentioned. This idea that outside factors determine the course of one's life makes team members less participative problem solvers. On the other hand, because most other cultures have strong tendencies toward collaboration, group problem solving and decision making can fit right into cross-cultural norms. In fact, the Japanese use consensus a great deal. The complaint that it takes forever to reach a decision is sometimes made by Americans who do business in Japan. While the process may be time-consuming, it also gives you maximum support for decisions because it gets the buy-in of the whole group.

Regarding decision making, there is one caveat about consensus other than the fact that it is time-consuming. Many people use the term, but few know how to use the process correctly. Here are a few rules that should prove helpful. In a group that has been well trained to use consensus, these rules become culturally neutral.

Rules for Consensus

1. Define *consensus* as reaching a decision where all people can "live with it" at least for a period of time. That doesn't necessarily mean that everyone loves it or that it won't come up later for reevaluation.
2. Consensus is a decision-making strategy reached through discussion of alternatives with absolutely no voting. Voting only polarizes participants by creating winners and losers. Avoid that at all costs.
3. Consensus is best used when you have, or need to create, numerous alternatives. It is inappropriate and too costly to use for either-or decisions.
4. Define your terms. When consensus doesn't work, it is often because people don't bother to clarify language first. Once semantics are clear, progress is easier

9. Commitment to a Common Goal

A team's cohesion is significantly helped along when the team has a common goal it deems meaningful. The most dramatic and clear-cut goals are found on athletic teams—the 1991 Chicago Bulls winning their first NBA championship, or the long-shot 1980 U.S.A. Olympic hockey team winning its gold medal. In business, "winning" may be harder to quantify. Is it increased market share? Greater profitability? Getting that new product to market in a timely manner? Being first out with the latest technological advancement? Whatever the answer is, your team will be more cohesive and effective if together members strive for a goal that is clear, achievable, and meaningful.

In one community hospital where we are currently working, the common goal is to deliver quality care with top-notch service at a profit to the institution. It has not been hard to rally people around the idea of keeping patients alive and well in a high-service environment. The hospital's survival is at stake. The manager of the environmental engineering department, a Filipino immigrant, feels that his staff, made up entirely of people of color, contributes to the positive experience patients have at this hospital. Employees make a real effort to help their department reach both quality and service goals.

10. Diagnostic Processes for Assessing the Health of the Team

Part of what keeps any excellent team effective over the long haul is its ability to look at its own operation and make changes as necessary. The very process of analyzing a team's content (what it's doing) and its process (how it's doing whatever it does) is a very mainstream culture paradigm. North American culture is analytical and linear. It assesses and solves problems. This nuance of culture suggests that if you have a team, some systems or tools must exist in order to keep it highly functioning or make it more so. While American business has much to learn from other cultures, it also has much to teach. And one area where we can make a contribution is in helping work teams understand their dynamics with an eye toward improving their functioning.

We have included three diagnostic tools here. In different ways, they all advance teamwork. The first, *Window on the Team,* gives individuals a chance to look at the team and its functioning. It also provides an opportunity to look at individual comfort and skill development. This will be a good tool to use when there is some level of trust and acculturation. It will be premature before team members understand the concept of working as a team or before they have a sense that cohesion and participation are of value. To use this tool and lessen the discomfort, have team members fill it out by themselves and then process it in small groups where there is high trust. Have a recorder put everyone's data, unattributed, on a large sheet of paper that duplicates the four quadrants. Then the data can be processed more anonymously and safely for employees who do not want to offend the boss. Chapter 5, on meetings, will give you various suggestions for processing diagnostic tools similar to this one.

Window on the Team

What's going well on this team?	**What are areas of concern?**
What skills would help you be a better team member?	**What kind of support helps you be a more productive team member?**

Suggestions for Using *Window on the Team*

Objectives:

- Stimulate individual thought and discussion that will lead to usable information for the whole team.
- Gain perspective and information about the team.

Intended Audience:

- All members of any functional work team.
- Managers, facilitators, consultants, or HR professionals who can facilitate the activity.

Processing the Activity:

- Ask participants to fill out information in all four quadrants.
- Pair up to discuss.
- Get information in top two quadrants from everyone and chart it on an easel and flip chart.

Questions for Discussion:

- What does this tell you about our (your) team?
- What kinds of support would help you be a better team member?
- What do the data suggest you (we) used to do to be stronger?

Caveats and Considerations:

- In a small group (six or seven people) you can share data from everyone.
- You can change the questions or areas of focus to suit any need you have at a given time.

The second diagnostic tool, the *Team Development Survey,* we developed years ago for working with any team that senses there might be some weak link in its team functioning. This sample tool gives the team a place to start its assessment. These are standard team-building questions we designed for our clients, but you can change them and substitute other questions more pertinent to your issues. We combined numbers and words in the analysis to provide comfort for all team members because some members put faith in objective data, some in subjective. In the sense that the responses come from individual perception, they are all subjective, but using both numbers and words should allow all participants to feel comfort somewhere in the diagnostic process. The variety gives you a better chance to hit each person's comfort level.

Team Development Survey

Please respond to items 1 through 6 by circling the appropriate answer. There is no right answer, only your answer, honestly given, based on your perception. Data will be reported collectively so the anonymity of each person is assured.

1. I am clear about our team's goals and priorities.

1	2	3	4	5
Rarely		Sometimes		Almost always

2. I am influential in setting priorities and making decisions.

1	2	3	4	5
Rarely		Sometimes		Almost always

3. As a team, we are effective in dealing with our differences.

1	2	3	4	5
Rarely		Sometimes		Almost always

4. On this team, it is safe to honestly express my values and ideas.

1	2	3	4	5
Rarely		Sometimes		Almost always

5. We have clear roles and responsibilities.

1	2	3	4	5
Rarely		Sometimes		Almost always

6. The goals of this team and this organization are meaningful to me.

1	2	3	4	5
Rarely		Sometimes		Almost always

Please respond to the following questions by writing down your candid responses on the lines below.

1. The strengths of this team are

_____

_____

2. In order for this team to be more effective, it needs to

_____

_____

3. What I expect from this day, or what would be most helpful to me is

_____

_____

Suggestions for Using the *Team Development Survey*

Objectives:

- Give the team feedback about itself in a number of different areas.
- Gain information objectively and subjectively through numerical responses and open-ended statements.

Intended Audience:

- Members of any functional work team.
- Any facilitator, manager, consultant, or HR professional leading a team through trust-building or feedback activities.

Processing the Activity:

- Ask team members to fill their responses out; you collect the worksheets.
- The facilitator compiles data and feeds the compiled data back to the group.

Questions for Discussion:

- What does this information tell you (us) about what the team is doing well and what it is not?
- How do you account for the range in numbers (from a low score of 2 to a high score of 5, for example)?
- How do the objective data fit with your open-ended responses?
- Based on this information, what issues does the team need to address?

Caveats and Considerations:

- You can collect this information ahead of the session and use it to plan the agenda of an initial team-building session. It legitimizes the direction you take with a group because the content comes straight out of their information. But you can also use this right at the session and tabulate the data on the spot and use the information to generate discussion on various dimensions of team effectiveness.

Finally, we offer the *Group Experience Rating Form*. This makes a good pre- and post-team-building tool. You can have individuals evaluate the team on all 20 items for starters; then, once the data indicate areas of strength and weakness, the team can focus on specific areas for improvement. Identify the skill areas team members need in order to add more value to the group. Each of these methods can be valid and effective.

Group Experience Rating Form

Instructions: Rate the problem-solving performance of your group by responding to the questions below. Indicate for each question the rating (1–5) that most nearly describes your observation of the group experience. Simply circle the appropriate number. The scale is as follows:

1	2	3	4	5
Seldom				Always

Members in this Group

1. Take time to find out what the problem really is.   1 2 3 4 5

2. Listen and try to understand my viewpoint.   1 2 3 4 5

3. Understand the feelings I may be experiencing.   1 2 3 4 5

4. Help me to clarify my thinking.   1 2 3 4 5

5. Repeat and clarify what I have said before making their own statement.   1 2 3 4 5

6. Ask clarifying, insightful questions.   1 2 3 4 5

7. Share their feelings about the team's strengths and weaknesses.   1 2 3 4 5

8. Offer loyalty, support, and encouragement to me.   1 2 3 4 5

9. Give me a chance to talk and encourage my contributions.   1 2 3 4 5

10. Help me explore alternatives without pushing their own solutions.   1 2 3 4 5

11. Set out to find the facts.   1 2 3 4 5

12. Take time to set goals and objectives.   1 2 3 4 5

13. Take time to evaluate how we are doing individually and collectively.   1 2 3 4 5

14. Put talk and decisions into action.   1 2 3 4 5

15. Seek and accept help from others.   1 2 3 4 5

16. Provide different functions to the team at different times (e.g., leader, clarifier, summarizer, etc.).   1 2 3 4 5

17. Say clearly, but sensitively, what they need or expect from me and others.   1 2 3 4 5

18. Face disagreements and seek to understand them.   1 2 3 4 5

19. Seem to care about me and other team members and whether or not we accomplish our best goals.   1 2 3 4 5

20. Give honest, nonjudgmental feedback.   1 2 3 4 5

Suggestions for Using the *Group Experience Rating Form*

Objectives:

- Assess the function and behaviors of the team.
- See which behaviors add to team effectiveness and which detract.
- Get a sense of the various perspectives team members hold.

Intended Audience:

- Members of any functional work team.
- Any facilitator, manager, consultant, or HR professional leading a team through trust-building or feedback activities.

Processing the Activity:

- Ask each team member to rate the team by responding to the 20 items.
- Discuss responses in pairs or small groups first, then in large groups.
- Based on responses, determine an area to work on.

Questions for Discussion:

- What are the areas of greatest strength? Greatest weakness?
- What does this rating form suggest this team needs to do differently?
- Focusing on what item will help this team the most?

Caveats and Considerations:

- If 20 items feel like too many, divide items in half or quarters. Start smaller and eventually work through all 20 items.

Feel free to use the items as they are, or adapt them to your own group. Remember that being analytical and linear (''The team has a problem; . . . let's fix it'') is very Western, as is the directness of the tools. But using small groups to process the tools can increase safety and security for members from different backgrounds as all team members try to acculturate to the collective norms of the organization and their own team.

Five Ways to Foster Appreciation of Difference

Not all differences and not all sources of team conflict will be a result of racial, gender, ethnic, cultural, or life-style differences. But some may be. It doesn't matter what the source of the differences is. The first step in creating a cohesive team is to start with the premise that individuals are unique. Any work group will naturally reflect the differences. Step two is to realize that in spite of the predictable differences, we're all human. There will also be areas of sameness that can provide a fragmented group with bridge-building opportunity.

We remember when we were consultants on Project Change, the Title IV C project for the Los Angeles Unified School District, a program that was designed to facilitate good education in the face of great change during mandatory integration. We were two members of a five-person team charged with the task of helping different schools and communities in Los Angeles deal with a mandate perceived by most parents and educators alike as anathema. There was no shortage of animosity between and among almost every sector of the educational community because people felt angry and powerless.

What enabled these disparate groups to come together were their common feelings, some positive and some negative. Parents and teachers resented the legal system for issuing the mandate that caused them to feel out of control in their own lives and perhaps ruin their kids' education. Despite many obvious differences, the strong feeling of victimization created a common ground: the need to regain power. More important, there was a shared concern for kids and the desire to ensure a good education. Part of your talent in being an effective team builder is to get people to see and appreciate the strength in differences. There are five ways to foster that mind-set.

1. Value It

You can talk all you want about valuing differences, but what you *do* will convey a megaphonic message. If someone on your team is known to be a lesbian, how is this person treated? What kind of discrimination or judgment does she face? Can your team accommodate differences such as sexual preference? Physical disabilities? Race? Ethnicity? It is hard to have a cohesive team without doing so. Employees will take their cue from the manager. It is easy to demonstrate that you think differences are positive, if in fact you really feel that way. Differences are an advantage, but only if you perceive them to be. If dealing with differences is hard for you, start increasing your own comfort by looking at the exercise regarding gains and losses in Chapter 7, on corporate culture. Focusing on the gains in dealing with differences can assist you in seeing the positive side.

One person who clearly sees differences as an advantage is Chief Executive Raymond W. Smith of Atlantic Bell. He was quoted as saying that the U.S. Bells would beat the Japanese. The reason? "Diversity is our competitive edge." He stated, "If you take a handful of Carnegie-Mellon engineers like me, you're going to get a particular slant on a solution. But with a diverse group in terms of race, age, and sex, you'll get a much better array of options."[29] Valuing differences is a critical first step in melding a team, and since every human being is different, we've all had a lifetime of practice. Hopefully, we'll get good at it.

2. Acknowledge It

There are those who live in denial about the differences between us. They try to be color-blind in an attempt not to be prejudiced. This denial, however well intentioned, is not helpful. Senator Bill Bradley of New Jersey believes that the United States could make more strides in our racial behaviors and attitudes if we acknowledged and dealt with race. Instead, we are busy explaining how irrelevant it is in the choices we make, the people we promote, or the new hires we bring on board. George Bush, denying that Clarence Thomas's race had anything to do with his nomination to the Supreme Court, is a perfect example. We would move ahead on this volatile issue more quickly if we dealt with it. There is a saying in Gestalt therapy that is appropriate here: "The only way out is through." You can't get beyond the differences until you first acknowledge they exist and then deal with them. Either course of action, acknowledging or denying, will affect team performance and morale.

3. Model It

Talk has always been the cheapest commodity around. Modeling an appreciation of difference means taking demonstrable action. If you manage a team, you may have to listen to, consider, and implement suggestions that don't agree with yours. Sometimes it will be hard for you to walk that proverbial mile in another person's moccasins, but a person who models an appreciation of differences can't afford knee-jerk rejection of others' ideas when they're suggested. They must at least be given serious consideration. Allowing your staff to implement solutions they believe in, even when these ideas aren't your preference, is an excellent way to make good on the example of modeling behavior that shows appreciation for different perspectives.

4. Reward It

When staff members demonstrate, through their discussions and decisions, that they see and appreciate each person's uniqueness, your group is on the way to becoming a team. You need to reward their behavior. We saw this work with an executive director and his 17 department chairs. Their common ground was the shared goals and unequivocal commitment to achieving them. Their differences surfaced in the various styles of how they went about accomplishing their results. The director functioned like the quintessential racehorse. He wanted everything done yesterday. In fact, this mixed male and female group humorously but honestly told him that he was their biggest source of stress. They acknowledged that they were different from him, particularly in pace and intensity of behavior, and perhaps time consciousness as well. But they also told him that they expected to and wanted to get the job done on time, in their own ways. He was smart enough to know if he didn't back off, he would lose their commitment, efficiency, and productivity.

The director got the results he wanted. He reinforced and rewarded the behavior he sought by continuing to give the department chairs the space they needed to do the jobs in their own ways. And smartly, the department heads also rewarded the director's behavior. First, they kept producing good results. But they also kept giving the boss feedback, telling him how much they appreciated the trust and the opportunity to do their job without his constant pressure. This example of reward is very mainstream American. The idea of giving the boss feedback that tells him how his behavior gets in your way would be appalling in most other cultures, as would the idea of giving him feedback, saying, "Thanks. You're doing great. Keep up the good work." Nevertheless, it did work well for this group, and on an acculturated team, it could also work for you. You may have to adapt the reward to suit your group, but it is doable and critical on any team.

5. Learn from It

Using what you learn from staff whose value base and experiences are dissimilar from your own will send a powerful message that you find worth in differences. In fact, it is one of the best strategies for creating a climate where others also want to learn from you and feel they can do so without losing their own culture. We've seen this operate dramatically in the area of language acquisition. Managers who have learned Spanish, for example, tell us it motivates their Spanish-speaking staff members to try to use English more frequently because they have less fear of sounding foolish. What develops when you are willing to learn from others is more acculturation by all parties, greater rapport, and mutual respect.

Trust: The Indispensable Element on Any Potent Team

The ability to guide any team, but especially one that is comprised of staff from diverse backgrounds, rests heavily on the trust and credibility of the leadership. Jack Gibb, in his book, *Trust: A New View of Personal and Organizational Development,* says, "Trust begets trust, while fear escalates fear."[17] One of the most important organizational insights Gibb makes is that "When trust is high relative to fear, people and people systems function well."[17] That idea makes a good case for helping your staff get comfortable with differences. If they don't, fear levels will rise, trust levels will plunge, and a cohesive team will be almost impossible.

Trust is a complex phenomenon. Most cultures develop it, or expect it to develop, more slowly than Americans do. The best way to cultivate it is to begin with realistic expectations about the lengthiness of the process and the slowness of the progress. Think *patience* and *long term,* not 30-second sound bite. In addition to having a realistic time perspective, you can engage in a number of concrete behaviors that will fuel the trust-building process.

For openers, come through on your commitments. In building trust, there is no substitute for honoring your word, and no technique can overcome an absence of integrity or character. If you have people in your group from different regions of the world, find out how trust is identified in their respective cultures. For example, in Japan, employees rank trust, warmth, and the interest of employees very highly. That means allowing latitude in how the job is carried out: "The worst thing a supervisor can do here is to seem to be watching people too closely.

It gives us the idea that we are not trusted. Without trust, we cannot keep our faces.''[10] The dominant culture in the United States takes words and statements literally. We have the expectation that people will follow through on their words. They don't always, but as a culture we value that and don't know how to develop trust without it.

Think back and try to remember promises you have made to colleagues and co-workers. Have you delivered the goods? Have they done the same? How do you teach them to be part of a trusting relationship? We suggest that you explain to any employees who are not members of mainstream culture, and to all employees who need to learn how to be trustworthy, that trust is defined in this country by coming through on your promise. Trust might show itself in some of the following ways:

1. A team member promises completion of a project by a certain deadline. Trust in this culture means the individual must meet the deadline. If he can't, he must renegotiate it before the deadline approaches. It is essential to the let the boss or contact know ahead of time. In cultures where time is more elastic, not meeting a deadline might seem like no big deal. When such a difference arises, teach people the correlation between time and trust in mainstream culture.

2. Someone tells you something in confidence. Respect that person's privacy by not passing on the information. If you violate that trust, it will be very difficult to recover. Wise old Benjamin Franklin said, ''Three can keep a secret if two are dead.'' Prove him wrong.

3. Reputation is a indicator of trust. What's the word on the street about your credibility with your staff? If a homosexual member of your team asks for bereavement leave to go to the funeral of his/her partner's parent, what do you do? Do you tell the employee that only funerals of relatives qualify for this kind of leave? Or do you sit down and try to figure out a way to meet this employee's needs and yours at the same time? How you deal with these kind of situations will either build or dismantle trust.

In addition to coming through on commitments and being believable, there is another thing you can do to build trust. There is no substitute for nurturing relationships. How much of a relationship nurturer are you? In the following box, put a check by any of the behaviors you engage in on a regular basis.

How Much of a Relationship Nurturer Are You?

____ I spend time with every staff member each week.

____ I make it a point to circulate through the areas of my department every day.

____ Employees often come to see me.

____ I often eat lunch or take breaks with my employees.

____ I know a little about the personal lives of each of my staff people.

____ I can usually tell when someone needs to talk.

____ Employees seem relaxed and comfortable around me.

____ I sometimes talk about non-work-related topics with my staff members.

____ I let my staff know I appreciate them.

____ I greet each employee every day.

____ I help staff through the rough times.

The more of these you engage in, the more trust you'll reap. Any effort on your behalf to nurture relationships will build trust and increase cohesion and commitment to the team and the task.

Building High-Performance Work Teams in a Diverse Environment: Six Key Ingredients

As you've read in this chapter, the factors involved in building a powerful work team are numerous and complex. There are a few simple principles worth remembering that will help you get started on the right foot as you team-build in a diverse environment.

1. Acknowledge Differences

Today's work force in not homogeneous by race, age, religion, ethnicity, gender, physical ability, world view, sexual preference, values, or much of anything else. Start your attempt at team building with that reality. It is helpful to acknowledge these real differences and the opportunities they present because then you can move on to find the strength in your sameness as well.

2. Find the Common Ground

Even members of nuclear families who love one another have their interpersonal rubs with each other. Your team won't escape the rough spots, either. But just as the differences are a reality, so is the common ground. In spite of all the differences just mentioned, if you work for the same boss on the same team in the same organization, you already share significant commonalities. Undoubtedly, there are others. Make those your glue and build on them.

3. Identify Individual Interests, Strengths, and Preferences

Identifying individual interests, strengths, and preferences will help you identify individual talent to be used for the good of the group. Focusing on individual strengths needn't conflict with cultures that emphasize the group. Any group is only as talented as the individuals who comprise it. This is your chance to ensure that people are in the right jobs based on their interests, talents, and strengths. In so doing, you gain commitment to the team as well as top-notch performance.

4. Clarify Expectations

There is a legitimate tightrope to walk between having clear standards of performance and being flexible enough to accommodate differences. You're the only one who can determine where to bend and when you break. Decide what issues are worth going to the mat for as you mold your team. Everything can't be a do-or-die issue, but some things must be. Once you are clear about what your expectations are, tell the troops and reinforce the standards.

5. Collectively Shape Group Culture

As leader or manager of a team, you are a very critical piece of it, but you aren't the whole of it. The effective group reflects the experiences and values of all its members. Make room for the richness of the totality. Humans are not static; don't expect groups to be. Even in a group of first-line staff that prefers everything spelled out, you can help team members grow and increase their input.

6. Create a Feedback Loop

When all is said and done, a team is measured by how it performs. Is the job getting done? Where are the levels of excellence? What areas are ripe for improvement? Utilize the suggestions we have made in other chapters about getting and giving feedback. They will enable individual team members and the group itself to learn and grow on the job. Ultimately, feedback on job performance is the organizational insurance policy for achieving peak performance.

In truth, each individual is a minority of one. The challenge and the joy of team building lies in taking diverse individuals and forging their uniqueness into a whole that is greater than the sum of its parts. Doing so is critical. The good news is that by using the techniques offered here, it is also doable.

Chapter 5

Making Meetings Work in a Culturally Diverse Environment

This chapter will give you:

1. A formula for structuring effective, involving meetings.
2. A chart that explains cross-cultural norms impacting your meetings and how to deal with them.
3. Tools to measure the openness of the meeting environment and evaluate your meeting effectiveness.
4. Information about eight different types of meetings and when to use each.
5. Proven techniques for getting participation.
6. Tips for dealing with dysfunctional behavior.

That moaning and groaning heard in most organizations is not due to the latest strain of the flu. It is the response to another bout of meetings—endless, long, and nonproductive. Meetings are almost universally held in disfavor, and they are viewed as even more difficult in an environment where cultural differences bring confusion and frustration. However irritating they may be, meetings are a staple of organizational life. The need to plan, problem solve, make decisions, and in general operate companies and the separate divisions within them requires communication between a sizable number of people.

How you run your meetings frequently determines the productivity, morale, and esteem of a group. Designing and developing norms for effective individual and group behaviors can be difficult under optimum circumstances. When you overlay different cultural programming on to normal egos and individual differences, the potential for dysfunction becomes even greater. Do any of the following difficult-to-deal-with behaviors show themselves at your meetings?

- A staff reluctant to participate in decision making.
- Employees reluctant to speak out.
- Cliques that segregate themselves by ethnicity.
- People uncomfortable with active participation.
- Greater interest in socializing with co-workers than in getting the job done.

This chapter is designed to help you solve these problems and understand the essential elements in designing and implementing effective, productive meetings. Special attention will be paid to general cultural patterns or behaviors that could interfere with a group's ability to tap its full talent in a meeting environment.

The "No-Fail" Meeting Essentials

When we ask people in our meeting seminars to describe the meetings they attend, geography and industry are irrelevant. We always hear the same answers: "too long," "boring," "useless," "a waste of time," "irrelevant." Every once in a while, we hear words like "purposeful and necessary" or the phrase "get a lot done." But the negative descriptions so far outweigh the positive ones that we need to start with some bare-bones essentials to meeting management. A couple of significant questions need to be answered before a meeting is even called.

1. Purpose: Is There a Reason to Have This Meeting?

To paraphrase the old movie title, *If It's Tuesday, It Must Be Belgium*, we could say, "If it's Tuesday, it must be another meeting." Begin by asking yourself why this group of people needs to come together. Do you have a very clear purpose? The "habitual Tuesday" is not a clear purpose. If you were to define your outcome in concrete terms in no more than one sentence, what would it be? If you can't do that with clarity and precision, go no further in convening the troops, but do read on in this chapter. There are, however, some valid reasons for having meetings. Look at some of the answers we have received to the question "Is there really a reason to have the meeting?"

Some Reasons for Having Meetings

- We have little chance to communicate, and we need the relationship building and interaction. There is validity to the fact that people who work together and need to accomplish a common goal also need some structured time to communicate and interact, whether for the purpose of dealing with issues, disseminating information, sharing ideas, or just plain touching base.
- We needed to make a decision on an issue we had been investigating. A group setting was the most efficient communication system.
- We have a systems glitch that is sapping our productivity. When the homework on a particular issue has been done, then the group needs to hear a clear presentation of the issues and make a decision. In this case, you may need a series of problem-solving meetings. Data need to be collected, perspectives about the issue compared, and the problem defined. Then alternatives are suggested and reality tested. A course of action is then implemented, and finally, there is an evaluation to see what worked and what didn't.

2. People: Who Are the Appropriate Employees to Have in Attendance?

Who should attend the meeting is no small question, and it deserves serious consideration. You do not want to waste the time of people not involved in the issue. At the same time, you don't want to exclude people who will be charged with the responsibility of implementing changes that are a result of decisions made at the meeting. If so many people are involved in the implementation that not all can be included at the meeting, whom do you involve and how do you select participants? Criteria for choosing a representative sample to attend the meeting will involve many issues: Who are the informal group leaders? In some groups, it may be the person with the best command of English or the one who has been in America the longest. Among Hispanics and Middle Easterners, it may be the oldest group member, who is respected for the wisdom his age brings. Are different points of view represented? They need to be. Do you have what we call reluctant cynics? That group must have representation if meeting results are to have any credibility at all. Organizational realities such as prior work commitment and work load may help select meeting participants. When you look at the issue of who should attend, in light of cultural differences, know that there are cultures where the group takes precedence over the individual. In these groups, it is especially important to know the informal leaders. Any successful implementation or solution to a problem will depend on their input and buy-in. Slighting these leaders will not bode well for group effectiveness.

3. Clear Time Frame: Have You Set Aside Specific Time Limits and Do You Respect Them?

One of the most difficult of all cultural issues to deal with is that of time consciousness. The Germans are perceived to be on one end of the time consciousness spectrum. It is often said that the efficiency and exactness of time can be seen in the predictability of the German trains. On the other end of the continuum, Mexican time consciousness is more relaxed and more concerned with people than with punctuality. To extend our last metaphor, if the train doesn't arrive at 1:00 P.M., don't worry. It will arrive sometime this afternoon. If you call a meeting for 8:30 A.M., it is possible that employees from Latino or Middle Eastern cultures will wander in sometime between 8:30 and 9:00 and feel that this is perfectly acceptable. What does this have to do with you and your meetings in a diverse environment? Meetings are an opportunity to instruct all staff, but especially those who may have been reared with a different set of rules, on what the group norms and expectations are. Time is a concrete issue and a good beginning point in the acculturation process.

The meeting is a supportive place for you to help staff understand how you view time. For example, if you call a one-hour meeting, how you respect that one-hour time limit will tell staff volumes about the importance of time. If you say the meeting starts at 2:00 P.M. and you start it at 2:20 because that is when most people saunter in, you will reinforce cultural rules more comfortable in Mexico than in Germany. That may be okay with you, but realize the pattern you are setting. Be clear about your expectations regarding time. Work with the informal leaders so they will help others understand that being there on time is important. Determine what you want, teach to it, count on it, and *honor* it. If you expect people to be on time for a one-hour meeting, then don't make the meeting one hour and 10 minutes.

4. Participation: Have You Constructed Processes Designed to Ensure Involvement and Empowerment?

How you structure a meeting to get everyone involved and participating is one of the trickiest aspects of working with different cultures. In cultures that are hierarchical, speaking out, challenging authority, and participating on equal terms in decision making are tough behaviors to learn. When you add to the influence of hierarchy a reverence for experience and age, you can see why some new immigrants, or those not fully acculturated, have a difficult time participating. It goes against some of their most important values and learned behaviors. But there are processes and ways to structure groups that will elicit participation and in so doing, help people to feel empowered and move beyond the cultural programming that would otherwise make it difficult for some people to participate. Paying particular attention to native-born women, people of color, and the differently abled is essential because their ideas have historically been less valued.

While there are many factors involved in creating effective meetings amid different cultural values and behaviors, these four "no-fail" meeting essentials are a critical starting point. Having a clear need and purpose, convening the appropriate people, setting clear time lines, and designing processes that involve all participants will certainly start you on the right track.

The Four Dimensions Critical to Effective Meetings

In order to design effective meetings, it helps to understand the dynamics that exist every time you get two or more people together. *The Meeting Environment* model shows you four factors that interact to influence your meeting results: climate, content, process, and productivity.

The Meeting Environment

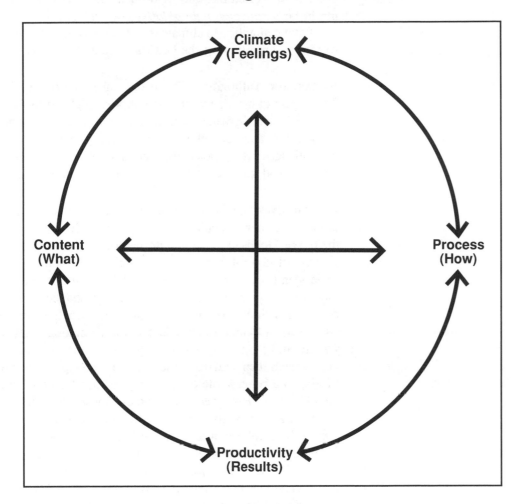

Climate: The Tone of Your Meetings

Climate is defined as the emotional tone of your meeting. Think about groups you have been a part of, or task forces you've joined to investigate and solve some organizational problem. When you reflect back on those groups, what words come to mind? Describe the tone or atmosphere. We can think of a terrific model from our own experience. We currently serve as board members for the Los Angeles Commission on Assaults Against Women, which is an extremely diverse group racially, religiously, and ethnically. It is also diverse regarding age, sexual preference, and the differently abled.

This group is a model for the best of what diversity can be, and the words we would use to describe the climate of those meetings are *open, trusting, accepting, free of tension, clear respect for differences,* and *warm*. This does not mean that we always see things eye-to-eye. We don't. A few years ago when we were doing some strategic planning, we reviewed our mission statement. There was intense discussion over the word *feminism*. But the climate was such that these very real differences could be discussed in an environment of respect and acceptance. In an environment like that, you have the chance for excellent results because people will not be inhibited about suggesting ideas, nor is there a likely chance that they will feel stupid. However, we have also been in groups where the tension was so thick that you could cut it with a knife. In a climate like that, where there is little or no trust, vested interests, and unchecked egos, words that describe the climate might be *suspicious, manipulative,* or *self-serving.*

Paying attention to climate is critical in running meetings cross-culturally. The following are a few of the cultural values that might impact the climate.

Respect for Authority.   This is one value that is very dominant in other cultures. The impact of having respect for authority might be to shut down communication by creating a more formal, closed environment. You may see people favoring a hierarchical structure and not feeling that it is appropriate to contribute ideas, ask questions, or challenge existing practices. Deference to authority can hinder an environment of openness and trust, as well as one that says all people's ideas may have equal value.

Control over One's Environment.   Most cultures are more fatalistic than the dominant American culture. Being born in "the land of the free and the home of the brave" tends to foster an internal locus of control. Americans are imbued with a sense of control over their own destiny. Tracing American history helps one understand how this mind-set evolved. The American Revolution and the westward movement are two historical events that shaped the American psyche so that Americans think that they control their own lives and choices. The dominant culture has a "can do" philosophy where you don't just accept your fate. Instead, you go and "fight city hall." If you don't like the forces influencing your life, you harness them and make the necessary changes. The perception exists that your life is, to a remarkable degree, in your hands. Predestination is not a dominant belief system. However, the same cannot be said for most other cultures, which believe more strongly in God's will and in that way are far more fatalistic. Their locus of control is external. According to this cultural teaching, the responsibility for what happens to people in their lives depends less on what they want or what they do than it does on what fate has in store for them. How does this difference of world view affect your meeting environment? If you want to solve an organizational problem and believe you can do so, you may get varying amounts of buy-in or investment of energy depending on people's perception of what they think they can, or cannot, influence in their own environment.

Assigning Individual Responsibility.   Harry Truman said, "The buck stops here." The message of this famous quote is compatible with the dominant attitude in American business that assigns individual responsibility. In other cultures, group responsibility is more common. Blame and praise are doled out collectively. This reinforces and is compatible with the emphasis on collaboration and harmony seen in the Asian-Pacific and Latino cultures rather than the individual competition that is so pervasive in the dominant American culture. The desire for harmony and collaboration found in most other cultures can be one of your best cultural assets as you look at creating a productive climate in meetings. Working together as a group is what you want in your climate, and in most cultures this is a natural.

Climate: How Warm (or How Open) Is Your Environment?

Asking people to adapt and change some of their long-held habits and beliefs is asking a lot, especially if they like what they have and believe how they have lived to date has worked for them. At the very least, these patterns have created security. Now employees are in a work group where there are a lot of different ways to behave. Creating a climate where being different is not only okay but actually valued can give a lot to the organization and the employees who are a part of it. Meetings offer you a splendid opportunity to structure an environment where differences can show themselves in positive ways that are useful to everyone. Creating an inclusive, accepting environment is possible when there is trust and openness. Spend a few minutes answering the *Meeting Climate Survey* to see how open your meeting climate is.

Meeting Climate Survey

Directions: Identify a group with whom you have regular meetings, either as a leader or a participant. Think back to the last six meetings you have had with this group. Then respond to the questions below with the most appropriate answer. To make this tool even more useful, pass it out at one of your meetings when your goal is to assess how you are doing as a group and how effective your meetings are. Once your participants have responded, you can see where your climate is thriving and where it also might be sagging.

Questions	Almost Always	Sometimes	Almost Never
1. The environment is easy and comfortable, even when discussing thorny issues.	____	____	____
2. Enthusiasm and participation at meetings is high.	____	____	____
3. New, unconventional ideas are suggested.	____	____	____
4. Different points of view on any issue are welcome and encouraged.	____	____	____
5. Many ideas are cultivated; none are ridiculed.	____	____	____
6. People speak their minds.	____	____	____
7. It is no secret where everyone stands on the issues that come up.	____	____	____
8. There is respect for principles of others, however unpopular the view.	____	____	____
9. Clarifying, and sometimes challenging, questions are asked in warm, unhostile tones.	____	____	____
10. Positions change as a result of discussions on the issues.	____	____	____
11. Feedback is given sensitively and constructively.	____	____	____
12. Relevant and appropriate self-disclosure on any issue occurs.	____	____	____
13. Group members build on the ideas of others, and they volunteer to help when help is warranted.	____	____	____
14. There is a "can do" attitude.	____	____	____
15. Group members follow through on their responsibilities.	____	____	____

Meeting Climate Survey *(concluded)*

Directions for scoring: Record the appropriate point count for each of you answers.
- Each "Almost always" answer is 3 points.
- Each "Sometimes" answer is 2 points.
- Each "Almost never" answer is 1 point.

1. _____   9. _____
2. _____   10. _____
3. _____   11. _____
4. _____   12. _____
5. _____   13. _____
6. _____   14. _____
7. _____   15. _____
8. _____   Total: _____

The closer your point count is to 45, the more open your climate is.

Trust and openness:	**numbers 1, 7, 10**
Morale:	numbers 2, 11, 14
Responsibility:	numbers 3, 6, 15
Support:	numbers 4, 9, 13
Freedom:	numbers 5, 8, 12

Trust and openness: The amount of safety and security one feels in giving an honest opinion and trusting these views will be valued and respected; this also looks at how open participants are to new ideas.

Morale: The feelings of confidence in the group's ability to accomplish its goals and get the job done in the face of the predictable roadblocks. There is also the sense that differences will be dealt with in sensitive and productive ways.

Responsibility: The willingness of participants to follow through on their tasks and be held accountable; also the willingness to take initiative in putting forth ideas and voicing reactions to any ideas suggested.

Support: Both emotional and task support are involved. The first shows appreciation for the person who sticks his neck out to say something unpopular. The latter involves taking the initiative without being asked.

Freedom: A real tolerance for differences without fear of recrimination or ostracism; the feeling that you can be honest about ideas or reactions and it won't cost you in your relationships or opportunities.

The questionnaire will evaluate your group in these five areas. The information you get will show you how open and trusting your climate is. Once you get the diagnosis from the group, you can then determine appropriate courses of action.

Suggestions for Using the *Meeting Climate Survey*

Objectives:

- Get a sense of the climate in which your meetings are conducted.
- Evaluate meetings in five areas: trust and openness, morale, responsibility, support, and freedom.

Intended Audience:

- Managers seeking feedback from the work group on the climate at meetings.
- Any facilitator, internal or external consultant, HR professional, or trainer helping managers understand the importance of an open climate in creating a productive meeting environment.
- Trainers, facilitators, consultants, and HR professionals who want to assess the climate they create at their workshops and seminars.

Processing the Activity:

- Ask participants to think of their last six meetings with one particular group and then respond to the questions.
- Have participants score the questionnaire.
- Discuss each of the five concepts being measured and discuss their connection to an inviting climate.
- Have people break up into small groups and discuss their own responses, paying particular attention to one-point answers. If participants have no one-point answers, suggest they look at two-point answers.
- Have participants do an item analysis to determine their meeting climate weaknesses.

Questions for Discussion:

- Is there any pattern to your one- or two-point answers?
- If so, what is it?
- What does this survey suggest you need to do differently to improve your meeting climate?

Caveats and Considerations:

- This questionnaire can be facilitated by a manager wanting a work group to evaluate their own meetings, but it can also be used as a training tool for managers focusing on their meetings and how to improve them.

Content: The What of Your Meetings

The next aspect of the meeting environment is content. In a word, content is the *what* of the meeting. Content answers the fundamental questions: Why are we meeting? What are we trying to accomplish? What is our subject matter or task? It might be any number of things. Are you trying to define a problem? Perhaps you want to evaluate the new system you have designed. Or you may have some new procedures to explain. Maybe you defined a problem at your last meeting and your content this week is to generate possible solutions—not decide them, but generate alternatives.

There are several types of meetings; determining what type of meeting you are having will clarify your content. The trick is not to keep the content a surprise to the participants. Tell them before the meeting so they will be prepared. Tell them at the meeting once you have welcomed them and tell them again at the close of the meeting exactly why it is you met and what you got accomplished. You can also determine at that time what the focus of the next meeting will be if you need another meeting.

The following types of meetings are commonly seen in organizations. They lend themselves to a time frame of one to two hours. There may be times when you combine several purposes in one meeting.

1. Problem Solving

A problem-solving meeting is a large umbrella that can cover various steps in the problem-solving process. Many of these steps have rated their own kind of meeting (e.g., idea generation and evaluation). One thing is certain: A problem-solving meeting involves clearly defining the problem and, once alternatives are suggested, also includes reality testing. Some examples of problem-solving questions are ''What can we do to minimize errors?'' ''How can we reduce the time lag in responding to requests?''

2. Idea Generation

Idea generation involves brainstorming or other creative techniques you may want to use as a way to generate alternatives. One of the strengths of brainstorming, particularly in a diverse environment, is that it allows for no evaluation or judgment. This can help in an environment where employees might be worried about loss of face.

3. Decision Making

Once you have investigated possibilities and evaluated information, you are finally ready to make a decision. This might involve determining which information system to purchase or deciding when it is appropriate to use languages other than English in the workplace.

4. Information

While straight dissemination of information is the least valid and least productive reason to have meetings, there are times when the sensitive nature of information or the potential impact of this information necessitates a meeting environment as the best way to get the word out. This kind of meeting is especially helpful in times of rapid change, when the rumor mill works overtime and people spend more time looking for information than getting work done. Make sure there is two-way communication so people can ask questions. Also, be sure you check for understanding. Nods and smiles do not necessarily mean you get your message across in a diverse environment. Our last tip regarding information meetings is to suggest alternatives such as voice mail, bulletins, or newsletters when your method is one-way communication and your goal is to give "the facts ma'am, just the facts."

5. Data Generating

A data generating meeting is very effective in team building and before problem-solving sessions. By asking questions such as the following, you will get data that show different perceptions.

- What is the best thing about being a part of this team?
- What does this team need to do differently to create more harmony?
- Where are the breakdowns occurring on the assembly line?
- Where are the areas of overlap in our functioning?

Asking questions in less direct ways will get you better results in a diverse group. For example, the question about how to create harmony would probably be asked more straightforwardly in a group that is highly acculturated to the American way of doing business. But taking a more indirect approach, such as "Let's talk a little about how we might work together and cooperate with one another," might be easier for Asians, Hispanics, and Middle Easterners. A good facilitator will structure the meeting in ways that get everyone to participate so that data come from every corner. We discuss more about how to do that in the next section of this chapter.

6. Sharing

Sometimes people need to get together just to renew contact with one another and share perceptions about what's going on. When we did a customer service program for a local health-care institution, several of the units had short meetings after the training to share their reactions to the techniques they were using and to compare the results they were getting. It's a good way to help people feel they are in the same boat, and to make certain the boat is not the *Titanic*. Regarding meetings in diverse groups, intercultural rubs between groups can be very disruptive. Sharing can be a proactive way to build relationships and minimize conflicts.

7. Planning

Planning is a process of rethinking mission statements, figuring out what the organization's purpose and values are, and determining where it's going and how it's going to get there. Strategic planning is not a one-meeting or one-session process. There can also be short-term or specific planning as it relates to particular issues. One advantage to having planning meetings is that it indicates the organization's desire to involve people in critical issues. Planning also helps in the acculturation process, as it reinforces cause-and-effect thinking, a cornerstone of American culture.

8. Evaluation and Follow-Up

Problems that get solved, decisions that get made, and plans that get implemented need to have some criteria to determine whether or not they are effective. Your evaluation and follow-up meetings are used for taking stock: Have we done what we set out to do? Is it working? Should we stay the course? These critical sessions can keep the best-laid plans from falling through the cracks. It's a way to hold people accountable and keep the organization on its self-determined track. The only caveat regarding a diverse work group is to make sure people whose first language is not English understand what is taking place and what is expected of them. In some cultures, the respect for authority and a fear of loss of face might result in the participants agreeing to everything that goes on at the meeting while not understanding anything. Or the emphasis on harmony might prevent employees from voicing any negative comments. Collecting comments and evaluations from small groups rather than individuals might circumvent this barrier.

Look at the eight types of meetings and determine which you use the most.

The last meeting I ran was a _____ meeting.

To improve my meetings and integrate my work force more fully, I need to use more _____

_____

_____

types of meetings.

When I look at the range of meetings, and when I consider the dynamics of my diverse group, on thing I can do to improve the content of my meetings is to _____

_____

_____

Process: The How of Your Meetings

Process looks at how your meetings are structured and how communication takes place. No matter what your content is, your process can be interactive. The more interactive it is, the more open and trusting your climate will become. Take the *Group Process Questionnaire* to see how you currently use interactive processes in your meetings.

Group Process Questionnaire

Answer the following questions by putting a check in either the Yes or No column. If your answer is yes, estimate the percentage of your meetings where you use what you've checked off and enter that percentage in the frequency column. For example, if you use the random count method about two thirds of the time, put 65%. If you use pairs in every meeting, your response might be 100%.

Use of Small Groups	Yes	No	Frequency
Method of Configuring the Group			
Random count			
Job alike			
Mixed groups			
Self-selection			
Numbers of People in the Group			
Pairs (can be someone you trust, or maybe just someone you are sitting next to)			
Triads (you can count off randomly or ask participants to find two people they feel comfortable with)			
Any number of people but it depends on purpose, number of participants and other factors; 7 to 9 are ideal for problem solving while groups of 4 or 5 are excellent for processing information and seeking input on various issues			

Group Process Questionnaire (*concluded*)

Use of Small Groups	Yes	No	Frequency
Publishing Data			
Collect data at central point and use flip chart			
Collect data on overhead or blackboard at central point			
Have various subgroups; generate data, record on board or flip chart, then report			
Synthesize data at central point after each group has recorded and reported its data			
Input-Seeking Techniques			
Open-ended statements given from overhead, easel, or on a handout (e.g., The best thing about this policy is . . .)			
Paper-and-pencil questionnaires			
Index cards (3 × 5 or 5 × 8) as a tool for writing questions/concerns, information, or organizing thoughts			

Suggestions for Using the *Group Process Questionnaire*

Objectives:

- Determine how interactive the processes are at your meetings.

Intended Audience:

- Managers who want to evaluate their own meetings.
- Trainers, facilitators, consultants, and HR professionals who want to get a sense of their own group process in meetings or the training sessions they design.

Processing the Activity:

- Have participants fill out the questionnaires.
- In small groups, discuss the results and implications.
- After you've looked at the data, indicate what changes need to be made in order to more effectively use group process.

Questions for Discussion:

- Which techniques and methods do you use the most?
- Are there some you rarely use that might make your meetings/sessions more interactive?
- What one would you be willing to try at your very next meeting or seminar?

Caveats and Considerations:

- Use of small groups where trust is high is critical to helping newcomers acculturate to American business norms.

Responding to the *Group Process Questionnaire* will give you information about whether or not you are currently using some of the process tools available to you. Once you have this general information, we can help you structure groups with a diverse cultural mix so that you get the results you want. Remember what we said in the section on content. Most cultures in the world value collaboration and harmony. They are also loyal to their employer. The most important thing to remember about process is that the ''group'' is your natural ally. Use it!

Productivity

The three previously mentioned components of the meeting environment—climate, content, and process—significantly impact the productivity in your meetings. In turn, the productivity influences the group climate by creating a sense of hope, possibility, and confidence. All four areas, when they work together like a well-oiled machine, can bring you results well worth the time and energy it costs to have a meeting.

Interaction: It May Be Cultural, but It Doesn't Have to Be Intimidating

The key to the success and effectiveness of any meeting will ultimately be measured by the results. When participants are involved and invested in dealing with the content at hand, results are better. Participation and commitment will best be achieved when there is interaction. Your job as a manager or a facilitator running your group's meetings is to design processes and create a climate where interaction is the norm, no matter what culture people originally come from.

There are a couple of cultural practices that could sabotage your group's willingness to interact. As we have already mentioned, respect for titles, authority, age, or experience could pose a problem for a boss who really wants the group to wrestle with any pertinent but thorny issues such as a new staffing policy, a flexible schedule, or a shift in roles and responsibilities. If it is not in a person's cultural program to offer suggestions or even feedback to a boss because of that person's title and position, getting the feedback you desire can be difficult.

But another cultural value can neutralize the respect for authority. Loyalty to the company and the group is also a strong value. If you position the need to assess a company policy as being in the best interests of the company, you will work in sync with the cultural differences that confront you. Furthermore, collaboration is more valued in most cultures without America's strong sense of rugged individualism. By working with the informal leaders to help them understand how important their input is in making the group or the company more effective, your group can come out a real winner. Over time, the expectations for feedback and suggestions become the norm, and this exchange of ideas in a group will not seem so intimidating. We saw this work very well with a local hospital where most of the staff in a particular unit had come from different parts of the Asian Pacific. Some immigrants had been here for 20 years; some were newly arrived. All of them wanted some improvements in the areas of staffing and flextime. Directly complaining to authority and challenging the system simply was not in their experience, but group problem solving, done in several meetings over a few months, was. By working with the informal leaders, by using the safety of the group, and by assuring all that it was for the benefit of the organization, participation was maximized and the experience was a very positive one even for the most initially reluctant employees. As the experience yields positive results, any residual intimidation will diminish. Group safety and mutual respect can work wonders.

The other cultural norm that makes participation intimidating is the issue of face saving. No one, in any culture, likes to look stupid. There are plenty of people at our seminars and meetings who are reluctant to speak up, and they are usually American born and bred. Imagine how much more difficult any of these behaviors would be in a culture where you don't yet feel comfortable and where shame is the end result of losing face. That fear is a great intimidator. It takes a lot of patience on a facilitator's part to help newcomers acculturate.

We previously mentioned *brainstorming*. It can be your ally in structuring interaction so that people don't lose face. It works very well in the idea-generation stage of problem solving, and some of the principles of brainstorming can be transferred to other areas of your meetings. All you need teach your group are the following few rules:

1. No judgment or evaluation of any ideas.
2. Write each idea down where everyone can see it, exactly as it is given.
3. "Freewheel"—which means encourage people to give bold, unconventional suggestions, many of which may seem totally impractical. Remember, just write them down as is!
4. Set a time limit and seek a certain number of suggestions with a given time frame. You may tell a group that they have 10 minutes to come up with 75 suggestions. The idea is that a short, concentrated time span will enable people to spark ideas off one another.

The "no judgment or evaluation" rule is especially helpful for a varied cultural group. It creates a climate in which it is impossible to look stupid because every idea is valid and all, particularly the "weird" ones, have the kernel of some potentially creative and unique solutions to organizational issues.

Brainstorming is an extremely collaborative process and addresses the two fundamental needs identified by Norman R. F. Maier and Rick Roskin, creative academicians from the University of Michigan who have done extensive work on group problem solving and decision making. The needs are *ego* and *affiliation*.[29] If you structure your group environment so that participants feel as though their contributions are valued (ego enhancement), and they belong to a collaborative, supportive work team (affiliation), the participative interaction will be welcome, not intimidating. There is a caveat, however. Brainstorming is a spontaneous process, and in a culture like the Japanese, for example, where people don't throw out off-the-cuff suggestions, it may be difficult for an individual to freewheel by uninhibitedly suggesting ideas. Imagine how difficult this process would be for someone from a culture that respects silence and in which words are chosen very carefully before they are uttered. While the concept of brainstorming is used in Japan, it won't necessarily be used at all levels of the organization. It is best used with a functional team that has a long history, significant trust, and an investment in coming up with new ideas, solutions, or products. Even then, the Japanese style is different from the American style. Raucous and uncensored shouting of ideas is not the Japanese way. Expect and respect that difference.

Make Sure that *Long* and *Boring* Do Not Describe Your Meetings

The only way that *long* and *boring*, or other equivalents, won't describe your meetings is to make the meetings interactive. The key to maintaining people's interest is to hook them; they have to see the relevance of this meeting to their work lives. Our teacher and mentor, Dr. John E. Jones of Organizational Universe Systems in San Diego, uses what he calls the PIT model. In designing an agenda, he starts with the *P,* which is the *personal* hook, then goes to the *I* for *interpersonal* relevance. Finally, he focuses on the *T,* or *task*. Some examples of questions that have personal relevance are the following:

- What are the most interesting and exciting challenges you face as part of a multicultural work force?
- How does this new policy affect the work flow efficiency in your job?
- What questions and concerns do you have about this new procedure?

An effective way to get to the personal aspect is to start your meeting with a warm-up that encourages participants to open up. Once personal relevance is established, then John gets to the *I,* or interpersonal issues. The questions here center on how a given issue impacts group relationships and interactions. An example of a question having relevance to the group would be ''What one operational change could create more ease and efficiency between the auditing and tax departments?'' Only then is it possible to focus productively on the task at hand, figuring out the specific implementation details of the procedure in question.

Let us give you an example of using the personal, then the interpersonal focus. We did some work with a health-care facility a few years ago that had a low census and rising costs. As a result, each department was told to trim its budget. We worked with the dietary unit which had the challenge of eliminating the equivalent of one full-time position. When this financial information and its impact were presented, staff members first had a chance to respond to this issue very personally. What concerns did the potential job loss mean to the individuals and their life-styles? Their families? Individual goals and aspirations like going back to school? Once those personal apprehensions were acknowledged, the group dealt with the issue of what one less position would mean to the unit in terms of work load as well as psychological comfort. Because they dealt with the personal and interpersonal issues first, they were free to get to the task of designing a solution that would work for the unit as a whole. To their manager's credit, she let them determine how they would meet the financial objectives. The group decided to cut everyone's hours a little rather than any one position totally.

Obviously, the issue described above was so central to the participants' well-being that they could hardly have been bored. But don't miss the relevance of the PIT model because of the seriousness of the content. When a meeting is structured so that the content is seen as having both personal and interpersonal relevance, the session has the promise of being anything but boring. In order to make certain that promise is fully realized, let's look at creating an effective agenda. This gives you the opportunity to use the PIT model. What's more, it's your blueprint for insuring that *long* and *boring* are never mentioned in the same breath as your meetings.

The Agenda: Your Blueprint for Success

There is a tried-and-true formula for planning an agenda that will help keep your meetings tightly structured and very effective. Use this agenda planning guide for all your meetings to keep you on track.

Agenda Planning Guide

Purpose.   What is the reason for this meeting in the first place?

Objectives.   What specific goals do you want to accomplish?

Process.   How is the meeting structured so you meet those goals?

- *Warm-up:* Use quick, relevant questions at the beginning for focus. *The Hows and Whys of Warm-Ups* chart gives you numerous options and examples.
- *Activity:* This involves some process that gets to the issue.
- *Grouping:* How and why do you divide people in certain groupings?
- *Leadership:* Facilitation skills are critical here. Consider having different staff members rotate leadership or take responsibility for part of the meeting.
- *Closure/next steps:* Who is responsible for what? Next meeting?

Logistics.   An old maxim states that the three most important things in real estate are location, location, location. The same might be said for meetings. Location (and facility) have a great deal to do with the results you achieve. For a retreat, location is probably given a lot more consideration than for a regular meeting. What is important regarding cultural differences is paying attention to an environment that helps people feel comfortable. We learned recently of a business owner who wanted to show his employees how highly he values them and so planned a company get-together at a very fancy, expensive hotel. His employees are people of simple means. Many felt they had to buy new clothes in order to attend, and in general, it was too ritzy an environment for the staff's blood. The intentions of this entrepreneur were noble. He tried to do something that he felt would elevate staff morale and help them feel appreciated. But in truth, they really just felt uncomfortable.

In addition to comfort, when you pick a place, think about purpose, who is attending, your objectives, time, money, and all other pertinent resources. Room size is critical. The room should offer flexibility in style of setup as well as mobility of chairs for different group configurations. On many occasions, we have been asked to work with midsize groups on issues that require several different small-group configurations within a given meeting. In one case, our contact person told us that the only facility available was the big auditorium with its permanent seats. This is definitely not optimal. Do yourselves a favor. Neutralize any negativity

The Hows and Whys of Warm-Ups

Purpose

- Focus participants on task or topic

- Get initial, immediate involvement of participants

Methods (Depends on size of group, time available, and amount of involvement required)

- Question to think about
  (Think of the most successful work unit . . . .)

- Polling the group
  (How many of you have . . . .)

- Random responses from group
  (What are some examples of . . . .)

- Individual oral response
  (Good management is . . . .)

- Share/interview in pairs
  (Assorted topics.)

Forms

- Open-ended statements
  (My biggest concern about _____ is . . . .)

- Respond to question
  (What behaviors do you see in good managers?)

- Topics for sharing/interviewing
  (High/low points of year, best/worst aspects of this plan/project, what I want to achieve/avoid in doing this project.)

- Analyze incident from experience
  (Think of your most successful/unsuccessful meeting.)

- Goal setting
  (Expectations, what I want to get, what is the best/worst that could come from this session?)

Tips for Warm-Ups

- Remember to keep warm-up relevant and quick

- Only chart information if it will be used

that may come from the environment by paying attention to size, chair mobility, room temperature, and lighting. If you want the staff's undivided attention, make certain the meeting is held in a location where participants won't be interrupted or called away every two minutes. Also make sure the meeting site is physically accessible for all staff.

Time. We have already mentioned the importance of sticking to your boundaries for both starting and ending times as a way to reinforce norms and expectations. The time of day to hold meetings can be flexible, but avoid calling heavy, serious sessions right before the day ends, when energy level and commitment are at best uneven and frequently nonexistent. On the other hand, brainstorming sessions at day's end can energize the troops and spark their productivity. Respect cultural differences in setting meeting times. For example, to call a meeting late Friday afternoon when Orthodox Jews observe Sabbath is exclusionary. Learn about and honor the differences of the people in your work group.

Preplanning.

- *Publicity:* How are you going to notify people about the meeting? Will you try newsletters? Written notice? Voice mail? Phone calls? Memos? An announcement on the bulletin board? Use them individually or in combination, as appropriate. One thing is certain: The more lead time, the better. Give people plenty of notice before the meeting, unless of course you need to call an emergency get-together.
- *Materials:* If you are dealing with an issue that involves a lot of information and you want people prepared to talk about it, be certain they have received all the material enough ahead of time so they can read it, digest it, and seriously think about it. Remember to have a few extra copies so you aren't caught short. The motto *semper paratus* is a good rule of thumb here.
- *Refreshments:* Food and beverage always soften the mood a little bit and seem to extend people's patience. More than that, in cultures where hospitality is important, it is offensive not to have refreshments. The good news is that in a diverse environment, food from different cultures is one of the most interesting and effective ways to build bridges. Food is a social lubricant and has been for eons. The Bible talks about breaking bread together. In this day and age, we can also break tortillas, rice, dolmas, bagels, or whatever. We do have one caveat regarding food. Learn about cultural food restrictions and individual preferences. Jews and Muslims, for example, don't eat pork. Some people drink only tea, not coffee. Others are vegetarians. Refreshments are one place where a little sensitivity can go a long way toward furthering intercultural knowledge and understanding, and toward creating a climate of inclusivity.

Paying attention to each part of the *agenda planning guide* before you ever conduct a meeting is like having a good insurance policy. As you follow our sample agenda, think about what content you would insert if you were filling this out for your next meeting. Then use the *Agenda Planning Worksheet* to plan your own agenda.

Sample Agenda

Purpose: To begin the process of improving interdepartmental communication.

Objectives: To identify the strengths and weaknesses of the interdepartmental communication process as it currently exists.

Process:
  Warm-Up: Each participant in the meeting responds to the following open-ended statements while the facilitator charts all responses on the flip chart at the front of the room.

  1. **The best thing about our interdepartmental communication is**

    _____

  2. **The most frustrating thing about it is**

    _____

After the facilitator records all the responses to these two questions on a flip chart, lead a group discussion about their responses to the data. Center the responses around three areas: (1) reactions, (2) surprises, and (3) insights. It may be helpful to write those three words on the flip chart in order to focus the discussion. Use the group's comments as a lead to get into the next part of the agenda, which is the _Personal Focus Activity_. While this worksheet offers a sample of a data gathering technique, you can change the content to make it relevant for you.

The Process

The steps in the agenda-planning process are described further below.

Activity. The _Personal Focus Activity_ is the heart of your meeting because it is the vehicle for getting to the question or issue you would like to deal with. Using the example on the next page, you would ask each participant to fill out this sheet by himself or herself first so the person has a chance to think about the problem from an individual perspective. Armed with that data, you can then decide how you would like to structure the groups so that you can process the information.

Grouping. Depending on who the participants are, the grouping will vary. If you have people from each department involved, mix the participants so that the differences in perspective are shared. If you and the other manager decide that each of the groups need to get a handle on their own perspectives first and bring the two groups together later, then you can count off randomly. If your group is small, about 8 to 10 people, you can use pairs or triads, or even split the group in half. When you start getting 12 or more people, form groups of 4 or 5. Give clear directions with a very clear time limit. Here's an example of how you might structure the groups to process your main activity:

Personal Focus Activity
(Interdepartmental Communication Process)

	My Department	Other Department
Procedures that Get in the Way		
Procedures that Help		

1. Have chart paper on easels or taped to walls. You can also use black boards . . . . anything so that each group can chart the collective data. By replicating the 4 quadrants on the chart paper or board, a recorder from the group can help distill the groups' responses in one central place. Once the data is visible, discuss the results and issues that surface. It is hard to say for sure how much time people will need for their discussion. Give them approximately 10 or 15 minutes in their small groups and keep checking with all groups to see if that is enough time.

2. At the end of that time, with an easel and flip chart at the front of the room, go around the room from group to group, getting one suggestion at a time from each group, till you have them all. You can suggest that when there is repetition of ideas, the reporter from each group lets you know so that you can check the idea off in a different color marker each time it is mentioned. That will give you a visual picture of the strength of some of the ideas.

Leadership.   Your leadership shows itself in how you collect and process the information. Once you have everyone's data, then you want to ask pertinent questions. Here are some samples:

1. What do you make of these data? What do they tell us about the communication process as it currently exists?
2. What areas can we leave alone because they seem to be working?
3. What areas seem to be ripest for problem solving?

Next Steps.   A discussion of the difficult communication areas should lead you to some problem solving. Determine which issues will be addressed at the next meeting. Depending on how many of the communication systems you decide to tackle, you may form sub groups to look at various parts of the problems. Determine a date for your next meeting and let people know that you expect them to come with the information they have collected from their investigations.

Closure.   Always wrap up your meeting in a neat little package. This doesn't necessarily mean that you completed all your business but it does mean that you need to review what you did accomplish, restate next steps and end with some quick closure, similar in technique to a warm-up. It should be fast and help pull things together. Depending on the number of people present, you may go around the group and ask everyone to respond, or you may just get random responses. Open-ended statements like the following are helpful closure techniques:

1. The best thing that came from this meeting is . . . .
2. What makes me feel most hopeful about this situation is . . . .
3. The one area I'm going to focus on before the next meeting is . . .

Regardless of the different cultures involved, when you structure this meeting based on the agenda planning guide, and when you use the interactive techniques we've mentioned, you will get participation.

Agenda Planning Worksheet

Purpose:

Objectives:

Process:

  Warm-up:

  Activity:

  Grouping:

  Leadership:

  Closure/next steps:

Logistics:

  Place:

  Time:

Preplanning:

  Publicity:

  Materials:

  Refreshments:

Suggestions for Using the *Agenda Planning Worksheet*

Objectives:

- Provide a structure to design effective meetings.

Intended Audience:

- Any person who plans meetings, training sessions, workshops, or seminars.

Processing the Activity:

- Offer this as a suggested structure that people can use over and over again.

Questions for Discussion:

- Are there any pieces of the agenda planning guide that are unclear?
- What questions do you have or what clarifications do you need?

Caveats and Considerations:

- Help people see the application. Sometimes only managers think this applies, but task forces and ad hoc committees can also use this information.

We suggest that this agenda planning guide and the *Agenda Planning Worksheet* function as your own "Thomas Guide" on the road to good meetings. Using them will undoubtedly improve meetings with diverse populations, and even meetings of homogeneous groups.

Skills for Running Productive Meetings

Using your *Agenda Planning Worksheet* starts you out on the right meeting-planning path. But what separates the proverbial men from the boys are facilitation skills. The consummate facilitator is one who maintains objectivity, regardless of the breadth, diversity, and intensity of viewpoints. That is easier to do when you truly are an outsider as opposed to being a part of, or manager of, the group. Most managers don't have the luxury of having that outside facilitator at their disposal, so they are forced to wear two hats. One is the "invested manager hat" that cares a lot about outcomes of meetings, decisions, and problem solving. The manager wearing that hat has definite preferences. The other hat the manager wears is the "objective facilitator" hat. When wearing that hat, the manager is focused primarily on using group process skills and being sensitive to cultural differences as he/she designs meetings to get the best from the group.

The words *facilitator* and *objective* go hand in hand. But that reality "ain't necessarily so" when you're talking about a manager as facilitator. Objectivity will be much more difficult to achieve in this situation. There will be times when you want to make a statement because you have a strong preference, or when you want the group to know how you feel. That's the time when you need to say something to the effect of "I'm taking off my facilitator hat for a minute and putting on my manager hat. I do have some concerns I'd like to share." When you've had your say, you can tell the group you will be putting on your facilitator hat again.

Whether you're the invested manager or objective facilitator, your role in leading effective meetings should be the same. Your job is to design and manage the meeting, lead the group through processes so that it can accomplish its task, and help the group maintain its health and equilibrium through the process. Rate yourself on the following critical facilitator skills from 1 to 5 to indicate how adept you already are at the behaviors we mention. The closer you are to a *5,* the more you have mastered the art of effective facilitation.

How Effective a Facilitator Are You?

Directions: Rate yourself from 1 to 5 on the following facilitator skills. The closer you are to a *5*, the more skilled you are at facilitation.

Facilitator Behavior	1	2	3	4	5
1. Remains neutral					
2. Does not judge or contribute ideas					
3. Keeps the group focused on common task					
4. Asks clarifying, helpful questions that suggest alternatives					
5. Creates a climate free of attack or criticism					
6. Encourages and structures participation					
7. Helps the group find win/ win solutions					

Suggestions for Using *How Effective a Facilitator Are You?*

Objectives:

- Evaluate facilitation skills.
- Determine areas for growth.

Intended Audience:

- Managers facilitating meetings.
- HR professionals, facilitators, consultants, and trainers who lead meetings, problem-solving sessions, or workshops where their neutrality is essential.

Processing the Activity:

- Distribute the questionnaire and ask participants to focus on a meeting or seminar they recently led.
- With that session in mind, ask participants to rate themselves on a 1 to 5 scale, 5 being the best.
- Have participants then pair up (or use small groups) and discuss their evaluations.
- Ask them to focus on what this questionnaire suggests their facilitation strengths and weaknesses are and what they need to do differently.

Questions for Discussion:

- How did you feel while you were filling this out?
- What good news did you discover about your facilitation skills?
- What do you think those who attend your workshops and meetings would say about your skills?
- What do the data suggest you need to do differently in order to improve your skills?
- What suggestions can you give one another (in pairs or small groups) that will be helpful to you?

Caveats and Considerations:

- Small groups increase safety and security when having people discuss their insights and then get feedback.
- Putting two sets of pairs together for the last discussion questions may increase the number of ideas offered.

The following is an explanation of each of the items on the questionnaire.

1. *Remains neutral.* Whether you're the manager or the facilitator, objectivity is critical. Restraint is advisable because if you voice your opinions, your position or title would be reason enough to squelch group participation. Remaining objective is especially critical in a diverse group for the reason we already mentioned—in numerous cultures, it would be unthinkable to challenge a boss.

2. *Does not judge or contribute ideas.* Judging ideas, even positively, will shut down participation. The minute you say, "Great idea!" you lose the appearance of objectivity. More important, those who do not think the idea is great may be intimidated or feel alienated. As a facilitator, your objective is to guide the group to its conclusions by the processes you use, not with your opinions. The results of negative feedback are well documented. No one in any culture likes to feel stupid or be put down, and a person who thinks he has been will likely withdraw commitment and participation.

3. *Keeps the group focused on a common task.* Maybe the question you are dealing with is "How are we going to stop creating cliques?" It might just as easily be "How are we going to increase productivity and profitability?" Whatever the question is, the facilitator has the job of designing processes that keep your meeting on track. If the group starts to derail, she brings you back to the task at hand. An example of what the facilitator might say is, "We're getting ahead of ourselves. That comment will be relevant when we generate solutions, but right now we're still analyzing the problem." If the whole group is involved in the discussion, then no one particular person will take such a comment personally and feel as though he or she has lost face or done something stupid.

4. *Asks clarifying, helpful questions that suggest alternatives.* A facilitator might ask questions such as the following: "If you take this approach, what will the impacts be, . . . both good and bad?" "If you do nothing, what will happen?" "Are your decisions going to impact people who aren't here and have no say?" "What might the fallout from that be?" Asking pertinent questions at the right time is an essential facilitator skill.

5. *Creates a climate that frees individuals and their ideas from attack or criticism.* The facilitator can set ground rules at the beginning that will tell people what is expected. One of the helpful ground rules is "No finger pointing or blaming." When looking at cultures where face-saving is significant, this protection is essential. You might need to stop and remind the group, "Right now we're generating ideas. We'll evaluate them later."

6. *Encourages and structures participation.* Using small groups is the best way we know to ensure the involvement of everyone from any culture or background. The cliché "variety is the spice of life" has relevance when we talk about different group combinations. Whether you pair people, put them in threesomes, or put them in some small group configuration, let your task objective determine the grouping. Are you trying to create a safe environment at the beginning, particularly for people who speak broken or heavily accented English? Then try using pairs. That is the most secure structure. To increase the security, tell people to find a partner they know well and with whom they feel comfortable. Are you trying to illustrate to everyone that there are a wide variety of perspectives? Then try randomly counting off so groups are all about four to six people in size. The random count should ensure some difference of

perspective. If, on the other hand, you are trying to teach a skill and then want people to practice, three is a good number—two to engage in a role-play using the skills while the third member acts as an observer and gives feedback. All of these variations on a theme will encourage the participation you want for an effective meeting in a way that will make cultural differences less relevant and meeting content paramount.

7. *Helps the group find win/win solutions.* As a facilitator, one of your greatest challenges and most important functions is to keep people from polarizing into rigid positions. We remember that before the peace treaty was signed after the Vietnam war, the biggest concern was the shape of the table and who would sit where. In similar ways, people in organizations attach symbolic meaning to issues and viewpoints. It is easy, especially in an era of insufficient resources, to take hard and fixed positions on symbolic things. As a facilitator, your job is to give feedback when you see that happening, and to ask questions that keep opening the options. Where diversity is concerned, sometimes in group-on-group conflicts, people from various groups attach themselves to outcomes that have nothing to do with the issue itself. Symbolic issues, or power issues, are the hidden agenda. This happens in homogeneous groups too, but it can be especially sensitive in diverse groups where some people feel disenfranchised. Again, we're back to asking questions that help people stay focused on the goal and still get to some of the underlying issues. Here are some samples:

> What might the effect of this policy be?
>
> How could it build bridges? Whom might it alienate? How?
>
> What do you want to do about it?
>
> What are some other alternatives?
>
> How will this policy help the group accomplish its objectives?
>
> How might it derail your efforts?

Which of these facilitator skills are your strength and which do you need to work on to be a more effective leader? Target one skill to work on at your next meeting.

Being a facilitator isn't necessarily easy, but it can be enormously satisfying. If you use the *Agenda Planning Worksheet*, become very clear about your content and processes, and design an agenda that is very interactive, you will lead meetings that are more interesting and productive. What's more, your group, no matter how diverse, should also increase its level of trust and openness. All of these skills, plus an awareness of and sensitivity to cultural differences, will enable you to really shine as a manager, supervisor, or leader of meetings with any group of people.

Paying Attention to Cultural Hot Spots in Meetings

We have come across many open, sensitive people in companies all over the country who experience frustration when faced with different cultural norms. In seminars we've taught, people have said things like, "I want to make everyone feel welcome but I don't know the customs of the Hmong, for example, and I don't want to offend them." A lot of well-intentioned managers don't do anything because they aren't sure how to run a meeting or bring a group together. Let's start with this reality. There are different cultural norms, and not identifying or acknowledging these norms can inhibit productivity, in or out of meetings. Identifying these norms can make your life easier and your meetings much more productive. The chart *The Impact of Cultural Norms on Meetings* on pages 184 and 185 should give you a lot of help.

Three Techniques for Getting Participation in a Diverse Group

The profound but subtle differences in how culture programs us can create some very interesting group dynamics, which often show up in your meetings. As we have already mentioned, how we interact, communicate, solve problems, and see the world will differ depending on our "software." These differences, at least initially, can cause reluctance on the part of some group members to participate. For that reason, we want to give you three easy-to-use and very effective techniques for getting everyone involved.

1. Pass the Hat

In order to guarantee anonymity and not make anyone feel uncomfortable, one manager we know has all participants write their suggestions or reactions to certain issues on a piece of paper. Participants are then asked to fold up the paper, unsigned, and put it in a hat as the manager or someone else collects it. Then the manager gives the hat to one person who becomes the starting point. That person picks a suggestion, and the hat is passed around till everyone gets a piece of paper. One at a time, each suggestion is read and discussed. It is possible that some ideas will take a long time and merit much discussion. Some may be very short and simple. What makes this a good idea has nothing at all to do with the content of the suggestion. Its strength is in the participation it gets from all members of the group. It does so by minimizing the self-consciousness someone might feel if he/she has been taught that any hint of the need for improvement might be an affront to a boss or authority figure. "Pass the Hat" can be a real involvement enhancer.

2. The Suggestion Box

This technique is no novice to work groups looking for ways to increase input and psychological comfort at the same time. The trick is to make sure that you don't suffer "death by the suggestion box," when suggestions are left to die in the box because they are never attended to. In order to avoid that demoralizing end, place the box in a location that is central and easy to get to. Then read and act on them regularly. Depending on the suggestion itself, you may have any number of reactions. Those that are more complex can be read and processed at a meeting. Those that are simple, such as "Let's have healthy refreshments at meetings like fruit instead of brownies," are easy to handle. At the next meeting, explain the change in refreshments and ask the group members how they feel about it. This is not a biggie—if some want fruit and some want pastry, we bet there is a way to handle them both. Most suggestions will undoubtedly be more complex. When they are, divide the staff into small groups. Have the

The Impact of Cultural Norms on Meetings

Cultural Norms	Impact on Meetings	What to Do
Respect for authority	This norm leads to an unwillingness to challenge ideas from people of a certain age or title; may inhibit solutions to problem solving and can lead to a more formal climate.	State expectations emphasizing the need for participation because it will benefit the company. Loyalty is also a norm that you can use here. Show respect to the group's informal leader because of age, knowledge, title, and overall influence. Solicit this person's help and give leaders the same esteem groups do.
Emphasis on group over individual	This may lead some managers to assume people are unmotivated or lazy because they keep pace with the team rather than seek individual glory or promotion.	The group is your best cultural ally. Use it! Stress teamwork, harmony, and collaboration. Structure group tasks and focus on group accomplishment.
Fear of shame and loss of face	Because people are afraid to lose face or make mistakes, there might be less willingness to take risks or share unconventional ideas.	Talk about the importance of taking intelligent risks and reinforce this even when the group makes mistakes. Avoid finger pointing or blaming. Make the group motto be "We're all in this together." Encourage their risk taking and reward their efforts.
More contextual, less direct communication	It is harder in less direct cultures to figure out what is really on someone's mind. This can result in miscommunication, both in and out of meetings.	Develop a good, trusting relationship over time. It will take time to understand the subtle nuance as well as to get people to open up. You may never get the straight talk the way Americans give it. But you can pay attention to the subtle nonverbal cues. With trust and a good relationship you'll develop understanding over time.

The Impact of Cultural Norms on Meetings *(concluded)*

Cultural Norms	Impact on Meetings	What to Do
Value placed on harmony and collaboration	This norm mostly works to your advantage in having people create a positive working environment. The downside may be an unwillingness to discuss painful truths for the sake of harmony, even though it may be necessary.	Use the question asking skills presented in the chapter on interviewing. In sensitive ways and an unthreatening tone, seek information that may be necessary, and do so through the informal system. Remember to use the group. That provides safety and minimizes the sting.
Family as the first priority	There are times when people, particularly from Mexico and Central America, may need to leave to take care of family priorities. They may miss meetings, and more important, the assignments that result from them. Deadlines may not be met.	Work with people to find the middle ground. No one wants to be insensitive in times of family emergency. There are always trade-offs. Explain them. The group may pick up a person's slack for a short time. If a pattern develops that permanently inhibits work flow, some choices will have to be made.
Time consciousness: some cultures hold tighter time lines than the dominant culture, some looser	The rules need to be the same for everyone or there will be disgruntlement. Be careful not to interpret some laissez-faire behavior regarding time as indications of laziness or lack of caring.	Make clear what the meeting norms and expectations are. Once you decide how strict or loose you are going to be regarding time lines, reinforce your "rules." Position being on time as showing respect to other members of the group.
Problem solving that is less linear and analytical	You sometimes may feel like you aren't getting anywhere, because again, American directness likes to go straight for the solution. But lateral, intuitive thinking adds its own unique contribution to the process.	Learn to value and utilize different ways of thinking. This difference is truly one of the biggest gifts from diversity. Don't immediately discount nonlinear, nonlogical methods.
Goal setting and planning influenced by fatalism	The external locus of control mentality mentioned earlier may create the appearance in some cultures that people are less driven or motivated. Again, it's probably cultural. Belief in God's will is a powerful shaper.	Help your work group experience the direct connection between the responsibility they accept and the results they get. This will be a whole new way of viewing the world for some people whose life experience has not shown them that they have much influence over their own world. Patience, respect, and positive reinforcement will help.

suggestion written clearly on an overhead or an easel so that all can see it. Give the groups a specific length of time to discuss the issue and tell them to have a spokesperson ready to respond in one of three ways at the end of that time:

- We'd like to implement this suggestion as put forth.
- This suggestion has merit, but we still have questions. Let's discuss this further.
- We don't even want to mess with this suggestion, at least for now.

If you want to make your answers even simpler, you can ask for one of the following:

- Yes.
- Yes, with reservations, modifications, and questions.
- No.

As the facilitator, you may have lots of questions you want to ask as a result of the answers you get from each group. In that case, use the suggestions that we gave in earlier parts of this chapter to process the data. In both this technique and "Pass the Hat," the most important objective is your group's involvement, not how brilliant a solution you design to any particular problem.

3. Graffiti

Take chart paper with different questions or issues written on each in different color markers and tape them all around the meeting room walls. Then ask people to write their responses on the chart paper, using multicolored large markers. Depending on the size of your group, you can have people travel together as they go from station to station discussing the issues and charting their collective responses. You can also have each person write his or her own on an empty easel or piece of chart paper. Then everyone wanders around reading the responses. This can be done individually or in small groups. There are any number of variations on the "Graffiti" theme. For example, you can give each person scissors and a couple of magazines or newspapers. That way they can glue their responses to form a collage rather than color or write them. In one organization where we were members, we were asked to cut out words or pictures that illustrated the mission of this organization. Then we glued these on the chart paper covering the walls. It was fascinating to see the varied perspectives. The pictures are a particularly helpful way to work in bilingual settings. They can create a wonderful common bond. Whichever one you use, make sure that everyone sees all the data. Here are a few sample questions:

1. What common themes or concerns emerged?
2. What were the most surprising or striking differences you noticed?
3. What do the data suggest as an appropriate next step?

You have the option of processing the information in small groups or handling the discussion from a central point by getting random responses from either individuals or groups. In any case, you can chart the collective data as you do so. The wonderful part about each of these three techniques is that they guarantee safety and involvement at the same time.

Beyond what we've already suggested, one idea is to spend some time looking at the individual members in your meeting, particularly when you have an ongoing group. Realize that dysfunctional behaviors aren't always cultural. Individual personality differences can also account for some of the problem behaviors you are experiencing. Isolate or identify some of the dysfunctional behaviors that could be blocking a more productive, open climate. In the lists below, we give you the most common examples we see and five ways to deal with them.

Common Dysfunctional Behaviors in Meetings of Diverse Groups:

Dominating the discussion.

Arriving late.

Leaving early.

Kibitzing.

Speaking a language many others don't understand.

Making under-breath or snide comments.

Eye rolling.

Joking and teasing.

Arguing.

Verbal attacks or personal criticism.

Using sarcasm.

Discounting ideas because of someone's race, ethnicity, or gender.

Showing reluctance to participate.

Five Tips for Dealing with Dysfunctional Behavior:

1. Give ground rules at outset.
   - "Everyone will be expected to participate."
   - "All ideas are acceptable without judgments."
   - "Everyone will have one minute to give views."
   - "If we start at 9:00 we will be out by 10:00."
2. Confront dysfunctional behaviors without labeling.
   a. Describe behavior/situation.
      "We're spending a lot of time on ___. Should we pursue it further?"
      "It seems we're accepting an either/or orientation."
      "We're getting into personalities rather than behaviors."
      "Many people are not contributing."
      "There are two conversations going on at once."
      "Many people in the group don't understand Spanish."
   b. Ask participants to describe behavior/situation.
      "Where are we?"
      "What just happened?"
      "What's getting in our way?"
      "Where did we get lost?"
   c. Give own reactions.
      "I get upset when we waste time discussing personalities."
      "I'm off the track/unclear/lost."
      "I find it difficult to concentrate when other conversations are going on."

    d. Ask the disrupter to share comments with whole group.
        "We'd all like to hear your suggestions."
        "Would someone please translate."
3. Discuss functional and dysfunctional behaviors with group.
- "How does this behavior affect you? The group?"
- "I feel best in the group when . . . ."
- "I don't like to speak up when . . . ."

4. Suggest alternative behaviors.
- "It would be more helpful if . . . ."
- "More people would be involved if . . . ."
- "We'd finish our task today if . . . ."

5. Co-opt the dominator(s).
- Interview before session.
- Include in planning and agenda building.
- Give a specific task (e.g., recording).
- Listen and reflect feelings: "It's clear you have strong feelings about this. We'd also like to hear how others feel."

Seven Ways to Boost Meeting Productivity

Ultimately, a productive and memorable meeting is like fine dining. You need for all the important ingredients to come together in elegant ways so that you are left with something truly distinctive and worthwhile. With that goal in mind, let us give you an international smorgasbord of well-seasoned meeting tips.

1. Let Staff Know What's Expected

Once you've identified the constructive behaviors you want to see from your staff, let them know. You might say, "It's our meeting, and all of our ideas count. I'm depending on you to speak out, ask questions, make suggestions, and listen openly to the ideas of others so that we can get the best results." But be realistic. The power of cultural programming runs deep. Recognize that all the changes won't come from staff. You may have to adapt as well. If someone is raised in a culture where praising an individual in public is taboo, find other ways to show that employee that he or she is valued.

2. Create a Comfortable Tone

No matter how good a relationship you have with your staff, the relationship dynamics change in a more formal setting. Meetings do intimidate some people, and cultural programming just complicates the matter. Setting a nonthreatening, accepting tone that allows everyone to feel safe and secure should be your first item of business. All your results (or lack of them) will depend on that tone.

3. Use Small Groups and Design Interactive Meetings

One of the laws of group dynamics is that the smaller the group, the greater the safety. If people are reluctant to speak in front of the whole group at first, and our experience shows us they will be, have people respond in pairs. Our teacher, John

Jones, told us years ago to trust the process, and he has been proven right time and time again. The use of small groups can be your major ally in overcoming cultural differences so that these differences don't sabotage the success of your meetings.

4. Group People Cross-Culturally

The cliche "Birds of a feather flock together" rings true when looking at human behavior. People do tend to group with people who are most like them. If you want to have productive, harmonious meetings, it is important to minimize the cliquishness that creates barriers between groups. Cross-cultural mixing can give your staff the opportunity to see how much they have in common with other employees when they have a chance to work together and talk face-to-face. It not only builds bridges between individuals but also gives you some of your most creative problem solving.

5. Write Down the Meeting Content

In a multilingual arena, giving employees two ways to absorb the information increases their chance to communicate and participate. Don't depend on getting your message across only through hearing. The "eyes" have it. Use easels, wipe-off boards, overheads, or even butcher paper taped to the wall. Write down the meeting agenda and major points of discussion so that people can integrate the information at their own pace.

6. Make Part of Your Objective the Development of Meeting Excellence, and Start with a Formal Evaluation

There is no substitute for an ongoing evaluation about the usefulness and relevance of your meetings. Some sort of quick-and-easy question, such as "On a scale of 1 to 10, how productive or useful has this meeting been?" will give you pertinent information. The *Meeting Planning Checklist* can serve also as a useful evaluation. It gives you something to work toward in improving your meetings by showing you where your meetings are most productive and where they fall short. Use the checklist to ensure your thorough preparation.

7. Value the Different Cultural Contributions of Each Group and Realize that Bringing All These Differences Together in a Harmonious Way Will Take Time

Rome wasn't built in a day, and cultural understanding won't be either. Teaching your staff to deal with differences such as time consciousness, problem-solving styles, or interpersonal communication norms takes time and attention. It also takes patience and a desire to build bridges. But it is doable, no matter what the composition of your staff. Seeing the growth and productivity that result among individuals, as well as the group itself, is a great reinforcer for all of you. Work doesn't get much better or more rewarding than this.

Meeting Planning Checklist

Use this checklist in planning your next meeting, then again as an evaluation after the meeting. Target weaker areas for improvement in subsequent meetings. You will find that more effective meetings mean not only greater productivity but more enthusiastic followership, both keys to your success as a leader.

Preplanning

_____ Have facilities and equipment reserved, set up, and functional.

_____ Suit room size and seating arrangements to group size and activity.

_____ Have materials prepared and distributed when necessary.

_____ Make accomodations for refreshments and offer alternatives (e.g., tea, decaf, juice, etc.).

_____ Make sure location is accessible.

Clarifying Purpose and Objectives

_____ Have clear outcome in mind for each meeting.

_____ Prepare participants by giving clear expectations of the purpose of the meeting.

_____ Realistically match desired objectives to available time.

Agenda Planning

_____ Use a relevant warm-up that is quick, purposeful, and focusing.

_____ Include a variety of activities (e.g., writing, listening, discussing).

_____ Structure activities which require everyone to participate.

_____ Make sure data collected are visible to all (e.g., on blackboard, flip chart, etc.).

_____ Summarize the accomplishments of the meeting and indicate next steps.

Getting Participation

_____ Use small groups for discussing and sharing information to increase input and output.

_____ Use different groupings appropriately (e.g., random, like-job, work units, etc.).

_____ Break down large tasks into small steps with progress checks throughout.

_____ Encourage passive participants to join in activities.

_____ Pay attention to the needs of the participants.

Evaluation and Closure

_____ Clearly define responsibilities resulting from the meeting.

_____ Set the time and place for progress checks.

_____ Get feedback from participants about the meeting (oral or written).

_____ Do a personal analysis of the meeting, focusing on accomplishment and participation.

Suggestions for Using the *Meeting Planning Checklist*

Objectives:

- Provide a meeting evaluation tool.

Intended Audience:

- Managers or executives who plan and lead meetings.
- Trainers, consultants, or HR professionals who plan training seminars, workshops, or meetings.

Processing the Activity:

- Think about the last meeting/training seminar/workshop you planned.
- With that session in mind, use the *Meeting Planning Checklist* as an evaluation tool.
- Put people in pairs to discuss their evaluations.
- Note the items where you were able to put checks. More important, note the items where you had none.

Questions for Discussion:

- What does this tell you that you did well at your last meeting? What could you have done better?
- What area on this list could most use some improvement?
- What will you do differently before your next meeting?

Caveats and Considerations:

- Wherever the word *meeting* exists, a trainer or consultant can substitute *workshop* or *seminar*.

Chapter 6

Performance Evaluation in a Diverse Organization

This chapter will give you:

1. An understanding of cultural and diversity-related variables that impact the performance evaluation process.
2. Information about the sources of resistance to performance evaluation and how to overcome them.
3. Ways to overcome cultural blind spots in performance evaluation.
4. Examples of effective and ineffective performance evaluation.
5. A step-by-step guide for planning performance evaluation sessions.
6. Techniques for getting employee buy-in and commitment in the process.
7. Self-assessment tools to help you analyze and improve your effectiveness as an evaluator.
8. Tips for avoiding common performance evaluation pitfalls.

It is a rare person who doesn't find the performance evaluation process difficult and tension producing. On both sides of the desk, apprehensions and nervousness are apt to be felt. The evaluator worries about being accurate and fair, avoiding hurt feelings, and not producing conflict. The evaluatee, on the other end of the process, anticipates potential criticism, judgments, and embarrassment. Yet for all its difficulties, evaluating employee performance is the only way organizations have found to maintain accountability and to reward employees equitably. Like it or not, this system is generally accepted as standard procedure in American business life. At its best, the process gives employees a chance to find out how they are doing so they can improve their performance. It also gives them an opportunity to highlight their accomplishments and reap the rewards of their hard work.

Why Diverse Employees May Resist Performance Evaluation

Employees who are not part of the dominant culture of the organization may have even more apprehensions about the performance evaluation process. Knowing the source of their tension can help you overcome some of their resistance. Think for a moment about how you might feel if you were

- An older female employee being evaluated by a young male boss.
- A young Filipina nurse with a temporary work permit, awaiting your green card, being evaluated by an American nurse manager.
- A long-term Latino factory worker being evaluated by your African-American female supervisor.
- A paraplegic male engineer being evaluated by your able-bodied male manager.
- A male Vietnamese immigrant bookkeeper being evaluated by your boss, a Euro-American female accountant.

What assumptions would you make? What expectations would you have as you approached your evaluation session? Some of the following factors might contribute to the resistance you might be feeling.

1. Fear of Repercussions

All of us feel less safe in any organization or culture where we are not the dominant group. Diverse employees, knowing they are not the power wielders, may experience fear when being evaluated by those who are in power. They may perceive they have no recourse to any judgment. They may also fear losing their jobs or their green cards. They may see the evaluation itself as a formalized reprimand, a wrist slapping for past mistakes, and hence they may be reluctant to participate.

Suggestion for Managers:

- Explain the purpose of the evaluation, emphasizing that it is not a disciplinary meeting and that the employee is not going to lose his/her job.

2. "Not One of Us" Syndrome

The American judicial system mandates that every person on trial be judged by a jury of his/her peers. It is felt that only those in similar circumstances can make a fair judgment. In diverse organizations, the evaluator is not necessarily of the same group as the evaluatee. The employee may feel that it is not possible to be fairly evaluated by someone who may have little understanding or empathy for the problems of the employee. When individuals do not perceive they will get a fair shake, they are apt to resist.

Suggestion for Managers:

- Sit next to the evaluatee at a table or in chairs rather than across a desk. Show empathy; for example, you could state, "People sometimes feel a little nervous at performance evaluation time. I feel that way, too, when I get evaluated."

3. Lack of Understanding of the Process

Employees of all stripes often see performance evaluation as a reprimand or dressing-down session. Because they do not fully understand the reasons behind the evaluation, nor the actual form and process, they may balk. In addition, the forms used may be confusing and intimidating for someone not used to such administrative paperwork.

Suggestion for Managers:

- Explain the performance evaluation process to the whole staff, telling them the reasons for it, how it can benefit them, and how they can help. Explain this again briefly at the beginning of each evaluation session.

4. It Is a Foreign Experience

For employees who are from other cultures, the whole process may be strange and confusing. In many countries, rewards such as promotions and raises are a result of seniority or family connections rather than performance. They may never have experienced this kind of formalized feedback process. The employee may have little experience with the notions of individual responsibility, goal setting, and monitoring of performance that underlie the evaluation process in American firms.

Suggestion for Managers:

- Use the evaluation as a teaching opportunity, explaining how individual performance and accomplishing goals leads to rewards.

5. All Task and No Relationship

In the more structured setting of an evaluation session, the employee may be taken aback when the task takes precedence over the relationship. Suddenly the evaluation form with its boxes and categories seems more important than the person. If the employee has had a comfortable relationship with the boss, he/she may feel betrayed, as though the boss who was so friendly this morning is now cold and all business.

Suggestion for Managers:

- Try to maintain the same tone in the evaluation session that you generally have in relating to the employee. Talk about each section in normal everyday language, making sure to avoid using "legalese."

Why Existing Performance Evaluations Don't Work with Diverse Employees

Performance evaluation generally has three major functions. First, it serves as a tool to help improve performance by giving employees clear feedback about what they are doing well and where they need to improve. Second, it gives the organization a measuring system to help in doling out rewards equitably. Finally, it helps employees in their own career growth, giving them feedback and assistance in professional goal planning.

Performance evaluation fails in accomplishing these objectives when employees do not understand the constructive purpose for evaluation. Furthermore, when they see the feedback as hurtful rather than helpful, they do not use it to grow. Finally, when they are faced with a different system of standards for reward than they are used to, confusion, frustration, and irritation build on both sides. Both bosses and employees find themselves required to go through the motions of a process that seems to be missing its mark, a waste of time at best, and a morale and productivity sapper at worst. For performance evaluation to serve its purpose with diverse employees, it needs to be clearly explained and perceived as constructive.

Helping Diverse Employees Understand the Evaluation Process

Imagine that you have suddenly been transported to England and find yourself in the middle of a cricket field. You are dressed in the regulation white outfit and have an odd-shaped bat in your hands. All the players speak English, though with a different accent. The game is about to begin, and you are told to play. How would you feel? Bewildered? Embarrassed? Anxious? What would you do? Start asking other players? Walk off the field? Observe and try to figure things out?

Some of your reactions might be similar to those of diverse employees attempting to "play the game" in your company, and making sense of the performance evaluation process is one more perplexing part of that game. It may be just as foreign an experience. Just as you would have been helped by a pregame briefing, so does the employee need to be explained the rules of the game. Since most of us are more receptive when we understand the reasons, the first place to start in the performance review process is to explain its purpose.

Emphasize the benefits that both the organization and the employee can derive from the evaluation. Using an analogy can help. If the person is interested in sports, for example, you might use a basketball analogy: "How would you learn how to make more baskets, if you had to play in the dark? You'd never know when you made a basket and when you didn't, so you wouldn't know how to improve your shots. Performance evaluation is a way of telling you how close you're getting to the basket, which balls are making it, and which aren't. Without the feedback you get in performance reviews, you'd always be in the dark."

You might want to talk about something that you learned in a performance review that helped you improve your own productivity. It is also important to explain that everyone in the organization goes through this experience, and that you and your bosses get evaluated, too.

How Diversity Impacts Performance Appraisal Systems

Managers and employees bring their diverse backgrounds and cultures to work, and these variations touch every part of the organization's systems. Performance appraisal is no different. Both cultural and experiential variables of diverse employees have a significant effect on the process of evaluating employee performance.

The following chart outlines the effects of diversity-related variables on performance evaluation. Once you have reviewed it, you can analyze one of your own performance appraisal experiences by using *Pinpointing Diversity-Related Influences that Impact Performance Evaluation*. Recall a recent review session, then check any of the factors that you felt influenced the process. Then jot down the employee behavior that indicated this factor was operating. In the far right column, write any actions you could take to improve communication and get buy-in from the employee.

The Impact of Diversity-Related Variables on Performance Appraisal

Cultural Factors	Impact on Appraisal	Behavior
Avoidance of loss of face	Anxiety on the part of the employee and unwillingness to discuss any criticism.	Smiling and laughter may be signs of embarrassment; missing conferences or absenteeism on performance evaluation day may be signs of avoidance.
Emphasis on harmony	Agreement to items not clearly understood.	Saying yes even when not understanding or disagreeing.
Respect for authority	Unwillingness to question the review or disagree with any points made by the evaluator.	Lack of eye contact and not entering into a dialogue with the boss.
External locus of control	Difficulty in seeing the consequences of behavior; not connecting the review with one's own behavior.	Comments may show that the employee does not make the connection between his/her performance and the evaluation ratings.
Emphasis on relationship rather than task	Task accomplishment not seen as the critical variable in job success; relationship with boss, seniority, and group status takes precedence.	Attempts to please the boss as well as bewilderment shown by a blank facial expression.
Difficulty in separating self from performance	Taking the review personally and finding comments hurtful; "But I thought you liked me" attitude; individual sees criticism as an affront rather than as helpful feedback.	Showing feelings of hurt, betrayal, or embarrassment.
Emphasis on group over individual	Difficulty in distinguishing own performance from team's as evaluating individual performance may be a different paradigm for employee used to group results being the focus of evaluation. Calling attention to individual contributions is perceived negatively. Employee may also find calling attention to him/herself awkward and disloyal to co-workers.	Signs of discomfort, confusion, or embarrassment such as smiling, withdrawal, or clamming up.
Other Diversity Factors		
Lack of common base of experience	Employee may feel misunderstood and unfairly judged if evaluator has not had to deal with similar obstacles or outside of work problems (e.g., older worker, single parent, or employee with elder-care responsibilities).	Sulking silence or defensiveness.
Previous discrimination	Employees who have experienced discrimination in the past are apt to be mistrustful and skeptical of the value and results of formal appraisal systems.	Lack of participation, sarcasm.

Pinpointing Diversity-Related Influences that Impact Performance Evaluation

Cultural/Diversity-Related Factors	Employee's Behavior	Manager's Action
Avoidance of loss of face		
Emphasis on harmony		
Respect for authority		
External locus of control		
Emphasis on relationship rather than task		
Difficulty in separating self from performance		
Emphasis on group over individual		
Lack of common base of experience		
Previous discrimination		

Suggestions for Using *Pinpointing Diversity-Related Influences that Impact Performance Evaluation*

Objectives:

- Identify diversity-related variables affecting performance evaluation.
- Gain information that will help determine actions to take to overcome diversity-related obstacles to performance evaluation effectiveness.

Intended Audience:

- Managers wanting to increase effectiveness of performance evaluation with diverse employees.
- Trainees in a managing diversity seminar.

Processing the Activity:

- Individuals analyze a recent performance evaluation experience with an employee from a different background using the worksheet. They check any of the variables they perceived as influencing the process, then jot down the employee behaviors that indicated this factor was operating. In the final column, they write any actions the manager could take to improve communication and get buy-in from the employee.
- Small groups can discuss those variables checked and behaviors observed, and then brainstorm additional actions the manager could take.
- The whole group discusses brainstormed suggestions for managers.

Questions for Discussion:

- Which variables had the most impact?
- What was the effect these variables had on the performance evaluation?
- What could the manager do to deal with these variables and overcome any potential obstacle?
- What insights have you gained?

Caveats and Considerations:

- This worksheet can be used as a coaching tool in helping managers develop more effective performance evaluation skills.
- This worksheet can be used by managers as a planning tool when setting up future performance evaluation sessions.

There Is No Culture-Free Performance Appraisal System

Try a little experiment with yourself. Close your eyes and imagine the ideal employee in your department. Picture the individual at work in your organization's setting. Notice everything about the way this person goes about working and interacting with others. Now, answer some questions about this ideal worker. Was the person male or female? What racial, ethnic, or cultural group did the person belong to? Did the individual have any physical limitations? How old was the employee? How close are you to this ideal image? What does this experiment tell you about your own performance expectations and their relationship to diversity? If you are like most people, that ideal worker bears a not so surprising resemblance to you. This experiment illustrates how difficult it is to have a culture-free performance evaluation.

Four types of performance evaluations most frequently used in organizations appear to be those that utilize

1. Rating scales.
2. Forced distribution.
3. Critical incidents.
4. Performance-based criteria.

All four of these share characteristics of the mainstream American culture. Because that culture reveres logic and linear thinking as well as fairness and task accomplishment, there is an emphasis on the objective, rational, and nonpersonal nature of appraisal. These systems are attempts at quantifying and objectifying a very subjective process. Yet, no matter how one analyzes the ratings or manipulates the statistical comparisons, the difference between an "excellent" and a "very good," between a "3" and a "4," or between employees ranked 5 and 6, is a subjective judgment. In addition, these evaluation systems presuppose an acceptance of the American cultural notion that performance is separate from the person. This view is contrary to that held in most other cultures such as those of the Middle East, Mexico, the Philippines, and much of Asia, which make no distinction between the person and his/her behavior. Americans tend to believe you are worthwhile because you do; others believe you are worthwhile because you exist. Finally, appraisals rest on a solid foundation of cause-and-effect, find-the-problem-and-fix-it thinking, which relies on an internal locus of control, the belief that achievements are the result of one's effort and ability. While this paradigm is prevalent in more developed countries, it is not a universal one. In many areas of the world, outcomes are seen as the result of fate, luck, or other factors out of the control of humans. These cultural foundations often present "blind spots" for those from other backgrounds who are unacculturated to American norms.

Overcoming Diversity Blind Spots in Each Type of Performance Appraisal

Overcoming diversity blind spots means teaching employees a different way of thinking and looking at the world. One way of doing that is to help employees understand the overlap areas between their thinking and that of the dominant culture. You can emphasize common ground, for example, by showing the employee how the American performance evaluation is subjective at its base, too, and that feelings about people do enter into the judgments. It might also help to ask the employee to evaluate the performance of some hypothetical employee who is a nice person but a nonproductive worker. Discussing these differences might highlight the separation between performance and the person. Showing employees the results of their work and giving them tangible and immediate rewards helps them mentally connect their performance with consequences. Another way to empower employees and help them develop a more internal locus of control is to ask them what they can do or would suggest about a particular problem. Continuing to pose the what-can-you/we-do-about-it question works to develop the employee's inner sense of capability and responsibility. It also builds rapport and relationship.

Specific performance review systems, however, pose special problems. The forced distribution method, similar to placing employees on a bell curve by ranking employees against one another, is a case in point. It would be like asking which fruit is the best—an apple, cantaloupe, strawberry, or mango. Not only does the answer depend on the rater's preference, but it has meaning only to the evaluator. In addition, comparisons generally put those who are different from the norm at a disadvantage. If this method is used, there need to be specific behavioral performance standards on which the comparisons are based. Even in using the rating scale method, which allows the evaluator to independently rate employees using a number scale, there is an implicit comparison between workers. Are Mohammed, Erik, and Rosario all *4*'s even though they work differently? If I rate Tranh a *5*, does that mean everyone else is a *4* because Tranh is always finished first?

The critical incidents method may be more difficult to use in jobs where the product depends on group effort and individual contributions are not as clearly distinguishable. This may be especially true among employees who value group loyalty and harmony over individual achievement. The workers themselves may make it impossible to determine which individual is responsible for which product, step, or part. Another difficulty with this method arises because those who are not in the mainstream may stand out and be noticed more than other employees. Examples of both superior and inferior performance can be exaggerated: "Wow, that was a dynamic presentation, and I thought Asians were not good at this sort of thing." In addition, incidents that reinforce the evaluator's expectations are apt to be noticed, while those that do not may be ignored: "I knew he'd have trouble with this because of his wheelchair."

No evaluation method is ever completely unbiased as long as human beings do the evaluating. However, using performance-based criteria leaves the least room for bias against diverse employees. Performance objectives are results-oriented, for example, "Customer complaints were reduced 25 percent," rather than "Communicates well with customers." Care must be taken to make sure criteria relate to the specific job responsibilities of the role. This method requires careful explanation to the employee of the standards expected as well as the levels of competency. Once the employee understands these, he/she can choose how hard to work and at what level of excellence. Practice in writing performance-based criteria is given in tip 4 on the list that follows. In addition, the examples of an ineffective and an effective performance evaluation are given on the following page.

Ineffective Sample Performance Evaluation

I. General Information

Name _____   Review Period _____

Reviewer _____   Date of Review _____

II. Performance

Objectives	Rating
1. Learn foreign side of business	Exceeds expectations
2. Participate in in-house training	Meets expectations
3. Respond to company reports	Meets expectations
4. Reduce operating costs	Exceeds expectations

Effective Sample Performance Evaluation

I. General Information

Name _____   Review Period _____

Reviewer _____   Date of Review _____

II. Performance

Objectives	Results Achieved	Rating
1. Learn how to contact foreign clients and negotiate international contracts.	Negotiated two successful international contracts.	Exceeds expectations
2. Complete in-house managing diversity seminar and put information to use in own department.	Completed course and made three changes in department due to learning in seminar.	Exceeds expectations
3. Respond via memos to monthly regional reports.	Writes and distributes accurate, informative memos within three days of receiving reports.	Exceeds expectations
4. Reduce departmental operating costs by 5% each year.	Reduced operating costs by 7% by consolidating forms and streamlining reporting procedures.	Exceeds expectations

Employee Evaluation Tools that Can Enhance Performance in Any Culture

1. You

As manager, you are the most important tool that you use in evaluating employees. Your ability to build relationships with staff, show them respect and appreciation, and value them as human beings is not something you do only at performance review time. Relationship building with staff is an everyday process. This doesn't mean you need to socialize with staff outside of work or become best friends. Doing so may, in fact, cause problems and has been shown to decrease productivity in work groups where employees come from traditional cultures that respect a hierarchy and show deference to authority figures. What it does mean is that you show employees dignity by such behaviors as the following:

- Greeting them every morning and saying good-bye at the end of the day.
- Noticing them as human beings and speaking to them about the details of their lives.
- Helping them solve problems.
- Listening to their complaints and suggestions and taking action to respond to them.
- Asking for and using their input appropriately.
- Teaching them new skills and showing confidence in their ability to learn and grow.
- Trusting them with responsibility.
- Noticing and rewarding their accomplishments in culturally valued ways.
- Suggesting new opportunities for growth and learning.
- Recommending them for special projects, programs, and awards.

When employees feel accepted and valued, they are more open to learning and adapting. When they do not, their energies will be directed at resisting, whether actively or passively, organizational procedures and processes. When this happens, performance review becomes a useless task that produces negative results for the organization and the employee.

As a manager, it is important that you get honest with yourself about your own feelings, assumptions, and biases about your employees. Your staff probably already know them and are reacting to them. You will be in a stronger position if you are aware of them, too, and work on them. In one organization, for example, the manager of the legal department was honest enough to admit that he had difficulty accepting the fact that one of the lawyers working for him was gay. Because the boss was able to face his own biases and admit his own stereotypes, he was in a better position to keep them from directing his behavior and influencing his decisions. This meant he could be a better, fairer, and more effective boss to this employee. To help yourself in this process, make it a point to look for examples of behavior that break the stereotypes you hold about particular groups. Watch for performance that exceeds your expectations. Try to prove your prejudices and biases wrong, not right.

2. The Employee

The second most important tool is the employee. Only the employee has the ability to use the performance evaluation information to improve performance.

Evaluations that do not include the employee in self-evaluation, goal setting, and action planning miss the mark. Without real employee involvement, you've gone through the motions and filled out the forms, but you have not achieved the results you intended.

Getting this kind of involvement may be difficult if the employee is from a culture that does not support this kind of participation. In more traditional settings, where hierarchies are more rigid and authority is not questioned, there is no expectation of employee input. Helping individuals become active participants in their own growth and development is a teaching/coaching process done a step at a time. Use every opportunity, from staff meetings and one-on-one conferences to informal lunches and breaks, to talk about the employee's plans, goals, dreams, and accomplishments. It is important to remember that you may need to be the initiator.

3. Talk First, Paper Second

Overemphasis on the evaluation forms can be off-putting to employees from cultures that emphasize relationships over tasks. Spend time at the beginning of the evaluation session in ice-breaking small talk, and then proceed to talking about the employee's performance in general. Invite the employee to loosen up and participate by using open-ended questions such as the following:

- How have things been going for you here?
- What have you been learning?
- How do you feel about your progress?

Also give your own views using *I* statements such as the following:

- I've noticed an improvement in . . . .
- I've been pleased with your progress in . . . .
- I've appreciated the way you . . . .

Once you have each given a general overview, then you can get into the specific performance criteria on the evaluation form.

4. Performance-Based Criteria

Ratings based on traits and characteristics evaluate the individual and tend to produce a defensive response from the evaluatee. This type of evaluation also allows for more subjectivity on the part of the evaluator, making room for charges of discrimination and accusations of prejudice. This system may also trigger resistance in managers who balk at "playing God" in making these judgments. Ratings based on performance and behavior on the job are less personally focused and so tend to produce less defensiveness. Behavior is the topic, so both boss and subordinate can discuss performance in a more detached manner. In addition, behavior can be observed, quantified, and measured in more objective and equitable ways. Try your hand at changing these trait/characteristic criteria into performance behavior statements. Then compare your responses to the suggestions at the end of the chapter.

Performance-Based Criteria

Trait/Characteristic	Performance Behavior
a. Careful and conscientious	*Continuously monitors quality of work, stopping to correct errors immediately.*
b. Neat and well-groomed	_____ _____
c. Cooperative and congenial	_____ _____
d. Responsible	_____ _____
e. Productive	_____ _____

5. Patience

While we may in theory subscribe to the axiom that patience is a virtue, few of us in the mainstream American culture practice it. However, it is a virtue that can bring you surprising payoffs in a diverse environment. Having patience in listening in the evaluation session makes the employee feel attended to. When you get impatient with a circuitous explanation that sounds to you like "beating around the bush," the employee will feel rushed and put off. Make sure you set aside enough time for the evaluation so you do not have to keep looking at your watch because you have the next appointment in 20 minutes. Also, in evaluating performance, be patient with the rate of growth you notice in the employee and yourself. None of us changes or learns overnight. Watch for incremental steps that show progress rather than huge transformations. When you look back over time and trace the growth, you may see some significant change.

Guidelines for Conducting the Performance Review in Any Culture

Seat-of-the-pants performance review is a setup for frustration and failure. Having a plan gives you confidence and a clear process. It also gives the employee security in an anxiety-producing setting. There are three areas in which to focus your planning. First is the preplanning arena, which sets you up for success. The second part involves the steps in conducting the review itself. Finally comes the aftercare portion, which ensures that outcomes of the review bear fruit.

Preplanning for Productive Performance Reviews

1. *Set performance standards.* Analyze the job, writing the desired standards in relationship to performance behaviors and conditions, not personal qualities.
2. *Explain and clarify the standards to the employee.* It is critical that employees understand what the job requires and on what criteria they will be evaluated. Get employee input and involvement in that process.
3. *Help employees understand the review process.* Explain the reasons for reviewing performance and the part they play in the process. Show employees the forms with samples of criteria.
4. *Observe employee performance periodically.* Make notes about examples and instances. There is a tendency for evaluations to reflect the few weeks just before the evaluation session rather than the total six-month or one-year period covered by the evaluation. By making notes all year, you will have ample information to write a complete, representative review.
5. *Give the employee the forms for self-evaluation.* Clarify the criteria and evaluation rating system to be used. Discuss any questions or areas of confusion. Remember, most employees won't ask when confused, so give an explanation without requiring them to ask for it. "Lots of employees ask about this part of the review," or "This part may seem confusing. Let me show you how it works," might be ways to open up the subject.
6. *Set the time and place for the review session.* Give both yourself and the employee enough time to prepare the review forms. Set aside enough time in the review appointment for discussion, and reserve a private location in which to meet.

Conducting the Performance Review Session

1. *Explain the purpose of the review session.* Emphasize that it is not a disciplinary meeting. Give the employee a brief idea of the agenda of the session so he/she knows what to expect.
2. *Set the tone.* Start with a general discussion about how things are going from both your perspectives. Take enough time to make a human-to-human connection and get used to the sound of each others' voices. Coffee, tea, juice, or soda might also help create more warmth and feeling of hospitality. In addition to the inherent inequality in boss-subordinate relationships, be sensitive to diversity-related reactions that may affect the climate of the meeting. A man being evaluated by a woman boss, for example, may feel discomfort. It may be the first time he has been evaluated by a woman since his mother or teacher did so years ago. A person of color being evaluated by a dominant-culture boss may carry memories of past experiences of prejudice into the session.
3. *Have the employee present his/her self-evaluation.* Listen carefully to the employee's assessment. Do not interrupt or refute the employee's analysis at this point. Be careful even in asking clarification questions such as "What do you mean . . . ?" because they are apt to sound like disagreements and can produce defensiveness.
4. *Present your evaluation.* Make sure to give specific examples of behaviors and conditions. Give a balanced view, beginning with the good news. Emphasize both positive, productive performance as well as areas of needed improvement. Identify points of agreement between the two evaluations. Use the techniques learned in the feedback section of the communication chapter such as using the passive voice and giving positive directions.

5. *Jointly identify problems and obstacles to improved performance.* Put your heads together and discuss improvement needs.
   - What seem to be the problem areas?
   - What task seems to be the most difficult?
   - Where does performance slip?
   - What is getting in the way?
6. *Jointly make a plan for improving performance.* Continue discussing, now focusing on problem solving.
   - How can the obstacle be overcome?
   - What does the employee need to do differently?
   - How can you help him/her in that process?
   - What are the employee's goals for growth?
   - How can these be worked on?
7. *Agree to the evaluation and commit to a plan of action.* Both employee and manager need to work together until there is agreement and commitment to it.
8. *End on a positive note.* Complete the session with a summary of the evaluation and next steps and a final positive comment. Show appreciation, give a compliment, show you value the employee. Thank the employee for participating, and end with a handshake or a formal closure.

Aftercare

1. *Assess yourself as a performance evaluator.* Use each review as a dress rehearsal for the next so you can continue to improve your own performance as an appraiser. The *Evaluating Yourself as a Performance Evaluator* checklist can help you assess yourself as an evaluator.
2. *Set checkup times with the employee.* Put notes in your tickler file to check back with employees periodically about how they are doing on their plans in both new goal achievement and performance improvement. Have a minievaluation session at these checkups. You will need to initiate these sessions, as it is rare for employees of any culture to do so.
3. *Help the employee work through any difficulties.* Perhaps the goal needs to be reassessed. Maybe a different solution is in order. Help the employee figure out what to do.

Evaluating Yourself as a Performance Evaluator

	Yes	Sometimes	No
1. I explain the performance expectations of the job to employees.	____	____	____
2. I check employees' understanding of the role and performance expectations.	____	____	____
3. I explain the reasons for performance review to employees, emphasizing benefits to the organization and the individual.	____	____	____
4. I explain the steps in the evaluation process from the setting of standards and the use of forms to the actual evaluation session.	____	____	____
5. I give employees the time and the opportunity to do self-evaluation before the joint session.	____	____	____
6. I listen openly to employees' perceptions of their performance.	____	____	____
7. I remain objective and nondefensive in the session.	____	____	____
8. I observe the employee in action throughout the year and make notes on my observations.	____	____	____
9. I use performance criteria based on observable behaviors and measurable results.	____	____	____
10. I give myself time to prepare the evaluation document with thought and care.	____	____	____
11. I plan the evaluation session, setting it for the most productive time and place.	____	____	____
12. I create a comfortable, inviting climate at the evaluation session.	____	____	____
13. I spend a few minutes initially in the session talking with the employee to break the ice and open communication.	____	____	____
14. I am willing to modify my evaluation, incorporating ideas and comments from the employee's self-evaluation.	____	____	____
15. I require the employee to set his/her own goals and make an action plan for achieving them.	____	____	____

Suggestions for Using *Evaluating Yourself as a Performance Evaluator*

Objectives:

- Assess one's strengths and weaknesses as a performance evaluator.
- Identify behaviors that could enhance one's effectiveness as a performance evaluator.
- Trigger thinking about self-development regarding this management responsibility.

Intended Audience:

- Managers seeking to increase their effectiveness as performance evaluators.
- Trainees in a managing diversity seminar.

Processing the Activity:

- Individuals rate themselves by placing checks in the appropriate column on the worksheet.
- Individuals share, in pairs or small groups, their ratings, identifying strengths and weaknesses and discussing potential areas for development, responding to the following questions:

  What did I do well?

  What do I need to work on to do better next time?

  What is one specific way in which I can make the next evaluation more effective?

- Group discusses reactions, insights, and learning.
- Individuals make a contract for self-development by targeting one or two behaviors to work on that would increase their effectiveness as performance evaluators.

Questions for Discussion:

- Which behaviors are easiest/hardest for you to do?
- What is the consequence of not doing those that are hardest?
- What would be the consequence of incorporating these?
- Which behaviors are you willing to do more often to make your performance evaluations more effective?

Caveats and Considerations:

- This worksheet can be used one-on-one in coaching sessions with managers as well as in supervisory/management training sessions focusing on performance evaluation.
- It can be used as a self-evaluation tool after each session and as a guide in planning future evaluation conferences.

Avoiding the Five Most Common Performance Review Pitfalls

1. Catching Their "Disease"

Anxiety and nervousness are catchy. So is defensiveness. As a manager, it is easy to pick up on your employees' emotional state and respond in kind. It is not uncommon for managers to catch the tension or defensiveness their employees bring to the performance review process. First, deal with your own nervousness. It is normal to feel some anxiety. Admitting it to yourself takes some of its power away. Also, look at the positive side of your feelings. Your nervousness may come from a concern for fairness and your desire to do a good job. Next, don't take it personally. Defensiveness on the part of the employee is not an attack on you or your assessment. It is an attempt to restore lost self-esteem. You can avoid this trap by not judging, accusing, or threatening the employee. You can also keep out of quicksand by not responding with your own defensiveness, but rather by showing empathy and listening to what the employee is saying.

2. Fearing Being Seen as Unfair or Prejudiced

All human beings have a need for approval. We have yet to meet the person who wants to be ignored, rejected, or talked about. Yet when your need to be perceived as a nice person takes precedence over your responsibility to give clear, direct, and honest feedback, you sabotage the process of performance evaluation. Not giving employees accurate feedback does a disservice to all. The employee does not know how to improve and may be confused by your mixed messages: "You tell me I'm doing great, yet you seem irritated with me." And you build resentment because the employee is not intuiting your desire for improvement. Remind yourself that you are not helping employees when you allow them to get by with less than they are capable of or less than is required. Take the acid test. Ask yourself, "Would I make this assessment if the person were of a different group?"

3. Assuming Employees Understand the Performance Review Process

Employees of all colors often see the evaluation as a test they are nervous about passing. They worry about failing, getting reprimanded, and losing face. In a diverse staff, many employees may have little or no experience with such a process, so it is even more important to make sure employees understand the purpose for the review. Help them see how it serves both the organization and themselves and how it is tied to rewards and promotions. Finally, employees need a clear understanding of how the process will be handled. Showing samples of past reviews, having them meet with employees who have experienced the process, and discussing performance review at staff meetings are examples of ways you can do this. You may even do a mock review session as a role-play at a staff meeting to give employees a taste of what it is like. Having employees share the best thing they got out of their last review and brainstorming benefits they can derive from the review process are two other ways you can help further employees' understanding of performance evaluation.

4. Missing the Coaching/Teaching Opportunity

One of the richest and most overlooked benefits of the performance review process in a diverse staff is the chance to teach employees and help them acculturate to the norms of the organization. The joint problem-solving and goal-setting process helps employees develop a more internal locus of control. Setting standards and self-evaluation helps employees develop skill in participating in shared decision making and giving input. Recognizing that these may be new and uncomfortable experiences for the employee can help you use them as teaching opportunities, or perfect chances to show employees the ropes and develop rapport at the same time.

5. Going It Alone

No matter how difficult it may be to get employee involvement in performance evaluation, involvement is essential. If it is your responsibility and your review, there will be little investment from the employee to use it for improvement. Make the review a joint project from the setting of the performance standards to the targeting of goals for the future. Work on getting this across to the employee in as many different ways as you can. You can say, "While I'm responsible for evaluating you as your boss, you're the real expert on your performance. I need your help and input in this process," for example, or "I can help you in achieving your goals if I know what they are."

Building Managing Diversity into Managers' Performance Reviews

If diversity is to be made an organizational asset, then management's ability to capitalize on a diverse work force must be developed. One way organizations can put teeth into their commitment of valuing diversity is to evaluate managers on this aspect of their role. In organizations that have made progress in creating a more inclusive environment, managers are evaluated on and rewarded for their effectiveness in managing diversity. Performance standards reflect such behaviors as those in the checklist titled *Diversity-Related Performance Standards for Managers*.

Diversity-Related Performance Standards for Managers

_____ Hiring, retaining, and promoting individuals from diverse backgrounds.

_____ Coaching and grooming diverse individuals for advancement.

_____ Building cohesive, productive work teams from diverse staffs.

_____ Resolving diversity-related conflicts between staff members.

_____ Maintaining a low rate of discrimination and harassment complaints.

_____ Developing staff through delegation.

_____ Planning and leading effective meetings with a diverse staff.

_____ Learning about the cultural norms and values of employees.

_____ Helping new employees acculturate to the organization's norms.

_____ Providing cultural sensitivity training for staff.

_____ Attending cultural awareness training and applying learning with own staff.

Suggestions for Using *Diversity-Related Performance Standards for Managers*

Objectives:

- Identify appropriate performance standards for managers regarding dealing with diversity.
- Assess existing and/or desired practices regarding the management of diversity.
- Assess one's own effectiveness in managing a diverse staff.

Intended Audience:

- Managers wanting to increase their effectiveness in leading diverse staffs.
- Executives seeking to increase their organization's effectiveness in managing diversity.
- Trainees in a managing diversity seminar.
- Task forces charged with the task of designing performance standards for managers.

Processing the Activity:

- Individuals can utilize this checklist in a number of ways. They can check those criteria that are presently part of their performance standards. They can star those they think need to be added. Executives can do the same with regard to subordinates' standards. Task forces can be asked to rank order these to identify top-priority criteria. In still another variation, individuals can use these standards to measure their own performance, checking those they do or rating themselves on a scale of 1 to 5 (low to high) on each criterion.
- Groups can discuss their responses, ratings and/or priorities. If they are groups such as task forces making proposals about performance standards by executives deciding on those to be included, they can work toward consensus on a decision.
- Individuals can also identify those performance standards they would like to add to their own review and make plans for their own development in those areas.

Questions for Discussion:

- Which of these are/are not part of your performance standards? Performance standards in your organization?
- Which do you think should be included in your evaluation? Other managers' evaluations?
- What other performance criteria related to managing a diverse staff would you add?
- Which do you need to work on to be more effective with your team department or work unit?

Caveats and Considerations:

- This tool can be used as an assessment for individual managers as well as an activity to prime the pump of those designing standards to support organizational strategy regarding the management of diversity.

Which of these are part of your performance standards? On which is your boss evaluated? How would you rate yourself and your organization against these standards? Which do you need to work on to be a more effective manager of your diverse staff? When performance in these areas is made part of the manager's job duties and responsibilities, to be evaluated periodically, its importance is validated. It is one way in which organizations show real commitment, not lip service, to diversity.

Performance evaluation is an important management tool that, when used effectively, can enhance employee performance, increase commitment, and strengthen the relationship between manager and employee. However, cultural differences and other diversity-related variables can sabotage the effectiveness of the process if not understood and dealt with. Using the information, techniques, and approaches given in this chapter can help you maximize the output of your performance evaluations with all staff.

Examples of Performance-Based Criteria

The following are suggested performance behavior statements (p. 206):

b. Dresses in a manner that inspires customer/client confidence in his/her ability.

c. Helps others with work without being asked.
    Responds positively to delegated tasks.
    Volunteers for task forces and special projects.

d. Completes projects on schedule.
    Takes initiative to correct errors, fix equipment, and/or solve problems.

e. Fulfills job responsibilities completely.
    Accomplishes assigned tasks within given time frames.

Section II

INTEGRATING DIVERSITY
INTO YOUR ORGANIZATION:
MODIFYING THE SYSTEMS TO
CAPITALIZE ON THE
BENEFITS OF A PLURALISTIC
WORK FORCE

Chapter 7

Creating a Corporate Culture that Embraces Diversity

This chapter will give you:
1. An explanation of how to create an inclusive culture.
2. A model of the change process and the losses that make people resistant to it.
3. Tools for assessing the openness of your organizational climate and the barriers to diversity.
4. Examples of two organizations that do embrace diversity.
5. Training materials that help employees come to terms with loss and change.
6. A model that explains stages of integrating new employees into the organization.

Progress is impossible without change; and those who cannot change their minds, cannot change anything.

George Bernard Shaw

There is much talk about creating a "new world order." Embracing diversity is about creating a new organizational order. Finding a way to do so in a time of rapid change is the challenge. James Baldwin astutely said years before the demographic revolution, the information revolution, the technological revolution, the women's revolution, worldwide political revolutions—and most of the other major revolutions we have recently witnessed—that "any real change implies the breakup of the world as one has always known it, the loss of all that gave one identity." He was a wise man. He understood the subtle but complex issues involved in trying to harness change. Demographic trends portend change in the culture of your organization. That change needs to include a psychological climate that is open and valuing of differences. It's a tall but necessary order. Nothing less than your organization's survival is at stake.

Inclusivity: A Mind-Set that Pays Dividends

Inclusivity is a term bandied about where people have a diverse work environment. It implies a comprehensive openness—an environment that welcomes any person who can do the job, regardless of race, age, gender, sexual preference, religion, ethnicity, or physical ability. How does this attitude show itself in real organizational life? For starters, it means that if I'm 55 and applying for a job, it is not automatically assumed that I'm unemployable because I'm too old. If I'm a male who wears an earring, it is not assumed that I'm gay and therefore an undesirable employee. Rather, my sexual preference and my earring, whether or not I'm gay, are viewed as irrelevant to my ability to do the job. It also means that when promotions are made or opinions are sought, it won't be assumed that women are too soft and too nurturing to handle the bottom-line tasks, that Asians will be too silent or too meek to make good managers, or that African-Americans will be too aggressive to be team players. In an inclusive environment, what counts is a person's ability to do the job, and no one is disadvantaged because of background.

Symptoms of Inclusivity

Smart leaders and managers know the value of creating an inclusive environment. They also know it isn't easy to achieve one. In order to achieve a more open culture in your workplace, start by measuring your organization's mind-set against the criteria titled *Symptoms of Inclusivity*.

Symptoms of Inclusivity

Directions: Put a check next to any itmes that currently exist in your company.

_____ Employees are welcome and accepted regardless of life-style variations.

_____ All segments of your population are represented in the executive suite.

_____ Air time at meetings is not dominated by any one group.

_____ Ethnic, racial, and sexual slurs or jokes are not welcome.

_____ Cliquishness between groups is absent.

_____ Variety in dress and grooming is the norm.

_____ Warm, collegial relationships exist between people of diverse backgrounds.

_____ There is sensitivity to and awareness of different religious and ethnic holidays and customs.

_____ Selection of food and refreshments at organizationally sponsored functions or food facilities takes into account religious and personal preferences.

_____ Flexibility exists to accommodate personal responsibilities outside the job.

Suggestions for Using *Symptoms of Inclusivity*

Objectives:

- To assess the openness of your work group or organization.
- To identify a starting point for creating more openness.

Intended Audience:

- A CEO or vice president of human resources who wants to stimulate a discussion among executive staff about opening up the organization.
- Managers of work groups who want to create a more open environment among staff.
- Trainers teaching managers to create a more open climate.

Processing the Activity:

- Explain the directions as stated in the inventory. Ask each participant to check off those items that indicate inclusivity.
- Put people in pairs or small groups and ask them to discuss the symptoms they see. Suggest illustrating their perceptions with concrete examples.
- Tell participants to use all perceptions, no matter how similar or different, as data for group discussion.
- Bring all the small groups back to the big group. Discuss as a whole.

Questions for Discussion:

- Where are your perceptions about symptoms of inclusivity the same as others'? Where are they different? How do you account for the differences?
- Think about the places where your work group or organization lacks openness. What does it cost you in individual and team performance?
- Think about times when you have felt excluded. What has been the impact on your performance?
- If you were to begin creating more openness by focusing on one of these symptoms, what one would you choose?
- What can you do to start the process?

Caveats and Considerations:

- Remind participants that culture change is slow. Small starts, reinforced over time, can add up to bigger change, but it won't happen overnight.
- Openness and flexibility need to be modeled. Employees learn behavioral norms more from what you and other leaders do than from what you say.

Focus on the inclusivity symptoms you don't see. Are there others you'd like to see? What does their absence cost your company? Your work group? Identify one symptom you'd like to work on as a starting point toward creating a more inclusive environment.

What might you gain in productivity and commitment if, for example, it was no longer acceptable to tell jokes at some group's expense? What would be the result of acknowledging the different holidays or celebrations of your employees in a company newsletter or in the cafeteria? These things are not hard to do, but they do have to be valued to be realized. What's in it for you to embrace diversity?

Increased Creativity Yields Better Product Development and All-Around Better Results

In our increasingly small world, the prize will go to the most resourceful, talented, productive organization. Your performance and productivity will increase with a rich staff mix. Historically, interaction between cultures has always been a source of knowledge, growth, and progress. The Crusades marked a turning point in European history and ushered in the Renaissance because of the knowledge, ideas, and products the crusaders brought from the Moslem world. Coastal trading ports have preeminence in every country in the world because they are a point of contact between cultures. When different cultures interact, increased creativity is the by-product.

Organizations tell us their biggest benefit (other than the fabulous ethnic restaurants!) from a diverse work force is the problem-solving results. When East meets West, wonderful differences occur in thinking, and work groups see it in the problem definition and solutions. The East has a highly intuitive thinking style, while the West is known for its highly developed analytical skill. The blend produces great results. For example, the total quality movement is a hybrid. What W. Edwards Deming transported to Japan after World War II has been adapted in a uniquely Japanese way to make Japan the most progressive and productive industrial power in the world today.

Organizational Vitality Is in the Adaptability to Change

Alvin Toffler, author of *Future Shock* and *The Third Wave,* said, "Change is not necessary to life, it is life." Economic survival in this day and age depends on an organization's ability to make corrections and change directions at a moment's notice. Entrenched attitudes and practices will only yield obsolescence. Truly diverse organizations are very fluid.

An Inclusive Environment Captures Commitment

An inclusive environment has as part of its bone marrow the acceptance of people as they are. That doesn't mean that feedback is not given, but it does mean that theoretically, each person is accepted for who he is and is valued for the talent he brings to the task at hand. Employees rarely produce their best work when they have to fit into someone else's mold. An atmosphere that has as its credo acceptance of a person's genuine self is an atmosphere that will get top performance from its staff. It will also minimize resistance and maximize commitment.

Identifying Organizational Barriers to Diversity

If creating a diverse and inclusive workplace is beneficial, how come there is so much resistance to doing so? For starters, there are numerous concerns that erect strong barriers to moving forward with diversity.

Cost of Implementation

Milton Friedman's quip "There are no free lunches" applies to organizations as well as individuals. If a company is serious about creating a culture that embraces diversity, does this necessitate a full-time minority recruiter? How much will outreach to colleges and universities cost in order to create and cultivate the connections that give you first crack at top talent? And what about training? There will be a need for management training to help managers handle the predictable difficulties that arise as diversity grows. There will also be a need for awareness training to sensitize employees of all backgrounds to one another, and training to help new employees acculturate to the organization. If all of this very necessary training takes place—and it is necessary if the diversity effort is going to be successful—who will be cranking out the work while staff is being trained? We can make a strong case for saying that the short-term cost may be high but the long-term benefits are worth it. Since the dominant American culture is notoriously short term in both thinking and the desire for gratification, a commitment of time and money can be a major obstacle. However, organizations that talk a good game but fail to make a real commitment risk losing the trust of their employees and the market(s) they serve.

Fear of Hiring Underskilled, Uneducated Employees

In our work with numerous clients, the biggest issue in diversity hiring is the presumption that hiring women, people of color, and other segments of population that fall under the diversity banner will mean sacrificing competence and quality. Common stereotypes hold that members of some groups are uneducated and therefore inadequate in a work environment. It is no secret that high school dropout rates in this country are disgracefully high, and they are even worse in communities where there is poverty or little support for education from parents at home. Business leaders are concerned about the investment they will have to make in bringing potential employees up to speed. And their even bigger concern is, "If we make the investment, will the employees stay and will they be able to do the work?"

Strong Belief in a System that Favors Merit

There is a bias toward equal treatment in this country that in itself is commendable. What makes this otherwise admirable attitude a barrier toward diversity can be seen in the subtle aphorism we've been raised on that advocates "the best man for the job." In the United States, not only has the best, *or only,* person for a job traditionally been a man, but it has been a white man. Organizations have been dragged kicking and screaming toward affirmative action as a way to level the playing field, but the perception still exists that any affirmative action candidate is someone chosen to fill a slot, not because she may happen to be the best candidate for the job. Our socialization is so strong and our biases so subtle that rarely is a women or person of color actually considered the best person for the job.

Annoyance at Reverse Discrimination

Reverse discrimination raises the hackles of those fair play advocates who say that it doesn't help to end discrimination of one group at the expense of another. So long as one person's gain is perceived to be someone else's loss, fears of reverse discrimination will provide very strong resistance to diversity. In interviewing people about their recruitment practices, organizations that were effectively dealing with diversity were looking for employees from very diverse backgrounds. Sometimes the applicant pool did not allow them to be as diverse as they liked. They did not sacrifice quality, but what they did do, when they found a number of excellent candidates from different groups, was take into consideration the ethnic makeup of their employee base.

Perception that There Has Been a Lot of Progress

In the eyes of some, any progress that exists is proof the system is opening up. It if opens at a snail's pace, so what? The thought goes something like this: Women, people of color, the differently abled, the older worker, and whoever else is not part of the dominant group should all appreciate the crack in the door. "Be satisfied with the progress you've made" is the implied message. Our view is that somewhere between the slow evolution some advocate and the revolution others want is a median point that would serve American business well. But as long as there is an attitude that you should be satisfied with the crumbs you've been thrown, we will cheat our organizations of talent and create a disenfranchisement from the American system that will only be harmful down the road.

Diversity Is Not Seen as a Top-Priority Issue

In a long list of organizational priorities, diversity may not be seen as crucial. The organizational complaint mill usually works overtime with any change, but expect it to work longer and harder regarding diversity. The psychological adaptations required of employees in the work force today are numerous and demanding. Globalization and downsizing are already problematic, and this is just one more issue heaped upon others that make people dissatisfied. The beef will be, "If it isn't crucial [and some think embracing a more open and diverse culture is not], then why mess with it? It only saps energy and resources when we need to be applying both of those things to the really significant issues at hand."

The Need to Dismantle the Existing Systems to Accommodate Diversity

The sheer weight of rethinking or changing existing systems is frightening to many people. Some fear the changes because of what they perceive they'll lose. "If, for example, the selection process or reward structure or performance review system is changed to create a more inclusive environment, what will that mean to me?" worries the employee. If you are charged with the task of modifying the existing system, it means one hell of a lot of work to develop a plan and get buy-in. If you are charged with implementing the new system, it means learning and teaching new methods of operation to others and then setting up a feedback system. And if you are an employee impacted by these changes, you don't know what it will mean, and that might be the scariest position of all.

The Sheer Size of the Organization

Your organization is like the 2,000 pound elephant. It can't turn on a dime, nor can it change direction quickly like the hummingbird. Bulk will inevitably weigh both individuals and organizations down. For starters, that weight is characterized by an organizational history, its systems, its norms, and a whole lot of mythology and folklore. Change alters them all in some way. Your organization is analogous to a human system whose primary function is to sustain and perpetuate itself. Any outside intervention is viewed as threatening, so the system closes to protect itself from intrusion. The result? Sheer inertia will keep the system moving on its own steady course; hence, organizational and personal responses to change almost guarantee that reversing or changing direction will not happen easily.

Consider how all of these factors play out in your organization. Which obstacles seem to be the most intractable? Is there currently any support for dealing with any of these barriers? If so, which seems the most hopeful place to begin? If you are truly determined to create a more open and responsive organization, these issues will have to be acknowledged, dealt with, and overcome. Try the exercise *Identifying Organizational Barriers to Diversity* in order to pinpoint your obstacles.

Identifying Organizational
Barriers to Diversity

Directions: Rank the following list of obstacles as they occur in your organization. The most significant obstacle rates a 1 and the least important an 8.

_____   Cost of implementation.

_____   Fear of hiring underskilled, uneducated employees.

_____   Strong belief in a system that favors merit.

_____   Annoyance at reverse discrimination.

_____   Perception that there has been a lot of progress.

_____   Diversity not seen as a top-priority issue.

_____   The need to dismantle existing systems to accommodate diversity.

_____   The sheer size of the organization.

Suggestions for Using *Identifying Organizational Barriers to Diversity*

Objectives:

- To identify obstacles that partcipants think prevent the organization from dealing with or paying attention to the issue of diversity.
- To compare perception of various participants to determine consensus on barriers and future courses of action.

Intended Audience:

- An executive staff willing to work on removing obstacles to becoming a more open organization.
- Top management of a division willing to do the same.
- A change agent who works with top management to identify barriers to diversity.

Processing the Activity:

- Ask all participants to rank order the obstacles from 1 to 8. Number 1 is the biggest obstacle; number 8 is least important.
- Have participants discuss their responses in groups of 7 to 10 participants. Have the group reach consensus on what the biggest obstacles are and determine a starting point for change.

Questions for Discussion:

- Are there any barriers you would like to add that were not on the list?
- What is the impact to the organization of not dealing with each of these barriers?
- Based on answers to the last question, which three obstacles are most significant or costly?
- What do you see happening to morale and productivity if you do nothing?
- What needs to happen in order to tear down some of these barriers?
- Where is a good place to begin?

Caveats and Considerations:

- Make certain in a group of 7 to 10 participants that all participants have their say. Everyone needs to contribute to the discussion.
- Keep asking questions that help participants see the high cost of exclusion.

Assessing Your Culture's Openness to Change

Identifying the barriers to diversity is important, but it is really part of a larger issue that involves your organization's openness to change. The measure of any successful organization in today's world ultimately rests on how adaptive that company is to the changing times. If you want to find a clear example of how adaptation means survival, you need look no further than "Big Blue" and Apple. Their recent efforts to cooperate and design new technology are in the infancy stages, so it is too soon to predict the success of these ventures. Because of their vastly different corporate cultures and the volatility of the computer industry, success is far from certain. But the outcome is irrelevant to our point. What matters is that both organizations see a need to change. Their survival depends on it. This is akin to David and Goliath pooling their resources to build a better weapon. They wouldn't change from a competitive to a collaborative relationship if they didn't think they had to. Spend a minute thinking about your own industry in general, and your own company in particular. How far would you go to remain competitive? How open is your organization to change? The tool entitled *How Open to Change Is Your Organizational Culture?* will help you see how adaptive and flexible you are.

How Open to Change Is Your Organizational Culture?

Focus on your organization as you read questions 1 through 15. Then place a check in the appropriate column.

Questions	Almost Always	Often	Sometimes	Almost Never
1. In my organization, change is viewed as a challenge and an opportunity.	____	____	____	____
2. Policies are reviewed annually to assess effectiveness.	____	____	____	____
3. Rewards are doled out to suit the preference of the rewardee.	____	____	____	____
4. Our personnel department is creative in finding new ways to attract top talent among diverse groups.	____	____	____	____
5. There is an openness to suggestions from people at all levels of the organization.	____	____	____	____
6. Our strategic plan is evaluated once a year and revised as needed.	____	____	____	____
7. "We've always done it that way" is a philosophy that describes my company's response to new ideas.	____	____	____	____
8. When problems emerge, there is a willingness to fix them.	____	____	____	____
9. Our products and services reflect the awareness of a more diverse consumer base.	____	____	____	____
10. My boss values new ideas and implements them quickly.	____	____	____	____
11. Performance evaluations in this organization measure an employee's adaptation to change.	____	____	____	____
12. Top executives in this company are innovative and approachable.	____	Often	Sometimes	Never
13. We can and do make midcourse corrections easily.	____	____	____	____
14. There is little variation in style of dress among employees.	____	____	____	____
15. People at all levels of the organization are continuously trying to build or rebuild a better mousetrap.	____	____	____	____

Directions for Scoring *How Open to Change Is Your Organizational Culture?*

Numbers 1–6, 8–13, and 15	Almost always	4 points
	Often	3 points
	Sometimes	2 points
	Almost never	1 point
Numbers 7 and 14	Almost always	1 point
	Often	2 points
	Sometimes	3 points
	Almost never	4 points

1. ____   6. ____   11. ____

2. ____   7. ____   12. ____

3. ____   8. ____   13. ____

4. ____   9. ____   14. ____

5. ____   10. ____   15. ____

Total: ____

Answer Key

50 to 60: The culture of your organization is open to change. You are able to react and adapt quickly, and are open to new ideas.

40 to 49: Your organization understands that change is a reality. In some ways you are open to it, but you haven't fully embraced it, nor are you harnessing change to make it work for you.

30 to 39: Your organization understands the value of change, but you need to be more open to its reality and quicker in the implementation process.

15 to 29: If you don't get better at adapting, you won't be around long.

Suggestions for Using *How Open to Change Is Your Organizational Culture?*

Objectives:

- To help a work group or part of an organization assess how open its culture is to change.
- To identify places where an organization or group is not open.
- To determine what, if anything, needs to be done to make the culture more open and flexible.

Intended Audience:

- Executive staff conducting its own assessment of the climate.
- An internal or external change agent working with the CEO and executive staff or management staff of any division.
- An internal or external change agent using this assessment at various levels of the organization to gather feedback that can be fed upward to top management and compared against their collective perceptions.

Processing the Activity:

- Distribute questionnaire to each participant and clearly identify the group being evaluated. Is it the whole organization? One division? A smaller work group?
- Ask participants to check the most appropriate answer for all 15 questions.
- Explain directions for scoring, and ask each participant to come up with a total.
- On a flip chart, record all the scores so the group can get an idea of how varied the perceptions are. There is no need to match names to scores.
- Then, depending on the size of the group, have small-group discussions. Anything from pairs to foursomes is good. Have participants look at their one- and two-point answers.

Questions for Discussion:

- Look at your one- and two-point answers. What do they indicate about the openness of your culture?
- What areas are ripe for change as you review your responses?
- What are you willing to do to begin the process of becoming more open?

Caveats and Considerations:

- The higher the level of management acting on data from this questionnaire, the more permeable the culture will be to change.
- This tool can provide valuable feedback from all levels of the organization. How it's presented to top management will influence receptivity. Get their buy-in before you use it.

The numerical score is a beginning assessment of how fluid your organization is. An even more instructive way to use this questionnaire is to do an item analysis. Circle all your one- and two-point answers. Then reread the questions and think about the issues embedded in them. For example, if your score on item number 12 was either one or two points, is it because top executives are too insulated? Maybe their creativity never filters down to the lower levels. More important, maybe employee creativity never floats upward. If executives operate as phantoms who are figuratively and literally out of touch with the troops, that would account for the score. Being unapproachable precludes an open environment because executives will have limited access to full information.

Item number 14 looks at variance in dress. If the norm is so strong that navy suits and white shirts are almost a prescribed uniform, what effect might that have on creativity? Or individual talent? Or unorthodox ideas? If this unwritten code exists, how open is your culture to a supremely talented, creative man who comes to work in casual clothes and tennis shoes? Will the fact that this person may be a marketing genius be obscured by his appearance? And if so, might that cost your organization something? By going through the questions where you score one or two points, you can get clarity about where your organization is vulnerable in being open to change and embracing diversity.

As you contemplate some of your answers, think about why your organization or work group scored low in certain areas. People resist change for many reasons, but underlying them all is the fear of loss. If you want to create a more change-oriented culture, you will need to come face-to-face with the losses people fear.

Acknowledging these losses is a critical first step. Later in this chapter, we present an activity that will help you or your work group deal with these losses. It is tempting to look for a way to short-circuit the pain of these losses, but that is not possible. The fact that there will be hurt and discomfort in this process is unavoidable. These losses are personal and real to the human beings that make up most organizations. Before you can create an organization that truly embraces diversity, both losses and gains need to be dealt with and acknowledged. To help yourself sort through the issue and achieve some clarity, fill out the four quadrants in the *Losses and Gains Experienced during Change* chart. The questions to answer are, "What do I stand to gain and to lose in a more diverse organization? What does the company stand to gain and lose?" A sample answer is listed in each square in order to help you fill out your own answers. You can use this exercise with your own work group if you detect resistance to becoming more open.

Sample Losses and Gains Experienced during Change

	Losses	Gains
Me	*Career opportunity*	*Marketable experience in managing and functioning in a multicultural work environment*
Organization	*Low employee morale*	*Creates opportunity to respond to employee needs and increase job satisfaction*

Losses and Gains Experienced during Change

	Losses	Gains
Me		
Organization		

Suggestions for Using *Losses and Gains Experienced during Change*

Objectives:

- To foster the idea that change can be positive as well as negative.
- To help people impacted by change get a broader perspective and thereby lessen the stress and resistance.
- To explore with co-workers different views of change and the gains/losses that accompany it.

Intended Audience:

- Managers helping individuals or a work group adjust to change.
- Any training professional who needs to do a seminar on change.
- Internal or external consultants who have to help resistant work groups or organizations deal with change and move beyond resistance.

Processing the Activity:

- In each of the four quadrants, have participants list perceived losses and gains for themselves and the organization.
- In pairs, have participants discuss their losses and gains in each area.
- On a flip chart and easel, list the losses and gains from the random responses of group members.
- Conduct a discussion with the whole group about the data that surface.

Questions for Discussion:

- What losses have you experienced for yourself? The organization?
- What gains in each category?
- What strikes you about these lists?
- What can you take from this experience to the next change?

Caveats and Considerations:

- There will be some participants who adamantly refuse to see any positive element in some of their changes. Acknowledge their anger and accept their feelings or reactions.

Losses: The Seeds of Resistance to Change

Let's pretend that you're at a meeting and an enlightened manager is trying to enlist your support in helping her create an environment that embraces diversity. Among her arguments for this openness are the following:

1. You can be seen and valued for who you really are—no hiding or censoring yourself.
2. The psychological safety and freedom you feel will enable you to be more creative and productive.
3. The organization will be more permeable, and because it is, your ideas may exert more influence.

Once your manager puts these benefits forward, would you sign on to bring about change? The answer ought to be a knee-jerk yes, but it isn't. Change frightens people and saps them of conviction. Why this resistance? William Bridges, Ph.D., provides a list of losses in his book, *Surviving Corporate Transition*.[7] See which of the perceived losses ring truest for you.

Perceived Losses during Change

1. Loss of Attachments.   Change in the work force means you can no longer count on the people you work with looking, sounding, or seeing the world the same way you do. As human beings, we tend to gravitate to and develop rapport with people who are our mirror images. Working with people who are different may make it harder to form relationships initially. It may be less comfortable to get to know someone with an accent or a different skin color.

Attachments to home, loved ones, and the familiar run deep. Several years ago, when GTE was downsizing, we conducted seminars that helped their middle managers deal with the significant changes attached to relocation or job loss. Some longtime employees were being laid off. Others could keep their jobs if they were willing to move to Irving, Texas. A few would still remain at the offices in Thousand Oaks, California, but with fewer colleagues and more work. The only certainty was that when the dust settled, everything would look different. Our goal was to help seminar participants deal with their anger or fear so they could move on. From approximately 40 seminars, we heard a catalog of memorable and moving stories related to personal and family loss or disruption. One such story in Lee's seminar moved her because the attachment was both deeply personal and very unusual. One of her participants mentioned that he had purchased a house years ago in Camarillo, California, with enough space for him to grow rare apple trees. He was a gardener by avocation. He was grafting a dozen different kind of apples that were so unique you would never find them in your supermarket. It had been a five-year process, and he was just starting to see the literal and figurative fruits of his labor. He was proud. There was a lot of him invested in this orchard. As we were talking about change and the loss of attachment, he said that he was very clear about not wanting to keep his job at the expense of moving and leaving his trees. He said, "I can't go into my boss and say, 'I don't want to move to Texas because I don't want to leave my apple trees.' But I can tell you that I don't want to move to Texas because I don't want to leave my apple trees." Attachments come in all sizes, shapes, and colors. All of us, native borns and immigrants, have them. Any change that forces us to leave these is threatening.

2. Loss of Turf.   Gang wars are literally fought over turf. In organizations, turf wars may not be fatal, but they can be devastating. One of the most volatile turf issues often centers on which languages are used in the workplace. Beyond the obvious loss individuals might feel in their ability to communicate, the greater loss is in the areas of power, dominance, and organizational influence.

In South-Central Los Angeles, after the Watts riots in 1965, the city built Martin Luther King Hospital for the African-American community. It was both a symbolic and real statement about rebuilding hope and pride in the black community. But it is no longer 1965. The immigration patterns in 1991 favor the Latino population. What was at one time a hospital to serve African-American patients by mostly African-American employees has become a hospital that now operates in a community that is 50 percent Latino. There are struggles over who gets the jobs because the Latino population wants its share of the work. African-Americans had the turf originally. Sheer numbers of Latino immigrants are forcing a change. The perception of the African-American community is that a hospital built for them is no longer theirs. They grieve the loss and the conflict over their turf.

3. Loss of Structure.   The loss of structure gets to the heart of some key organizational systems—promotional, accountability, and reward systems, for starters. Answers to questions like ''What do you have to do to be promoted in this organization?'' or ''What behaviors get rewarded in this company?'' will change if the organization is more open and inclusive. If you are a talented, competent white male who has been working hard to move up the ladder, and the new structure rewards an able, competent woman with the position you have coveted, you will feel cheated and angry that these systems no longer automatically favor you. Loss and frustration will be among the paramount feelings as you adjust to this change.

4. Loss of Future.   The demographic shifts portend a different racial/ethnic/cultural configuration, hence a different power structure. Being white and male no longer guarantees preeminence. On the other hand, if you are a woman or a person of color, your professional future might hold more opportunities as sheer numbers shift the balance of power. This loss is the most direct hit on the career opportunities of those who have been favored in the past. If several candidates are of equal talent and experience, a person of a diverse background will likely get the nod in an environment that wants to be more inclusive. Getting beyond the predictable organizational resistance necessitates that a truly inclusive organizational culture doesn't exclude talented white males; rather, it finds a way to select appropriate job candidates from a wide variety of backgrounds.

5. Loss of Meaning.   All human beings have a set of operating principles by which they live their lives. These assumptions act as bedrock and function smoothly in times of stability, but they are severely challenged in a time of change. These principles lend fundamental meaning to people's lives by assigning significance and order to the world. For example, if it gives meaning to a person's life to be loyal to a company and have that loyalty reciprocated through the promise of lifetime employment, in a time of downsizing, a 25- or 30-year veteran will very likely feel betrayed at being laid off. The loss of meaning comes from assumptions that are violated. A person whose professional goals are unrealized may feel that a lifetime of loyalty given to the organization is not loyalty returned.

The issue of meaning spills over into other losses such as those of structure and future. Meaning is the most subtle of the losses, and very powerful. Changing your assumptions and expectations is key to opening the organization up to change. It also is intimately connected to the sixth fear, loss of control.

6. Loss of Control.   The overriding loss during change is the loss of control that encompasses all the other losses. Seeing the increase in diversity at the most concrete and fundamental level, we know that our borders are uncontrollable. But knowing that we're failing to stem the entry of undocumented immigrants hasn't helped those in charge figure out how to plug the holes. Closer to home, when working in organizations where significant numbers of people around us don't speak English, we may feel like strangers in our own house. Not knowing how to give directions to a blind employee might make you feel out of control or inadequate. Fear of a female employee's crying as a result of feedback may make you question your ability to handle a situation.

When we don't know how to manipulate our world anymore, we feel threatened and powerless. What follows is anger. If organizations are populated with people who feel they can't control demographic changes, the push for affirmative action, or the need to create a more inclusive environment, there may be enough anger and resentment about diversity to resist it rather than accommodate it. The issue of control is not limited to white males. One African-American called us after reading a magazine article we had written on today's multicultural work force. She was a deeply angry woman because, in her view, the implied promise made to blacks about securing a bigger piece of the pie has never been fulfilled, and now she has to share limited resources with so many other immigrant groups. She feels her own opportunities are diluted. Again, change comes—she can't control it. Her anger makes it hard for her to be open to creating an inclusive climate.

In an environment that is attempting to become more inclusive and change its hiring and promotional patterns, some in the organization will feel their informal contract was broken. We have met countless women who bought into the assumption that they would be judged, evaluated, and promoted by the job they did. They strove to deliver continuously excellent performances, but when promotion time came around, the prize was not there. Again, a "contract" broken, an assumption violated.

Because our assumptions are so much a part of who we are and how we think, it is sometimes difficult to define them. A fish and water are inextricable, and that's how we are with our assumptions. But there is a difference. A fish can't survive if it changes its basic environment, while we won't survive if we don't. Our assumptions can and must change if individual and organizational health are to be maintained. To see how adaptable you are, try the exercise *Common Career Assumptions*.

Common Career Assumptions

In order to start assessing your assumptions, look at the seven samples below and circle any that are appropriate for you.

1. If I am competent and work hard, I will get ahead.

2. If I am loyal to the organization, it will be loyal to me.

3. There is a lifetime commitment between me and the organization.

4. The organization will take care of me (e.g., benefits, vacations, sick time).

5. People will be judged by the job they do.

6. The organization will remain stable enough that I can accomplish the career goals I've set.

7. I will work with people who share my values and life-style.

Some of Your Career Assumptions

Once you have circled the career assumptions listed above that apply to you, write any other relevant career assumptions that are appropriate.

1. _____

2. _____

3. _____

As you look at your assumptions, see which ones need to change in order to accurately reflect today's changing reality. Here's how to do this exercise, using the first two assumptions as examples.

Assumption: If I am competent and work hard, I will get ahead.
Accurate rewrite: If I am competent and work hard, I may get ahead, but nothing is certain.

Assumption: If I am loyal to the organization, it will be loyal to me.
Accurate rewrite: The organization and I will have a mutually satisfying relationship so long as it meets both our needs.

Now, take three of your assumptions. First, write each assumption as you have held it. Then rewrite each to reflect today's reality.

Currently held assumption:

_____

_____

Rewritten assumption:

_____

_____

Currently held assumption:

_____

_____

Rewritten assumption:

_____

_____

Currently held assumption:

_____

_____

Rewritten assumption:

_____

_____

Suggestions for Using *Common Career Assumptions*

Objectives:

- To help participants rethink their basic assumptions and expectations about work.
- To provide insight about the subtler changes in expectations and the anger or frustration that can result from a "broken contract."

Intended Audience:

- Anyone in any organization who is trying to deal with losses from change.
- HR practitioners and trainers trying to help organizations through downsizing efforts.
- Managers trying to help their own work groups through rapid change in organizations that are downsizing or involved in other changes.

Processing the Activity:

- Ask participants to look at the list of common career assumptions listed in the learning activity and list any others they would add.
- Rewrite the assumptions to accurately reflect today's reality.

Questions for Discussion:

- Which work-world myths have to go by the wayside?
- How do you feel about the changing reality?
- How long ago did this reality change?
- What can help you come to terms with this new reality?
- What is the relevance of this process to you or your work group as you deal with future change?

Caveats and Considerations:

- Focus your discussion on subtle change and the betrayal you feel when unwritten contracts or expectations are violated.
- Help participants see that the new expectation, constant change, has an upside and a downside. They can make change work for them.

Dealing with the Losses from Change

Directions: Think about the diversity you and your work group are dealing with. In the boxes below, make notes about how this loss impacts both you and your group.

Loss	Impact on You	Impact on Your Work Group
1. Attachment		
2. Turf		
3. Structure		
4. Future		
5. Meaning		
6. Control		

Suggestions for Using *Dealing with the Losses from Change*

Objectives:

- To help individuals and work groups identify the losses they experience from rapid change.

Intended Audience:

- Trainers and managers who can help individual employees and work groups deal with the frustration, stress, and anger sometimes associated with change.

Processing the Activity:

- Ask participants to write down perceived losses as an individual and as a member of a group.
- In pairs or small groups, have people discuss their comments.
- Discuss perceptions among the whole group, looking both for common viewpoints of loss as well as different reactions.

Questions for Discussion:

- Where do you feel the greatest loss personally? In the work group?
- Were there some areas where you felt no loss?
- What was your reaction to writing this down and seeing your thoughts on paper?
- What were the most interesting reactions that surfaced in your group? Any surprises?
- Based on comments you heard from others, are there any of your losses you are willing to rethink? If so, which ones?
- How can you use this mental process next time you feel a loss?

Caveats and Considerations:

- People have strong feelings about these losses. Provide enough time for venting and good discussion.
- Create a trusting climate, but suggest people group themselves with those they don't know too well in the discussion segment. It might offer a varied perspective.

Several things should become obvious from analyzing your losses from change.

1. Expect both gains and losses. The surprise to most employees who do this exercise is the number of gains they come up with.
2. Perception is critical. Often the only difference between a gain and a loss is how someone sees it.
3. Whether the changes result in a loss or a gain depends on how they are handled. A manager can do some problem solving around areas where there are perceived losses such as fear of shrinking resources and fewer career opportunities. Those feelings can create an opportunity for some team building that will be to everyone's advantage.

Losses and gains are an inevitable part of facing the diversity issue. They are also a central issue in dealing with change and the resistance to it.

Moving through Change: Stages in the Process

The human species seems to have a love-hate relationship with change. We crave the adrenaline and stimulation it thrusts our way, but we flee from the disorientation and fear that are the natural outgrowth of transition. We are more open and responsive to change when we seek it, or have some control over the process. It becomes an intimidating experience when we see ourselves as its victims. It is the latter situation that has relevance to diversity. Seeing change as a three-stage process (as in the figure *Normal Transition Curve*) can help you and your organization increase your feelings of control and create a climate where change is less threatening.[22]

Stage I: Denial—It Works for the Ostrich; Why Not for Me?

Demographic changes in the United States have happened relatively quickly. As numbers of immigrants continue to increase, there is a perception that our borders are out of control. Feeling overwhelmed by increased population density as well as the unfamiliarity of "home" causes people to react in stage I with a combination of shock and denial. This changing workforce composition is one example of change. There are others.

We remember being consultants on a federally funded Title IV C project that helped the Los Angeles Unified School District work its way through the mandatory integration process. Fifteen years ago, Los Angeles dealt with segregation of blacks and whites rather than the diverse mix the city has today. "White flight" was the most concrete form of denial. In Southern California, suburban school districts were flooded with new white students and those that didn't move went to the private schools that literally sprang up overnight. Leaving the school district was a way of denying the change. We saw this same phenomenon happen several years ago when we were invited to speak to a group of doctoral students at the University of LaVerne. When we presented the demographic predictions compiled by the Hudson Institute in their book, *Workforce 2000,* the statistics were chal-

Normal Transition Curve: How We Deal with Change

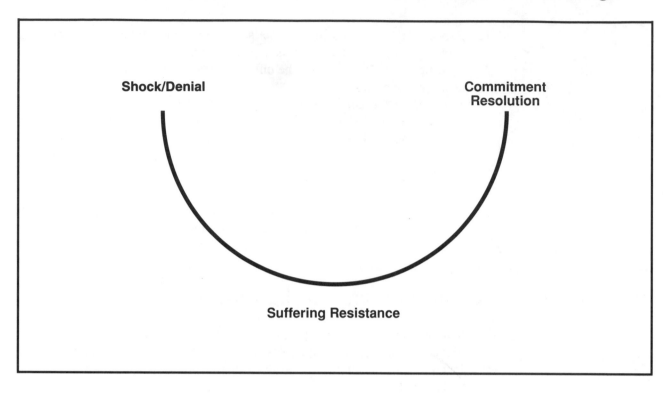

lenged by one angry white male. Ultimately, the safest response for him to make at the time was to simply get up and walk out of our session. His was a strong case of denial.

In organizational life, denial is expressed by those who keep hoping that "these people will go away so the city (or the neighborhood, or the school, or the workplace) will go back to how it used to be." Short-term denial is healthy because it allows you time to muster the necessary resources to deal with loss. But the short-term is not eternity. The most important objective of the shock and denial stage is coming to terms with a new reality. In the case of diversity, it's a simple reality. The work force is no longer predominantly white or male.

Look at the list of typical behaviors during the typical shock and denial stage: Which ones do you see around your organization?

Stage I Behaviors that Indicate Shock and Denial

1. Acting as if it's business as usual. You hear phrases like "What change? These people are coming here—they just have to adapt."
2. Refusing to talk about the changing composition of the work force and the need to become a more inclusive company.
3. Showing no feeling. (Denying this change causes the denial of other feelings as well.)
4. Talking as if change will affect others but not you (e.g., "Boy, does environmental engineering have problems! They speak three different languages in that unit and none of the different groups get along").
5. Making more errors than usual.
6. Acting and feeling bewildered.

Recognizing these symptoms in you or others will give you an indication of whether or not you are still in stage I or ready for the next stage.

Stage II: Dealing with Resistance—A Predictable Response to Change

The second stage is the suffering and resistance stage. This is the transition process that goes from what was to what will be. It means acknowledging the losses and trying to find the gains. The previous activity, *Dealing with the Losses from Change*, will help you do this. Regarding diversity, there are legitimate losses that need to be mourned. For example, if you are a white male who is used to having great promotional opportunity and you now find that you are the one who is the wrong color, that's a loss and you are entitled to mourn. No one likes losing opportunity. If you used to live in a city that was less densely populated and the influx of immigrants has brought more crowding so that you sometimes feel suffocated, you're entitled to mourn. If you have worked in your current company for a very long time and it used to seem like a home away from home but it no longer does because the employees are so different from you, you are also entitled to mourn the loss of comfort and ease you used to feel. If you are a person of color who no longer feels you can get a promotion based on your competence or talent, but only to help round out some statistical report on the HR manager's desk, you have a right to feel the loss of being looked at and evaluated as an individual, not just the member of some particular group.

The person who hates so much population density can recognize that new immigrants create a stimulating, cosmopolitan city that brings both artistic and culinary delights. The white male who now feels endangered and the person of color who questions being promoted due to his own skill and ability both feel deficits—for a time. You will be ready to move on to stage III when you no longer exhibit the typical behaviors associated with the resistance stage.

The following are typical behaviors during resistance. Again, notice which ones you see in your organization.

Stage II Behaviors that Indicate Suffering and Resistance

1. Increased absenteeism. (Escapism is an acted-out version of anger and frustration.)
2. Angry outbursts. (The threat of potential losses and the betrayal felt toward an organization that is no longer what it used to be create feelings of powerlessness and anger.)
3. Complaints about why things won't work. (Listen to the pronouns: a lot of "us versus them," "They don't do . . . ," or "If only they would. . . .")
4. Seeing only the negative. (The losses are more personal, while the gains are more organizational.)
5. Less communicative. (People who are suffering may withdraw.)
6. Performance drops. (Preoccupation with the frustration saps energy and performance.)

The turning point at this stage comes when you stop saying, "Ain't it awful," and start asking, "What can I do about it?" Taking back your power moves you to stage III.

Stage III: A Commitment to Action

By stage III, the organization as an entity and most of the people in it have agreed that a new reality does exist, and there's a commitment to make this new reality successful. That reality is a diverse work force, which can mean many things: Being over 50 is no longer over the hill; sexual preference is (or should be) irrelevant to one's competence on the job; and jobs exist for people of limited physical mobility, with lower IQs, or with different accents. It should mean that men can be secretaries and nurses without facing scorn and that women can be vice presidents of something besides community relations or hold something other than a staff job with no line responsibility. In *Surviving Corporate Transition*, Dr. William Bridges says that change "is nothing less than the death and rebirth of a person's world."[7]

No wonder it's so difficult. Dr. Bridges goes on to say that "people's resistance to change is really the difficulty of letting go of who they were, or difficulty with the ambiguities and emptiness of the neutral zone, or difficulty with the challenge of beginning anew."[7] In stage II, employees witness the death of the organization as they knew it, with the reward system favoring white males. In its place will emerge an organization that taps everyone's talent more fully and values all people more fully for who they are. The gains can be enormous. But as we view the massive changes in what was the Soviet Union as we knew it for the last 70 years, we see that the dismantling of one system isn't necessarily the simultaneous rebirth of another. There is a period of trial and error, of groping and experimenting while you try to rebuild. That will very likely be your organization's reality as it tries to change corporate culture.

The following are a number of concrete actions and commitments that indicate you are moving forward beyond the suffering stage. You'll know you're in the third stage when you see the following:

Stage III Behaviors that Indicate Commitment

1. There is a surge of energy. Instead of complaining and withdrawing, people are thinking forward.
2. There is a "can do" attitude. The negativity of stage II is gone. There is hopefulness and a problem-solving mentality.
3. Instead of asking, "Why are we . . . ?" employees ask, "How can we . . .?" In keeping with a productive problem-solving attitude, staff no longer focuses on reasons. They accept reality and just want to make it work.
4. Increased communication exists. The communication issue is always a tough organizational challenge, and in an inclusive environment, it will be even more so because the value will be against withholding information.
5. Planning is in the air. The energy surge results in constructive projects. Work is getting done. There is a feeling of hope as people see that diversity really can be good for everyone. There is renewed involvement and investment.

No one says that getting through these three stages is easy, nor is changing corporate culture. If you get cold feet, screw your courage to the sticking place, as Shakespeare would say. Then reflect on the massive changes that took place in the Soviet Union in 1991. Your job should immediately look easier. Margo Parker, corporate vice president of employee relations and communication at Northrop, says this about change: "In 21 years, I never learned how to change culture . . . only how to work with it." It is in this transition stage between what no longer exists, and what you are building anew, that Margo's perceptions have relevance. The moving on and commitment stage is a call to action. It means looking at some of the existing systems and modifying them to accommodate and encourage a diverse and inclusive environment.

First, look at the composition of your work force. See what changes you need or want to make. How diverse is middle management? Upper? What is the turnover rate at all levels of the organization? How does it differ among your diverse population? Attracting a diverse work force is like a 10-kilometer race. Keeping them is a marathon. Also, in a truly inclusive organization, white males are not made to feel like the enemy. Yes, they inherited the power, . . . and yes, it needs to be shared, but no group willingly gives up power. Sensitivity to the changes they are going through is critical if everyone is to benefit from the change.

Next, provide awareness and training. Oliver Brown, one of the organizational effectiveness (OE) change agents for the city of San Diego's exciting diversity effort astutely says, ''You can't change culture with a four-hour seminar.'' But he would also agree that training and awareness have to be part of the change effort. Training that focuses on behaviors is essential. It is not okay, for example, to tell racist and sexist jokes. Making people aware that one person's laughter is another person's pain can be done through training. Learning how to give feedback in culturally sensitive ways is helpful. It is also important to have awareness training that focuses on what culture is and its pervasiveness in shaping us. That awareness will help employees come to terms with their own cultural preferences and turnoffs. Do your employees understand enough about culturally influenced behaviors not to misjudge co-workers because of their culture? Do they know enough about cultural etiquette to put a potential employee at ease during an interview and not violate any cultural norms? How about the best ways to address people as you greet them?

Finally, analyze your existing systems and fold appropriate changes into them rather than starting from scratch. The biggest threat employees feel comes from losses that affect their career opportunities, reward structure, and perceptions of loss of control. For starters, look at your promotional system. What kind of career development system do you have? How much mentoring goes on? Since the pyramid always gets narrower at the top for everyone, what alternative career paths can you create to reward people and tap their talent? Is your criteria for success or promotability both broad and fluid enough to include top achievers? Do you mostly reward direct, analytical problem solvers? What kind of plums exist for more intuitive, lateral thinkers? Do you conduct exit interviews to find out why diverse people leave your organization? How do you reward managers who strive for and accomplish an inclusive environment? Is there any penalty for continuing to tell racist or sexist jokes long after there has been a declared taboo? Changing organizational culture and creating new norms is a daunting task but well worth the effort.

From Monocultural to Multicultural: Designing Incentives that Work

Commitment to becoming an organization that embraces diversity necessitates going from a monocultural to a multicultural organization. The road to hell, as the saying goes, is paved with good intentions. In most of our organizations, that road is littered with diversity efforts gone sour, stopped midstream (and midsteam). Some companies and personnel just had no idea of what they were getting into and what kind of resources would be required to make a real effort work. Good intentions and noble objectives were not enough. Before you embark on the long journey from monoculturalism too multiculturalism, take a reality check. Every organizational journey of 1,000 miles begins with a single step. The following list presents your first dozen. Use these 12 steps on the road to multiculturalism as a checklist to guide your own change effort.

Twelve Steps on the Road to Multiculturalism

1. A Long-Term Change Effort Is Required.　In our 30-second-sound-bite culture, sustained long-term effort requires more tenacity than we are normally willing to invest. The kind of change we are advocating impacts the bone marrow of the organization. It can be successful, but it will not be quick, it will not be easy, and it will need eternal vigilance. It is not an effort for the faint of heart. Set clear expectations with employees from the very beginning so they understand you are embarking on a several-year, systemic change as opposed to eight hours of diversity training.

2. Time, Energy, Money, and Emotional Commitment Are Essential.　If so many resources are involved, and if commitment is usually only lukewarm, why do it? In a word, *survival.* To paraphrase the L'Oréal commercial, it may be expensive, but you're worth it! Smart, competitive organizations will not look at this as only a diversity effort. They will frame it as it should be framed—a change effort designed to produce a quicker, leaner, more open, and more competitive organization. Becoming more inclusive is just one piece in the global powerhouse puzzle.

3. Support from the Top Is Critical to Success.　No one can dispute that support from the top is critical to success. What's also critical is to determine what that support looks like. Is the CEO willing to continue financial support for this change effort in tough financial times? How accessible will she be to consultants, internal or external, who facilitate the change? When you get to the training sessions, does she need to kick them off—all of them? Does she need to do so in person? Is video an acceptable medium to indicate that this is a top organizational priority? These are tough questions. Lip-service support is easily detectable, and it won't work. Don't make the mistake Paul Newman talked about in the movie *Cool Hand Luke.* Newman's character said, ''What we have here is a failure to communicate.'' In an organizational effort of this magnitude, that failure can be deadly. The stakes are too high, the cost too great, and the consequences too important not to define the terms very clearly ahead of time.

4. Don't Raise Expectations that May Eventually Be Dashed.　We meet a lot of cynical people as we travel around in our work. Most have been hurt over the course of their professional lives by organizations that raised their hopes but didn't come through. The result? Lowered expectations and cynicism. You are better-off to never start the effort of revamping the organization and making it more responsive to employees if you don't plan to go where the path leads. Tokenism will be detected. Contrary to what P.T. Barnum said, suckers are not born every minute, or if they are, don't count on the fact that they live in your organization. If you start this effort, you need to be open enough to go where the data take you, have ego enough to not be defensive, and have courage enough to implement changes. There are no sacred cows once you start the process.

5. Expect Discomfort: Change Is Unsettling.   Organizational transitions lead the troops, at least for a time, to a no-man's-land. This is not a comfortable place to be. It's that undefined area between what you are as an organization and what you are striving to become. The human species likes predictability and homeostasis. Change disrupts them both. Your effort should be centered on creating an organization that's nimble. If you can create a psychological climate open to diverse people, you will also end up with an organization that is more open to new and different ideas. You don't want old wine in new bottles. Expecting some ferment when you go from fruit on the vine to mellow wine is what it's all about.

6. Be Clear about the Depth and Breadth of the Effort.   Whether the people guiding the change effort are internal or external, they need to coach, facilitate, and guide the organizational leadership. It is not hard to imagine a CEO that signs up for a top-quality workplace with the promise of achieving a highly talented work force from diverse backgrounds that conducts business productively and profitably together. Who wouldn't want that? What he might not ask, however, is, "At what price?" Few people would turn down a Mercedes if all things were equal. But all things are not. A Mercedes and a Toyota Corolla are not in the same price range, and probably not in the same performance range. Even with the most elaborate plans, all outcomes cannot be anticipated, but you will do yourself a favor if you define your commitment level before you ever start.

7. Work to Modify the Systems You Already Have in Place.   Don't throw out the baby with the bathwater. If you need a new promotional system to encourage broader representation among diverse groups, look at your existing system. What parts are working? What adaptations have to be made as your objectives change? If you have performance reviews conducted in a way that is offensive to people from certain cultures, see what communication norms are incompatible or offensive. Determine what kind of changes need to be made in giving feedback so that employees will be open to suggestions that are useful. Revising systems you already have is much smarter and less threatening than starting from scratch.

8. Help Employees Understand the Big Picture and Get Beyond Themselves.   Helping employees understand the big picture may not be so easy to do in mainstream American culture because we focus so extensively on individual need fulfillment. It will be a much easier task in most immigrant cultures where personal satisfaction usually takes a backseat to the collective good.

9. Set Measurable Criteria.   As you struggle to become multicultural, what are your criteria for success? What results need to occur in order for staff to determine that the efforts are warranted? Your chances of success are greater if you determine the criteria before you get started, not after the fact. If you are trying to create a more inclusive culture, there needs to be something in it for everyone. Get data from the troops. Find out what needs revamping. Does the flexible benefits package need a new look? How about career development? Or a mentoring system? Money spent on stock options or employee training? There may be other issues that indicate a closed, exclusive system. Opening up the system anywhere will change it everywhere. Diversity can simply capitalize on, or dovetail with, other issues.

10. To Get Support for the Changes, Employees Must Be Shown Something Better Will Result than What Currently Exists. The city of San Diego is involved in a major change effort to value and embrace a diverse work force. As so often happens in these efforts, the perception initially exists that what the organization is really after is just "slotting minorities" into management positions. When two of the organizational effectiveness consultants from the city's organization effectiveness program went around to various groups to explain the program, they talked about many things, among them the flexible benefits package that gave every employee in the city an extra $600. This was initially intended to help with child care, but each employee could use the money as he or she saw fit, even taking it in cash. Additionally, a child-care coordinator was hired by the city to investigate different child-care centers and contracted with several of them to give city employees discounts of between 10 and 25 percent. At the end of one of their briefings that explained the change program, a white woman told one of the consultants how glad she was they had come to talk to her group because before they explained the program, she thought this was just designed to help certain people. Now she can see this effort is for everybody. You want yours to work? Then it, too, has to be for everybody.

11. Training Is Necessary but Not Sufficient. Training is undeniably an important part of any long-term change, particularly as it relates to systems changes that revise organizational culture. Your training content should fall into three areas: (1) awareness, (2) knowledge, and (3) skills. Employees need awareness about their own reactions to different cultures specifically and to change generally. They also need knowledge about what culture is, about how it impacts everyone, and about change as a universal human phenomenon. Lastly, managers need skills in areas such as managing intercultural conflict, structuring an effective work team or task force, and leading meetings in a diverse group.

12. There Is No "There" There. After all your effort, you will see some wonderful, satisfying results. You'll also undoubtedly have experienced some frustrations. But the most sobering reality will be the realization that as you have created openness and solved certain problems associated with closed systems, inclusivity presents its own set of challenges. New problems will be spawned, new answers needed, new products developed to meet competition in the market place. There is no laurel on which to rest. At best, you get a temporary stopping place for a moment, where you can feel the warmth of the sun and the satisfaction of accomplishment. But organizations are rapidly changing and are always in evolution, so your best bet is to look at this a little bit like Tom Sawyer's fence. You've got some willing and committed painters, but by the time they get to the end, they may need to go back and touch up a few spots.

Surviving the Transition and Moving On: A Case in Point

Agreement is widespread that organizations are very different entities than they were 5, 10, and 15 or more years ago. The revolutions in the workplace are well known. The changing work force takes its place alongside the emergence of the information age, the dual-career family, and global competition, to name a few. Clearly, these changing times call for a new response.

One corporation that has successfully adapted is Northrop. Our assumption was that a mostly male, analytical, traditional defense contractor would lag behind in adapting to the changes wrought by diversity. Happily, we can report that rather than lagging behind, Northrop is leading the way. When questioning Margo Parker, corporate vice president of employee relations and communications, about how this traditional company had pried itself open, she says with exquisite simplicity, ''We take our existing systems and add diversity. You build from what you have.''

It all sounds so simple. How does it work? What kind of resistance does Margo face as she tries to include more people in the decision-making process? We threw some of these and a couple of dozen other questions at her. For starters, she does her homework and is always prepared. She engages in a number of smart but subtle actions, conducting literature searches on diversity-related topics. She then inundates senior management with these timely articles. She attaches letters, notes, or Post-its on the articles, and therein lies the beginning of an education and awareness project. The education is both subtle and low-key. These articles plant seeds, create awareness, and raise consciousness. Her approach of working to refine or modify the existing systems works well for Northrop. She would not offer it as a wholesale remedy for another organization's approach to diversity. But Margo insists all systems are interconnected, and she wouldn't even address individual diversity-related questions for us. What she did do is show us how her approach works within a system. We looked at the promotional system because it is an issue that engenders heated emotion. The subtle (or not-so-subtle) perception exists that any affirmative action promotee is less qualified than a white male. Nevertheless, to get support for broadening the satisfaction of new hires, Margo traveled around the organization presenting the HR department's best effort at a system that would meet legal mandates and maintain quality at the same time. Then the employees at her meetings were asked to shoot holes in the program. She encountered some predictable resistance. Managers felt they would lose control in hiring decisions. They also worried about getting competent people on board. First, she listened. She also made it clear that Northrop still wants and expects the same high quality in all their recruits and promotees. She told managers that diversity-related criteria must be met. Once they are, managers can hire whomever they want without consideration to gender or background. To the complaint ''We just can't find qualified people,'' Margo said, ''You will eventually . . . go back and try again till you get the quality you want. Keep looking. You will find excellence.'' And they have.

To illustrate how the recruiting system and diversity work together, Margo mentioned two important programs that impact hiring and promotion. One is Northrop's college relations program. It is an ongoing program that seeks potential employees from local colleges, as well as targeting schools in other areas. Northrop identifies key minority schools as a way to increase diversity. They also have a scholarship program with a certain percentage of the scholarships going to women and people of color. They offer these scholarship recipients summer employment, which serves as a trial run for both the organization and the employee. It is one of the least costly and most effective ways to broaden the work-group composition. These two outreach programs look for talent in all segments of the population. While the initial push may come from affirmative action, the results speak for themselves. Resistance no longer exists. Managers have seen that they keep their hiring freedom. They recruit and promote quality staff, and Margo has not had even one grievance all year in regard to hiring. The key is that Margo and her staff designed a system, got input and critiquing from all divisions, and then rolled the changes out.

As we mentioned earlier, Margo makes a point of not talking about diversity separately. She just makes certain that it exists. Her most concrete example came from talking about the company newsletter or videos they have made. She wants a visible example of Northrop's diversity reflected in the pictures shown in the newsletter. That means the people in pictures can't be all male, nor can they be all white. Margo chuckled as she talked about how she has raised sensitivity among staff. When they started putting the visuals together, she wanted a balance of young and old, male and female, all colors and cultures. She used to have to remind the people who put this material out. She would say, "Where are my older workers?" She hasn't had to say anything about demographic composition in a year. The staff is in tune now and aware of the importance of showing Northrop's diversity, so Margo is on to other things.

When we asked her the question about how she justifies the cost of diversity and how she measures its success, she was very clear. She says, "The right question to ask is not how can we afford to become more diverse, but rather how can we afford not to? We measure diversity efforts the same way we measure our anything else . . . grievance rate, turnover, promotion." She made Northrop's efforts and the results sound so simple that we finally said, "What about resistance? Do you have white males or others who are resentful?" Margo believes the resistance to diversity is the same as resistance to affirmative action and she bases it on people's lack of understanding. She attacks this lack systematically and starts by showing her organization the benefits from diversity-related efforts. In Northrop's case, legal mandates are a strong incentive for compliance. But to dismiss Northrop's change and growth as strictly a reaction to contractual obligations would be to shortchange the steady and real changes taking place.

Margo has support from senior management and admits that affirmative action has changed the composition of the senior management staff. For example, she is currently conducting an employee attitude assessment. As recently as five years ago, if that tool were used at all, it would be viewed merely as an interesting exercise. Today, this survey will be fed upward to top management as a useful feedback tool. If action is suggested, action will be taken. The feedback could be about flexible benefits, for example. Maybe information will surface that says the hiring and promotion system needs attention. Maybe task-oriented issues related to quality or the manufacturing systems will suggest certain changes. What's important is that top management's ears are opened.

There are other changes visible today that weren't there several years ago. When Northrop is represented at community events, the table is staffed by a diverse group. When a group of Vietnamese workers wanted to cook lunch at Northrop's Anaheim facility, they found out that due to health laws, they couldn't. The compromise was to buy a microwave, the best solution in an imperfect world. Problem solving, change, people's unique needs mattering in a large organization—clearly, Northrop or any other organization with its eyes opened realizes the rapidity of change and the interconnectedness of the world. American business is in uncharted territory. But there are a few organizations that have a map and know they are on the right path.

Maintaining a Balance between What Was and What Is to Be

We thought the adage, "When in Rome, do as the Romans do" was immutable. But all things change, including Rome. The saying still has validity, but in the competitive organization of today, it has an add-on. Effective relationships in a diverse environment (and in fact, *all* relationships) are two-way streets. They require give and take; they also require sensitivity. They require newcomers to learn to adapt to a culture or environment that is different from their own, but effective relationships also require the organization to broaden its base of acceptable behaviors.

At its best, acculturation involves a willingness to accommodate some of those differences. The very issue of acculturation is a heated one. It implies building a base of common experience and understanding. But it also means cultivating the unique contributions made by different people. Walking that tightrope between holding on to existing norms and creating new ones is central to your organization's ability to create an open, inviting culture where every employee gives a best effort. An organization's ability to maintain this balance will significantly impact its ability to be productive, and to retain the diverse workers it hires. The task is doable, but it is not easy.

The most striking example of this balance on a large scale involved the coalition troops stationed in Saudi Arabia in January of 1991. Because of so many conflicting values and practices, maintaining this balance was like dancing on the head of a pin. With Desert Storm, we saw a U.S. military used to having women in its ranks as well as troops drinking beer and other alcoholic beverages. How could practices in the American military coexist with some different values and norms in Saudi Arabia? The solutions required dual sensitivity. We respected their prohibition of drugs and alcohol. With some modifications, they accepted women in our military. Women could not go out jogging alone, nor could they walk around in short-sleeved T-shirts. The accommodation made a tough situation workable for all parties because there was acceptance of and adherence to the values and norms of each culture.

This same accommodation and sensitivity is required in your organization. Here's an example of something Avon did to create more sensitivity. The company holds an annual outing or retreat that has historically been called President's Golf Day. There are women who entered the upper ranks of management who felt excluded because they did not play golf. There was no conscious attempt to leave them out, but Golf Day held no allure. The implication was that golf is the ticket to becoming a member of ''the club.'' Avon's sensitivity is shown in the subsequent change. The day is now called President's Day, and instead of playing only golf, you can swim, jog, play tennis, or just relax by the pool.[26] Expanding the activities and changing the name of the day are symbolic gestures that have real value. A positive message about valuing uniqueness is sent. You no longer have to recreate in cookie-cutter fashion. You are not relegated to invisibility if you don't play golf.

Avon also used to buy season tickets to sporting events. The message they inadvertently sent was, ''You're welcome to our club so long as you're just like us.'' Being like us means you have to enjoy sports. Avon no longer buys sports tickets. Instead, they go to the ballet, symphony, or museums. However, a truly inclusive organization makes just as much room for sports as it does for ballet. The point of cultural, gender, racial, or any other kind of sensitivity is that a wide range of behaviors or priorities is valued.

Take what could be a modern day Tower of Babel, Los Angeles County, a geographic region in which approximately 90 different languages are spoken. Many of the people show up at the county's medical center, either as employees or as patients. They bring with them not only language differences, but cultural differences as well. To deal with those differences, LA/USC Med Center offers flexibility in scheduling people's work for a variety of reasons, some cultural and some not. Some employees want fewer hours so they can go back to school. Others have ailing parents who need elder care. Many Latino employees wanted to visit their families in Mexico after the earthquake. Add these requests to the predictable family vacations and other commitments outside of work and you can see the vastness of the issue. Nevertheless, LA/USC has found that the more flexibility you offer, the more stable your work force.

The Med Center also offers a stipend for employees who function as translators for commonly spoken languages such as Spanish, Chinese, Korean, and Tagalog, the language spoken by Filipinos. This is both smart and sensitive. Translation is necessary; it is also time-consuming. Compensating employees for their knowledge and skill that goes beyond the scope of their technical job is a way to help the acculturation process for everyone. Furthermore, language and literacy classes are paid for. Schedules are juggled so employees can take the class on work time, which means for all practical purposes, they are getting paid to learn. It is not uncommon for older workers to resist learning English and enrolling in the class because they say it is very difficult for them to learn and they feel embarrassed by their accents and lack of proficiency. Nevertheless, they are given incentives to attend. The classes help both the employee who is trying to acculturate, and the organization that needs, literally and figuratively, some common language to function productively. This is a win/win for everyone.

In the past, literature has focused on the need for the "minority to adapt." But we know that trying to get round pegs into square holes is a losing battle—and the important word here is *losing*. In organization after organization where minorities have been hired and recruited, unless the culture is both inclusive and accommodating, new hires don't stay. Some employees feel like they can't be their authentic selves; others plateau and resign due to dashed expectations and the feeling they are on a fast train to nowhere. Being sensitive as an organization, and helping the newcomer learn the organizational norms, is a step in the right direction.

Teaching New Employees the Ropes

In Voltaire's *Candide,* the reader experiences the "best of all possible worlds." If that best-of-all-worlds concept were applied to the issue of helping new employees learn the ropes, this is what you'd see. Both the organization and the employee would be in simultaneous transition, molding to one another. The organization would demonstrate more flexibility—in schedules, the identification of acceptable norms, and how employees are rewarded. At the same time, the new employee would be making adjustments and changes as well. That scenario paints a picture of productive and healthy acculturation. However, human nature long ago laid its claim to resistance, defensiveness, and egos run amok.

From the work of Eileen Morley, we have adapted a predictable process of integration experienced by an outsider to a new organization.[31] It spells out what behavior you can expect from individuals at each stage of this adaptation. You will also get a sense of how an organization can appropriately respond. This model is designed to give you perspective. If you expect initial rejection or resistance, you can handle it better and take it less personally. New employees to the organization will likely go through the five stages described below and summarized in the box entitled *Stages of Integration.* As you read the stages, think about newcomers with whom you are working. How can you help them adapt?

Stages of Integration: Helping New Employees Fit In[31]

Stage 1 Behavior: Rejection/Resistance.   Organisms instinctively protect themselves from that which is new and different because it is threatening. In the case of a work group or organization, if this differentness feels like an assault, the group will close off and protect itself, keeping the newcomer out. At an individual level, resistance may be strong. The newcomer may fear acculturation because in the past, people's original culture was sublimated. The perception by those not part of the dominant culture is that the cost of becoming so is one's own self-esteem. If the stakes for belonging are seen as too high, rejection or resistance may last a long time.

Stage 1: Suggestions for Managers.   Understand and accept initial rejection or resistance. Pushing employees or work groups to move beyond these reactions before they get a chance to articulate fears or loss, as we illustrated earlier in this chapter, will exact a strong reaction. We remember very well the doctoral student from Nigeria who came to study in the United States for what he thought would be a seven-year stint. He came with his wife and 2-month-old son. Part of his resistance to this culture was his well-articulated concern that his son would be Americanized by the time they went back to Nigeria. He feared the loss of his proud Nigerian culture.

Stage 2 Behavior: Isolation.   The second stage is characterized by withdrawal, both physical and psychological. Passive hostility is also seen in this stage. In work groups, we have seen perfunctory acceptance of newcomers. There is sometimes a we-have-no-choice-but-to-include-you attitude. For the newcomer and the group, contact has a veneer of politeness and a lot of superficiality. If a newcomer feels excluded, she might cluster with those of her same background.

Stage 2: Suggestions for Managers.   As human beings, we have more similarities than differences; therefore, it is important to structure opportunities that bring people together. This is the time to activate a network, take the newcomer around, formally introduce this person to others, and provide assignments that are central, not tangential or irrelevant. The sooner connections are structured, the better. Familiarity will lessen isolation and offer opportunity to learn the informal rules.

Stage 3 Behavior: Assimilation.   Adjustment to the work group norms is taking place. By this stage, the norms, behaviors, and customs of the organization should become clear to the new employee. Clarity may be gained through observation, a buddy system, a question-and-answer exchange, or a crash course in "Here's how we operate around this place." The most difficult of these behaviors cross-culturally will be getting the newcomer to ask questions.

Stage 3: Suggestions for Managers.   The hard part for the new employee is knowing what to adapt to and what rules may violate his own sense of identity. If we were to drive in England, the adaptation would need to be immediate or the consequences might be life threatening. On the other hand, some English customs will be less critical for our survival as well as for our enjoyment and success in the travel experience. Help new employees by telling them about the critical adaptation points.

Only time will tell which adaptations are healthy and which go against the grain. Having to listen to jokes told about diverse groups, whether it's your brand of diversity or someone else's, may be deeply offensive to you. If you think assimilating means being one of the boys in order fit in (even if you're a woman) over time, that adaptation will be very costly. The organization can help by expanding its criteria of acceptable and rewarded behaviors. Also, performance needs to be judged on results rather than style. Don't discount the worth of the message because the messenger speaks, thinks, or behaves in ways different from you.

Stage 4 Behavior: Coexistence.   It is in the coexistence stage that new employees find ways to exist within the dominant culture without sacrificing themselves. The new employee can get support and information from support groups or cultural networks.

Stage 4: Suggestions for Managers.   The organization can adapt successfully by setting up parallel options, as Avon did in the example discussed earlier in this chapter where President's Golf Day became a kind of multifaceted fun-and-games-for-all day. Include people. Acknowledge their uniqueness. Find a way to utilize and capitalize on their strengths. Avon's gesture showed flexibility and respect on the part of the organization. Its behavior said, "It's okay to be different." At the same time, the company found a way to create activity together so they could build a common culture.

Stage 5 Behavior: Integration.   The new employee now feels like a regular member of the team, not a token, not the odd person out, and not an exotic specimen. Relationships are real and fluid. That means some days involve conflict, some cooperation. But whatever the problem, diversity is no longer the issue.

Stage 5: Suggestions for Managers.   Continue to model respect for differences, both organizationally and individually. This is hard to do, with or without diversity. Create a feedback and reward system that produces the behaviors you want.

An Example of Inclusivity in Action

It is fashionable to talk about diversity, but examples of organizations that actually engage in the practice of creating a more diverse and inclusive work force are few and far between. The city of San Diego is one shining example. To begin with, the city's leaders have crafted a statement that shows their slant on diversity. It is a philosophy that is not hard to rally around:

> The City of San Diego's Diversity Commitment:
> To create an environment where differences are valued
> and all city employees are a productive part of
> a high-performing team delivering services to our citizens.

They believe that the city can become an even better place for everyone, and the diversity program is a positive step in that direction. The history of this program delineates the factors that are making it work. It began several years ago when former city manager John Lockwood had convened an annual meeting of the top managers in the city. It was at that time that Lockwood learned there were many

Stages of Integration

Stage 1 Behavior: Rejection/Resistance

Characterized by fear of acculturation due to sublimating one's culture. The stakes for belonging are seen as too high.

Stage 2 Behavior: Isolation

Characterized by physical and psychological withdrawal. There is a perfunctory politeness, but superficial interaction.

Stage 3 Behavior: Assimilation

Characterized by adjustments toward group norms. There is a clarity about the operating rules.

Stage 4 Behavior: Coexistence

Characterized by an ability to become part of the mainstream while maintaining sense of self and uniqueness.

Stage 5 Behavior: Integration

Characterized by a sense of belonging. Relationships are real and fluid and involve conflict and cooperation.

Source: Adapted from Eileen Morley, "Management Integration," paper presented at OD '80—A Conference on Current Theory and Practice in Organizational Development, San Diego, 1980.

strong feelings about limits to equal opportunity at the middle and top levels. For years, management positions had been filled in a way that did not sufficiently reflect the diversity of the community. John Lockwood made a concerted attempt to change the composition of the management ranks and then began a renewed commitment to a diverse work force. The beginning was not easy. There were deep pockets of resistance but there was also *strong* support from the then assistant city manager who was head of the diversity effort. When Jack McGrory later became the city manager, he made it clear that diversity was still a high priority for him and would play an important part in his tenure at the helm of San Diego.

In January of 1991, the Organizational Effectiveness (OE) Program sent out requests for proposals (RFPs) to consultants who were thought to be the best in the area of change in general, and diversity in particular. They selected the firm of Kaleel Jamison Consulting Group and Southwest Communication Resources to begin working with the internal consultants.

Of the 10,000-plus people who work for the city, data were collected from almost 1,000 employees. Seventy-five focus groups were held. The data collection culminated in a two-day effort attended by the consulting firm and the appropriate people from the city, one of whom was the city manager. Their goal was to determine emerging issues and themes that needed attention. Findings and recommendations were presented, both short-term and long-term. One of the most important things that Oliver Brown, the on-board OE person, mentioned is that the results were important because the diversity-related feedback gave San Diego a chance to capture important organizational issues that have systemwide impact. For example, their data suggest that one of the major problems in the city revolves around career development issues. The findings have resulted in a number of changes in that area and in other areas as well:

Career Development:

1. Change interview panels to include a more diverse interview board.
2. Change the process whereby people are notified about openings. All positions will be posted so that people will know job availabilities.
3. Employees who go through the promotion process will be given more complete and useful feedback from both their written tests and their interviews.

Communication:

1. The perception exists that there are gaps in communication top to bottom and that no communication seems to float up to the top of the organization. As a result, each director in the city will work with his or her group to improve the communication process in that particular unit.
2. A directory will then be published that makes this communication procedure part of a group's policy.

Ease with Which Employees Can Obtain Information:

1. A resources booklet for employees will be put together to provide information about benefits packages, personnel policies, or any additional information.
2. The city is setting up an 800 number so that employees may have easy access to any information they need.

Help in Dealing with Accents:

1. A task force has been formed to study accents, translation, and language barriers due to accents.
2. The perception exists that accents have made people nonpromotable. The task force will look at the issue of promotability in relation to accents and work with an eye toward helping both customers and employees.

You can see by the four short-term goals already mentioned that San Diego's change effort has an impact on a number of areas. The diversity program is still in progress, so final results have not yet been measured, but even San Diego's initial learnings are worth passing on.

Early Realizations from San Diego's Diversity Effort:

1. Systemic changes that are making life better and easier for all employees are beginning to convert even the most skeptical. The concrete benefits such as more accessible child care and increased tuition reimbursement have a positive impact in the areas that people value most—their time and their money.
2. Two critical factors have made this an effective program so far: personal and financial commitment from the top and the expertise of the consulting firm. The latter laid the ground rules. The former has demonstrated commitment by continuing the funding for this effort in less-than-easy financial times. A special position was created in the OE department. There was also the cost of the consultants, advertising, a newsletter, lapel pins, logo, and so on. In a time of cost containment, such a venture takes vision, wisdom, and guts.
3. The decision to create an inclusive climate makes good business sense, but the results are hard to quantify. San Diego got support for this effort by looking at demographics, defining an open environment as part of good management, and acknowledging that the city is a service organization. It also showed that individual and organizational productivity would increase if employees felt they were valued for who they genuinely are.
4. San Diego's accomplishment and employee support did not come easily. This is an organization with real people who have real egos and real prejudices— as well as real fears, ambitions, and mortgages. San Diego doesn't claim to have created utopia, nor does it claim to have found the definitive answer to creating a more diverse and open climate. It is a city government made up of human beings, many of whom have a difficult time dealing with change. Some of the most intractable problems center on gender differences among blue-collar workers. Sexist jokes and posters still exist, as does nepotism and favoritism. But these problems are being addressed. The other difficult issue is that white males now feel disadvantaged because they are white. Hiring and promotion practices are perceived as favoring women and people of color. There is no easy or particularly satisfying answer to this dilemma. But at the City of San Diego, the dialogue has started. The vision has been articulated, and the doors previously slammed shut are now open a crack. This is a city on the move, and it is moving in a wonderfully positive direction.

Chapter 8

Conducting a Diversity Audit: Taking an Organizational Snapshot

This chapter will give you:
1. A clear understanding of the advantages and disadvantages of three types of assessment methods.
2. A series of diversity assessment tools—questionnaires, checklists, and opinionnaires.
3. Guidelines for conducting focus groups and interviews.
4. Sample questions to use in focus groups and interviews.
5. Tools for pinpointing diversity-related problems and training needs of managerial and nonmanagerial staff.

"Know thyself" is as important a dictum for organizations as it is for individuals wanting to increase effectiveness. Before your organization or work group can figure out how to manage diversity, it needs to examine and assess existing conditions, practices, attitudes, and skills. Without accurate baseline information, plans and changes are built on unstable foundations.

The Role of Assessment: What It Can Do

Assessment is a tool for diagnosing organizational conditions. It is analogous to a physical examination where a patient's temperature and blood pressure are taken and lab tests and X rays are done to check the body's functioning. Many different methods of checking are used to give the doctor critical information needed in making a diagnosis. Likewise, the many tools of organizational assessment provide information that serves your organization in five ways.

1. *Provide feedback.* Assessment data reported back to the organization function much like biofeedback for an individual. By seeing information in black and white, with words, charts, graphs, or other visual depictions, managers and other staff get an accurate picture of the aspects of the organization. This information serves as a springboard for making decisions and taking action. Seeing these effects and conditions is a first step in doing something about them. Often, having this information made public within your team, management group, or whole company is enough to get change started.

2. *Determine baseline data.* Assessment also provides information that serves as a "state of the union" report. This baseline information is essential for strategic planning and as a reference for future comparison. "How far have we come?" can't be answered unless we know where we started.

3. *Make latent issues public.* Assessment also uncovers problems, concerns, and obstacles that might not have been openly discussed before. Like underground reefs, unseen on the smooth surface of the sea, they can be treacherous if not discovered. Assessment brings them out into the open where they can no longer be ignored.

4. *Identify staff development needs.* Data from assessment also uncover areas of needed development of staff, both managerial and nonmanagerial. Attitudes, skill levels, and knowledge can be assessed and determinations made about needs for training and growth experiences.

5. *Generate commitment through input.* Because data come from people in the organization, staff are more apt to "own" the information and feel committed to any plans or actions built on it. Getting input in this initial stage sets the tone for participation throughout any change process.

In understanding the positive outcomes of assessment, it is important to heed a caveat. As one colleague of ours sagely cautions, "Don't open up a can of worms unless you have the recipe for worm soufflé." Assessment can open up volatile issues. If an organization is not prepared to deal with the information, the result may be expectations initially raised, then dashed or, said a little differently, morale raised then lowered. Unless an organization is ready to make use of assessment data and has a clear purpose for doing so, it is better not to embark on the process of data gathering in the first place.

Before you begin the process, the following questions can help you plan and structure the most effective audit for your purpose.

1. What do you want to find out? For example, do you want to assess staff attitudes about the many cultures in the workplace, perceptions of employees from nonmainstream groups, or skills of managers in working with a diverse staff?

2. What part does this data collection play in your larger organizational plan? Assessment needs to be in the service of a larger goal. Is it part of a plan to increase diversity at all levels in your company? Or perhaps the development of more cohesive work teams is part of your quality improvement program.

3. Who needs to be involved? Your purposes and your budget will help you decide the answer to this. Do you need an organization-wide survey, focus groups from certain segments of the work force, or a questionnaire for managers, for example?

4. How will data generated be used and communicated to others? Will information be used by a diversity task force or executive management? Will the data be fed back only to those who participated or communicated to all staff? How will that process be managed?

5. What methods will be used to collect data? The answers to the questions above will help you decide the most appropriate assessment options.

6. Who will be most appropriate and effective in collecting data? What staff personnel or outside resources are best suited to conduct the process or aspects of the process?

7. What cultural factors may influence the audit process? The language and reading level of any instruments, the values at the base of the process, and the methods used will all be influenced by the cultural backgrounds of those involved—designers, data collectors, and participants. This chapter will help you formulate your own answers to these questions.

Three Types of Assessment: Paper and Pencil Isn't the Only Way

Assessment generally calls up images of paper-and-pencil instruments such as your last employee attitude questionnaire or your customer satisfaction survey. While such written assessment tools represent one way to collect data, there are two others. A method borrowed from marketing research and being used more frequently in internal assessment is that of focus groups. These group discussions serve as a kind of group interview. Questions are posed for participants that enable them to share their opinions, perceptions, and feelings on the topic being investigated. Finally, a third avenue of assessment is through individual interviews with appropriate staff members. The table *Assessment Methods Compared* takes a look at the advantages and disadvantages of each.

There is no need for exclusivity when choosing an assessment method. A combination of two or all three methods may be used in one assessment project. For example, interviews with top executive staff members and a random sampling of managers may help determine the areas to be investigated and questions to be asked on a written questionnaire. Even further, this information may be used

Assessment Methods Compared

Method	Advantage	Disadvantage
Questionnaire	Data can be obtained from everyone in the organization in a cost-effective way. Data are collected anonymously so employees feel free to be more honest. Provides data in comparative form from all respondents that can be quantified and statistically analyzed. Takes relatively little time from employees and can be done simultaneously in many locations. Simple to administer.	Requires literacy and possibly translations into other languages One-way communication offers no way to get clarification or explanation about responses. Responses tend to be limited by information requested in questionnaire. May get lip service and perfunctory answers rather than thoughtful responses. Impersonality and lack of human touch may put off employees, especially those from other cultures.
Interviews	Interviewees may feel freer to speak openly without others present. Problems and issues surfaced can be explored in depth. Permits collection of examples, anecdotes, and stories that illustrate the issues and put them in human terms. More personal touch allows for person-to-person communication.	Least time-efficient and most costly method. Requires skilled interviewer to guide sessions. Data collected from a limited number of people may provide a narrow slice of information if only staff at certain levels are interviewed. Affects the least number of staff so may generate only limited commitment.
Focus Groups	Serve as a teaching tool, building respondee awareness about diversity. Produce richer data through in-depth discussions about topics and issues. Two-way communication permits clarification and explanation of information given. More personal and human. Subtle information from nonverbal clues and body language can be picked up. More time-efficient to get information from groups rather than individuals one at a time. Interaction generates more data. Comments spark other ideas so new information may emerge. Participants' hearing of each others' views may expand their understanding of the issues.	Require skilled facilitation in sessions. Generally only provide a sample of views, not everyone's. Peer pressure may influence participants' comments. Takes time to coordinate sessions and schedule the pulling of employees from jobs. People may be uncomfortable in a new setting and an unfamiliar experience. Participants may be reluctant to open up and speak freely for fear of repercussions or because of cultural norms that discourage negative or critical comments.

to set up focus groups. Then a two-pronged approach—using focus group data collection and an organization-wide questionnaire survey—can be used. Combining the two provides breadth and depth.

An important consideration is whether to use internal or external data gatherers. Using in-house resources such as staff in human resources or EEO/affirmative action departments may seem more cost-effective. Insiders have a greater knowledge of the organizational culture and so may have a sense of which issues to pursue. Their informal networks and information pipelines can help in getting beyond the level of superficial observations. However, their association with existing programs, such as affirmative action, may cause employees to question the purpose and objectivity of the assessment process. On the other hand, an assessor from the outside has greater objectivity and clarity in looking at the organization. This outsider usually has no vested interest, no relationships with other staff, and no history with the organization to color his/her thinking. Assessment may get more honest, candid responses from employees who have greater trust in the objectivity of an outsider. Having an external data gatherer may also cause employees to see the assessment in a larger organizational context, not just another project from a particular department. Deciding who should conduct the various aspects of your assessment does not have to be an either-or. The assessment can be a collaborative effort of insiders and outsiders, getting the best of both worlds.

Once you have decided on the *who* and *how* of your organizational audit, there is a need for the *what*, the tools and techniques that will help you get the information you want and the answers you need.

Assessing How Effective Your Organization Is at Managing and Capitalizing on Diversity

In examining an organization's overall management of diversity, three areas need to be investigated. First, because organizations' effectiveness and productivity depend on the human beings who work in them, there is a need to look at individual attitudes and beliefs. Such issues as how open employees are to people who are different and how comfortable staff is with change are important areas of assessment. Beyond the individual level, it is essential to look at organizational values and norms. How do organizational practices encourage or discourage diversity? Is diversity tied to the vision and strategic goals of the company? Finally, it is critical to look at the place where the organization and the employees interface, the management practices and policies. How do managers use such organizational systems as accountability, reward, and decision making to capitalize on diversity? How adept are managers at getting maximum commitment from all segments of the work force? *When all three of these levels of organizational functioning work in concert, diversity is effectively managed as a corporate asset*. The *Managing Diversity Questionnaire* can be useful to you in assessing an organization at these three levels.

Managing Diversity Questionnaire

	Very True	Somewhat True	Not True
In this organization:			
1. I am at ease with people of diverse backgrounds.	____	____	____
2. There is diverse staff at all levels.	____	____	____
3. Managers have a track record of hiring and promoting diverse employees.	____	____	____
4. In general, I find change stimulating, exciting, and challenging.	____	____	____
5. Racial, ethnic, and gender jokes are tolerated in the informal environment.	____	____	____
6. Managers hold all people equally accountable.	____	____	____
7. I know about the cultural norms of different groups.	____	____	____
8. The formation of ethnic and gender support groups is encouraged.	____	____	____
9. Managers are flexible, structuring benefits and rules that work for everyone.	____	____	____
10. I am afraid to disagree with members of other groups for fear of being called prejudiced.	____	____	____
11. There is a mentoring program that identifies and prepares women and people of color for promotion.	____	____	____
12. Appreciation of differences can be seen in the rewards managers give.	____	____	____
13. I feel there is more than one right way to do things.	____	____	____
14. Members of the nondominant group feel they belong.	____	____	____
15. One criterion of a manager's performance review is developing the diversity of his/her staff.	____	____	____
16. I think that diverse viewpoints make for creativity.	____	____	____
17. There is high turnover among women and people of color.	____	____	____
18. Managers give feedback and evaluate performance so employees don't "lose face."	____	____	____
19. I am aware of my own assumptions and stereotypes.	____	____	____

Managing Diversity Questionnaire (concluded)

	Very True	Somewhat True	Not True
20. Policies are flexible enough to accommodate everyone.	___	___	___
21. Managers get active participation from all employees in meetings.	___	___	___
22. I think there is enough common ground to hold staff together.	___	___	___
23. The speaking of other languages is forbidden.	___	___	___
24. Multicultural work teams function harmoniously.	___	___	___
25. Staff members spend their lunch hour and breaks in mixed groups.	___	___	___
26. Money and time are spent on diversity development activities.	___	___	___
27. Managers effectively use problem-solving skills to deal with language differences or other culture clashes.	___	___	___
28. I feel that working in a diverse staff enriches me.	___	___	___
29. Top management backs up its value on diversity with action.	___	___	___
30. Managers have effective strategies to use when one group refuses to work with another.	___	___	___

Scoring:

Items 5, 10, 17, and 23: Very true = 0 points, Somewhat true = 1 point, Not true = 2 points.
All other items: Very true = 2 points, Somewhat true = 1 point, Not true = 0 points.

___ Individual attitudes and beliefs: Items 1, 4, 7, 10, 13, 16, 19, 22, 25, 28
___ Organizational values and norms: Items 2, 5, 8, 11, 14, 17, 20, 23, 26, 29
___ Management practices and policies: Items 3, 6, 9, 12, 15, 18, 21, 24, 27, 30
___ Total score

Suggestions for Using the *Managing Diversity Questionnaire*

Objectives:

- Assess three levels of an organization's effectiveness in managing a diverse work force: individual attitudes, organizational values, and management practices.
- Increase awareness and knowledge about aspects of managing diversity.
- Target areas of needed development.

Intended Audience:

- Staff at all levels in an organization that is working to increase effectiveness in managing diversity and that desires to understand perceptions of employees about the issues.
- Executive and/or middle management involved in planning diversity development strategies.
- Executive staff members charged with organizational strategy regarding diversity.
- Trainees in a managing diversity seminar.

Processing the Activity:

- Individuals are asked to respond to the questionnaire based on their perceptions of the organization and how it functions. They are told that responses are anonymous and are asked to be candid. They are also told how the data generated will be used, who will see them, and what will be done with them.
- Questionnaires are collected and scored.
- Data are compiled and analyzed by item, by the three levels of functioning, and by demographic groupings of staff.
- Data are reported to appropriate executive and or management staff, and a summary of findings is communicated to all participants along with an indication of next steps.

Questions for Discussion:

- What are our organization's strengths and weaknesses?
- How similar or disparate are perceptions of different groups, divisions, or levels within the organization?
- What issues need further investigation or clarification?
- What issues need attention?
- Who or what (positions, levels) needs to be involved in dealing with the issues surfaced?

Caveats and Considerations:

- Do not embark on a process of this type until you have a clear plan about how the data will be used and a commitment that they will be considered in planning.
- This questionnaire can be used as an awareness builder for managers who want to increase their own effectiveness and/or for those involved in diversity task forces. It can also be used as a jumping-off point for discussions about managing diversity in execution and/or management staff meetings.
- Questionnaires can be coded by level, department, length of time with the company, type of work, and so on to give more specific categories for analysis.

The overall score has a range of 0–60. The higher the number of points, the more effectively the organization is managing and capitalizing on diversity. However, analyzing scores by item and by the three levels—individual, organizational, and managerial—provides additional information. Item analysis can help you pinpoint diversity weak spots, your organization's figurative Achilles' heels. For example, if the lowest-scoring item is number 15, then perhaps including managerial performance standards about developing diversity might need to be addressed. If number 7 is a collective low point, your company might want to consider providing cultural awareness training to staff so they can learn about the cultural backgrounds of groups with whom they work. The information gained from this survey can be fed back to executive staff so they can make use of it in their strategic planning. It can also be fed back to managerial staff so they can problem-solve around the weaknesses surfaced, for example, coming up with ways to offer more appropriate rewards to a diverse staff.

Analyzing scores at the three levels of organizational functioning can give you additional information. If, for example, the individual attitudes and beliefs score is lowest, then training might be called for to help staff understand and accept differences. If the organizational values and norms score is lowest, then perhaps a feedback session with executive staff is called for, giving top management the questionnaire data so they can use them in their strategizing. Finally, if the management practices and policies score is low, then perhaps management development training regarding diversity and problem-solving sessions are called for. In one organization that used this audit, scores showed a large disparity between executive and first-line staff perceptions about management policies and practices. Sharing these respective realities might be a place to begin dealing with diversity in this organization. In all cases, top management needs to see the data and be involved in setting a course of action.

The most critical aspect of any organizational assessment is using the data. To conduct this type of a process and then to merely report the findings misses the point. Something needs to be done with the information gathered. Analysis needs to be done, and "so what" questions need to be asked.

- What does this tell us about our organization?
- Where do we need to improve?
- What do we need to do to improve our effectiveness?

Having staff at appropriate levels grapple with these questions is a critical step in milking assessment tools such as this for their full usefulness.

If an organization is in the initial stages of addressing diversity as an issue, there may be a simpler and more basic question to answer: "How do we know if we need to address this issue at all?" One straightforward way to get a collective answer is to use an uncomplicated checklist that requires respondees to indicate any of the problems they are experiencing; see *Symptoms of Diversity-Related Problems: Internal Checklist*.

Symptoms of Diversity-Related Problems:
Internal Checklist

Check any of the following situations you notice and/or are experiencing in your organization:

_____ Lack of a diverse staff at all levels in the organization.

_____ Complaints about staff speaking other languages on the job.

_____ Resistance to working with or making negative comments about another group (ethnic, racial, cultural, gender, religion, sexual orientation, or physical ability).

_____ Difficulty in communicating due to limited or heavily accented English.

_____ Ethnic, racial, or gender slurs or jokes.

_____ EEOC suits or complaints about discrimination in promotions, pay, and performance reviews.

_____ Lack of social interaction between members of diverse groups.

_____ Increase in grievances by members of nonmainstream groups.

_____ Difficulty in recruiting and retaining members of different groups.

_____ Open conflict between groups or between individuals from different groups.

_____ Mistakes and productivity problems due to employees not understanding directions.

_____ Perceptions that individuals are not valued for their unique contributions.

_____ Ostracism of individuals who are different from the norm.

_____ Barriers in promotion for diverse employees.

_____ Frustrations and irritations resulting from cultural differences.

_____ Other diversity-related problems. Explain: _____

Suggestions for Using *Symptoms of Diversity-Related Problems: Internal Checklist*

Objectives:

- Identify diversity-related problems within the organization.
- Raise awareness and spark discussion about such issues.
- Provide a jumping-off point for taking action to deal with diversity-related problems.

Intended Audience:

- Managers, supervisors, and first-line staff in a diverse organization.
- Trainees at a managing diversity seminar.
- Executive staff attempting to identify obstacles to productivity and morale.
- Human resource staff attempting to reduce turnover and grievances.

Processing the Activity:

- Individuals are asked to check any of the problems they have experienced within the organization. They may also add others that are not listed.
- Groups can discuss problems checked to get an idea about which issues seem to be most prevalent. They may also assign priorities regarding dealing with the problems, discuss how widespread the problems are, and/or determine which parts of the organization seem to be most affected by particular issues.
- Follow-up will depend on the group involved. Data can be used by managers in solving the problems in their own departments/divisions. They can be used by executives in developing or modifying plans or policies. They can also be used by human resource staff in making recommendations to executive management and in modifying their own procedures. Finally, data can be used in planning management development activities.

Questions for Discussion:

- What seem to be the most frequent problems surfaced?
- How widespread are they? Which sections of the organization seem most affected?
- What is the cost to the organization of these problems? What will happen if these go unaddressed?
- What additional information do we need in order to address these? From whom?
- Where/how do these issues need to be dealt with?
- What do we need to do to address these problems?
- What support, skills, and training do managers need to deal with these issues?
- What organization systems or policies need to be examined and possibly modified?

Caveats and Considerations:

- Be careful not to make any premature commitments regarding actions to address these problems. Undoubtedly, further clarification about the problems is needed before solutions can be planned.
- This activity can be modified for use by a manager to get feedback from his/her work group.

The beauty of this tool is that it is quick, is easy to administer, and can be used to pinpoint the organization's problem areas related to diversity. Pay particular attention to the frequency with which problems are identified. When the same data surface repeatedly, they are sending a message. This checklist can be used in deciding whether diversity does present problems to the organization and, if so, what those obstacles are. If problems are uncovered, more investigation and assessment would be needed to answer such questions as the following:

- How widespread is this problem?
- Which groups are most affected?
- How is the problem getting in the way of productivity? Morale?
- Is the problem a result of individual attitudes, organizational norms, and values or managerial policies and practices?
- How can these issues best be addressed?

Answering these questions may require the use of a survey questionnaire and/ or focus group data collection. They may also be addressed at management staff meetings.

Stages of Diversity Survey: An Organizational Progress Report

Dealing with the phenomenon of diversity is an evolutionary process, not a revolutionary one. No organization has a homogeneous work force one week and a diverse staff the next. In fact, the evolution is a gradual process of change that involves a shift in not only the demographics but attitudes and practices in the organization as well. An organization can have a very diverse staff yet continue to function as a monocultural system, as though its staff were all of similar backgrounds. Bailey Jackson and Evangelina Holvino hypothesize that organizations experience three stages in this evolution: monocultural, nondiscriminatory, and multicultural.[16]

In the *monocultural stage*, the organization acts as though all employees were the same. While staff may be somewhat diverse, there is an expectation to conform to a standard that is, in most cases, the white male model, which puts white men at an advantage. Success is achieved by following the expectations and norms of this model. Women, people of color, and immigrants are expected to assimilate, to adopt the dominant style of the organization. The motto might be "When in Rome, do as the Romans do." Differences are underplayed, and there is an attempt to be "color blind."

As the organization evolves, it reaches the second stage: the *nondiscriminatory stage*. Usually because of governmental regulations and the threat of employee grievances, organizations begin to pay attention to affirmative action requirements and EEO regulations. In this phase, there is much attention paid to meeting quotas in hiring and promotion and in removing roadblocks that inhibit diverse groups from moving in and up. The goal is to eliminate the unfair advantage of the majority group. Generally, the two groups that have been most affected at this stage are women and African-Americans. Training in gender equity and reducing stereotypes and prejudice is often done during this period. For diverse employees, there is a push-pull between the need to assimilate and a desire for the organization to accommodate to their needs. Compromises are usually the method of resolving these conflicts, with each side giving in a little in order to gain some as well.

Sooner or later, because of work-force changes in ethnicity, life-style, and values, the organization comes to the third stage: the *multicultural stage*. In this stage, there is not only a recognition that there are clear differences of culture, background, preferences, and values, but a valuing of those differences. Assimilation is no longer the model for success. Rather, new norms are created that allow more leeway for employees to do things their own way. Organizational policies and procedures are flexible enough to work for everyone, and no one is put at an exploitive advantage. This nirvana-like state is a worthwhile goal, but we have yet to see an organization so evolved that it fits entirely in this stage. You can use the *Stages of Diversity Survey* to assess where your organization is in its evolutionary process.

Stages of Diversity Survey:
An Organizational Progress Report

Directions: Check each response that is true of your organization. You may check more than one response for each item number.

1. **In this organization:**

   _____**a.** There is a standard way to dress and look.

   _____**b.** While there is no dress code, most employees dress within a conventional range.

   _____**c.** There is much variety in employees' style of dress.

2. **In this organization:**

   _____**a.** Newcomers are expected to adapt to existing norms.

   _____**b.** There is some flexibility to accommodate the needs of diverse employees.

   _____**c.** Norms are flexible enough to include everyone.

3. **In this organization:**

   _____**a.** Diversity is an issue that stirs irritation and resentment.

   _____**b.** Attention is paid to meeting EEO requirements and affirmative action quotas.

   _____**c.** Working toward a diverse staff at all levels is seen as a strategic advantage.

4. **In this organization, dealing with diversity is:**

   _____**a.** Not a top priority.

   _____**b.** The responsibility of the human resource department.

   _____**c.** Considered a part of every manager's job.

5. **People in this organization:**

   _____**a.** Downplay or ignore differences among employees.

   _____**b.** Tolerate differences and the needs they imply.

   _____**c.** Value differences and see diversity as an advantage to be cultivated.

6. **Demographics of this organization show that:**

   _____**a.** There is diversity among staff at lower levels.

   _____**b.** There is diverse staff at lower and middle levels.

   _____**c.** There is diversity at all levels of the organization.

7. **Money is spent on training programs to help employees:**

   _____**a.** Adapt to the organization's culture and learn "the way we do things here."

   _____**b.** Develop diverse staff's ability to move up the organization ladder.

   _____**c.** Communicate effectively across gender and cultural barriers.

Stages of Diversity Survey:
An Organizational Progress Report (concluded)

8. Managers are held accountable for:

_____**a.** Motivating staff and increasing productivity.

_____**b.** Avoiding EEO and discrimination grievances and suits.

_____**c.** Working effectively with a diverse staff.

9. Managers are held accountable for:

_____**a.** Maintaining a stable staff and perpetuating existing norms.

_____**b.** Meeting affirmative action goals and identifying promotable talent.

_____**c.** Building productive work teams with diverse staff.

10. Managers are rewarded for:

_____**a.** Following existing procedures.

_____**b.** Solving problems in the system.

_____**c.** Initiating creative programs and trying new methods.

11. This organization:

_____**a.** Resists change and seeks to maintain the status quo.

_____**b.** Deals with changes as they occur.

_____**c.** Is continually working on improvement.

12. In this organization, it is an advantage to:

_____**a.** Be a white male.

_____**b.** Learn to be like the "old guard."

_____**c.** Be unique and find new ways of doing things.

Directions for Scoring:
Count the total number of checks next to each letter (a, b, c) and fill in the totals below:

_____ **a.** Monocultural
_____ **b.** Nondiscriminitory
_____ **c.** Multicultural

Suggestions for Using the *Stages of Diversity Survey: An Organizational Progress Report*

Objectives:

- Determine an organization's stage of development in dealing with diversity.
- Give feedback to executive management about the organization's status regarding dealing with diversity.
- Provide data for strategizing regarding organization development.

Intended Audience:

- Middle- to lower-level staff in a diverse organization.
- Management and supervisory staff.
- Members of diversity task forces or planning teams.
- Executive staff involved in strategic planning.

Processing the Activity:

- Individuals are asked to check each response that they perceive as a true statement about the organization. They may check more than one response for each item.
- Questionnaires are collected and scored. If used by a task force or planning team, they may be scored in the group.
- Scores are analyzed, and data are interpreted and then presented to planning group.

Questions for Discussion:

- Where is our organization in its development regarding diversity?
- What surprises or new information is there?
- What issues are uncovered that need to be addressed?
- What kind of planning or development is indicated for growth?

Caveats and Considerations:

- While this instrument leads to a score that places the organization in a particular stage of development, its purpose is not to label the organization but rather to serve as a tool for exploration and growth. Help those with the information utilize it for that purpose.
- Individuals may disagree with some of the statements. They may also find some indicators of particular stages not desirable. In these cases, use disagreement to provoke discussion of desired organization goals and indicators of their achievements.

The *a* responses describe an organization in the monocultural stage, the *b* responses describe an organization in the nondiscriminatory stage, and the *c* responses depict an organization in the multicultural stage. The category in which you have the highest number of checks indicates the probable stage of the organization. However, scores of the other two categories are important as well. Because organizations function at many levels simultaneously and evolve unevenly, most will have some points in all the stages. The most instructive part of this questionnaire may emerge not from the score but from an examination of the specific responses checked or not checked. Which of the *c* responses were not checked? What goals or strategies might that suggest?

Diversity Readiness: Analyzing Individual Awareness

"Awareness precedes choice," contends our friend and mentor, organization development theorist, author, and consultant John E. Jones. A beginning point in dealing with diversity is awareness about differences, about individuals' attitudes and prejudices, and about the impact of diversity in the workplace. The *Diversity Awareness Continuum* can give you a quick assessment of the awareness level of a group or staff. Armed with this information, you can proceed to design a diversity training program that meets people where they are.

Diversity Awareness Continuum

Directions: Put an X that represents where you fit along the dotted line for each continuum below.

I am not knowledgeable about the cultural norms of different groups in the organization.	....	I am knowledgeable about the cultural norms of different groups in the organization.
I do not hold stereotypes about other groups.	....	I admit my stereotypes about other groups.
I feel partial to, and more comfortable with, some groups than others.	....	I feel equally comfortable with all groups.
I gravitate toward others who are like me.	....	I gravitate toward others who are different.
I find it more satisfying to manage a homogeneous team.	....	I find it more satisfying to manage a multicultural team.
I feel that everyone is the same, with similar values and preferences.	....	I feel that everyone is unique, with differing values and preferences.
I am perplexed by the culturally different behaviors I see among staff.	....	I understand the cultural influences that are at the root of some of the behaviors I see.
I react with irritation when confronted with someone who does not speak English.	....	I show patience and understanding with limited English speakers.
I am task focused and don't like to waste time chatting.	....	I find that more gets done when I spend time on relationships first.
I feel that newcomers to this society should adapt to our rules.	....	I feel that both newcomers and the organizations in which they work need to change to fit together.

Draw your profile by connecting your Xs. The closer your line is to the right-hand column, the greater your awareness regarding diversity. The closer to the left-hand column, the less aware you may be about diversity-related issues.

Suggestions for Using the *Diversity Awareness Continuum*

Objectives:

- Assess individual awareness and attitudes about diversity.
- Give management information about staff attitudes and potential sources of resistance to diversity.
- Give individuals information about potential areas of personal/professional development.

Intended Audience:

- Members of diverse and/or changing work teams.
- Managers dealing with diverse staffs.
- Trainees in diversity awareness and managing diversity seminars.

Processing the Activity:

- Individuals place an *X* representing where they fit along each continuum on the sheet. They then connect their *X*s.
- In groups or in a team, they discuss their responses, focusing on the farthest left and farthest right marks. Discussion continues about reactions and feelings about diversity and consequences of those reactions.
- Individuals target one or two areas for personal development.

Questions for Discussion:

- Where are you most/least aware and knowledgeable about diversity?
- What do you need to learn?
- Where are your greatest strengths? Weaknesses?
- What are the team's/group's greatest strengths of weaknesses regarding diversity?
- What do you need to do as a team to grow? As an individual?

Caveats and Considerations:

- In addition to its value as a tool for growth for the individual and team, this activity can provide data to training and development professionals developing diversity training programs.
- It also serves as a subtle teaching tool, suggesting areas of development regarding diversity.

This tool can serve as a jumping-off point in beginning discussions about diversity. It can also show you the degree of acceptance or resistance that exists regarding diversity. Armed with this information, you can tailor your intervention to suit the group. A more aware group may be able to jump into experiential training activities right away. A more resistant group, conversely, may need a more cognitive approach initially. Beginning with statistics and demographic data supporting the need for dealing with diversity would be a less threatening first step and would probably give you the best chance for acceptance with a less aware, more resistant group.

Measuring Employee Perceptions: How Much Is Diversity Valued?

Perceptions and attitudes are difficult to measure with self-report assessment tools because most people are "test wise" and smart enough to pick up on which is the "right" answer. In addition, most of us are uncomfortable with our own prejudices, so we often deny them, even to ourselves. However, there is value in having people respond to questionnaires such as the *Diversity Opinionnaire* to get some information on professed attitudes as well as to open people's minds to some of the issues involved in dealing with diversity.

Diversity Opinionnaire

Please respond with a rating that represents your feelings about each opinion below. 5 = strongly agree, 4 = agree, 3 = uncertain, 2 = disagree, 1 = strongly disagree.

_____   1.   Everyone who works in this organization should be required to speak English.

_____   2.   Diversity brings creativity and energy to a work group.

_____   3.   Immigrants should be expected to forsake their own cultures and adapt to American ways.

_____   4.   Multicultural teams can be stimulating, productive, and fun.

_____   5.   People should leave their differences at home and conform to organizational standards at work.

_____   6.   Showing flexibility and accommodation to people's individual needs and preferences increases commitment and motivation.

_____   7.   Diversity only brings unnecessary conflict and problems to a work group.

_____   8.   Women and people of color are underrepresented at higher levels in this organization.

_____   9.   Increasing work-force diversity has led to a decline in quality.

_____   10.   People are more motivated and productive when they feel they are accepted for who they are.

_____   11.   Women and minorities are oversensitive to prejudice and discrimination.

_____   12.   Stereotypes exist about all groups.

_____   13.   Minorities tend to stick together.

_____   14.   Differences often make people uncomfortable.

_____   15.   Some groups are more suited for or talented at certain jobs.

_____   16.   There should be no double standards. The rules should be the same for everyone, regardless of gender, race, age, ethnicity, and so on.

_____   17.   America would be a better place if people would assimilate into one culture.

_____   18.   America would be a better place if people were allowed to preserve their individual cultures.

_____   19.   People are reluctant to disagree with minority group employees for fear of being called prejudiced.

_____   20.   Training is needed to help employees understand each other and overcome communication barriers.

Scoring:

_____   Total score for odd-numbered items
_____   Total score for even-numbered items

Suggestions for Using the *Diversity Opinionnaire*

Objectives:

- Assess attitudes about openness toward diversity.
- Identify potential sources of resistance to diversity.
- Uncover personal prejudices and feelings about diversity.

Intended Audience:

- Staff at all levels in a diverse organization.
- Managers dealing with a diverse staff.
- Trainees in a diversity awareness or managing diversity seminar.
- Individuals wanting to increase their own awareness and sensitivity regarding dealing with differences.
- Members of a diversity task force or planning group needing to ''get their own house in order'' before working with the organization about this issue.

Processing the Activity:

- Individuals respond by assigning a number, from 1 to 5, to each of the statements.
- If used as an organization assessment, questionnaires are collected, scores are tabulated and analyzed, and then data are reported to the appropriate planning group.
- If used by individuals or groups for their own information and growth, individuals score their own, then discuss results and their significance.
- Individuals can target areas for personal growth, while teams or groups can pinpoint areas for group development.

Questions for Discussion:

- What is the workplace impact of these attitudes?
- How can these opinions affect relationships with diverse groups?
- How do they affect manager/subordinate relationships?
- Which attitudes represent obstacles to making diversity an asset to the organization or team?
- What needs to be done to deal with these perceptions? How?

Caveats and Considerations:

- Discussion is apt to be heated, and there may be a tendency for individuals to want to defend their opinion, attack another's, and/or argue for their own point of view. It is important to remind people that attitudes and perceptions are neither right nor wrong; however, they are realities for those holding them. Keep the discussion centered on the effect of the attitudes and the consequences of the behaviors they provoke. Focus on the cost to the organization, team, and individual.

The odd-numbered items are opinions that represent a more monocultural view and a resistance to diversity. The higher the total for these items, the stronger this view is held. The even-numbered items are opinions that represent a more multicultural view and a valuing of diversity. The higher the total for these items, the stronger this view is held. An overall score for comparison purposes can be obtained by subtracting the odd score from the even score. The result may be a positive or negative number. The higher the number on a positive scale, the greater the acceptance and receptivity to diversity. Again, as with all the other tools offered, this data can be a catalyst for and can legitimize action.

Staff Diversity Needs Analysis: Awareness, Knowledge, and Skills

In order for individuals of many backgrounds to work productively together, they need information and abilities on three levels: *awareness, knowledge*, and *skills*. First they need awareness. It is critical that they recognize differences and are aware of their own assumptions about those differences: "What are my unconscious expectations of African-Americans? Latinos? Women?" "Am I surprised when all secretaries and nurses are not women or when I meet doctors or executives who are?" Beyond awareness of their own subtle expectations or assumptions, there is a need for knowledge about different cultural norms, life-style needs, and personal preferences of individuals from different groups.

Second, they need knowledge. Information is needed to answer such questions as the following: "Why do people nod and say yes when they don't understand?" "Why do gay men and lesbians feel the need to come out of the closet?" "What are the myths and realities about aging?" "Why do some employees speak their native languages at work even when they know English?" "Why do others react negatively when I speak my native language on the job?"

Third, they need skills. Employees need to have the ability to deal with one another in sensitive ways: "How can I resolve a conflict with someone who won't admit anything is wrong?" "How can I communicate with a co-worker whose English is limited?" "What can I do when I encounter racist remarks or ethnic slurs?" The *Staff Diversity Needs Analysis* can give you an idea of the training and development needs of your employees at these three levels.

Staff Diversity Needs Analysis

Please respond to the questions below by answering *true* or *false*.

_____ 1. I am comfortable working with individuals who are different from me in race and cultural background.

_____ 2. I am sometimes confused by the behavior of employees from different backgrounds.

_____ 3. It is difficult for me to understand people who speak with thick accents.

_____ 4. I'm reluctant to disagree with employees of different groups for fear of being considered prejudiced.

_____ 5. I know about my own cultural background and how it influences my behavior.

_____ 6. I am able to resolve conflicts with employees who are different from me in cultural background, gender, race, and life-style.

_____ 7. My behavior is influenced by gender differences.

_____ 8. Prejudice exists in every individual.

_____ 9. I feel comfortable talking about differences in race, culture, and sexual orientation.

_____ 10. Racial and cultural differences influence my behavior.

_____ 11. Stereotypes are held about every group.

_____ 12. I'm not sure what labels to use in referring to different groups.

_____ 13. My behavior is influenced by differences in sexual orientation.

_____ 14. I understand the different cultural influences of my co-workers.

_____ 15. I get frustrated when communicating with limited-English-speaking individuals.

_____ 16. I am most comfortable spending time with people who are similar to me in background.

_____ 17. I find the behaviors of some members of diverse groups irritating.

_____ 18. I'm fearful of offending individuals of diverse groups by saying the wrong thing.

_____ 19. People of diverse groups are treated differently because they act differently.

_____ 20. I find myself thinking, "Why don't they act like us?"

Staff Diversity Needs Analysis (concluded)

_____ 21. I'm able to resolve problems easily with co-workers who are different from me.

_____ 22. I recognize my own biases and prejudices.

_____ 23. Certain behaviors of diverse groups bother me.

_____ 24. I am able to work with people so I feel I fit in, no matter how different we are.

_____ 25. I wish we were all more the same.

_____ 26. I understand some of the reasons why there is cultural clash and conflicts between groups.

_____ 27. When dealing with differences, I am able to "walk in someone else's shoes."

_____ 28. I find differences among us interesting and stimulating.

_____ 29. I understand the reasons for my own reactions to others' differentness.

_____ 30. I find many similarities between me and my diverse co-workers.

Scoring—Give each answer a point value as follows:

Items 1, 5, 6, 7, 8, 9, 10, 11, 13, 14, 21, 22, 24, 26, 27, 28, 29, 30: True = 1 point, False = 0 points.
Items 2, 3, 4, 12, 15, 16, 17, 18, 19, 20, 23, 25: True = 0 points, False = 1 point.

_____ Awareness = Total score for items 1, 4, 7, 10, 13, 16, 19, 22, 25, 28

_____ Knowledge = Total score for items 2, 5, 8, 11, 14, 17, 20, 23, 26, 29

_____ Skills = Total score for items 3, 6, 9, 12, 15, 18, 21, 24, 27, 30

_____ Total

Suggestions for Using the *Staff Diversity Needs Analysis*

Objectives:

- Identify training and development needs of staff regarding diversity.
- Pinpoint specific areas for development.
- Give information to individuals regarding personal training and/or development needs.

Intended Audience:

- Staff at nonmanagerial levels in a diverse organization.
- Trainees in a diversity training seminar.
- Individuals wanting to increase their own ability to deal with diversity.

Processing the Activity:

- Individuals respond to the statements by marking them true or false.
- Questionnaires can be collected and scored for use as a training needs assessment.
- Questionnaires can be scored by the individuals, then discussed in groups. Discussion can focus on strengths and weaknesses and areas of needed growth.
- Individuals can prioritize needs and target specific areas for growth.
- Training and development professionals can analyze scores to determine appropriate training content and design.

Questions for Discussion:

- What strengths and weaknesses emerge?
- Where are the greatest growth needs—awareness, knowledge, and/or skills?
- How do weaknesses in these areas affect productivity? Morale? Service?
- What does this tell us about training needed by staff in specific departments/units?
- What do we need to find out more about?

Caveats and Considerations:

- This questionnaire can serve as a catalyst for discussion within a team dealing with diversity. The group can identify collective weaknesses and target areas for growth and development.

There is a possible total of 10 points for each of the three areas. The higher the score in each, the greater the mastery of that area. The lower the score, the greater the need for training and development in that area. Overall totals may be compared, by group, staff, age, ethnicity, gender, and position to see if there are significant differences. For example, it may become apparent that employees in the customer service department need help in dealing with limited-English-speaking clients/customers or that certain groups are more aware of their own attitudes and prejudices than are others. The data can help you in tailoring training sessions and in structuring problem solving at staff meetings to help employees develop the awareness, knowledge, and skills they need.

Management Development Diversity Needs Analysis: Awareness, Knowledge, and Skills

Managers have many of the same awareness, knowledge, and skill needs as other employees when it comes to dealing with a diverse staff. However, they have additional skill needs in the area of management responsibilities such as giving feedback, reviewing performance, and building productive work teams. They need answers to such skill-related questions as the following: "How can I give directions to someone who won't tell me when he/she doesn't understand?" "How can I give a performance review that does not cause a decline in motivation because of hurt feelings?" "How do I keep my staff from segregating into separate ethnic, racial, or gender groupings?" The *Management Development Diversity Needs Analysis* can give you an idea of the training and development needs of managers regarding their awareness, knowledge, and skills in managing diversity.

Management Development Diversity Needs Analysis

Please respond to the questions below by answering *true* or *false*.

_____   1.   I am comfortable managing individuals who are different from me in race and cultural background.

_____   2.   I am sometimes confused by the behavior of employees from different backgrounds.

_____   3.   I'm able to resolve problems easily with employees on my staff who are different from me.

_____   4.   I'm reluctant to disagree with employees of different groups for fear of being considered prejudiced.

_____   5.   I know about my own cultural background and how it influences my behavior and my expectations of employees.

_____   6.   I know how to give feedback so employees of different cultures don't "lose face."

_____   7.   My behavior toward employees is influenced by gender differences.

_____   8.   Prejudice exists in every individual.

_____   9.   I feel comfortable talking with my staff about differences in race, culture, and sexual orientation.

_____   10.   My behavior toward my staff is influenced by racial and cultural differences.

_____   11.   Stereotypes are held about every group.

_____   12.   I am able to give constructive performance reviews with employees of different groups.

_____   13.   My behavior toward my staff is influenced by differences in sexual orientation.

_____   14.   I understand the different cultural influences of the people I manage or supervise.

_____   15.   I get frustrated when my staff segregates into subgroups along cultural or racial lines.

_____   16.   I am most comfortable managing people who are similar to me in background.

_____   17.   I find the behaviors of some members of diverse groups on my staff irritating.

_____   18.   I'm fearful of offending employees of diverse groups by saying the wrong thing.

_____   19.   People of diverse groups are treated differently because they act differently.

_____   20.   I find myself thinking, "Why don't they act like us?"

Management Development Diversity Needs Analysis
(*concluded*)

_____ 21. It is difficult for me to manage people who speak with thick accents.

_____ 22. I recognize my own biases and prejudices.

_____ 23. Certain behaviors of diverse groups on my staff bother me.

_____ 24. I am able to resolve conflicts between employees of different cultural backgrounds, genders, races, and life-styles.

_____ 25. I wish my staff were all more the same.

_____ 26. I understand some of the reasons why there is culture clash and conflicts between employees and groups of employees.

_____ 27. I'm not sure what labels to use in referring to different groups.

_____ 28. I find differences among us interesting and stimulating.

_____ 29. I understand the reasons for my own reactions to others' differentness.

_____ 30. I am able to build a cohesive work team from my diverse staff.

Scoring—Give each answer a point value as follows:

Items 1, 5, 6, 7, 8, 9, 10, 11, 13, 14, 21, 22, 24, 26, 27, 28, 29, 30: True = 1 point, False = 0 points.

Items 2, 3, 4, 12, 15, 16, 17, 18, 19, 20, 23, 25: True = 0 points, False = 1 point.

_____ Awareness = Total score for items 1, 4, 7, 10, 13, 16, 19, 22, 25, 28

_____ Knowledge = Total score for items 2, 5, 8, 11, 14, 17, 20, 23, 26, 29

_____ Skills = Total score for items 3, 6, 9, 12, 15, 18, 21, 24, 27, 30

_____ Total

Suggestions for Using the *Management Development Diversity Needs Analysis*

Objectives:

- Identify management development needs regarding diversity.
- Pinpoint specific areas for training.
- Give information to individual managers regarding personal development needs.

Intended Audience:

- Managers dealing with a diverse work force.
- Trainees in a management development series or a managing diversity seminar.
- Management teams wanting to increase their effectiveness in dealing with diversity.

Processing the Activity:

- Individuals respond to the statements by marking them true or false.
- Questionnaires can be collected and scored for use as a management development needs assessment by the training department.
- Questionnaires can be scored by individuals, then discussed in groups. Discussion can focus on strengths, weaknesses, and areas of needed growth.
- Groups and individuals within them can prioritize needs and target specific areas for growth. They can even brainstorm ways to accomplish that growth.
- Training and development professionals can analyze scores to determine appropriate training content and design.

Questions for Discussion:

- What strengths and weaknesses emerge?
- How do the weaknesses impact management effectiveness? Productivity? Morale?
- Where are the greatest growth needs in general areas (awareness, knowledge, skills) and/or specific issues (e.g., communication with limited-English-speaking staff).
- Where do we need to focus our own development?

Caveats and Considerations:

- Dealing with the issues in this questionnaire may provoke heated discussion if there has been no previous groundwork laid regarding managing diversity. This is best used after a general session discussing changes in work force demographics where venting can be done and where executive management explains organizational goals and strategy regarding diversity.

There is a possible total of 10 points for each of the three areas. The higher the score in each, the greater the mastery of that area. The lower the score, the greater the need for training and development in that area. Overall totals may also be compared by age, ethnicity, gender, education level, and position to see if there are significant differences. It may be that supervisory level staff have different skill needs than middle management, or that younger managers have different attitudes toward diversity than older managers, for example.

In addition to using this questionnaire, the *Management Development Diversity Needs Assessment Checklist* can be filled out by managers as part of your training and development needs assessment process. This gives managers a chance to give direct input about their training needs and to participate in their own development.

Management Development Diversity Needs Assessment Checklist

Check any of the following you would like to learn more about.

_____ Understanding attitudes about race, culture, gender, sexual orientation.

_____ Dealing with prejudice and stereotyping.

_____ Understanding norms, practices, and values of different cultures.

_____ Understanding communication differences among groups.

_____ Learning to reward appropriately amid diversity.

_____ Using nondiscriminatory language and labels.

_____ Communicating with limited-English-speaking individuals.

_____ Motivating effectively in a diverse environment.

_____ Resolving cross-cultural conflicts.

_____ Dealing with prejudice on my staff.

_____ Building multicultural work teams.

_____ Giving feedback in culturally sensitive ways.

_____ Enhancing trust in a diverse staff.

_____ Communicating more effectively with diverse employees.

_____ Coaching, grooming, and mentoring diverse employees.

_____ Conducting productive performance reviews with diverse staff.

_____ Recognizing the special needs of different groups.

_____ Creating an environment where all employees feel included.

_____ Other: _____

Suggestions for Using the *Management Development Diversity Needs Assessment Checklist*

Objectives:

- Identify management development needs regarding diversity.
- Give information to training and development professionals regarding perceived needs.
- Increase awareness about skills and knowledge essential in managing a diverse staff.

Intended Audience:

- Managers and supervisors dealing with diverse staffs.
- Potential trainees in a managing diversity seminar.
- Executive staff wanting to increase the effectiveness of managers and supervisors in dealing with diverse staffs.

Processing the Activity:

- Managers check those aspects of managing diversity in which they need development.
- Groups can discuss items checked and assign priorities to them.
- Training and development staff can then use this information in planning training for managers.
- Executive staff can discuss data and assign priorities for management training.

Questions for Discussion:

- Which items were checked?
- What themes or issues do these items relate to?
- What is the effect of these deficiencies on the job?
- What are the consequences if these go unaddressed?
- Which are most/least widespread? Critical?

Caveats and Considerations:

- This tool gives only preliminary data. More information is needed before action is taken.
- If managers responding to this checklist are new to dealing with diversity, they may not recognize needs they have.
- This checklist can also be used as a self-assessment by managers by changing the directions and having them rate themselves, either with a plus/minus or on a scale of 1 (not very good) to 5 (very good) on each of the items.

The data produced by this checklist can help the human resources department target and focus management development activities. Using the checklist in this fashion not only gives you information about training needs, but also serves as a diversity awareness builder for managers and can lead to insightful discussions as managers begin to grapple with these challenges.

How to Use Focus Groups to Get Information about Diversity

Focus groups can be a rich source of information about diversity. In a small-group setting, where there is comfort and safety, employees are often willing to be more candid and open about diversity problems and concerns. In addition, issues can be explored in greater depth through discussion than through a questionnaire. In order to get the most from your focus group needs assessment, a number of factors need to be considered. Attention needs to be paid to selection of participants, group composition and size, time and location of sessions, facilitation of discussions, and topics and questions on which to center discussions.

Selection of Participants

Since focus group participants represent a larger constituency, they need to cover as wide a spectrum of views as possible. In a large organization where a number of focus group sessions will be held, selecting participants by random sampling techniques—every 20th employee from an alphabetical list, for example—might be appropriate. In smaller organizations, or where only a few groups will be conducted, selecting members from different opinion ''camps'' and diverse groups would help ensure a wider spread of views and inclusion of employees from all groups. Accepting only volunteers skews your sample. While those who would volunteer probably have a greater interest in the issues surrounding diversity, they may also have some of their own axes to grind or their group's vested interests to promote. They may not be representative of the larger group of employees. While you may include some volunteers, you may need to recruit more reticent employees to get divergent views.

Group Composition and Size

Different groupings will serve different purposes in your needs assessment. If you want the specific views of different groups—Latino, African-American, Korean, or Filipino employees; middle managers; immigrant employees; assembly-line staff; or differently abled workers, for example—then forming like groups would be indicated. In these groupings, individuals are more apt to be open and candid about their true views and feelings about prejudice, discrimination, and other touchy topics because they can feel safer and more accepted while not having to worry about offending someone from another group. On the other hand, like groupings may reinforce stereotypes and not give participants a chance to hear the perspectives of other groups. Having mixed groups allows participants to hear how different co-workers experience diversity at work. For example, it might be eye-opening for Euro-American males to hear the frustrations of Latino, African-American, or female employees, and vice versa. In one organization where diversity was being discussed in a culturally mixed group of peers, the Euro-American males were shocked to hear one of their colleagues, an Asian-American, talk about his experiences with prejudice and discrimination in what they thought was an open, accepting, and equal environment for all. It can also be insightful for different groups to realize they are not alone in some of their concerns and frustrations. Finally, it may be surprising for groups to learn that they are both the victims and the perpetrators of prejudice. It is important to choose the type of grouping that best suits your purposes.

Group size is another factor that will affect results of focus group data collection. The smaller the group, the greater the comfort and participation. However, if the group is too small, there may not be enough energy and divergence to spark a lively discussion. Generally, groups of 8 to 12 make for optimum discussion.

Time and Location

Since the purpose of focus groups is to elicit feelings, attitudes, and perceptions about a topic that is apt to generate strong emotional responses, enough time needs to be allotted for the discussion. It is frustrating for both participants and data collectors to have to cut off a lively and informative discussion midstream. Therefore, schedule at least 1½ hours per focus group session with a 30-minute cushion between sessions in case the discussion goes over the scheduled time frame. If it seems that there is more discussion needed, you always have the option of scheduling a follow-up session with the group. The 30-minute cushion also gives the data collector time to jot down observations and reactions.

Another important logistical element is location. Focus group discussions will tend to be more open and honest if held away from the work environment, far from the possibility of eavesdroppers, curious passersby, and work distractions such as beepers and phone messages or other interruptions. A meeting or conference room that allows for chairs to be arranged around a conference table or in a circle is also helpful so that participants can face one another.

Capturing Data

Information from discussions can be captured for later use in a number of different ways. With the permission of participants, the discussion can be taped and comments transcribed later. Comments can be charted or notes taken; however, this usually necessitates two facilitators—one to lead the discussion and the other to take notes or chart information. Another method sometimes used is for the facilitator to make notes immediately after the discussion. However, this may result in some data being lost.

Facilitation

Sessions need to be led by experienced and skilled facilitators, either in-house staff in the human resource department or outside consultants. The role of the facilitator is to keep discussion focused on the topics being investigated, to encourage active participation of all individuals present, and to set and enforce the ground rules of the discussion. In addition, the skilled facilitator is adept at questioning to probe for additional information and feelings about points made. The advantages and disadvantages of both in-house and outside facilitators have been discussed earlier in this chapter. Whichever is chosen, sessions need to have a structured agenda so that participants feel a sense of security and so that the objectives of the discussion are achieved. Notice the facilitator's role in the *Sample Focus Group Agenda*.

Topics and Questions for Discussion

In formulating focus group questions, remember that open-ended questions stimulate the most discussion, while topics related to issues of real concern for participants will elicit the most participation. Questions should then be formulated that will give you data about the issues you are investigating. Because they will produce much response, it is probably a good rule of thumb to limit the number of questions to four or five. Depending on your objectives, the *Sample Focus Group Questions* can give you examples of questions to stimulate discussion.

Diversity Quotient: Analyzing Organizational Demographics

One source of fruitful information in the overall assessment plan is in the area of organizational demographics. Statistics about your work force can give you an unvarnished look at diversity within the company. Some of this information may be on file in your human resource department; however, some may not have been collected. Before embarking on the collection of the data, be aware that you may get some resistance to this kind of assessment. In one organization, for example, many managers refused to respond to the surveys about the ethnic and racial composition of their staffs because they felt it was both irrelevant and an invasion of individuals' privacy. Ethnic labeling brought images of totalitarianism and government identity cards. It is important to tell staff why you are collecting this information and how it will be used so you can allay fears and reduce resistance. "We need to find out about the composition of our staff so we can meet the needs of everyone. That's why we are gathering information about all employees. The data will remain anonymous and will not be connected with anyone's name."

As a first step, you will need to determine which demographic statistics you require and where you can obtain this information; see the *Analyzing Organizational Demographics* chart.

Sample Focus Group Agenda

1. Introduction of facilitator and explanation of the general purpose of the focus group sessions, as well as who will see the data.

2. Self-introduction of participants by name.

3. Objectives of the group discussion:
    *   Gain employees' perceptions about how the organization is dealing with a diverse work force.
    *   Learn about diversity-related barriers to teamwork, productivity, and motivation.
    *   Hear employees' concerns, ideas, and suggestions about dealing with diversity.

4. Ground rules of the session:
    *   Confidentiality of sources, with input reported anonymously.
    *   Each person speaks for self.
    *   Every perception is valid; no arguing with perceptions.
    *   One person speaks at a time.
    *   Get permission to tape if desired.

5. Present questions for discussion, giving participants time to jot down ideas and points. (Questions may be on an overhead transparency, flip chart, and/or handout.)

6. Facilitate discussion.
    *   Keep participants focused on the questions asked.
    *   Chart comments and responses as stated.
    *   Clarify points and ask for specific examples when vague comments or generalizations are made.
    *   Maintain objectivity and do not enter into the discussion.

7. Wrap up the discussion, summarizing themes or making a concluding statement that refers back to objectives.

8. Thank participants and tell them what will happen with data.

Sample Focus Group Questions

These questions are examples of the kind of discussion "pump primers" you can use to get people talking and to focus their comments on the areas you are investigating.

- What are signs that this organization values a diverse work force?

- What are the obstacles in the way of employees who are different from the mainstream?

- What organizational practices, policies, or norms keep diverse groups from succeeding and/or moving up?

- As a member of a minority group in this organization, how do you feel you are treated?

- What kinds of prejudice or discrimination have you faced, if any?

- What do you wish members of other groups knew about you or your group?

- What do you wish your manager understood about you?

- What do you wish management understood about your group?

- What contributions and behaviors are most valued and rewarded in this organization?

- What do you need to do and/or know to get ahead in this organization?

- What would you like to know and/or learn that could help you succeed here?

- How comfortable, accepted, and valued do you feel in this organization? Why?

- What groups are easiest/hardest for you to work cooperatively with?

- What behaviors of other groups are most difficult for you to deal with or most irritating?

- What do you think the organization could do to get the best from everyone?

Analyzing Organizational Demographics

	Executives Number/ Percent	Managers Number/ Percent	Supervisors Number/ Percent	Staff Number/ Percent
Staff Composition				
Gender:				
Male	___/___	___/___	___/___	___/___
Female	___/___	___/___	___/___	___/___
Total	___/___	___/___	___/___	___/___
Ethnicity:				
Euro-American	___/___	___/___	___/___	___/___
African-American	___/___	___/___	___/___	___/___
Latino	___/___	___/___	___/___	___/___
Middle Eastern	___/___	___/___	___/___	___/___
Asian	___/___	___/___	___/___	___/___
Pacific Islanders	___/___	___/___	___/___	___/___
Native American	___/___	___/___	___/___	___/___
Other	___/___	___/___	___/___	___/___
Total	___/___	___/___	___/___	___/___

Languages Spoken

	Number	Percent
Native English speakers	___	___
Fluent, accented-English speakers (strong accent)	___	___
Limited-English speakers (strong accent)	___	___
Non-English speakers	___	___
Bilingual	___	___
Spanish/English	___	___
Tagalog/English	___	___
Japanese/English	___	___
Vietnamese/English	___	___
Chinese (Mandarin)/English	___	___
Chinese (Cantonese)/English	___	___
Arabic/English	___	___
Korean/English	___	___
Armenian/English	___	___
Hebrew/English	___	___
Russian/English	___	___
_____/English		

Personal Data

	Men Number/ Percent	Women Number/ Percent
Married	___/___	___/___
Single	___/___	___/___
Dual parent	___/___	___/___
Single parent	___/___	___/___

Suggestions for Using *Analyzing Organizational Demographics*

Objectives:

- Examine organization demographics related to diversity.
- Provide data for analysis and decision making regarding diversity.

Intended Audience:

- Human resource professionals collecting data for diversity planning.
- Diversity development task forces gathering baseline data.

Processing the Activity:

- Data collectors gather statistics about each category, compiling information and computing percentages. Data can be gathered through self-report questionnaires, personnel records, and/or management observation.
- Data can be analyzed, summarized, and reported to appropriate planning group.

Questions for Discussion:

- How do organizational statistics compare with those of the work force in the area? Population in the area?
- What surprises or questions are there?
- What do these statistics indicate for the organization in terms of needs, potential opportunities, and possible problems?

Caveats and Considerations:

- Some individuals may regard information requested as too personal and may balk at the categorization.
- Some individuals will see the categorization as divisive rather than as a first step in remedying deficiencies that may exist.
- Careful explanation of the purposes of this survey and its use in identifying organization needs is required.

What does your survey of demographic data tell you about diversity within your organization? Having a meeting with executive and/or management staff to discuss the following questions might be useful:

- What do our demographics say about the diversity of our staff at each level?
- How closely do our percentages mirror the local population? Our client/customer base?
- Are there groups that are underrepresented? At what levels?
- What surprises are there in the figures?
- What challenges does this information present?
- Are there changes called for in light of demographic trends in the larger society? In our client/customer base?

Analyzing Turnover Statistics for Clues to Diversity Management

Another method of getting information about an organization's diversity management is to analyze existing statistical data regarding turnover. In analyzing this data, you may be able to zero in on specific causes—whether diversity-related or not—which can only be addressed once they are uncovered. In one organization, for example, an African-American female professional was recruited away by another organization. Even though this "raiding" of employees is not an uncommon practice, management spent time investigating her reasons for leaving. Though the new position was exciting and challenging, it involved a move to another city. Management wanted to know what factors influenced her to accept the offered position. What they found was that she had continuously felt she was bumping up against a brick wall in this white-male-dominated organization and was frustrated by the constant inability to get people to hear what she was saying. When asked why she had never complained, she said it was obvious to her that this "deaf ear" to the concerns of women and nondominant group members was sanctioned organizational practice. While it was too late to keep this employee, management got some critical feedback that led them to question their communication and promotion practices and begin working on making conditions more inclusive. Though on the surface things look fine, these kinds of subtle underlying issues and problems can be the undoing of even the best diversity efforts. This kind of information often emerges only through in-depth exit interviewing.

Organizational feedback can also be obtained from turnover statistics by searching for answers to such questions as:

- What are the rates of turnover in each department, section, division, or unit? How do these compare to other units? To industry or profession standards?
- What is the gender, ethnic, and racial breakdown of the turnover percentages? Are they at parity with overall turnover percentages within the organization?
- Are there departments, groups, or areas that stand out because of their higher or lower percentages?
- What factors within these groups might lead to these higher or lower turnover rates?
- What information is uncovered in exit interviews? What reasons do employees

give for leaving? (Is there in-depth exit interviewing to get beyond superficial responses?)

- To what do managers attribute the high or low turnover rates of diverse employees?

Information obtained from this analysis may be able to give you clues about how to retain diverse employees and why they leave. This information can be helpful feedback for individual managers and valuable input in designing management development training programs.

Observation Checklist for Assessing Morale and Work-Group Cohesiveness

As a manager, you may not be in a position to institute organization-wide programs in diversity training or the development of diversity at all levels of the company. However, you can and do manage the work-group environment of your staff. In that role you may need a tool to help you assess the morale and cohesiveness of your staff. Many of the tools you have already learned about can be used or adapted for use with your staff. You may also be able to assess these factors without questionnaires or focus groups by using your own observation skills. The *Morale and Work-Group Cohesiveness Observation Checklist* can help you in that process. It can also be used as a work-group checklist by simply asking staff members to react based on their own observations.

Morale and Work-Group Cohesiveness Observation Checklist

Check those statements that describe your staff most of the time.

_____ Employees of different groups help one another without being asked.

_____ Staff members eat lunch and spend breaks in mixed groups.

_____ Employees talk freely and openly with one another.

_____ There are no cliques or in-group/out-group divisions among staff.

_____ Employees take initiative in solving problems and making suggestions about improvements.

_____ Employees do not blame one another for problems.

_____ Employees freely voice their views to their manager.

_____ Employees are proud to work in this department/unit/division.

_____ There is low absenteeism.

_____ There is low turnover.

_____ There is laughter and good-natured humor in the work group.

_____ No employees are left out of work-group camaraderie.

_____ Employees of different backgrounds work together cooperatively.

_____ There is little friction between staff from different cultures or of different life-styles.

_____ There is seldom petty gossiping or backstabbing.

_____ Employees are willing to help each other out during stressful or demanding times.

_____ The workload is shared equitably by all.

_____ Employees celebrate together.

_____ Employees make an effort to help newcomers become part of the team.

_____ Employees go out of their way to understand employees whose English is limited or accented.

Suggestions for Using the *Morale and Work-Group Cohesiveness Observation Checklist*

Objectives:

- Assess work-group morale and cohesiveness.
- Pinpoint obstacles to teamwork.
- Identify employees' irritations, concerns, and problems that may be blocking productivity.

Intended Audience:

- Managers and supervisors seeking to increase the cohesiveness and morale of their teams.
- Trainees in a management/supervisory development class or managing diversity seminar.
- Members of a diverse work group seeking to strengthen the team.

Processing the Activity:

- Individuals check those conditions and factors they observe in their work team.
- Groups discuss those items checked and not checked, focusing on strength and weaknesses of the team.
- Items not checked are discussed with regard to their impact on the team.
- Weaknesses are listed and prioritized, and areas for development are targeted.
- Individual managers can target specific areas to begin working on to strengthen their own team.

Questions for Discussion:

- What strengths and weaknesses are indicated?
- What is at the root of the weaknesses?
- Which issues have highest priority for attention?
- How can these areas be strengthened?
- What can you/we do to begin working on the problems surfaced?

Caveats and Considerations:

- Managers making observations of their own staffs will tend to lack objectivity. It is helpful to suggest having a few other people in the group or the whole team respond to get a more rounded view.
- Weaknesses indicated need to be investigated further to find out underlying reasons, conditions, and organization systems that may be at the heart.

The more items checked, the greater the work-group morale and cohesion. Those descriptions not checked may indicate problems in motivation or relationships. Checking into these areas may turn up the underlying differences in cultural programming that are causing individuals to misinterpret each other's behavior, act on inaccurate assumptions, or make prejudicial judgments. These kinds of problems can signal a need for cultural sensitivity training and diversity-related team building. They may also be a sign that the manager needs to restructure roles and responsibilities so that people of different groups learn to work together. Assigning tasks or projects across race, gender, cultural, physical ability, and sexual orientation lines, for example, is one way to structure this work-group desegregation.

Using Interviews as a Method of Collecting Data

A third method of gathering assessment data is through one-on-one interviews. While time-consuming and expensive, interviews can be a rich source of in-depth information about attitudes, conditions, and problems. Interviews need to be conducted by individuals skilled in this process and those who have objectivity regarding the issues and personalities involved. The following tips can guide you in getting the most from this method. In addition, the material on interviewing found in Chapter 9 can be helpful.

1. *Know what you are after.* Determining what information you arc seeking helps you select the most appropriate individuals to talk with and the most relevant questions to ask. If you want to find out about problems between supervisors and their staffs, interviewing executive managers won't help, while asking supervisors about organizational diversity strategy will also miss the mark.
2. *Establish rapport and build trust.* Begin the interview with a few minutes of person-to-person contact, explaining the purpose of the interview, why the interviewee has been selected, how the data will help their organization, and how the information will be used. Assure the individual of confidentiality and anonymity in the reporting of data.
3. *Use carefully constructed questions.* Ask questions that get to the information you are after; however, be careful not to be so direct that you are perceived as intrusive. In addition, you may miss important data if your questions do not come at the issue from different directions.
4. *Use your questions as a guide, but be flexible.* Your objective is to get information, not to finish all your questions. Be careful not to have the interview become nothing more than an oral questionnaire. Listen to the interviewee's response and use that to prompt your next question. Ask for clarification, examples, and specifics as well: "Can you tell me more about that problem?" "Give me a specific example of that issue." "In what ways is that attitude a problem?"
5. *Don't be afraid of silence.* Jumping in with the next question to fill the void may cause you to miss important information. Interviewees generally give the safest and most superficial information first and get more candid as they talk. Wait and listen.
6. *Listen for the unstated message.* Pay attention to nonverbal cues. One of the advantages of this method is that it gives you the opportunity to pick up the

50 percent of the communication that is not in the words. Pay attention to tone and speed of speech. Also watch body language and facial expressions. You can pick up much about the feelings and attitudes—such as uneasiness, tension, irritation, or disbelief—from rolled eyes, crossed arms, and furrowed brows, for example.

7. *Capture the data.* Utilize the most comfortable and effective method for keeping the data from the interview. Either taping, with the permission of the interviewee, or taking notes during the interview is generally used. Waiting until after the interview risks losing some information.

While you will need to construct questions that suit your purposes, the three sets of sample interview questions (for leaders and policymakers, non-dominant-culture employees, and dominant-culture employees) can trigger your thinking.

Sample Interview Questions for Leaders and Policymakers

1. What have been the biggest benefits of having a multicultural work force? What are the biggest problems and frustrations?

2. With an increasingly diverse work force, what changes do you see in productivity? Interpersonal dynamics? Bottom line (e.g., training dollars spent on education)?

3. What challenges does this present to your organization?

4. What is your organization doing to help your managers meet these challenges? What do they need to learn to do differently?

5. How do you measure and reward your managers in this area?

6. What is your organization doing to enhance the upward mobility of non-dominant-group members? What obstacles prevent this mobility?

7. What processes do you have to identify and develop a diverse pool of talented employees?

8. What does your organization do that shows you value cultural diversity?

9. What is your organization doing to accommodate differences in values, norms, and mores?

10. What made you decide to invest your organization's resources (time, energy, money) in making diversity development a priority? What results have you seen?

11. What organizational systems, practices, and policies present obstacles to fully developing and utilizing your diverse work force?

12. If your organization does nothing to address the cultural diversity issue, what do you predict will happen?

Sample Interview Questions for Non-Dominant-Culture Employees

1. What do you like about the culture of this organization?

2. What do you find difficult about it?

3. What did you expect to find when you came to work here? What was your biggest surprise? Biggest joy? Biggest disappointment?

4. What kinds of experiences made you feel welcome in this organization? Unwelcome? What did you do to help the situation?

5. What is your professional goal? What do you hope to achieve here?

6. How has this organization helped you toward your goal? How could it help more?

7. Have you ever felt it was a mistake to come to work here? If so, what made you feel this way?

8. How have you been treated by bosses and co-workers (both good and bad news)?

9. How do you get along with people of other groups in the workplace?

10. On a scale of 1 to 10, how much do you feel a part of the organization? What needs to happen to make you feel more a part of it?

11. What is the most important thing the organization can do to help you adjust? What can you do?

Sample Interview Questions for Dominant-Culture Employees

1. What have been the biggest changes in this organization the past few years?

2. What have been the biggest benefits of being part of a multicultural work force? What are the biggest problems and frustrations?

3. How does diversity in the work force impact you? Your work group? This organization?

4. What has been the biggest "culture shock" for you in working with diverse groups?

5. What kinds of experiences make you feel comfortable with employees from different groups? Uncomfortable? What did you do to help the situation?

6. How have you been treated by employees of diverse groups?

7. What is the most important thing your organization can do to help non-dominant-group members adapt to this organization?

8. What is the most important thing these employees can do to help themselves adapt?

Bringing Your Organizational Snapshot into Focus

While this chapter has given you a variety of assessment techniques, all the tools in the world won't help if you don't ask the right questions in planning your audit and in analyzing the data once they are collected. The following can be helpful guides in designing your audit:

1. What do we want to find out?
2. What are the most useful tools we can use?
3. Where can we find the information we need? (Which organizational statistics? Which individuals? Which groups?)
4. Who should coordinate and conduct this audit for optimum results?
5. What kind of a budget do we have to work with?
6. What do the collected data tell us?
7. What next steps are indicated? Where do we go from here?
8. What kind of commitment are we willing to make? What are we willing to do about what we have found out?

An organizational audit will give you the clearest, most revealing picture of your organization if you choose the most appropriate tools, focus on the richest sources of information, and seek the most relevant data to answer your questions. The process involves careful planning, thorough implementation, and thoughtful analysis of the collected data.

Chapter 9

Recruiting for a Diverse Workplace

This chapter will give you:

1. Tools to use with groups or individuals who need coaching about how to create a less culturally biased interview process.
2. Strategies to enhance your recruitment and hiring of diverse individuals.
3. Suggestions for ways to expand your cross-cultural network.
4. Skills in asking interview questions in culturally sensitive ways.
5. Information about how values, assumptions, and biases impact hiring and recruitment efforts.

Actions Speak Louder than Words: Demonstrating Organizational Commitment to Diversity

There is a saying by Ralph Waldo Emerson pertinent to assessing an organization's commitment to recruiting and hiring a diverse work force. "I can't hear what you're saying because what you are rings so loudly in my ears." His use of language was appropriate in the 18th century. In today's fast-paced society, we say, "Actions speak louder than words" or, shorter still, "Walk the talk." What do any of these admonitions about practicing what we preach have to do with hiring or recruiting a pluralistic work force? Simply this: It is easier to talk about valuing a diverse employee base than it is to actually find, hire, and recruit one.

Make no mistake. Words are important in sending a message about the value of creating diversity in your environment, but beyond the rhetoric, a key question remains: What is your organization doing to secure and develop a diverse work force? What we aren't talking about here are quotas where you find a person of a particular color, ethnic background, age, or sexual preference to fill a slot. What we are talking about is an organization's willingness to truly open up the applicant pool and provide hiring and promotional opportunities to talented, experienced people regardless of gender, color, age, physical abilities, or sexual preference.

We can already hear the chorus of people saying, "We want to hire a diverse staff—we just can't find the people." Well, this chapter is about helping you uncover creative ways to find the talent, and that's the easy part. The hard part lies in creating an organization where the environment is inclusive and accepting enough that a person who is different from the dominant group feels comfortable, wants to join you, and, more important, stays. As we said earlier, talk is cheap, but actions speak volumes. Your company's commitment to this issue is demonstrated in tangible clues. To find out if your company has this commitment, do a little investigative work. Put on your sleuth hat and respond to the following questions:

1. What is the ethnic, racial, and gender composition of your workplace?
2. What is the age span of the workers?
3. What percentage of top management are people of color, women, or those who are differently abled? How do the percentages change when applied to middle management? First-line staff?
4. Is the ethnic and cultural distribution the same from top to bottom in the organization, or are all white males in the executive suite and all Hispanics in environmental engineering?

Responses to these questions give you a partial answer to the level of your organization's commitment on this issue. But while some companies like Xerox and Corning have demonstrated their commitment for years through their hiring and promotional practices, others aren't yet sold on the idea of diversity being factored into the hiring equation. For them, the case still needs to be made.

Should Diversity Be Part of the Hiring and Promotion Equation?

The short answer to the job analysis question is yes, but only if you want your organization to survive and thrive. We say that, not because it is a moral or ethical imperative (although we believe it is), but because the demographics demand action. If you haven't read *Workforce 2000*, you can get a clear sense of the demographics by looking at Chapter 11 of this book. Beyond the data, let's look at some of the business imperatives that indicate attention to this issue is both warranted and critical.

Planning Requires Short- and Long-Range Goals

Remaining competitive in a globalized economy necessitates forecasting on any number of issues; among them are capital outlay, research and development, and the skill level and availability of the labor pool. It is this last that ties directly to the question of diversity as part of the equation. Whether we're talking about short-range goals, which are defined as planning for this year and next, or long-range goals, defined as three to five years in our rapidly changing world, your considerations regarding the labor pool lead to the same conclusion. This is not an issue that can be ducked in most companies. If you doubt the validity of that statement, consider this. John Lynch, worldwide affirmative action manager for Hewlett-Packard, made the observation that 30 years ago, most engineering graduates were white males. Those numbers are dramatically different today. If Hewlett-Packard and other companies as well want to remain industry leaders, there is no viable alternative to attracting, hiring, and developing the current diverse work force into effective managers.[11]

The Composition of the Work Force Changes before Our Eyes

The case cannot be made strongly enough for taking the issue of work-force composition changes seriously. Check out the following facts:

1. While the numbers of white males in the work force are declining, in the next decade, 64 percent of the growth in the labor force will be from women.
2. Gender is only one aspect of diversity. Age is another, and the reality of the aging work force, like age itself, is creeping up on us. In fact, age may be the quiet giant of the diversity issue. The Bureau of Labor Statistics indicates that of the 75 million people of the baby-boom generation, most are over 40 years old. And according to the Social Security Administration, the number of people age 65 or older is expected to more than double, from 30 million to 68 million, by the year 2040.[11]

The Diverse Employee Base Is Paralleled by a Diverse Consumer Base

The percentage growth of Hispanics and Asians is dramatic. Hispanics made up only 7 percent of the labor force in 1986 but will constitute 10 percent by the year 2000, according to the U.S. Census Bureau, and there are indications that in cities like Los Angeles, the growth in the Latino population has been underreported. It has grown from 8 million to almost 19 million, and this group runs more than 400,000 businesses in the United States. These businesses generate $18 billion dollars in sales.[11] What constitutes making an issue a bottom-line consideration?

Those kind of numbers and dollars, for starters. Smart companies will reach out to address the needs of the diverse communities that are part of their consumer base. How best to do that? By understanding the group you are trying to serve. This understanding comes most easily when you hire employees who are part of that community.

The "Grapevine" Never Rests—Your Reputation Will Precede You

Attracting the best talent in a seller's market occurs when the word gets out that yours is a comfortable, welcoming company in which to work—a company where talent and individual differences are respected and rewarded. Xerox and U.S. West, for example, do not have to cheerlead or shout about what inviting companies they are, or about how much opportunity they provide for people of any background who are willing and able to do the job. Their hiring and promotion decisions speak for them.

Neutralizing the Application Process

An organization truly committed to getting and maintaining a diverse work force will pay attention to just how "applicant friendly" the company really is. It is of little comfort to open the doors to applicants if they strangle on the application process. "Applicant friendliness" involves cultivating and welcoming talent among groups of individuals from different backgrounds whose norms, values, and customs may not be identical to those of the dominant group. Do employees in your company have to be stamped out of a cookie cutter to get ahead? Try to imagine yourself a different age, color, gender, or background. Would you feel comfortable working there? Walking the proverbial mile in another person's moccasins will give you some very important information about your organization's openness so that you equalize the process for everyone. Answering questions in the *Neutralizing the Application Process Checklist* will help you identify obstacles that exist in your organization's application maze.

Neutralizing the Application Process Checklist

Answer each of the questions below by putting a check in the column that most accurately reflects the behavior of you or your organization.

Questions	Rarely	Sometimes	Often
1. All applicants are given the same information and get their questions answered.	____	____	____
2. When language problems exist, our organization finds a way around them through the use of pictures, interpreters, or the like.	____	____	____
3. Every interviewee for a particular job is asked the same questions. While interview style may change due to personal and cultural differences, the interview process is standard.	____	____	____
4. Interviewers avoid prejudging applicants based on appearance.	____	____	____
5. Interviewers don't jumpt to conclusions about someone's ability to do the job based on race, gender, age, ethnicity, or physical ability.	____	____	____
6. Interviewers and managers recognize and compensate for their own hiring preferences.	____	____	____
7. Applicants are interviewed by a diverse team.	____	____	____
8. There is a male/female mix on the interview team.	____	____	____
9. Interviewers are aware of cultural "hot spots" and avoid issues that may offend applicants.	____	____	____
10. Written application questions have been tested for cultural bias and ease of understanding.	____	____	____

How to Score the *Neutralizing the Application Process Checklist*

For each *Rarely* answer, score 1 point. For each *Sometimes* answer, score 2 points. For each *Often* answer, score 3 points.

1. _____	6. _____	
2. _____	7. _____	
3. _____	8. _____	
4. _____	9. _____	
5. _____	10. _____	
	Total: _____	

Interpretation

Warm	27–30 points	You and/or your organization have an applicant-friendly environment, warm and open to differences. You are successfully creating a neutral application process.
Temperate	21–26 points	You (or your organization) are making progress in neutralizing the application process but you've got a way to go. Don't rest on your beginning accomplishments.
Cool	10–20 points	Yours is a cool organization, not applicant-friendly. Diverse talent will pass you by. If you want to remain competitive in this labor pool, start making your application process more friendly.

Use this information as a starting point. Your one-point answers will give you some clear indications of where your organizational Achilles' heels are in the interview domain. That can be the beginning of some helpful and necessary changes.

Suggestions for Using the *Neutralizing the Application Process Checklist*

Objectives:

- Gain a sense of the openness and neutrality of your organization's application process for new hires.
- Get feedback from those in positions to hire, or recent new hires.
- Educate those in a position to bring new people on board.

Intended Audience:

- HR professional in charge of recruiting and hiring or in charge of educating managers about hiring.
- Managers who do their own hiring.
- Work teams who interview and pick new hires.
- Vice president in charge of HR who wants to raise the issue at top levels of the organization.

Processing the Activity:

- Distribute the questionnaire to those charged with the task of interviewing and hiring new employees. This can be given in a workshop setting or to individuals one-on-one.
- Ask them to respond by putting a check in the appropriate column. Then score the checklist.
- Whether in a workshop setting or discussed one-on-one, ask respondent to look at one- and two-point answers.

Questions for Discussion:

- What do the data from this questionnaire indicate about your application process?
- Where can you or your interview team pat yourselves on the back for creating an open and neutral environment?
- What do you need to still do to make it more so?

Caveats and Considerations:

- If an HR vice president gives this to one manager, he or she may suggest that the whole interview team look it over and discuss it before the next interview.
- This would be a good tool to give to recent new hires for feedback. That information could be distributed to the appropriate sources.

How to Find, Recruit, and Hire a Diverse Work Force

The most common complaint we hear from companies who say they truly want to expand the diversity of their population is that they don't know where to find the personnel. For those of you who fit into this category, help is now on the way. Your search becomes much simpler when you realize that there are only two main scouting locations: *outside* the organization and *inside*. Both have benefits and costs attached.

Recruiting Outside

The biggest cost to recruiting outside the organization is not the recruiting cost itself, although that is not cheap. It is the demoralization of those who are on the inside. The unselected employee's question will be, ''Why not me? I know the organization, I'm committed to it, and I have a good track record. With a little training, I'd be perfect.'' There is no culture where feeling rejected is painless or comfortable. But in some cultures, the consequences are larger than in others. Those who are overlooked will probably feel they have lost face and be embarrassed. Some may even quit. This situation could lead to low morale and dissatisfaction among loyal friends of the employee who was not promoted. That doesn't mean, however, that the cost of employee discontent should deter you from not looking outside when it is appropriate.

Outside versus inside is one of the issues facing the Los Angeles Police Department, whose last chapter has yet to be written in its search for a new chief. What is clear is that the struggle for an appropriate replacement for the current chief involves the very issues we are talking about. Does Los Angeles need a chief untainted by the Rodney King incident? If the choice is for a ''breath of fresh air'' over an inside candidate, what will the morale in the department be? And if the selection committee doesn't go outside, what will citizen morale be? The department has never hired an outsider for its chief. Can an outsider well versed in policing even test well in this process if he or she doesn't know the ropes unique to this city? These questions show up in real-life organizations every day, and the answers are not cut-and-dried in the Los Angeles Police Department or in any other organization where they show themselves.

With so many potential negatives to outside recruiting, what might get an organization to do it any way? For starters, there may not be an existing pool of candidates from whom to draw. If you are actively seeking a broader employee base among women, people of color, the elderly, or the differently abled, you may have to look outside. In addition, organizations balance the inside/outside question when new blood is needed to get the organizational adrenaline pumping again or for purposes of gaining a different perspective. Maybe you are seeking skills or experience that no one currently employed seems to have. One thing is for certain: Egos transcend culture and language differences, so any promotion or recruitment needs to be handled with great sensitivity to all involved. With these considerations in mind, let us give you a number of places to scout the local talent. Among companies using creative recruiting strategies, Vons grocery stores in Southern California wages the battle for effective recruitment and retention on several fronts (see box titled *Recruitment and Retention Strategies of Vons Groceries*). *But there are other good strategies as well.*

1. Explore Community Nooks and Crannies. Estella Romero, president of

Estella Romero Enterprises, a consulting firm that specializes in marketing strategies and community outreach to the Latino consumer in Southern California, gets tremendous results by cultivating her local community. Some of the sources she mentions can be tapped in any community. Among them are the following:[34]

- *Adult education classes:* Many new immigrants congregate here for the purpose of learning English. Besides language skills, they also learn other skills in order to find gainful employment. There is a ripe and ready work force here, eager for training and opportunity.
- *Parent advisory groups and the PTA:* Some parents associated with local schools have skills, need, and drive but lack the confidence and know-how to convert these skills to paying jobs. Giving them an opportunity and some on-the-job training will result in loyal employees.
- *Local churches, synagogues, mosques, or other religious centers:* These are wonderful places to network because religious-based community groups and churches are among the most active in helping immigrants and disadvantaged groups get into the economic and social mainstream of life. Those in these religious centers are already being helped through the acculturation process, so their learning and adaptation curves accelerate.
- *Ethnic student associations on local college and university campuses:* This avenue provides targeted outreach to a specific population. It can be a good source of networking for both present and future jobs.
- *Government job training programs:* These programs provide skill and training, job preparation, and placement services.
- *Refugee resettlement agencies:* Such social service agencies help immigrants adjust to life in the United States. This might involve learning the language, finding a job, or taking care of others' resettlement needs. These agencies are nonprofit organizations that generally target one nationality or ethnic group.
- *Employee referrals:* Who you know can open doors at all levels of organizational life. In one utility company, a personal relationship got somebody a job in the housekeeping department. This is the first time the newly hired immigrant has ever had health benefits and a steady job without waiting on street corners every day looking for work. He was asked by a number of employees how he got the job because their brothers and cousins are on the waiting list. He played the innocent, but in truth, a professional colleague who worked with the division head pleaded his case, and he was hired. In your continuing efforts to attract top talent, one satisfied employee can be your best recruiter. In communities that have not always felt embraced by mainstream America, an endorsement by a fellow employee can mean a lot.
- *Elementary school outreach:* Chuck Canales, the personnel officer at Olive View Medical Center in the San Fernando Valley, starts recruiting in elementary school. He targets fourth and fifth graders at career fairs. Armed with balloons, pencils, and information, he plants the seeds early about good job opportunities in health care that are realistic and reachable for the kids he talks to.

Instead of going to a career fair, Sheriff Sherman Block of Los Angeles County did some unintended recruiting when he went to address the questions and concerns of a class of local elementary school kids. The indirect recruiting happened like this. The students are given a weekly assignment of writing a letter to someone in the news about an issue of importance to them. One particular week, after a

Recruitment and Retention Strategies of Vons Groceries (A Chain of Southern California Supermarkets)

Group	Recruitment Strategies
Minorities	Early school links
	Explain opportunities
	Identified career paths
	Image enhancement
	Role models
	Cultural awareness
Homemakers	Increased flexibility
	Child-care considerations
	School-term-only jobs
	Image enhancement
	Wage/benefit information
Retirees	Increased flexibility
	Image enhancement
	Role models
	Recruitment targets
	Wage/benefit information
	Part-time shifts
Students	Increased flexibility
	School-term-only jobs
	Image enhancement
	Wage/benefit information
	OJT programs
	Identified career paths
Mentally/ physically challenged	Agency contacts
	Explain opportunities
	Role models
	OJT programs
	Job content-flexibility
Retention Strategies	Employee orientation
	Service training
	Management training
	Literacy training
	Employee association
	Service awards
	Retention bonuses

young man had been shot and killed by the sheriff's department in a local housing development, this class of primarily Latino students wrote the sheriff about this incident, in search of answers to questions that troubled them. Rather than answer 35 separate letters, the sheriff called the teacher and asked for permission to come to class and talk to the kids face-to-face. He spent two hours answering their questions and making a pitch for a life of education rather than drugs and gangs as the best way to avoid this young man's tragic fate. When one little girl in a wheelchair asked Block if she could become a sheriff, he told her that if she got her education she could probably become anything she wanted to. At the end of the two hours with the class, Sheriff Block asked how many students might someday be interested in a career with the sheriff's department. Every hand in the class went up, including the teacher's. To her, he sent an application. To the students, he planted seeds about the value of education. In one way or another, law enforcement will hopefully reap the rewards. Recruitment is not a short-term strategy. Good recruiting is a combination of strategic thinking and the willingness to make a long-term investment.

2. Be Creative in How You Sell Your Company by What You Offer. Flexible benefit packages as well as flexible work hours can make your company very attractive. For example, looking at benefit packages that contain provisions for child care, or flextime that allows two new mothers to share one full-time position will not only help you hire an able work force but will enable you to retain them as well. To recruit female employees, offering provisions for elder care can also be an inducement.

3. Tap the Talent of Underutilized Groups. Two such groups come to mind immediately: One is our senior citizens and the other is the differently abled. Employment statistics on our aging work force make seniors a particularly interesting group to tap. With the over-55 market ballooning, this is an experienced, responsible group with much to offer. In a country that for years has extolled the virtues of the "Pepsi generation," an emphasis on age and experience rather than youth and potential may take some getting used to. Nevertheless, this group can contribute to an organization's bottom line in a full-time, part-time, on-call, or project basis. Seniors have the reputation of being devoted and dependable employees who still have the Protestant work ethic. Your company gains a dedicated worker, the senior gains a sense of being useful and making a difference, and all of society gains because we aren't discarding our human resources. We have seen this work magically in the field of education where retired "lifers" come back to tutor kids and work with teachers in a variety of ways, or in the fast-food industry where three generations of employees may be working side by side with those who have below-normal IQs. A little ingenuity can do the same for you with both seniors or the differently abled.

4. Build Ties that Bind. It's time to take a page from the book of organized athletics. For years, college coaches have been masters of building ties to local high school coaches, and the pros have done the same with the colleges and universities. Everyone who follows sports can recall some story about a heavy recruiting battle for top talent. While an athlete's high school coach can't make the decision about where his star athlete should play college ball, he very likely will have some influence. He can start the process by tipping off some college coach.

What works in sports will work in business, law enforcement, or any place else you need to recruit. Just ask Sheriff Sherman Block how he recruits in the Asian immigrant community. Recruitment there has been a difficult task for several reasons. First of all, for most Asian refugees, police were part of the problem in their former countries, so this is an occupation where there is no trust. Furthermore, particularly in the Chinese and Japanese community, police work is not viewed by parents as a desirable profession for their sons and daughters. Sheriff Block stated in an interview that recruiting in the Asian community is "analogous to recruiting star athletes. You sit down with the family and convince everyone involved that this is a worthy endeavor." Block uses Asian recruiters and gets help from Asian community groups. Nevertheless, his work is cut out for him. What brings him success is building the ties like coaches have done for years. It's time for you to systematically do the same—at universities, local community colleges, trade schools, community organizations, or wherever else you determine you can set up a talent pipeline.

5. Have a Full-Time Minority Recruiter.   Hiring talent from diverse populations becomes most efficient and effective when you have a full-time minority recruiter. As in any successful venture, building a network of good people who are trusted requires long-term effort, and targeting the minority recruitee is no exception. One company that has done this very successfully is Bristol-Myers. According to Lionel Stevens, the corporate director of equal opportunity and recruitment programs, the attempt to recruit minority members with specialized skills such as internal auditors or systems analysts requires doing unique things. Stevens sees this talent as a scarce commodity and his organization is willing to invest to get the results by having a full-time professional.[31]

6. Make Your Commitment to Minority Recruitment Visible.   In order to recruit people of color effectively, the effort needs to be more than just a spotty one. No one you hire will like being thought of as a statistic or someone who just fills a slot. In the case of a woman of color, she won't be any happier to think she fills two slots. A company like Bristol-Myers won't run into that perception by their new hires because of the visible long-term efforts they sustain. Bristol-Myers provides financial support to companies that develop talent among people of color and invests in educating gifted individuals. The company also has a well-established program that provides minority fellowships, both at universities and through personnel associations. They make it their business to invest in human capital. In so doing, their actions do shout very loudly about their commitment, and the end result is that they are a very attractive company when hiring time comes around. Make your effort both conscious and consistent.

Recruiting Inside

Looking inside the organization is the other invaluable way to promote and reward deserving talent. The main benefit of staying inside the company is that you build loyalty within the existing work force. It's also cheaper. The learning curve is shorter since your promotees are already acculturated to company mores. Rewarding those on board sends a message to other employees that hard work, good performance, and dedication will pay off. The downside of promoting from within is that you can miss some top talent by looking only inside. You can also become too inbred. Sometimes, that outsider can blow a much needed breath of fresh air through a musty environment. Deciding whether to promote from inside or hire from outside requires balancing the organization's objectives against the skills and experience of the existing labor pool. In some fields, companies are so desperate for personnel that they take whatever they can get. Regardless of where you look, there are five important values (see table) in mainstream American culture that are different from those in than most other cultures. It will be helpful for you to think about these alternative views so that cultural bias doesn't affect your hiring or promotion decisions, no matter where you find prospective employees.

Not recognizing these subtle but powerful aspects of culture may cause you to sell some applicants short and mistake a lack of self-promotion for a of lack of interest, or an emphasis on collaboration rather than competition as a lack of drive. Recognizing these cultural influences should help you to have more discerning judgment as you go through the finding, hiring, and promotion process.

Creative Cultural Networking: Your Ace Recruiting Tool

We recently wrote an article entitled "Who You Know Does Count!" for a newspaper in Los Angeles. It was directed to job seekers and touted the value of building relationships. Our article stated that in today's volatile job market, your only job security may be in the contacts you develop and nurture. As an employer, the proverbial shoe is on a different foot; nevertheless, some of the main points are still relevant. Your ability to attract the best and the brightest will be impacted in part by the extent of your contacts. Building a "rainbow rolodex" requires some creative cultural networking.

Cultural networking is your ability to develop individual relationships with people from diverse backgrounds, and in so doing, build a large bank of human resources that you can call on when needed. Some of your best leads can come from your own employees but you also want to be sensitive to becoming too inbred. We know one hospital that hired their first Filipino in the accounting department, and every hiree after that was a Filipino recommended by that first person. Not only does this not create a diverse work force, but it is a questionable practice because it can lead to a ghettoized workplace.

Joining professional associations may help you get personnel leads when you need them. Maybe someone will take the initiative and call you about the one person you absolutely *must* interview. Perhaps some contact can tell you where you can go to comfortably ask questions regarding diversity-related issues or find out about cultural norms as you try to educate yourself and minimize faux pas. This cultural network may lead you to developing good friends from various backgrounds, but whether or not that is either achieved or desired, what it should enable you to do is get access to the invaluable talent pool that exists in every environment. The *Creative Cultural Networking Checklist* can be helpful by showing you what you are already doing to build your network and what actions you may still need to take.

Recognizing Values Differences in Your Hiring and Promotion Process

Mainstream America	Most Other Cultures	Impact
1. Work and obligation to the job are a high priority for many.	Primary obligation is to family and friends.	This values difference often causes American managers to question the loyalty and commitment that diverse employees have toward the company, as well as their motivation to do the job.
2. An organization has the right to terminate an employee. An employee has the right to leave a company for a variety of reasons.	Employment is for one's lifetime.	If an employee from another culture is terminated for not meeting performance standards, it may disgrace the employee. In addition to loss of face for the individual, there is the possibility that members of the same group will interpret termination as an affront. It could demoralize and affect group commitment and loyalty. The expectation of lifetime employment may make some managers gun-shy when they consider hiring someone from a diverse background.
3. There is a strong drive for personal achievement.	Personal ambition is frowned upon.	People who frown on personal ambition and who place group loyalty before personal reward may be perceived as lazy or unmotivated. Individuals from cultures where "tooting your own horn" is discouraged may not feel it is appropriate to seek promotion or even mention an interest in doing so. Managers will need to keep a special lookout for these "diamonds in the rough" and encourage them to take advantage of developmental activities, or sign up for promotional exams.
4. Competition is a valued way of stimulating performance.	Competition upsets balance and harmony.	People from immigrant cultures may not indicate interest in promoting or setting themselves apart from the crowd because loyalty to the group and a harmonious environment are more important. The danger here for the American manager is the false assumption that the person isn't motivated to do an excellent job and that he isn't aggressive or assertive enough to get the job done.
5. Loyalty is to the organization.	Loyalty is to individuals such as bosses or informal group leaders.	Employees from cultures that emphasize personal loyalty may see promotion as an act of disloyalty and lack of gratitude toward one's boss. Organizations need to understand the strong pull of boss and peer group loyalty when offering promotions and understand why this opportunity might not be received enthusiastically.

Creative Cultural Networking Checklist

Put a check by any statements that reflect what you are currently doing.

_____ 1. I belong to professional or social group where the membership is very diverse.

_____ 2. I consciously attend group functions where I am an outsider, where I don't know many people, and where some of them are of a different group (e.g., gender, ethnicity, race, or religion).

_____ 3. I create collegial relationships, friendships, or arrangements at work with people who are different from me.

_____ 4. At meetings, functions, or professional conferences, I make it my business to expand my contacts with people from diverse groups.

_____ 5. I attend various cultural support groups such as the Black Employees' Association at work, even though by background I am not a member of those networking groups.

_____ 6. I attend community functions, lectures, art exhibits, or holidays that celebrate diverse cultures.

_____ 7. I join civic groups apart from work where I have a chance to broaden my contacts.

_____ 8. I have hosted a networking party where I invited people from diverse backgrounds and asked them all to invite a friend or colleague.

_____ 9. I keep nurturing the relationships I have already developed so that my base of contacts grows.

_____ 10. I have joined an organization or currently subscribe to a publication whose top priority is cultural diversity.

Directions for scoring: Count your checks. The more you have, the more productively you create your cultural network. Our suggestion is that you target one or two of these specific items as a beginning point toward expanding your cultural network.

1. One thing I will do to more creatively develop my diversity network is _____ and I will do so by (date) _____ .

2. One thing I'm already doing well but could improve on a little is _____. I plan to capitalize on this networking technique by doing the following: _____.

Suggestions for Using the *Creative Cultural Networking Checklist*

Objectives:

- Offer suggestions about various places to expand contacts and gain greater access to pluralistic work force.
- Assess current outreach efforts.

Intended Audience:

- Human resource professional or manager in charge of hiring and promoting.
- Affirmative action officers in charge of hiring and promoting.
- External consultants specializing in diversity management who want to expand their network.

Processing the Activity:

- This self-assessment tool is primarily designed for those whose responsibility it is to expand the mix of employees at all levels of the organization through recruiting and promotion efforts. A single individual can take this assessment, see the results, and use it as a blueprint for greater outreach.
- If there is a companywide or divisionwide effort to expand the employee mix, this could be useful in a workshop setting to determine an organization-wide strategy.
- Have participants check the response they are engaged in. See what activities are not being covered by the group; then determine what efforts need to be made.
- The facilitator can take each item, one at a time, and see who is doing what. Areas ripe for exploration will emerge in the discussion.

Questions for Discussion:

- How many of you are involved in item number _____?
- What have been your results?
- What makes this work well?
- Are there things that might make this strategy more effective?
- Where should we put our energy as a group?
- Let's define commitment more specifically. Where are you willing to put your energy?

Caveats and Considerations:

- This can be very effective as a tool for individuals. Vice presidents of HR may want to share it with appropriate people on an as-needed basis.

To give you a little extra help, the following section presents some networking tips. If followed, they will pay big dividends when you need help in either the find, hire, or promotion stage.

Creative Networking Tips

1. Focus on Building Excellent Relationships with Good People of All Persuasions

Invest your time in cultivating people. You have limited time and energy, so you need to be discerning about whom you invest with, but the effort can have a very high payoff. We Americans hurt our competitiveness because, while we know relationships grease the wheels of business, we're too short-term in our thinking to invest the necessary time in building strong bonds. Many other cultures pay more attention to building relationships and nurturing people. They realize that the ability to transact business rests on trust, which builds slowly. If you are genuine and treat people as though they are worth getting to know, you will end up with memorable interactions, worthwhile colleagues or associates, and the results you want when you need them. It is sometimes difficult to remember in our "Pampers society" (easily disposable) that genuine relationships pay dividends *over the long haul*. But the truth is they do. Creative cultural networking, unlike Federal Express, does not deliver the goods overnight.

2. Let People You Meet Know What Kind of Jobs Your Company Has Available

Networking can be a very cost-effective way of advertising or recruiting. If you are actively seeking candidates or contacts, don't keep it a secret. We frequently see this in our business. People call to find out whether we teach accent reduction or are bilingual and can work with different groups on a variety of organizational issues. When the work that is requested is not our area of expertise, we always refer the caller to other consultants. Sometimes the people to whom we refer the caller are not exactly right, but they usually know someone else who will be. It works for everyone. There is a method to this madness that has unwittingly been set to poetry. Part of a line from Robert Frost's "The Road Not Taken" is applicable here: "way leads on to way." One person will lead you to another, to another, to another, and eventually you'll hit paydirt.

3. Develop Patience and Realize Some Goals Are Accomplished Indirectly

The punctuality and goal orientation of mainstream American culture can come into direct conflict with the slower, more deliberate pace and emphasis on relationship building in Mexico, Central America, Asia, and the Middle East. It is difficult for a culture that espouses the aphorism "Time is money" to realize that the direct route is not always the fastest or best. We have an acquaintance who managed a project in Kuwait. He invested a full 30 percent of his time in building relationships. His bosses back in the United States were totally frustrated at the pace of the project, but he told them it had to be done his way or he'd leave. He understood the culture he was living in and was willing to live by Kuwaitis' values. By building trust and nurturing relationships, he brought the project in on time. Sometimes the shortest distance between two points is not a straight line.

4.   Give as Well as Take

Symbolic tokens of appreciation are significant in most cultures. Sometimes that means giving gifts. We remember a consultant who did a lot of work in Japan, and she spent a considerable amount of time investigating protocol to find an appropriate gift for her host. For people in your network, this kind of gift giving may not be relevant. But the generosity of time you spend helping people in little ways will be very meaningful, indeed. The saying, "What goes around comes around" is trite, but it is also true. Said a little differently, if you give the gift of time or information to others when they need it, particularly to those who may be reluctant to ask for it, they will be in your debt. They will also return the favor. Giving and getting help should be a win/win practice for all involved.

5.   Acknowledge and Show Respect for the Special Events of Different Cultures

All cultural groups have their own unique celebrations. By remembering to acknowledge those celebrations through sending cards, attending events, or simply wishing someone a happy holiday, you go a long way toward helping people feel validated. This kind of consideration builds goodwill and understanding. It is part of what cultural networking, and in fact all networking, is really about. Lee sees this all the time with her friends and colleagues who are not Jewish. When Passover or Yom Kippur roll around every year, she receives good wishes and holiday cards. Her non-Jewish friends of many years feel at home at the seders. Every January 7, Lee shares Serbian Christmas with Anita's family. We all feel richer for these exchanges.

6.   Become a Master of Follow-Up

When you meet someone who may be helpful in expanding your network, follow up the initial contact with a note, an appointment for lunch, or an after-work drink. Take the initiative. Show interest. And always let people know that you appreciate their help. We have been in business for a dozen years. In that time, we have been shocked by a lack of *common courtesy* on so many occasions that we have decided the very term is an oxymoron. We have also been delighted by uncommon gestures. Some colleagues of ours who are classy people and smart businesswomen always send a small box of chocolates when they get a referral. It's a nice gesture that distinguishes them from the crowd, but even a thank-you note will make you stand out. Anything you do to build and strengthen ties is a plus, and a gracious acknowledgment to someone for effort on your behalf crosses language and cultural barriers.

7. Put Yourself in the Appropriate Places to Increase Your Contacts

When we worked with the UCLA Business Operations Division in its diversity development effort, one of the many things that impressed us about this group was the diligence with which they made an effort to recruit people of color. Managers in this unit systematically socialized, joined organizations, and attended events or workshops with an eye toward meeting and networking with people who could lead them to the work force they were seeking. You never know where a contact may come from—or where it may lead.

8. Set Goals for Expanding Your Network of People Whose Backgrounds or Experiences Differ from Yours

It is human nature to feel most comfortable and secure with people who are like you. But skin color, physical abilities, or age are only some of ways in which people are the same—or different. Explore values, special interests, hopes, and dreams with people who are different from you, and you may be surprised at how similar you are. We know that all people are different, even those who look, or arc, a lot like us. Your own family can be a fertile learning ground for appreciating differences. Let the differences you discover be a source of stimulation and fun. Not only will you expand your network, but more important, you may expand your vision.

Overcoming Cultural Barriers in Interviewing

The most important tip for overcoming cultural barriers in interviewing can be succinctly stated. Part of being human is the increased feeling of comfort we all get from being with people who are most like us. Beware of this all-too-human response in the interview arena. It can shortchange your organization by keeping it from hiring excellent and talented people simply because they are different from the person conducting the interview.

Putting your interview process under a microscope will be helpful in finding out if you are unwittingly sabotaging applicants. Sensitivity and openness to different cultures are put to the test in an interview situation because our "shoulds" about behavior surface. Separating job incompetencies from irritating cultural differences requires vigilance on the part of the interviewer. The biggest barrier interviewees of any background face is that people tend to look for or hire their clone or mirror image. We have seen it time and time again. Whites are accused of wanting to hire only whites, but we have also seen African-Americans and Filipinos—in fact, every group—behave in the exact same way. While it is true that in the United States most hiring is done by whites, it is also true that hiring those who are most like us to the exclusion of others is a universal affliction. The good news in American business today is that the light is dawning. Companies are starting to realize that is in their best interest to expand the diversity of the work force at all levels of the organization.

When you are honest enough to realize that you might be guilty of excluding applicants based on cultural differences, then you're on the right track. Determine if some of the rubs are etiquette issues. Cultural etiquette is sometimes subtle, sometimes not. But it can have a dramatic effect on social interaction, relationships, and ultimately, hiring and promotion.

There are certain examples of this etiquette that will show themselves the first moment you see someone in an interview. Do you shake hands? If so, how much firmness is appropriate? How do you address prospective employees? If you are a woman interviewing a Middle Eastern man, are you prepared for the confusion or discomfort when he does not shake your hand? Culture has programmed you and the prospective employee with a different set of rules.

Tips for Not Being Sabotaged by Your Own Cultural Programming

1. Understand How Truly Powerful Culture Is and Have a Generosity of Spirit about the Differences.   Culture is powerful and pervasive. All humans come with a set of operating rules, but those rules differ depending on where we are reared. Simply hiring or promoting someone in your organization who came with a different "instruction manual" won't result in instant acculturation. You won't be able to negate that person's previous years of training or behavior, and hopefully you wouldn't want to. Just imagine yourself moving to a foreign land or even to a different part of the United States. We transport our patterns and habits with our move. The only difference between personal habits and the furniture we move is that you and others can immediately see the furniture—it is tangible while our patterns are more illusory and take longer to discover. But they are just as real. Moving to a different country is major culture shock. The adaptation process gets even tougher in stressful times. Remembering the effort involved in that acculturation can increase your sensitivity toward others.

2. Expect that People You Hire Will Be Reshaped by the Organizational Culture, and in Turn, the Company Will Also Become Different.   The people you are hiring or promoting are trying to become successful in an existing company with an already powerful culture of its own. To do so, they will need to fold into this organization. But the adaptation isn't strictly one-sided. Both the company and the individual will become a little bit different through the interaction. Both want to thrive, not just survive. The goal of thriving necessitates identifying a common set of operating rules that function like glue, keeping the place together. Making those rules elastic and inclusive enough so that all the people you hire or promote feel comfortable and stick around is essential to your company's financial health.

3. Be Tolerant and Respectful of Different Cultural Values.   Dealing with differentness is difficult, but it also can be infinitely rewarding. As we wrestle with the impact of these differences, it is important to remember that *all* values in *every* culture cut two ways.

As a case in point, look at the ways different societies view women. In Saudi Arabia, women don't drive, nor do they work outside the home unless there is some special circumstance involved. There are prescribed standards of dress and, in general, much less freedom than women in the industrialized world have come to expect. But while the lack of freedom can be problematic for a Westerner, it isn't for Saudi women, who esteem their role for its importance in transmitting the values of the culture. Having women manage the family helps the society maintain a tightly knit structure, and some of the West's greatest ills, such as drugs and crime, are almost nonexistent in Saudi society. The lack of freedom brings a control and order to their society that works for them. We can appreciate that it works for the Saudis and admire some of the effects of these dictates without wanting that cultural norm in the United States. And we can expect that if we went to Saudi Arabia, we would need to honor their customs, just as the coalition members of Operation Desert Storm did. Likewise, people coming to this country find different core values than they are used to. But tolerance goes two ways. A man coming to the United States from a different culture may not be used to reporting to female managers or even to seeing women in a professional context. However, if that man wants to live and work in this country, he will need to make the adjustment.

4. Read about, Learn about, and Become Familiar with the Cultural Norms of Your Employee Population.   Learning about different customs and the reasons behind them will make the ''rules'' less foreign and sometimes less irritating. You may find some different customs interesting and become more accepting. There may be others that are difficult for you to understand. We interviewed a number of American women who had worked and lived in Japan and, when they returned to the United States, had continued to work for Japanese companies. They talked about their adjustments. One that gave them pause and got a good chuckle was the one where they were not able to leave the company before their Japanese bosses at the end of the day. That took some getting used to because the Japanese have notoriously long days. Conversely, one woman described the shock her new Japanese boss got when he came to do his rotation in California. At 5:00 P.M. on his first day of work, he witnessed a mass exodus. Very perplexed and confused, he inquired where everyone was going. When he found out that all the hullabaloo was because it was 5:00 and time to leave, he could not fathom this. Adjustments are required all around.

5. Come to Terms with Your Humanness.   Part of being human is having limits and being imperfect. Acknowledge that some behaviors are hard for you to deal with and that's just the way it is. However, acknowledging the difficulty doesn't give you license to be intolerant. Understanding why certain behaviors are hard for you can be the beginning of dealing with them. For example, Lee is involved in a professional group with people who view their once-a-month meetings as a great opportunity for socialization. A strict time frame is not a big issue for them, but it is an issue for Lee. She tried to facilitate faster conclusions to these sessions. There was much teasing between the group members and Lee. Humor was a help—so was the group's commitment to end all meetings within two hours. But the fact is, Lee will always be impatient even with two-hour meetings and downright irritable when they go longer.

6. Be Willing to Ask Questions.   Within your organization, you have resources—people who can explain customs, educate you, and assign meaning to certain cultural behaviors unfamiliar to you. Use these resources so you can minimize your feeling of frustration or irritation at certain behaviors that don't seem very credible for someone job hunting. Finding out why an Asian applicant smiles all through the interview or why the African-American listens with no nonverbal affirmations (nods and "uh-huhs") would help you avoid misinterpreting the behavior.

7. Be Honest with Yourself. In many cases, a candidate's name gives you information about his racial, cultural, or ethnic background. The issue is not the applicant's background, but rather the interviewer's reaction to it. Do you immediately have expectations, both positive and negative, about what that person can do? Do you assume that any person with an Asian name will be a technological whiz? Do you just as quickly assume that any African-American seeking a promotion to management probably got into engineering school as an affirmative action candidate and therefore might not be fully qualified? Both high and low expectations based on anything but performance do all people an injustice. One of the easiest things in the world is pigeonholing people, but it is also one of the most costly. You can't afford to be anything but honest about your prejudices—that way there is less chance they will limit or control you.

8. Assess Your Cultural Awareness and Sensitivity. To see just how much awareness you have of the impact of culture on your evaluation of potential employees, respond to the *Cultural Awareness Questionnaire*.

Cultural Awareness Questionnaire
(How Culturally Knowledgeable Are You?)

Directions: Please respond to each of the questions below with a check in the appropriate column.

	Yes	No
1. I know that different cultural values and behaviors may influence my perceptions of a person's competence, confidence, and social graces.	___	___
2. I have ways of being less direct in asking questions of someone from Mexico or the Middle East in order to get information and help the interviewee feel at ease.	___	___
3. In cultures where the group is more important than the individual, I have ways to gain information about a person's performance by focusing on group goals and the individual's part in them.	___	___
4. Regarding introductions, I appropriately use first names and surnames.	___	___
5. I understand that not making eye contact is often a way of showing respect, not a lack of assertiveness.	___	___
6. I know when to use both sturdy and soft handshakes, depending on the culture.	___	___
7. I understand that vagueness in answering a question is often culturally correct.	___	___
8. I conduct the interview formally because the informality of American culture can be intimidating for an interviewee whose comfort comes partially from a hierarchical structure.	___	___
9. I am conscious of the fact that standing very close to someone is appropriate in Middle Eastern culture.	___	___
10. I realize that the loudness or softness with which people talk is often cultural.	___	___

Scoring the *Cultural Awareness Questionnaire*

The more *yes* answers you have, the more culturally aware you are. If any of the cultural behaviors embedded in these 10 questions surprised you, start paying attention to them as you see them in the work arena. Look at your *no* answers. Have you ever come across these behaviors? If so, can you remember your responses or reactions? In order not to have any of these behaviors impede your selection of new personnel, look at how some of them might be your own cultural barriers. Then respond to the questions below.

To Overcome Your Own Cultural Barriers in Interviewing:

1. Which of these behaviors are most troublesome for you?

_____

_____

_____

2. How do you interpret these behaviors? What is the reason they are problematic?

_____

_____

_____

3. What are you willing to do, or how are you willing to see things differently, in order to make sure this behavior does not negatively impact the interviewing you do?

_____

_____

_____

Suggestions for Using the *Cultural Awareness Questionnaire*

Objectives:

- Educate interviewers about cultural norms that may impact how they treat and view a potential employee.
- Provide an assessment tool that increases cultural and self-awareness.

Intended Audience:

- HR professionals or affirmative action officers in charge of interviewing and hiring or in charge of educating managers about interviewing and hiring.
- Managers who do their own interviewing.
- Work teams who interview and pick new hires.
- Vice president in charge of HR who wants to educate and sensitize the executive staff.

Processing the Activity:

- This tool can be used for groups being educated about cultural differences. It can also be given to managers of other individuals who need cultural awareness because they interview, hire, or promote.
- If used with a group, pass it out to participants, have them discuss in pairs or small groups.
- Discuss questions in whole group. Be sure that the last three questions, on overcoming culture barriers, are discussed as well.

Questions for Discussion:

- What cultural behaviors or values surprised you?
- Which of these behaviors are most troublesome for you?
- How do you interpret these behaviors? What makes them problematic?
- What changes are you willing to make in your own interviewing?

Caveats and Considerations:

- HR professionals or affirmative action officers can give this to managers of people who need it and discuss it one-on-one. It can be a useful coaching/ teaching tool.
- You can make this tool more culturally specific if you are trying to educate your staff to deal more effectively with a particular consumer or employee base.

Five Ways to Ask Questions that Set Up Any Candidate for Success

Awareness of the norms and customs of other cultures that impact the communication process is critical. These communication patterns are particularly significant when you look at the interview process and see how people from different cultures solicit information from one another. Americans, quite accurately, have a reputation for being very direct. The mainstream culture would say we are "efficiently so." Other cultures might say we are "aggressively or rudely so." Clearly, your style in asking questions, whether you are seen as efficient or rude, has a lot to do with culture and your effectiveness in communicating and soliciting information.

The process of asking questions is by nature a prying, intrusive one, so we can't stress strongly enough the importance of investing time up front to put people at ease. There are many people born and reared in the dominant American culture who are sometimes intimidated by the directness with which questions are asked. This process is even more difficult for someone from a culture that is more private and less open. As an interviewer, you have a responsibility to get the information you need in order to make a good hiring decision. But how you ask these questions, or elicit the information you want, is critical to your success. Using the five techniques described below and summarized in the table on page 340 should help you get the information you need.

1.   Open-Ended Questions

The open-ended question is designed to help a person explore options or design possibilities. By nature, it is an expansive technique and best used when you want to assess a person's judgment or critical-thinking skills. The question allows the interviewee to give a lot of information beyond the parameters of the question as stated. The following are examples of open-ended questions:

- How might an ideal educational system (or health-care system or university admissions policy, etc.) look if you could help design it?
- How would you structure a work group to create greater harmony?
- What are some possible ways for improving interdepartmental communication?

The open-ended question also helps people whose native tongue is in passive languages like Spanish or Arabic to frame questions passively. For example, you could ask, "How might the organization be made more effective by this policy?" rather than, "What do you suggest we do to improve this policy?"

2.   Closed-Ended Questions

The closed-ended question is not designed to explore as much as it is to get very specific answers. The point of closed-ended questions is to narrow the responses and get very concrete. An example might be, "Of the various procurement procedures mentioned, which do you favor and why?" Another might be, "Which information system did you select?"

3.   Speculative Questions

The speculative question asks the interviewee to think about possibilities and show vision. Using the speculative style will give a person the chance to reflect on possibilities that don't currently exist. Realize that though some groups, the Japanese for example, find speculative questions unfathomable, "How" and "What" are useful here. Some sample questions are

- How might hospital revenues be impacted if there were no more medi-Cal or medicaid?
- What future do you envision for our company's global competitiveness if we fully employ a diverse work force? What might happen if we don't?

4.   "Tell me . . . ."

The two words "Tell me" are a good starting point because they begin a question disguised as a statement. At the end of a "Tell me" statement is a period, not the traditional question mark. That simple punctuation difference sets a whole different tone in the request for information. This is a perfect strategy for working with diverse cultures because immigrants often feel defensive when asked questions. In cultures that are more closed than mainstream American culture, and most are, this style offers protection from intrusion and still allows you to get the information you need. Here are a few examples:

- Tell me what you liked best about your last job.
- Tell me about the most important accomplishment of your group at U.S. West.
- Tell me what your last boss did to bring out your best.

5.   "Describe . . . ."

The word, or questioning style, "Describe . . ." has the same advantage as "Tell me." It is invaluable because it solicits information without an intrusive style, and in a subtle, nondirect way, it may help define the interviewee and his priorities. The same cultural factors that make "Tell me" effective will also work with "Describe."

- Describe the best company you ever worked for.
- Describe the way you got support for your customer service program.
- Describe an effective quality control system.
- Describe the work environment that brings out the best in you.

These five questioning techniques will enable you to get beyond cultural barriers and get information from the people you interview in a nonthreatening way. They provide enough latitude for people to show their industriousness, creativity, and values because questions are posed in a culturally sensitive way. For example, asking someone from either Mexico or Japan to highlight his individual accomplishments would make the candidate uncomfortable. But if you ask a question about the effectiveness and productivity of someone's work group and ask a person to discuss that part of the project he was responsible for, you will get the information you seek and the interviewee will feel comfortable giving it.

Five Ways to Ask Questions
(That Set Up Any Candidate for Success)

Question-Asking Style	Advantage	Disadvantage
1. Open-ended questions	Designed to explore options or design possibilities. Good at the beginning of discussion process. In passive languages, easy to frame questions.	Time consuming; not designed to give specific information so getting to concrete answers can be a lengthy process.
2. Closed-ended questions	Narrows responses; gets very concrete.	Not designed to let you see the creativity or ability to suggest options that may be a strength in a candidate's thinking.
3. Speculative questions	Designed to encourage vision and reflect on possibilities that don't exist or may seem unlikely; can really showcase creative thinkers.	Some groups, particularly the Japanese, find this style unfathomable—not in their thinking style to deal with questions of this nature.
4. "Tell me . . . ."	Because these two words are a question disguised as a statement, it feels less intrusive. It will open people up who may not like to be questioned.	If people are not concise, they can ramble and go off on a tangent.
5. "Describe . . . ."	Like "Tell me . . . ," this also solicits information without seeming intrusive. It will create more openness and less defensiveness.	This also can be time-consuming if people ramble or go off on a tangent.

Our suggestion is to look at the *Sample Interview Questions*. Change any or all of the questions to suit your own style and organizational objectives. Also be sensitive to the cultural norms you have read about in previous chapters. Once you have looked at the list, rephrase five pertinent questions you normally use in interviews along the guidelines offered in each of these suggestions. Pay attention to the cultural implications of asking these questions. Try being less direct and more passive. Avoid asking a lot of questions that will force the individual to look only at individual accomplishment. Frame your questions with a combination of group accomplishment and the individual's contribution to it in mind.

We suggest that you take the 12 sample interview questions and get a cultural slant on them from knowledgeable people in your organization. We did by asking a few Japanese nationals on a tour of duty in the United States. For example, in Japan, question number 3 would not be asked of a new graduate because he is not expected to know about such things. Questions 5, 6, and 11 would rarely be asked because they would put the interviewee in the uncomfortable position of playing boss, and question 8 is unnecessary in Japan because résumés are so detailed. Our Japanese colleagues told us that question number 9 was a catch-22. If the interviewee enjoyed so much about his/her previous employment, why did he/she leave? And if nothing was enjoyed, what kind of miserable person is this human being? We suggest you seek the various cultural interpretations that reflect your interviewee base. It is indeed interesting.

Rolling Out the Welcome Mat: Using the Interview to Develop Rapport and Sell Your Company

Demonstrating courtesy and warmth is the best way to roll out the welcome mat. There is a good chance that you are an interviewee's first extended contact with a company, so the impression you make will be *the* definitive view this person has of your company at the beginning. By creating an environment that helps an interviewee feel welcome, she will be able to showcase her talent, skill, and experience in a way that lets you see her strength when she is not plagued by nervousness. Furthermore, you will make a good first impression on behalf of your company and increase your chances of attracting the candidate you'd like to hire. Before you can create a "global welcome mat," you need to reflect on your current routine. Does the following scenario look familiar?

1. You extend a warm, solid handshake and a smile. You call the interviewee by first name and say something to the effect of "It is nice to meet you."
2. You direct the interviewee to a seat, and in most cases offer the person coffee, juice, or something else to drink.
3. You then make a few minutes of small talk to relax the person, and that conversation usually revolves around weather, traffic, or any local happening that the parties involved may share in common. "Did you feel that earthquake?" works well in our neck of the woods, but each region has its own natural phenomena.
4. Sometime during that initial greeting, you make eye contact and smile to extend warmth and put the candidate at ease.
5. After a few minutes of small talk, you give the interviewee the parameters of the interview, including length of time, and a description of the interview

Sample Interview Questions

1. What makes this job opening interesting to you?

2. Tell me (or us) why you want to work for this company.

3. What things mean the most to you in any job? In what order of importance?

4. Describe the position as you understand the job. Talk about your experiences in these areas.

5. What qualifications would you look for in a candidate for this job if you were doing the hiring? What attributes do you think would be most essential to job success in this position?

6. How would you distinguish an outstanding employee from a typical one in any job?

7. What have you learned in your past schooling and training that you think would be helpful in the job you are currently applying for?

8. What has your group accomplished in your past position that you feel would be indicative of successful performance in this job? What did your group find most difficult?

9. What did you enjoy most about your previous jobs, co-workers, supervisors, departments, companies, and industries?

10. How did you happen to choose the jobs you have held?

11. Let me describe a situation that we are dealing with in this unit. What are your suggestions for dealing with it?

12. What has your past experience been in dealing with cliques? What has been the biggest impediment to a cohesive work team in your past jobs? How would you change that if you found the same circumstances here?

In the blanks below, rephrase your own questions to be more culturally sensitive.

1. _____

2. _____

3. _____

4. _____

5. _____

process. Then you begin by asking the easiest, least risky questions first for the best results because the candidate will be able to gain confidence as the interview progresses. You generally start with those that center on the candidate's education and experience. Your tone of voice conveys interest and cordiality.

Have you thought about how you might change this ritual if interviewing someone from a different background? The following list will give you areas for heightened sensitivity. No culture is monolithic, nor is any race; therefore, assuming that all people from Japan will respond the same to matters of cultural etiquette is a mistake. Nevertheless, knowing cultural norms can be helpful. As you find out about the background of the candidate you are interviewing, you may need to do a little bit of homework to learn about the specific customs of that person's culture.

Let us give you a suggestion first from a colleague of ours, Vicki Tomoush, who works for the Human Relations Commission in Pasadena, California. Because she is of Syrian and Lebanese ancestry, she is most familiar with Arab culture. One suggestion she makes is the need for extensive social interaction at the beginning. Small talk about general things is critical. It is considered rude and uncouth to just say hello, have one or two sentences of small talk about the weather or traffic, and then jump into the interview. She indicates it would be quite common in the Middle East to talk about things like the furniture in the room, the organization's history, or even things that may be inconsequential. The point of the conversation is to pass time, get used to each other's voices, and create a hospitable environment. There is one interesting postscript here. Vicki knows that weather is a favorite conversation opener in mainstream American culture. She indicated that acculturated Middle Easterners would talk about the weather, but in truth, Muslims look at weather as a gift from God and a blessing, so they don't judge or discuss it. The following caveats and suggestions are a few ways to help people feel comfortable.

1. *Caveat:* Smiles do not mean the same in every culture. Before you rush forward with your "hail-fellow-well-met" smile, check the person's background. Your smile may indicate a lack of respect or seriousness.

Suggestion: Temper your warmth and cordiality with an appropriate professional tone.

2. *Caveat:* Most cultures are more formal than the dominant American culture and prefer the use of last names, not first. They may also combine the first name with Mr., Ms., Miss, or Mrs., for example, as in Miss Susan or Mr. Juan.

Suggestion: You will provide greater comfort for most interviewees who are of immigrant backgrounds if you use your last name when you introduce yourself and use their last name in addressing them.

3. *Caveat:* The firmness of a handshake differs by culture. Germans have the firmest grip, while people from the Asian Pacific have a handshake that is soft. A sturdy American grip will do just fine with the Germans, and if you can soften yours a little in cultures where the handshake is less pronounced, you'll do just fine.

Suggestion: There are two important things to remember about handshakes, and all the symbols of etiquette we are mentioning. If you can match the interviewee's, do it. It will help him feel comfortable, and it will show your sensitivity and openness to differences. Also avoid making assumptions about a person's competence based on his/her handshake.

In our assertiveness seminars, the behavior participants find most irritating is what they call the dead-fish handshake. Labels such as *wimp* or *weak* accompany the description, and the weak handshake is viewed as a character defect. You don't have to like the soft handshake, but be careful about writing someone off because of it. That person may not like the firmness of your grip. There is an extra caveat here regarding the Saudi Arabian culture if you are a woman interviewing a man. In the Middle East, it is foreign to see women in the work arena. People who choose to live and work in the United States realize that women here do work. That doesn't necessarily suggest that someone is comfortable enough to treat women as equals or shake hands with them. And, as has been mentioned, some religions prohibit the handshake.

4. *Caveat:* Eye contact varies by culture. Of all the cultural differences immigrants bring to this country, lack of eye contact is probably one of the most well known. But knowing it intellectually doesn't mean that we don't still judge people negatively when their eyes don't meet ours. You may know that the interview candidate from Taiwan may have been "programmed" to avert your gaze as a sign of respect, but your own programming tells you that eye avoidance is an indicator of having something to hide. Remembering all of these differences and factoring them into your assessment is easier said than done, but your adaptation is critical to your company's success in the marketplace.

Suggestion: Remind yourself that someone from the Asian Pacific who will not look you in the eye is most likely engaging in the behavior he was taught, rather than being underconfident or dishonest.

Most important of all, remember that in a high-stress situation, both you and the job candidate will fall back on knee-jerk responses, regardless of how much you know and how hard you try to overcome your programming. Stress makes us reactive. Remembering that will enable you to be more compassionate and less intimidating as your probe for the information you need in getting the best candidate for the job. The following helpful hints will enable you to transcend the cultural barrier and welcome people from any background.

1. A formal manner is usually more comfortable for interviewees from different cultures, particularly if they have been in the United States a short time.
2. It is all right to ask about differences in etiquette. "How would you like me to address you?" is a perfectly legitimate question. It shows sensitivity to cultural differences.
3. In making small talk to put people at ease, be mindful of the need for privacy. Americans tend to be open, but Filipinos, for example, in an attempt to build connections, are sometimes viewed as asking intrusive questions. Questions that might be all right to ask a Latino employee about his or her family might be inappropriate in an interview with someone from Japan or the Middle East, who may view American openness as inappropriate or insincere.
4. Humor varies by culture. It is a risky tool that may be intended as a relationship builder, but when humor is misunderstood, it is confusing and can be offensive.
5. The spirit of goodwill you exhibit in an interview will be more important than any question you ask or any norm you observe. People can feel when they are treated with dignity and respect. Ultimately, your behavior and tone are the most important allies you have in rolling out a welcome mat.

Checking Your Own Biases at the Interview Door

We've talked about a lot of factors involved in the effective interviewing, hiring, and recruiting of employees from diverse backgrounds. We have looked at ways to neutralize the application process and have given you suggestions for networking creatively. We have talked about how to ask questions and have even given you sample questions to ask. We've looked at the impact of culture on an interviewee's behavior and suggested that you not determine someone is incompetent because he or she is operating under different cultural rules. What we haven't done is really to ask you to acknowledge your own biases and check them at the door. It is important to do that now because all our other suggestions will be for naught if you don't come to terms with your own preferences first. The purpose of this reckoning is not to accuse you or point a finger at you for having preferences. We all have them. Once you identify yours, they will be less likely to limit your perceptions of others. Ask yourself the questions in *Interviewing Assumptions and Biases*.

Interviewing Assumptions and Biases

Directions: Answer the following five questions. The more candid you are, the more helpful this information will be.

1. What behaviors do I currently expect to look for from someone I interview or hire? Consider the following areas specifically:

    • Language skills/usage

    _____

    _____

    • Communication style (verbal and nonverbal)

    _____

    _____

    _____

    • Etiquette (involves social norms such as handshakes, how people are introduced, and distance between people)

    _____

    _____

    • Social values (egalitarianism vs. hierarchical structure)

    _____

    _____

    _____

2. What assumptions do I make about potential interviewees and their competence when I see different behaviors than I want or am used to?

    • Language:

    _____

    _____

    _____

    • Communication:

    _____

    _____

    _____

Interviewing Assumptions and Biases (concluded)

- Etiquette:

  _____

  _____

  _____

- Values:

  _____

  _____

  _____

3. What differences are easy for me to handle?

   _____

   _____

   _____

4. What differences are a problem?

   _____

   _____

   _____

5. What does this suggest I need to do differently to be more sensitive when I interview people of color, the differently abled, older workers, or those with a different affectional orientation?

   _____

   _____

   _____

Suggestions for Using *Interviewing Assumptions and Biases*

Objectives:

- Identify biases or assumptions in areas of language, communication, style, etiquette, and social values that impact the interviewing and selection process.
- Determine where biases can sabotage recruitment efforts.

Intended Audience:

- HR professional or affirmative action officer in charge of recruiting.
- Manager in charge of recruiting.
- Work team that hires its own team members.
- Vice president of HR who wants to coach particular managers.

Processing the Activity:

- This can be used with teams who hire their co-workers or by HR professionals who want to coach a manager one-on-one. In either case, it needs to be filled out first.
- If a team uses this to broaden its awareness of biases, a facilitator would ask team members to share in pairs first, then discuss as a whole group.
- A group discussion would follow.

Questions for Discussion:

- Use the five questions in the questionnaire to guide your discussion, focusing on four areas: (1) language, (2) communication style, (3) etiquette, and (4) social values.
- All five questions are important, but ultimately, numbers 4 and 5 need to be discussed fully: What differences are a problem? What does this mean I (we) need to do differently?

Caveats and Considerations:

- Like all the tools in this chapter, this can be used with a group, but it can also be very helpful in coaching managers one-on-one.

In order to attract and keep top talent, an organization needs to demonstrate its commitment to searching out talented people with varied backgrounds, beliefs, and behaviors. Dedication to accomplishing this goal is essential from the top of the organization on down if you are going to create a truly open, welcoming company that retains recruits.

Beyond that commitment from the top of the organization, those people charged with the direct responsibility of hiring and recruiting need to have open minds, refined skills, and the energy it takes to go out, find the talent, and then sell potential employees on the idea that yours is an organization they can comfortably call home. The open attitude and energy you have to furnish yourself. But if you have them and utilize the strategies you just read about to rethink your application process, take a new look at the interview questions you ask and how you ask them, consider ways to enlarge your network, and rethink your values as you increase your cultural awareness, there is no doubt you will be a formidable competitor in the marketplace of top talent.

Years ago, we heard Dave Grant, a seminar speaker, talk about what he called *the law of the radiator*. The essence of that law is very simple. What you radiate is what you attract. This law has significant implications regarding recruitment.

Chapter 10

Making Room at the Top (and in the Middle, Too)

This chapter will give you:
1. An awareness of subtle assumptions that sabotage your diversity promotion efforts.
2. Tools to evaluate and determine what management characteristics are promoted in your company and what part gender plays in that promotion.
3. A model of career development.
4. Suggestions for effective coaching and mentoring.
5. An assessment that measures your organization's openness to promoting candidates other than white males.

The most exciting thing about women's liberation is that this century will be able to take advantage of talent and potential genius that have been wasted because of taboos.

Helen Reddy

Helen Reddy was an optimist when she made the above statement years before the current demographic revolution. We could substitute the word *people's* for *women's* and the quote would be equally appropriate. While the new work force is already upon us, the new management and leadership to match are still in metamorphosis. According to R. Roosevelt Thomas, Jr., "women and minorities no longer need a boarding pass, they need an upgrade. The problem is not getting them in at the entry level; the problem is making better use of their potential at every level, especially in middle-management and leadership positions. This is no longer simply a question of common decency, it is a question of business survival."[40] Recognizing the need for upgrades is a first step, but other variables impact the full utilization of employee potential, whether at the top or in the middle of the organization.

Quality versus Diversity: Not an Either-Or Proposition

The subtle message delivered by most corporations at midlevel management and above is that Euro-American males are the "A Team." When necessity demands, real talent may have to be diluted in deference to politics, demographics, or affirmative action. For a variety of reasons, organizations are being forced to the realization that all or mostly white male leadership or management teams must change. Having admitted that, the perception still exists that varying the complexion of the management team for reasons of equity and justice will most assuredly mean sacrificing quality.

We witnessed this perception firsthand when we worked with one of our clients, a team of 48 managers struggling with the question of how to widen the ethnic, racial, and gender composition of their team. While white males were the dominant group in positional power and numbers, the team was diverse. Most ethnic groups, including native Americans, were represented on the team, which was committed to the cause of diversity and to achieving parity at top echelons of the division. Even so, with all their awareness, commitment, and desire to move forward, when it came time to look at the valued management characteristics they promote or hire, the intensity of discussion on this issue showed how deep and difficult the resistance is. They had a hard time getting beyond the idea residing somewhere deep down that quality really would suffer if accommodations were made to promote diverse candidates.

Incorrect Assumptions that Sabotage Your Diversity Promotion Efforts

Part of what makes the *quality versus diversity* issue a difficult one is that human beings attach certain beliefs to the worth, talent, or performance abilities of certain individuals or groups. These assumptions are based on direct and indirect experiences such as the teaching we have received from our parents and the attitudes that permeated the environment in which we were reared. Societal influences may incorrectly indicate what certain groups of people are capable of or where they should be slotted professionally. For example, Asians may be seen as superior performers in the area of quantitative analysis. Does that mean they are always expected to go into computer science or engineering? Does it mean they are too technical to be good with people in a managerial role? What makes these kinds of assumptions dangerous is not only that they are limiting but also that they are unconsciously absorbed through osmosis. Assumptions are part of the air you breathe and are just as hard to get hold of. Yet they can exert a powerful influence. Think about the following four assumptions. Do you hold any of these yourself? Identify those that are operative at your company because until they are acknowledged, their negative impact can't be minimized and efforts toward building a truly diverse management team will be impeded.

1. *Women and people of color, gays and lesbians, or any people who come under the classification of affirmative action are not promoted because of job performance.* People of color frequently tell us that they are seen as token appointments because they were nondominant group members. It is rarely assumed that someone who is not white and male could be promoted on sheer performance and ability alone. The blanket but false assumption exists that a diverse promotion is a less qualified promotion. In truth, individuals of every race, religion, or nationality are qualified in some areas and not in others. The determiner of qualification is a coalescing of many factors—experience, innate talent, a passion to do the job, intelligence, developed skills and competencies, raw potential, and so on. Diversity-related promotions can be as good a fit and as right (or as bad a fit and as wrong) as any other promotion.

The best way to get beyond this obstacle is to pick people with excellent track records who are ready for increased responsibility and who have been coached. Furthermore, the organization only does part of its job when it picks a diverse candidate for the upward climb. The other part is to offer continued support, technically and emotionally. In that way, new managers can be set up for success, not be left hanging out to dry.

2. *Merit and competence in certain areas are the only salient qualifications.* Sometimes only certain job skills are emphasized as necessary when, in fact, the role requires multifaceted skills. For example, lifeguards have traditionally been selected on the basis of athletic performance. While no one disputes the importance of being a superb swimmer in order to rescue people, the job also necessitates being able to resolve conflict, solve problems, and communicate with the diverse public that utilizes the beaches. Swimming competence is only one part of the job. In some circumstances, resolving conflict and dealing effectively with different people may be more critical. These skills also need to be factored into the job description and given some weight.

3. *A diverse management team is a weaker team than an all–white male group.* No intelligent person would admit to this theory, but the battles for equity are fought and won in the deep recesses of our mind, not out in the open. Homogeneity may be comfortable, but it is no longer reality in the United States. It is also no guarantee of an effective team. Both homogeneous and heterogeneous teams can be effective and ineffective, depending on management's ability to tap the skills and commitment of the group as well as the innate talent on board. The obstacle arises when white males who have the power to open up the management team buy in to this assumption. The time is right for the leadership to realize that

talent and tenacity come in both genders plus a variety of sizes, shapes, and colors.

4. *Women, people of color, the differently abled, or any person of the non-dominant culture must sell out in order to make it.* The perception exists that the elevator to the top floor leaves a good part of a person's integrity behind as he or she travels upward. Questions abound: ''Did this individual sell out in order to make it? Can he or she be an authentic self and survive?'' The questions raised by these assumptions incorrectly put the burden for adaptation on the individual when, in truth, adaptation is a shared responsibility. Both the organization and the individual should change a little through their interaction.

One executive recently told us a story that illustrates this simultaneous and evolutionary change. She was at a meeting with her executive management team when her secretary came in and announced that she needed to take a phone call right then from her child's school. She took the call in the meeting. As she recounted this story, one of our colleagues asked her why she didn't take the call elsewhere. Her response was both quick and clear. It was important to her that her colleagues redefine their image of an executive to include being a nurturer. She is unwilling to deny that part of her and feels strongly that her male colleagues need to come to terms with both her maternal role outside of work as well as her executive role at the office. Meeting these issues head on is the only way society will change. What's more, in that way she can be her authentic self, not someone else's picture of who she should be.

A critical beginning step in making room at the top for diverse talent is to realize how the subconscious thinking of dominant and nondominant groups alike sabotages the diversity promotion efforts and results. When assessing your company's progress at midlevel and above, some important questions need to be asked. What elements influence promotion decisions? How subtle or overt are the selection criteria? Which ones can be measured and verified? Once you address these questions, there are four unconscious decision factors that strongly influence promotion decisions. They are simply another variable that sways candidate selection. They deserve some thought and attention as they rattle around your unconscious because they are influential by virtue of their being unrecognized or unarticulated. As you read these unconscious factors, note any that influence promotional outcomes in your organization.

Unconscious Factors that Influence Promotion

1. The Clone Effect. It is predictable and natural for human beings to value and appreciate those people who are most like them. When promotion time rolls around, appointing a carbon copy might feel like the most natural thing to do if you don't force yourself to think about the pros and cons of anointing your double. In countries with homogeneous populations the issue of racial or ethnic clones is less of an issue than in our immigrant nation. With Euro-American males holding the power positions in American businesses, most promotions have traditionally gone to other white males, and without some emphasis on the need to build a kaleidoscopic management team, nothing will change. When promoting people, be aware of the pitfalls of appointing someone just like you, not only in appearance and background, but values and thinking styles as well. There is strength in differences. Steve Bottcher, vice president of operations for Pepsi-Cola, said after a three-and-a-half-day diversity training course, ''A year ago, I might have automatically hired somebody who thought like me. Now I am much more likely to hire someone with a different point of view.''[27] As you deal with the natural tendency to hire clones, consider looking for similarities between you and potential promotees in less obvious ways than that of skin color and ethnic background.

2. Comfort Level. One reason why there is a tendency for individuals to promote or select "clones" is comfort level. We are most comfortable with people like us. When executives or managers add new players to their team, among the factors they consider are their own comfort and trust levels with those they're bringing on board. Jack Gibb, a management consultant, said years ago when talking about trust, "I like the me in you." There is safety in the familiar reflection. Trust is often a function of how similar people are. We feel safer in the company of those whose values, looks, traditions, or habits are like ours. So we keep adding them to our executive staffs. In this way, the clone effect and comfort level are tied together. Replicating yourself feels safe, but it doesn't necessarily produce the strongest management team. Since comfort is an important component of a high trust management team, find commonality in less superficial ways. Instead, focus on values, habits, hobbies, skills, and just plain human preferences.

3. Expectations and Socialization. One of the most harmful saboteurs of equal opportunity promotion has to do with our unconscious expectations and the prejudices we have about other groups of people. Most of us became acquainted with the self-fulfilling prophecy, or the "Pygmalion effect," years ago in some college classroom. It is the idea that we live up to or down to the expectations others have for us. But in reality, we have lived its effects all our lives from the teachings of the parents who reared us, the schools that educated us, and the communities that enculturated us. Over a lifetime, our brains have collected pictures and ideas about the capabilities of various groups and individuals. Through print and media, these ideas have been reinforced. The end result? Labeling individuals from various groups based on these ideas. The labeling often occurs in subtle ways, which can be helpful or harmful, depending on the level of expectations we set for others. The good news is that we can unlearn our harmful thoughts.

When we mention the subtle power of expectations and socialization in workshops, participants deny being affected by them. But we equate expectations from stereotypes to secondhand smoke. If you're in the environment, it impacts you. Lee learned this lesson from a personal experience. In 1981, she was going through surgery to move her jaw forward after five years of orthodontia. Her lesson in unconscious and harmful assumptions happened the second night after surgery at 2:30 A.M. when a kind and gentle nurse came in to check on her and take her blood pressure. In spite of the fact that Lee was still affected by anesthesia, she recalls this incident vividly. Even though heavily sedated, she wondered why this large man was a nurse. Her unconscious told her that since he was so big, he should be playing on the defensive line for the Los Angeles Rams. When Lee awoke the next morning, she remembers her thought process and how she stereotyped and limited this very able nurse. Awake and aware, she hopes she would have fought that programming. But she knows that deep down, there are still limiting expectations she must fight. Based on gender and size, she had determined that this man belonged in a uniform for football players, not nurses.

Most managers don't try to set limiting expectations on their staffs, but they sometimes do so without being aware. Do you ever catch yourself expecting Asians to be technical wizards while you expect Salvadorans to mop floors and clean rooms? If so, what effect might such thinking have on promotions for women or people of color? If you do find these expectations on automatic pilot, serve notice to your *expectation software*. It's about to be reprogrammed.

4. Double Standard.   Gloria Steinem once said that we'll know women have made progress in our society when they can be as mediocre as men. The idea that women, or other members of the nondominant culture, have to perform stunningly to pass muster when those in the dominant group can get by doing less has not gone unnoticed. You can look at most organizations in this country and find an example of a woman or person of color who has to jump through more hoops, win more battles, prove themselves in more arenas than those in power to even be considered for a promotion.

Deborah Tannen, Ph.D., speaks both eloquently and humorously about the double standard and miscommunication between men and women. She cites the example of women speaking up in mixed-sex groups being harshly described as "overbearing" or "hard-edged." On the other hand, when women are not aggressive in presenting their ideas, they are viewed as "pushovers." Tannen makes the point about women's double bind. "If they speak in ways expected of women, they are seen as inadequate leaders. If they speak in ways expected of leaders, then they are seen as inadequate women. The road to authority is tough for women, and once they get there it's a bed of thorns."[38] In a broader but equally relevant arena, Latinos and African-Americans are often considered passive if they don't speak up, but militant if they do.

On more occasions than we care to recount, even when the objective performance is stellar, due to factors like the clone effect and comfort level, diverse employees frequently lose out, or worse still, are simply ignored. Their behaviors and performance are interpreted or defined differently from that of white males. By helping those who have the power to promote become increasingly aware of these unconscious factors, they will have less influence on promotional decisions in your organization.

Promotable Qualities: What Does It Take to Move up the Ladder?

There is a disparity of opinion about whether or not traditionally perceived differences in leadership traits between males and females really exist. Tom Peters, author of *In Search of Excellence,* acknowledges that there is a difference when he states, "New survival traits for firms of any shape read like a portfolio of women's inclinations and natural talents."[33] Judy B. Rosener, Ph.D., of the University of California at Irvine, cites an article by Susan M. Donnel and Jay Hall, "Men and Women as Managers: A Significant Case of No Significant Difference," as convincing her to study sex differences in management style. While suggesting their data shows few male/female differences, Donnel and Hall casually mention that under stress, male managers become more authoritarian and female managers become more conciliatory.[35] Since most managers (as well as nonmanagers) spend a good part of their organizational life under stress, it seems useful to consider the difference. Dr. Rosener, in her own study of male and female leaders in a variety of organizations, found similarities and differences, and she considers the differences worthy of note. She looked at 456 male and female leaders across industry and geographic regions. The major differences were in leadership style and exercise of power. The men relied on top-down style, "where rewards are exchanged for services rendered or punishment given for inadequate performance."[35] Men used command and control as the primary methods of influencing others.

Rosener described the women's leadership style as an effort to "get subordinates to transform their own self-interest into the interest of the group through concern for a broader goal," and they use "power coming from personal characteristics like charisma, interpersonal skills, hard work, or personal contacts rather than organizational structure."[36] Rosener describes this leadership style as one that encourages participation as well as sharing power and information while also enhancing the self-worth of others. What makes her study salient is that at this time in our economic and political history, the characteristics associated with women's style seem particularly suited to improving performance in any organization by empowering the employees who work there. This is not to disparage some of the male traits that have worked effectively in the past. Without question, the most effective managers will combine the perceived strengths and traits of both men and women and learn to use them appropriately. The management blue ribbon goes to the leader with the largest repertoire of available skills and behaviors.

Let's take a look at managerial qualities that have traditionally been ascribed to both men and women. While each are valuable, the problem historically has been that women's leadership strengths, which very closely mirror the strengths of many of the world's cultures, have been given short shrift and deemed unimportant. They have been underutilized and undervalued. But to quote a line from Bob Dylan, "The times, they are a' changin'."

Promotable Qualities

The following list of promotable characteristics deemed male and female comes from the work of Dr. Judy Rosener. Her work is not meant to imply that no men are nurturing or that all male leaders are unskilled at encouraging information and sharing power any more than male characteristics are meant to imply that female leaders are neither action-oriented nor analytical. Nevertheless, socialization has taught men and women differently. These teachings have resulted in different rewards for each gender based on differing expectations. The purpose of looking at these characteristics is to provoke the awareness that leads to making certain women are not disadvantaged simply because they are women. The biggest gains come not only from developing androgynous leaders, but from rewarding them as well.

As you read this list, write down the names of managers or executives in your organization who seem to exemplify these characteristics. Is there a pattern to the qualities that get promoted? Are these perceived male qualities demonstrated equally by men and women? Do you see a real gender difference in management style? Note the strong task emphasis for male characteristics. While people and relationships may be strategically or pragmatically relevant, the emphasis is on task, task, task.

Promotable Qualities: Male Characteristics

1. Leading by Command and Control.[36]   Command and control work best in the military or other hierarchical organizations. Operation Desert Storm is the quintessential example of command-and-control leadership. The generals issued dictates, and the troops got the job done. General Norman Schwarzkopf was a master at his method, but he neutralized the perceived negatives of traditional command-and-control leadership by showing some female traits. He had great feeling for his troops and was not afraid to show that emotion when he said his good-byes. Because he was so clearly a man's man, he was able to let his aesthetic and nurturing side show through without ridicule. He is a great example of combining the characteristics traditionally attributed to both males and females.

Cross-culturally, this leadership style may have some benefits. In managing employees from the 70 percent of the world that values a rigid hierarchy, command and control would be more effective than a more participative management style. However, in managing across gender lines with American women, it has drawbacks.

2. Exchanging Rewards for Services Rendered. Exchanging rewards is the old-fashioned barter system. The implied, and sometimes stated, agreement is that, if you do your job well, you will be rewarded, and one of those rewards might be climbing the ladder of success. White male–style leadership rarely deviates from this cookie cutter, traditional promotional system. However, in the case of women or people of color, a closer look needs to be taken because the diverse population is frequently left out of the barter. If you can't trade your talent in the marketplace, you can't climb the ladder. Creating more flexibility in what an organization rewards is critical to helping an expanded pool of employees find the ladder's steps.

3. Reliance on Positional Power. White males in the United States overwhelmingly hold the power positions, so it is no wonder when we think of positional clout, our images are predominantly white and male. Ronald Reagan and Jimmy Carter couldn't be more different in their styles, or in a good many of their values. Jimmy Carter was an intellect who pored over the details of government; Ronald Reagan was an ideologue who didn't want to be bothered with details. The similarities lie in the position they held and the power it gave them. Cross-culturally, positional power is something people not born in the United States will probably respond to more favorably than native-born Americans. Here, if you rely on your position to move the troops, you've already lost the battle. Doing it because "I'm the boss" may give you short-term results. It's a poor long-term strategy with highly acculturated employees, but it does wield enormous influence in other cultures.

4. Following a Hierarchical, Quasi-Military Structure. Historically, the Western male style of getting the job done has relied on an organization with fixed lines of authority. That style is now less celebrated in American business, whose current management mantra is total quality management (TQM), which followed on the heels of other participatory movements like Quality Circles. The end result is a somewhat flatter hierarchy, though in truth, we see no evidence of horizontal organizations becoming the norm. Getting participation is very important for employees acculturated to mainstream America, but it will be uncomfortable for those newly arrived to this country, particularly at first-line levels.

5. Action Orientation. In the past, the take-charge, aggressive stance has been a big reason for America's success. It has enabled us to cross the continent, build cities, and forge a very powerful country in a relatively short time span. Action orientation can be constructive—but used inappropriately, it can also be wasteful. What Anita heard from one of her frustrated clients in a stress workshop is that this manager and his department are on the receiving end of management dictates that spew orders out in rapid-fire succession only to recall them regularly. This participant feels like his work is meaningless now because it always has to be redone anywhere from two to four times, depending on how often the objectives from upper management change. Being action-oriented is valuable. But organizations needn't reward action that is "ready, fire, aim."

6. Analytical Thinking and Linear Problem Solving. Analytical thinking and linear problem solving have a good track record. Breakthroughs in medical science and setting man on the moon are a few of the significant results. However, even veteran researchers relying on the most scientific of methods often concede that new ideas frequently come in an intuitive flash. Intuitive and lateral thinking have been viewed as more feminine and more closely reflect other cultures in the world. Each style has a great deal to offer, and any manager successfully incorporating the two would increase effectiveness in relating to a diverse staff, and achieving good results as well.

Promotable Qualities: Female Characteristics[36]

Going through the preceding analysis can show you clearly the costs and benefits of the traditional male management style. Every coin is two-sided, and this truth applies to traditionally feminine characteristics as well.

1. Sharing Power and Information. There is a perception in some quarters that power is a fixed sum. Either you have it or you don't. That thought is invalid. Power ebbs and flows, just like everything else in life. Simply having the position won't grant you long-term power. Such power exists in the influence exerted through relationships, and it is found wherever people have information or resources that others want and need. Women are skilled at maintaining power through relationships. They also, as a group, are more willing than men to share the goods. Dr. Rosener's study "Ways Women Lead" suggests that among female-associated leadership characteristics is a comfort with the sharing of power and information.[36] It is natural for women, based on their socialization and experience. It's not that men intentionally resist sharing. But what happened at Corning is not an atypical occurrence. During a gender awareness workshop, the female executives complained that because they were never invited to lunch with their male colleagues, they missed out on information that could lead to opportunities. Their problems were not feelings of rejection. Rather, exclusion at lunch often leads to exclusion of useful information such as job postings. The net result becomes no lunch, no info. Informal power sharing can critically but subtly influence promotability.[25]

2. Enhancing Self-Worth of Others. That female leaders tend to help build the esteem of people they work with is one of the findings that surfaced in Rosener's study.[36] This can be a powerful leadership tool. Article after article in professional journals pays lip service to the importance of human resources, yet real investment and nurturing of human beings remains just that—lip service. Empowering employees and helping enhance their esteem is a natural outgrowth of female socialization. It's hard to see how this leadership trait could do anything but generate employee commitment. This is especially critical in managing a diverse staff. People who come to the United States from cultures where family and relationships are important will benefit from the attention and investment made on their behalf, as will other previously excluded groups. In our own experience with clients, we have seen enhanced employee self-esteem result in the desire for increased responsibility, the chance to learn new skills, and the opportunity to grow when the employee's picture of his or her potential to perform is expanded.

3. Encouraging Participation.   For people who are acculturated or native born, participation will be an expectation and a desire for the majority of your staff. Not so for first liners who are immigrants. Of all the female characteristics we have mentioned, this is the most difficult for newcomers to deal with. Nevertheless, it is powerful and important. When we wrote our book *What It Takes* (Doubleday, 1987), for which we interviewed 100 of America's top business and professional women to see what characteristics they had in common, we heard a story relevant to this issue. We interviewed Barbara Corday, who was the cocreator of "Cagney and Lacey," a female-buddy-cop TV show that had a long run. At one point, Corday was also at Columbia Pictures Television and vice president of prime time programming at CBS. We could see she was warm and charming, but we did not want to paint a one-dimensional portrait, so we interviewed two of her subordinates. One of them, Andy Hill, had glowing things to say about Barbara. When asked what made Barbara stand out, his response was, "She says four words no male boss has ever said to me. 'What do you think?' " Encouraging participation may be difficult for new immigrants at first, but with help in acculturating, they will learn to value and depend on this.

4. Getting Others Excited about Their Work.   There is a value for most women, not just in getting the job done right, but in the process of how it gets done. You could say that female managers and leaders place great emphasis on process, not just product. They really want to enjoy the journey. We're not saying men don't want to motivate others and get them excited about their work or enjoy the process of task accomplishment. Coaching athletics is the most visible effort in this regard. However, when coaches get their teams excited, usually it's a means to an end—winning or gaining a championship. There is a different emphasis with women. They want their employees to find intrinsic value in their work.

Thinking about these general qualities or characteristics of male and female leadership and how effective each is evokes images of *The Doctor*, a movie that came out in 1991 starring William Hurt. It showed the power in combining masculine and feminine characteristics. Hurt is a cardiovascular surgeon with all the typical male attributes just cataloged. He is an excellent technician but not a complete physician because he is missing the human dimension. Patients and their illnesses represent problems to be overcome, and they usually are, but Hurt is more a technocrat than a healing physician. It is not until he becomes a cancer patient himself that he understands the indignities people suffer at the hands of these empty but excellent technicians. His experiences transform his approach to medicine and help him become the complete physician, technically and emotionally. While this example can be easily dismissed as Hollywood fantasy, it offers a case where life could and should imitate art.

As you reflect on both male and female characteristics, think about the strengths they offer and where each can be both effective and ineffective. Filling out the chart *Evaluating the Trade-Offs of the Male and Female Management*

Prototypes will give you a chance to clarify your own thinking. The hope is that once you have identified the gains and losses of such an approach, you will see that all of these qualities are at times necessary but not sufficient. More important, to open up your organization, more room needs to be created to reward those characteristics deemed female.

Evaluating the Trade-Offs of the Male and Female Management Prototypes

Directions: List the gains and losses you see in your organization from perceived male and female management styles.

Male

Prototype	Gains	Losses
Leading by command and control		
Enhancing rewards for services rendered		
Reliance on positional power		
Following a hierarchical quasi-military structure		
Action orientation		
Analytical thinking and linear problem solving		

Female

Prototype	Gains	Losses
Sharing power and information		
Enhancing self-worth of others		
Encouraging participation		
Getting others excited about their work		

Suggestions for Using *Evaluating Trade-Offs of the Male and Female Management Prototypes*

Objectives:

- Consider what the traditional male and female models of leadership give to and take from your organization.

Intended Audience:

- Executive or midmanagement staffs that want to address the issue of what qualities are rewarded and promoted.
- Executive or midmanagement staffs that want to open up the system and make a commitment to more diverse representation at the top.

Processing the Activity:

- Have individual participants fill out the worksheet first.
- Then have a group discussion about the gains and losses derived from each of the various characteristics.

Questions for Discussion:

- What do these stereotypically male and female characteristics contribute to the organization?
- What do we reward around here?
- What is it costing us?
- How can we open up the system?
- What management skills are missing from this list that we need to reward?
- How can we ensure a broadening of the skills we reward and more representation from all segments of society?

Caveats and Considerations:

- Participants may react to the issue of *male* and *female*. They'll say "All males don't . . ." and "all females don't . . . ." Setting up the activity by citing the studies from which the data came, and by acknowledging that they do not refer to "all males" or "all females" can help diffuse resistance. Explain that these are generalizations but that there is some reason they exist. Your purpose is not to label or pigeonhole either gender, but rather to open up the system.

By using this analysis, you should be able to see the upside and downside of prototypical female leadership. When companies err in their promotion efforts, they rarely do so by promoting too many employees who clearly demonstrate the feminine characteristics. With today's diverse labor force, ignoring these strengths puts your organization at peril. As you look at the characteristics that tend to be more dominant or natural in one gender than in the other, think about your own leadership or management style. Where do you excel? Where do you need to improve? In order to have a more rounded management team, what characteristics does your organization need to look for? These characteristics are the yin and the yang of effective management. Both matter and are useful, but with what we know about other cultures, the relationship-oriented style of leadership associated with women, frequently overlooked as "soft," can produce "hard" results among today's pluralistic work force.

Traditional American Management: Expanding the Mix

Part of the responsibility for being promotable falls on the shoulders of any candidate who wants a new, better, or different job. Part of the responsibility also falls on the organization. The problem is that in far too many cases, the overwhelming responsibility for promotion has been borne by the candidate, and the results for women, people of color, and the organization itself are not heartening. In an unyielding system, where one type of management characteristic is valued to the exclusion of others, you have high turnover and diminished credibility with the diverse population. To be successful in making room for non-dominant-culture promotions, the model of what constitutes successful and effective management must grow even beyond the typical male/female model discussed above, and the organization must do its part to ensure that result. Dr. Rosener paraphrases a colleague when she says that people who are blocked by the glass ceiling can't break it from below. Cracks are starting to appear in some ceilings. The question is, Are they big enough to squeeze through? You can ponder that question by reflecting on your own company. What leadership traits are currently being promoted in your organization? By filling out the *Valued Management Traits* list, you'll get a clear indication of your organization's management prototype.

Valued Management Traits

I. List the 10 most important traits your company looks for in someone it promotes to a management position:

_____   _____

_____   _____

_____   _____

_____   _____

1. Put a check by each trait that describes you.

2. Put an X by each characteristic that is valued by the dominant American business culture.

3. What is the flip side of each of these characteristics?

4. Are any of these traits more difficult for a woman? Person of color? The differently skilled? Someone of a different affectional orientation?

II. List traits that you see frequently in other groups on the job that "hold them back."

_____   _____

_____   _____

_____   _____

_____   _____

1. What are some advantages to these traits?

2. If you were to coach someone of another group for a management position, how would you help that person with traits that you perceive hold him or her back?

Suggestions for Using *Valued Management Traits*

Objectives:

- Identify management traits that are rewarded and promoted in your organization.
- See how similar you and other managers or executives are to that management model.
- Consider how difficult it might be for someone from the nondominant culture to succeed and be promoted in your organization.
- Get a sense that other cultures have traits we can learn from.

Intended Audience:

- Facilitator, consultant, or HR professional working with a middle management group to help look at opening their promotion process.
- Affirmative action officer or vice president of HR who wants to help an executive staff understand current promotability with an eye toward opening up the system.

Processing the Activity:

- Ask participants to fill out the worksheet. When working with an executive staff, discuss responses among the whole group. For a middle management group, break up into small groups first, then process with the entire group.
- Chart the list of characteristics on an easel in front of the group. Put checks by those characteristics.

Questions for Discussion:

- Discuss each of the other questions with the biggest focus on What are we promoting? How does this model of promotability hold a diverse candidate back? What can we do about it?

Caveats and Considerations:

- Do not even begin the analyses of valued management traits unless you are willing to do something about broadening the criteria. Looking at the issue will raise expectations, but doing nothing will create cynicism and hopelessness.

Determining what is rewarded and promoted in your company is one way to assess the informal structure for moving people up. But genuinely opening up the organization is a systemwide challenge that looks at many things—power shifts, utilization of resources, and alterations in the reward structure to name but a few. It requires looking at policies, practices, and procedures to see where deep, comprehensive change can begin. Take the questionnaire *What Does Your Company Do to Increase Promotions of Its Diverse Employees?* to see how your company stacks up.

What Does Your Company Do to Increase Promotions of Its Diverse Employees?

Directions: With your organization in mind, respond to the following questions by putting a check in the appropriate column.

Questions	Yes	No
1. Top management utilizes formal systems to meet with and encourage top talent from diverse backgrounds.	____	____
2. Teaching potential "stars" the rules is a top priority.	____	____
3. A balanced life is compatible with the demanding work load of those who move up.	____	____
4. Our company is attractive to diverse employees because we are flexible enough to accommodate differences.	____	____
5. Our company models change by welcoming diversity at all levels of the organization.	____	____
6. A formal mentoring system exists to nurture top talent.	____	____
7. The golf course is the best place to tap into the informal pipeline.	____	____
8. Taking parental leave is possible but frowned upon.	____	____
9. Our organization can sell itself to diverse employees by pointing out that 25 percent of top management are currently women and people of color.	____	____
10. Involvement in change is pushed to the lowest level of the organization.	____	____
11. Top management seeks advice from and contact with employees from all backgrounds.	____	____
12. Our organization reaches out to and is knowledgeable about the population it serves.	____	____
13. A reward structure exists to accommodate the different employee motivations.	____	____
14. Our company has an excellent reputation in attracting top talent because of our child- and elder-care policies.	____	____
15. Many of our systems are different today than they were one year ago.	____	____

Scoring: Items number 7 and 8 are *no* answers and all the rest should be *yes* if your organization promotes advancement of diverse individuals. Here are the concepts being measured:

Items 1, 6, 11 *Building connections:* Helps employees develop and maintain relationships that are sturdy and enhancing at all levels of the organization.

Items 2, 7, 12: *Political savvy:* Helps employees make use of the informal organization and pick up the unstated clues.

Items 3, 8, 13: *Dealing with multiple motivations:* Demonstrates a willingness to be flexible with today's work force, realizing that different employees are motivated by different things.

Items 4, 9, 14: *Positioning:* Indicates the organization's ability to make itself attractive by presenting outcomes in a value base employees respect and respond to.

Items 5, 10, 15: *Mastering change:* Attests to an organization's openness to new people, ideas, and systems.

Suggestions for Using *What Does Your Company Do to Increase Promotions of Its Diverse Employees?*

Objectives:

- Assess your organization's openness to promoting diverse employees.

Intended Audience:

- Executive-level staff to see how open they perceive the organization to be and where they can be more so.
- Middle management to give executive staff feedback about openness as they see it.

Processing the Activity:

- Have each participant take and score the questionnaire.
- In executive staff, discuss as a whole group; for midlevel management, break into small groups first.
- Collate results from midlevel management and feed upward.

Questions for Discussion:

- What item number and category do you see as this organization's greatest strength in opening up the system?
- Its greatest weakness?
- What, according to the data, needs to be done in order to expand the promotional system?

Caveats and Considerations:

- Don't give this to midlevel managers to send feedback upward if there won't be any movement. The disenchantment and disappointment will be too costly.

The organization may do its part to develop a system for implanting these strategies. But if it wants candidates from diverse backgrounds to succeed when they are promoted, these career strategies need to be taught and nurtured to up-and-coming managers. Having an advocate or mentor in the organization who will teach these skills can make the difference between success and failure in securing a job or being promoted. Building connections will help give potential managers the visibility and access to those at the top while learning the rules of etiquette, and the informal norms will help protégés increase political savvy. Beyond the first two skills, learning the rules that lead to reaping the rewards is critical. In some companies, 60-hour weeks are expected, while in others, time for family is valued and 45-hour weeks are sufficient. One of the hardest techniques for people to utilize is positioning, which enables an employee to sell his ideas by showing the "buyer" what's in it for him. It is particularly hard for immigrants from some cultures to use this technique to promote themselves. Developing the ability to frame opinions and ideas in values that others respond to is a hallmark of success at any level, but it is especially important for managers who must ask employees to continuously do more work with fewer resources. Finally, learning to embrace and harness change is increasingly important for survival in today's world. Flexibility and adaptability are as crucial for business survival as oxygen is for humans. A good mentor can help a potential manager find the opportunity associated with change rather than the fear. Anything short of this mutual investment coupling organizational strategies with the development of personal skills will set new promotees up for failure, no matter how sharp they are.

Mentoring: A Proven Way to Groom and Grow Talent

While coaching helps an organization grow talent through good one-on-one teaching and some cheerleading, mentoring can be counted on to provide the role modeling and career counseling. By definition, mentoring is the sponsoring or guiding of another person; it resembles the apprenticeship idea from days of old. The best mentoring takes place within a formal system in the organization even though the relationship itself can have an informal style or feel to it. While conclusive evidence on the value of mentors is still scant, Jerry Willbur, vice president of Service Master Company, states "For females and members of minority groups entering management, the chances for career success improve when these individuals obtain mentoring."[39]

Various companies are flirting with mentoring efforts. One of the most interesting is at Procter & Gamble, where as a result of "high turnover among black and women managers at a plant in Georgia, it set up a mentoring program that paired 23 minority managers with a senior employee of their choosing." According to Robert E. Cannon at P&G, the mentoring program gets credit for reducing the turnover. Furthermore, Cannon believes that career planning is where an organization puts muscle into their diversity efforts. In Cannon's words, "It's where the rubber meets the road."[12]

Mentoring is usually a less structured, less formal relationship than coaching. It is most successful when mentors act as a career counselor, while at the same time they are advocates who increase a protégé's visibility, accessibility, and promotability. The higher up a mentor is, the better, because he or she can do some PR work for the protégé and the advocacy will carry more influence. When interesting assignments come up, the mentor can throw out a suggested name. When a new job opportunity is in the offing, a mentor can guide a protégé through the process of meeting influential people, accumulating the right skills and experiences, or handling oneself in appropriate and flattering ways. A mentor can be the magnet that helps pull a protégé upward. And this relationship is not an all-give-and-no-take experience. The mentor garners loyal support that can increase his or her power base, as well as increase access to information through the lower-level pipeline. It provides an opportunity for the mentor to grow by polishing and refining some of his or her own skills.[46]

All in all, mentoring can be a winning strategy for everyone. If a company is serious about developing and retaining diverse talent, we suggest a few essential steps that can add some substance and structure to a mentoring program. It is based on a process we used eight years ago in working with the Council of Mexican American Administrators, a group of educators in the Los Angeles Unified School District. There were two clear purposes, the first of which was to teach and groom those already functioning as administrators to be mentors so they could help other Hispanics be promoted. The other purpose was to design a program that would build the skill and confidence of the potential administrators they were trying to promote. To meet both goals, we did the following:

1. Consulted with the leadership of the organization to determine concrete outcomes they wanted from the mentoring program. This was helpful in forming the nature of the training.

2. Designed the training content that explained the role of the mentor and that of the protégé. Each of the roles had different responsibilities. It was important to clarify expectations so accountability and success could occur. The training content was set up to increase self-confidence and performance by teaching specific skills such as risk taking, self-reliance, dealing with conflict, and giving feedback effectively. While all the administrators in our program were Latino, they were either born in the United States or had been here so long that their acculturation was a fait accompli. In most organizations, the cultural programming of mentors and protégés is different, and attention needs to be paid to the issue of acculturation.

3. Mentors and protégés were paired up in formal relationships. To ensure accountability, mentors sought answers to several questions in order to make the process effective. Some may be pertinent to your organization:
   • How do we ensure opportunity for both line and staff experience as we try to promote candidates?
   • Are we identifying generalists? Specialists? How do we build crossover?
   • How do we track the people we've identified as both mentors and protégés regarding the results we've gotten?

These are but a few of the questions that need to be addressed if an organization is going to use mentoring as more than a token tool to increase promotability and retention of minority candidates. Tracking the results is absolutely critical in order to find out what parts of the program are working and what needs to be improved. The dynamics between mentors and protégés can offer useful information in designing a continuously evolving program that increases chances of success.

Cross-Cultural Coaching for Top Performance

John Wooden, Vince Lombardi, Bear Bryant, and Pat Riley are but a few of the legendary coaches who stand out because they have gotten superior performance and results from their respective teams. While athletic coaches provide us with the most visible models of excellence in coaching, every field has its share of teachers who coax, cajole, instruct, support, nurture, and encourage individuals as they work with them to develop their full potential. Astute managers realize that the principles of a genius like John Wooden can apply to any coaching experience, from the court at Pauley Pavilion to any board room in the country. A coach is the equivalent of a private tutor or personal trainer. Applied to a company's diversity effort, it entails a tacit but demonstrable commitment to help women and other diverse employees flourish as they move up rather than wash out.

Selection of coaches should be based on job-related skills and professional relationship. The process begins when a manager identifies a person who has talent and potential, and then takes the oversight responsibility and time to invest in grooming an employee for management ranks. There are several overall functions that an excellent coach performs. As you think about the talented people who are able to teach and groom other employees with potential, see if you can identify some managers who might fit the bill. You might even look to see if it's right for you.

Functions of a Cross-Cultural Coach

1. Have Knowledge of and an Appreciation for Different Cultures.   This attitude is so basic that it almost doesn't bear mentioning. However, it is not uncommon to pair up people in organizations, ask someone to show another person the ropes, and then learn down the road that the training didn't work because the coach has a chip on his shoulder about immigrants or feels uncomfortable with blacks or cringes around gays. Goodwill can make up for less-than-brilliant coaching. What won't work well is selecting a coach who has an ax to grind about affirmative action, racial quotas, or whatever labels someone wants to attach to opening up the system.

2. Provide Support.   Giving support is one of the most important functions of a coach. *Cheerleading* is probably not too strong a term. As a cross-cultural coach, it will be important to encourage risk taking, assertiveness, and the ability to sell oneself or one's ideas. All three of these behaviors may be difficult for someone from a different culture or anyone who feels like an outsider in a system. By offering support and encouragement, you can help increase a protégé's confidence, visibility, and ultimately, promotability.

3. Give Helpful and Usable Feedback.   Imagine that as a coach you function like a Polaroid camera. You make it your business to give your student usable information based on behaviors you see firsthand. These behaviors focus on skills such as giving presentations, leading meetings, or representing the company at a public function. But the feedback doesn't have to be skill based. You may give your trainee useful information about cultural norms that he violated or common organizational practices that are inviolate. Be careful of how you give the feedback. Cross-culturally, this is a sensitive issue. Chapter 3 gives you hints on how to do so effectively, but most important, if you are a sensitive human being, you have a good chance of delivering useful information in a very helpful way.

4. Teach the Importance of Cause and Effect.   In a word, you are trying to teach *accountability*. In cultures where fatalism is a strong concept, it is more difficult to teach the idea that what you do has consequences and your behavior triggers them. It is helpful not only to teach cause and effect, but also to help the employee create more options so she rarely feels backed into a corner and will almost always see alternatives. In terms of professional growth and maturation, this is a critical concept. It will take patience, reinforcement, and the realization on your part that mistakes will be made.

5. Point Out the Big (or Whole) Picture.   Perspective is a healthy coping strategy. Excellent coaching necessitates that function. You can teach people to see both the macro and the micro view, make their choices, and then live with the results. Theoretically, the coaching function should help protégés warm up to the idea of risk taking with the recognition that if it doesn't work perfectly, that's all right. There were gains from the doing and the learning, in any case. Also, you can function effectively as a sounding board asking your student hypothetical questions so he can see different alternatives and consequences before he makes choices. Hypothetical questions may be hard for immigrants, particularly the Japanese. Nevertheless, encouraging a protégé to bounce ideas off of you is what good coaching is all about.

6. Teach Promotable Skills.   A top-notch coach is primarily an excellent teacher, and as with any good teaching, coaching someone for management involves an understanding of the learner. People in different cultures think and learn differently. Is one culture's learning style more didactic? Is another's more hands-on? How much participation might an employee be used to? The sensitivity required in teaching needed skills includes knowledge of customs and understanding subtle but significant nuances of the protégé's acculturation. How much adaptation would be required to get this individual ready to make a presentation? What might be a comfortable way for her to present ideas by herself when all the work she has ever done has been as a team member? Where might the adaptation required for promotion cross the line and result in behaviors so antithetical to upbringing that they foster self-hate? Teaching critical promotable skills in a way they will be heard is in itself a remarkable skill. It may mean borrowing a line from a song in the film *Mary Poppins:* ''Just a spoonful of sugar makes the medicine go down.''

7. Create a Collaborative Partnership.   As a coach, you can be a person's professional confidante. As a partner or collaborator, you can help an employee define her goals. If she wants to become a midlevel manager, start pointing out how midlevel managers dress. Ask her to look at differences in dress at each level of the organization. Focus on certain behaviors and customs such as how people introduce one another, or whether first names or surnames are used when addressing colleagues. The learning exercise entitled *Norms: The Unwritten Rules of This Organization* is an example of the kind of worksheet you can give your apprentice as you try to coach him/her up the organization. It's sort of an ''everything you wanted to know about promotion in this organization but were afraid to ask.'' Give the employee you are coaching worksheets like these that you create, focusing on all the norms the protégé needs to learn. Set up appointments to discuss any observations and what the learning means to your particular student.

Learning the "Culture" of Your Organization: Norms—The Unwritten Rules

One of the benefits of receiving good coaching is learning the unwritten rules. Breaking these norms can be a costly mistake, yet one you may not even know you are making. Investigate and discover the norms regarding dress and communication by working with a coach and filling in the information on the chart entitled *Norms: The Unwritten Rules of This Organization*.

Norms: The Unwritten Rules of This Organization

Dress
What is the organizational uniform? How do people dress? Who wears suits? At what level are jackets required? Do women wear pants?

	Men	Women
Top executives		
Senior management		
Middle management		
Supervisors		
First-line staff		
Other		

Communicating and Addressing
How are people addressed? (First name, title, etc.) How are people contacted? (Phone call, memo, appointment)

	Men	Women
Top executives		
Senior management		
Middle management		
Supervisors		
First-line staff		
Other		

Employee Gatherings/Interacting
Who interacts? Who invites whom? How much time is spent? Is promptness valued/expected?

	Format (Where, When, Interaction)	Participants (Who, Roles)
Meetings		
Breaks		
Lunch		
After work		

Suggestions for Using *Norms: The Unwritten Rules of This Organization*

Objectives:

- Help potential managers learn the unwritten rules of behavior in your company.

Intended Audience:

- Coaches working with potential promotees so they can teach them the "rules."

Processing the Activity:

- One-on-one discussion between coach and promotee.

Questions for Discussion:

- Whatever is on the worksheet and whatever other norms the coach suggests are important.

Caveats and Considerations:

- It is possible for a trainer to bring coaches together and use a seminar format to collectively determine what the norms are so that all coaches in a given organization teach and reinforce the same ones.

These are only sample questions. What else you choose to ask will depend on the norms you are trying to teach. These norms will vary from one organization to another, but the key to the success of this undertaking remains teaching any unwritten rules that could sabotage the success of your protégé. Working with an attentive coach can help a potential promotee learn the significant norms.

The next exercise, *Coaching for Promotion,* is designed to help potential coaches uncover any biases or hidden expectations they may have about certain groups. This learning exercise needs to be conducted in a group setting. Divide people into small groups; based on the background of the candidate, each group determines a coaching strategy. It is not until groups report on their respective strategies that participants realize that perhaps expectations based on background may have something to do with the coaching that takes place. How would you coach a person who is Latino? What differences would it make if that person with the same qualifications were gay? Differently abled? An elder worker? In terms of opening up the system, it is important to see if expectations influence coaching. When each group reports its coaching strategy, you may not notice any differences between groups at all, but if different strategies do exist, they may provide good opportunity for discussion. What does this tell you about the coaching, inclusivity, and openness of this organization? A good facilitator will help you maximize the learning and determine any accommodations that need to be made.

The candidate we have used in the sample is Maryann Ransom, a lesbian who is a member of the Gay and Lesbian Rights Association. We suggest a few other examples, such as Roberta Rothstein, a Jewish woman who is active in the American Jewish Federation; Luis Hernandez, a Latino active in the Mexican American Legal Defense Fund; and LaVerne Johnson, an African-American who gives her time to the NAACP. Make up candidates pertinent to your employee population. Only the names, extracurricular organizations, and backgrounds change. All professional experiences and qualifications are the same. Therein lies the learning.

Coaching for Promotion

As a unit manager in systems planning, Maryann Ransom, a lesbian, has just come to work for you. She has a B.A. from a state university and graduated in the top third of the class. Her first job out of business school was as a management trainee at Merck, where she received excellent training in basic supervisory skills and computer programming. Working with you, her job duties will involve budget planning and analysis, project management, and supervision of a small group of data processors. References indicate good peer relationships, initiative, creativity, and great promise. Maryann is also an active member of the Gay and Lesbian Rights Association.

The quality of her work has been excellent; however, she has had little experience in some key areas required for the new job such as personnel relations, EEOC and affirmative action guidelines, and hiring and interviewing skills.

1. What would you do to help groom Maryann for promotion?

2. How would you coach her to develop the skills and experiences necessary to move up in the organization?

3. List 10 steps you would take or suggest to enhance Maryann's development and career success.

Suggestions for Using *Coaching for Promotion*

Objectives:

- Determine whether people are coached differently because of ethnicity, race, gender, or other aspects of background.
- Detect any biases in who is promoted.

Intended Audience:

- Facilitator, consultant, HR professional, or trainer who is charged with the task of helping mid- and upper-level management see if there is any bias in how people are coached.

Processing the Activity:

- Use the worksheet, changing only the name and background of the person and keeping the criteria the same.
- Divide people into small groups. Have them discuss coaching strategy and then report back to entire group about their strategy. Write strategies on chart paper.

Questions for Discussion:

After each group reports its coaching strategy, discuss what differences emerge based on background.
- What differences in coaching exist? Depending on what factors? How can they be minimized?

Caveats and Considerations:

- Make certain that the different employee populations in your geographic area are represented.
- Don't let participants know that candidate names are different but qualities are the same.

Career Development: A Sure-Fire Way to Develop Your Talent Pool

Implementing systemwide career development across cultures calls for nothing less than a paradigm shift in how career development is conducted. The very idea of career development—with its ladder stretching upward and its assumption that you reward individuals who like recognition and take responsibility for their own life and career—flies in the face of many of the cross-cultural norms we have discussed throughout this book. The very idea of individuation and focusing on or rewarding the self for accomplishment is foreign to many cultures. By looking at values cross-culturally (see the table on page 381), you will increase your understanding of their impact and be able to use organizational systems to enhance career opportunities for all who fit under the diversity banner.

HR departments responsible for career development and promotion of diverse employees need to look at the formal systems such as performance review, interviewing, recruiting, and mentoring, as well as the informal systems such as socializing, networking, and support groups. For a career development system to work, it has to be both top down and bottom up. The *Career Development Model* on page 382 shows some of the major pieces it needs.

The importance of this model is in the realization that making room at the top involves not only systems changes with leadership and buy-in at the highest levels but also training for managers and entry-level employees. Managers used to dealing with a homogeneous work force need new skills and information, and those employees who are not mainstream need to learn how to adapt to the norms of American business if they are going to be successful. All employees can stand a course in learning to deal with change and cross-cultural norms. Attracting, developing, and maintaining the best talent requires nothing less than a full-throttle approach. The payoff will be worth it. What Stephen M. Wolfe of United Airlines says about women is applicable to each and every employee in an organization that makes room for diverse talent at all levels: "Fortunately, U.S. society is learning that not only can women succeed in just about any arena, but the qualities they bring to the competition raise the level of the entire playing field."[44]

Impact of Values on Career Expectations and Performance

Point of Contact	Mainstream Culture	Other Cultures
Interview	I need to showcase my experience, skills, and talents.	My track record and seniority speak for themselves. I need to establish a relationship and get comfortable with the other person first.
Performance review	I need feedback so I can do a better job.	Criticism could cause me to lose face and feel shame.
Meetings	Making suggestions and actively participating show I am motivated and take the initiative.	Contributing my ideas, asking questions, voicing complaints, or making suggestions look like I am showing off and may make my boss lose face. Besides, ideas and suggestions need to come from the leader.
Socializing/networking	I'm going to these events because you never know who will be there. The visibility can't hurt my career.	I will go to this event because my boss asked me to and I wouldn't let her down.
Mentoring	I'd like the CEO to be my mentor because he has the clout in this organization. If he's in my corner, it will certainly help.	I like my boss, Miss Shirley. She is a very nice person who treats me with respect.
Self-promotion	Expected and rewarded; to paraphrase American Express, "Don't expect a promotion without it."	Very difficult for other cultures; it would be embarrassing and a violation of some of the most sacrosanct norms to toot your own horn.
Forming alliances	Pragmatic in the dominant culture; people and organizations are political. This is a survival skill.	Inclusion in the group and relationships are critical. They are formed because of personal loyalty and affection, not because of position in the organization.
Social skills; ice breaking; establishing rapport	The dominant culture is short on social lubrication, long on getting right to the point. Self-introduction is accepted and sometimes expected.	This skill could be a natural ally for most other cultures where far more time is invested in relationships. Formal introductions are expected. Individuals may be reluctant to establish relationships outside of their own group.
Giving and getting feedback	Needed and expected skills for one's growth; "If you don't give me feedback, how can I know what I need to do differently or better?" Done in the good old American way—directly. Separation of the behavior from the worth of a person makes it more objective and less personal.	This is very delicate in other cultures. Loss of face warrants shame. People have left jobs because of negative feedback and the perception of disgrace. Feedback is often taken personally and seen as a personal affront.
Tapping the grapevine	Skeptical of informal communication. There is a tendency to believe what is in print and official.	Those out of power generally make the greatest use of the grapevine and are often skeptical of official information channels.
Scheduling/goal setting	Task and time consciousness, coupled with linear thinking and planning matter. Anything can be done or accomplished if the individual works hard enough. Each person is responsible for his/her own success or failure.	Time is relative and the accomplishment of tasks depends on more than the individual alone. Other priorities often change schedules and plans. Fate and the will of God play a part.

Career Development Model

1. **Top down:** Build career development through all the systems. Some examples are:

   • Performance review.

   • Recruitment/hiring/promotion.

   • Accountability.

   • Training.

2. **Bottom up:** Conduct skill training for managers and employees in various diversity-related areas. Some examples are:

Managers:

   • Giving performance reviews in culturally sensitive ways.

   • Handling intercultural conflict.

   • Running effective meetings in a diverse environment.

   • Conducting interviews in culturally appropriate ways.

   • Building effective multicultural work teams.

   • Recognizing cultural biases in making promotions.

   • Expanding the list of valued management characteristics.

Employees:

   • Building connections.

   • Becoming politically savvy.

   • Learning to position ideas effectively.

   • Managing and becoming comfortable with change.

   • Becoming comfortably assertive.

   • Gaining self-promotion skills.

Section III

ROUNDING OUT YOUR KNOWLEDGE BASE: REALITIES AND RESOURCES

Chapter 11

Diversity: Today's Demographic Reality

This chapter will give you:
1. Facts and figures about the demographic trends changing the American work force.
2. Myths and realities about this work force.
3. A delineation of primary and secondary dimensions of diversity.
4. Information about work-force trends—aging, feminization, immigration, and educational deficits.
5. The strategic advantages of effectively managing diversity.

Demographic Destiny: Work-Force Trends and Their Impact

Today's demographic revolution is radically transforming society and organizational life. The changes are fundamental and far reaching. How American businesses deal with the dilemmas presented by the five trends we describe will affect not only their success but also the survival of the national economy. The first place to begin in grappling with this massive societal shift is to examine the five major trends impacting the workplace.

1. Increase in the Number of Women

While working mothers, two-wage-earner households, and single parents are commonplace in our society, the Hudson Institute reports that by the year 2000, women will make up almost half (47 percent) of the labor force and 60 percent of the new entrants to the work force.[23] In addition, women are holding a larger share of jobs in management and the professions, especially in fields that have been traditionally male dominated such as law, medicine, and accounting.

Having more women in the work force and more women at higher levels means organizations have to deal with the needs and circumstances of women, who continue to bear the major burden for home and family responsibilities. Organizations have begun to respond with child-care options, flexible scheduling, elder-care programs, and cafeteria-plan benefit packages. However, they still need to make progress in creating career development options that meet the needs of women. Once satisfied to merely get in, women, like other previously excluded groups, are cracking the glass ceiling and demanding admittance to the upper echelons of organizations.

2. Increase in the Number of Minorities

Changing demographics are beginning to make the terms *minority* and *majority* invalid and irrelevant in many communities across the country as the percentage of Latinos, African-Americans, and Asians increases. According to Hudson Institute estimates, by the year 2000, nonwhites will make up 29 percent of the work force.[23] In order to capitalize on this sector of the work force, organizations will need to expand opportunities for nonwhites by creating more inclusive environments.

3. Increase in the Number of Immigrants

Immigrants are flocking to America's shores and over its borders in greater numbers than any period since World War I. However, today's newcomers are different from those of the early 1900s, who were mainly Europeans. Today's immigrants are not as visibly assimilable—they look different. They are mainly Latino, Asian, and Middle Eastern individuals, who, like all immigrants past and present, want a piece of the American dream, but not at the expense of their unique cultural characteristics and values. This steady flow of one half to three quarters of a million immigrants per year is felt most strongly in California, Texas, and New York, states where well over half of all foreign-born residents live.[23] The range in education, skill level, and ability is wide, from those who are illiterate in their native languages to those who are multilingual and who possess advanced degrees.

Language is one of the greatest challenges immigrants pose for organizations.

While some are fluent English speakers, most immigrants are not. Yet a survey of 645 American organizations by Towers Perrin and the Hudson Institute reported that fewer than 10 percent of the companies surveyed had English-as-a-second-language programs for employees.[41] Beyond dealing with language barriers, organizations are faced with the challenge of helping managers understand the cultures of their employees so they can motivate, reward, and build productive work relationships with their diverse staffs.

4. Aging

As the demographic bulge created by the postwar baby boom (1946–1961) passes into maturity, it moves a large proportion of the work force into middle age. While the majority of workers in the next decade will still be in their most productive years (35–54), the labor force is slowly getting older. This means fewer young, entry-level people, as well as more experienced workers who come with education and training as well as a higher price tag. Organizations will be called upon to help more mature employees maintain the flexibility and energy needed to deal with an accelerated pace of change. In addition, businesses will also have to find ways of dealing with the increased competition among older workers for midcareer promotions and management positions at a time when most companies are streamlining and trimming layers of management.

5. Rise in Education and Skill Requirements

Today's and tomorrow's jobs require a more highly skilled, more educated work force in a society where the education and skill levels of the population are declining. *Workforce 2000* predicts that the majority of jobs from now on will require education beyond high school.[41] This trend may prove a barrier to minority groups who have been educationally disadvantaged and who have traditionally entered the work force through unskilled or semiskilled jobs. Organizations will need to create bold new methods of training employees in both basic and job-related skills and retraining existing workers to keep up with the demands of the workplace.

Aging: Different Generations Equal Different Values

Morris Massey's film *What You Are Is What You Were When* has cleverly brought the topic of generational values into organizations across the country. With humor and insight he helps people understand how deeply programmed our values are by the era in which we grew up. Those of us with parents reared during the depression of the 1930s undoubtedly grew up hearing them praise thrift, hard work, and perseverance while viewing security as a prime value in a job. On the other hand, those reared in more affluent recent times are accused of being the "me first" generation with no patience for delayed gratification. "Enjoy now, pay later" is the current motto.

When we lead diversity seminars, participants often tell us that one of the hardest gaps to bridge is not one of culture or race, but one of age. Stereotypes, both positive and negative, abound. Younger workers are labeled irresponsible, ill-mannered, undependable, and not willing to pay their dues. Most damning of all, they are thought to have an inferior work ethic. Conversely, older employees are described as rigid, stodgy, uncreative, and resistant to change. While no one person of any generation is a carbon copy of others of the same age, there are values sets that characterize age groups. The differences between generations center on the following values and assumptions.

1.   Entitlement

Younger employees have grown up in an era of abundance and a climate of questioning authority. Where mature workers brought up in a more hierarchical and traditional society may follow directions because they are given by a boss, younger employees want to know why. In addition, with less fear of retaliation such as job loss, younger employees find it easier to challenge authority and demand that their concerns be recognized.

2.   Security

As older employees approach retirement, they are naturally concerned with making sure they are set for their ''golden years.'' In addition, many mature workers have a tacit ''signed on for life'' bargain with the organization. They may feel they have traded more lucrative opportunities for the security of a lifetime job guarantee. The threat of a job loss or layoff may be particularly devastating to an older employee who not only feels betrayed, but is at a loss in competing in a job market that discriminates against older workers. Younger employees, on the other hand, come from a generation that expects career mobility, job hopping, and many career moves. These individuals tend to build security through a strong résumé rather than through organizational stability.

3.   Achievement

Older workers tend to subscribe to the ''work hard and you'll get ahead'' school of thought. Achievement rests on stick-to-it-iveness. Their younger counterparts, on the other hand, subscribe to the ''work smarter, not harder'' theme. Clever thinking is seen as the ticket to success. This may lead to conflicts where older employees see younger staff members as conniving or lazy, while younger employees may see their older colleagues as plodding and unwilling to try new approaches.

4.   Loyalty

Perhaps as another legacy of the entitlement era in which they grew up, today's younger generation's loyalty is to themselves and their own prosperity, advancement, and well-being. Older workers tend to show more loyalty to the organization that has given them opportunities and so are willing to do what is asked, go the extra mile, and do more than is on their list of job duties. On the other hand, this same loyalty is often at the heart of the betrayal felt by these long-termers when organizations are forced to downsize and cut staff. The loyalty often brings with it the expectation that the organization will take care of the employee by guaranteeing lifetime employment.

   In dealing with a work force from different generations, it is critical not only to recognize the different values set each age group brings but also to find ways of working with rather than against those differences. One way to do that is to consider both the positive and negative aspects of each value in order to deal with the clashes in a more neutral, dispassionate, and objective way. For example, a strong value on personal entitlement may help the individual get ahead by stating desires and preferences clearly and openly. It may also make the individual a more productive team member who takes the initiative to give input and tell the boss about problems and complaints. On the downside, it may cause the individual to ignore the needs of others, causing rifts in a work group. Or it may lead to a reluctance to bear the extra work and pressure of the tough times that are part of every job from time to time. Conversely, a deemphasis on entitlement may make for an employee who is willing to bear any burden without complaint but one whose built-up resentment shows itself in passive resistance or stress-related illness.

Once seen in a more even light with a more neutral perspective, these value variations look less right and wrong than just plain different. What need to be negotiated are the tangibles such as schedules, hours, tasks, equipment, or supplies rather than the values themselves which are personal, deeply held, and powerfully defended.

Feminization of the Work Force

Gone are the Donna Reed days of apron-clad moms greeting their children with milk and cookies after school. Because of economic necessity, increasing options for women and personal career choices, the majority of women in America today work outside the home, making up close to half of the work force. This fundamental societal change has impacted organizations in significant ways.

1.   Dealing with Family Issues

Women in the workplace face double jeopardy—the regular pressures and work load of organizational life and the "second shift" they work when they get home. Because women remain the main caregivers and caretakers in our society, organizations have been forced to deal with family issues as strategic business concerns. Child care, return to work, and leave policies, as well as flexible scheduling options such as job sharing, have been organizational responses to the work/home conflicts faced by most working women. However, more progress is needed. A recent Towers Perrin/Hudson Institute survey reports that fewer than 10 percent of the organizations responding provided near-site or on-site day care or sick child care. Fewer than 15 percent had a gradual return to work policy, 20 percent provided paternity leave, and a little over 30 percent allowed sick days for sick children and maternity leave.[41] In competing for employees in the projected tight labor market, attending to these needs can be a strategic advantage for a farsighted organization.

2.   Meeting the Varying Needs of Working Women

Working women come in all shapes, sizes, and life-styles. Some come from dual-career households, while others are single parents. Child care, elder care, or college tuition may be their main concern. Some are midcareer and climbing, aspiring to executive levels, while others are nearing retirement or working to put a child through college. In order to attract and keep competent female employees, organizations have been required to become more flexible and creative in benefits such as health care, retirement, and educational reimbursement; incentives such as stock options and bonuses; and policies regarding leaves, work schedules, and the like. In the same Towers Perrin/ Hudson Institute report, a little over 20 percent of the organizations responding had job-sharing programs, though half offered flextime options.[41]

3.   Dealing with the Career Demands of Working Women

No longer content to fill the bottom layers of organizations, women are increasing their share of managerial and professional jobs. According to *Workforce 2000*, women account for nearly half of all professionals.[23] However, in addition to the discrepancy in earning power, women are angry at hitting the glass ceiling when they attempt to move beyond middle management. In order to retain talented female employees, organizations are recognizing the need to have both genders in the executive suite. Not only does promoting women give other women a sense of the possibilities within the organization, but it brings a different leadership style into upper management. Women at lower levels see that you don't have to be "one of the boys" and lose your own style in order to succeed. Equally important, the organization benefits from the other gender's approach to problems.

Polls continue to report only one or two women at the helm of major U.S. corporations. This area of career pathing for women is the most problematic for organizations and the one where least progress has been made because it deals with a central issue in diversity—power sharing. Making the most of today's and tomorrow's diverse work force depends on the ability of those in power, traditionally Euro-American males, to share power with groups who have been previously excluded from corporate decision making.

Back p. 38L

Immigration and Racial/Ethnic Shifts

If, as one student quipped, "Immigration is the sincerest compliment," then the United States is certainly much admired. The 1970s and 1980s brought the biggest tide of immigration to the U.S. since the great wave of the early 1900s. Changing immigration laws in 1965; the end of the war in Southeast Asia; and political and economic instability in Mexico, Central America, and the Middle East have resulted in a huge population influx. Somewhere between 500,000 and 750,000 new immigrants are predicted to enter the United States annually for the remainder of the century.[23]

Many of these new Americans bring languages and cultures that are non-European and non-Western. In addition, today's immigrant is generally more concerned with preserving ethnic identity than were many of those early 1900s pioneers who were eager to shed old-world ways. Finally, because of the large concentration of immigrants in certain cities, it is possible for people to continue to live in their native culture and language in this country. Los Angeles, for example, has the largest Spanish-speaking population in the world outside of Mexico City, the largest Filipino population outside the Philippines, and the largest Korean population outside Korea. The Los Angeles Unified School District reports that 80-plus native languages are spoken by its students.

The impact of this influx of newcomers on U.S. business is multifaceted. Immigrants often enter the work force at the lowest levels and provide a ready supply of low-wage workers for manufacturing and service jobs. However, language presents a problem, as newcomers generally lack facility in English. Organizations find themselves searching for ways to teach employees English while they teach supervisors and managers the skills needed to manage non-English-speaking workers. The mix of languages and cultures in work groups presents additional challenges for employers attempting to create harmonious and productive work teams. Finally, different cultural norms and values impact performance. How to relate to a boss, participate in a meeting, take criticism, solve a problem, or take initiative are all culturally influenced behaviors. What in one culture looks respectful may look lazy in another. What is polite in one may look deceitful in another. What is direct and clear to one person may seem rude and insulting to another. These cultural differences present significant challenges to managers of multicultural work teams.

While immigration has increased the diversity of the work force, native-born non-Euro-Americans also figure into the diversity mix. African-Americans, previously the largest minority, continue to make up approximately 12 percent of the population and will represent around 20 percent of the new entrants to the work force during this decade. However, other groups such as Latinos and Asians are growing at much faster rates due to immigration. This demographic shift has led to a fear expressed by many African-Americans that their hard-won gains in civil rights and EEO in the workplace will backslide and their concerns be preempted by other groups who by sheer numbers may prevail. One African-American woman who called our office expressed it this way:

> I'm black and frustrated. It seems to me that the concerns and issues of blacks have been lost in the shuffle due to all the attention focused on new immigrants from Central America and Asia. Our problems have never been fully addressed and now we're still getting the short end of the stick.

It is clear that America's work force is and will continue to be a heterogeneous, multicultural, polyglot mixture. As with any change, this shift brings with it both challenges and opportunities. It is our new reality to do with as we will.

Educational Deficits: The Gap between Organizational Needs and Work-Force Skill Level

The title of one *Business Week* article says it all: "Where the Jobs Are Is Where the Skills Aren't."[6] One of the biggest challenges for American business is the need for increasingly skilled workers in a population with decreasing education and skills levels. It is projected that over half of the decade's new jobs will require post–high school education and a third will require a college degree. As we shift from a manufacturing to a service economy, more brain than brawn will be called for. The fastest-growing jobs necessitate more language, math, and reasoning skills, while declining occupations have low levels of skill requirements. Entry-level workers are increasingly lacking in the basic skills to perform adequately on the job. High school dropout rates and slipping achievement scores, plus the need to import workers from abroad or ship clerical work overseas, demonstrate the educational deficits we are facing. For example, the *Business Week* article mentioned above reported that Chemical Bank in New York interviews 40 applicants to hire 1 who can be trained as a teller and that the New York Telephone Company had to test 60,000 applicants to hire 3,000 people.[6] The scenario is even more bleak for Latinos and African-Americans who have a greater educational disadvantage.

Organizations are beginning to respond by providing basic skills training for employees in reading, math, and other job-related competencies. A recent study reported fewer than 10 percent of companies provide preemployment training, but over 15 percent offer remedial education, over 30 percent partner with high schools and technical schools, and 40 percent offer on-site skill classes.[41] These percentages are bound to rise as organizational skill needs increase and workers' educational levels decline. In addition to bringing education to the workplace, business is going to the schools. In many communities, business/education partnerships are forming, bringing together leaders from both sides of the issue to solve one of society's toughest problems. With additional financial resources from corporations and more accurate information about the occupational skill needs of tomorrow, schools are trying to equip students for success after graduation.

Identifying Primary and Secondary Dimensions of Diversity

As fingerprints show us, each human being is unique, providing the world with infinite diversity. However, some differences are more important than others in the effects they have on individuals' opportunities in the world. Marilyn Loden and Judy Rosener, in their recent book *Workforce America!*, separate the major dimensions of diversity into two categories—primary and secondary.[28]

Primary Dimensions of Diversity:

- Age
- Ethnicity
- Gender
- Physical ability
- Sexual/affectional orientation

Secondary Dimensions of Diversity:

- Geographic location
- Income
- Marital status
- Military experience
- Parental status
- Religious beliefs
- Work experience

Primary factors are unalterable and extremely powerful in their effects. Secondary dimensions are significant in shaping us, but they are to some extent shapable in return, because we have some measure of control over them.

Janet Elsea, in her book *The 4 Minute Sell,* tells us that the nine most important things noticed about people in our society, in order of importance, are the following:[13]

1. Skin color
2. Gender
3. Age
4. Appearance
5. Facial expressions
6. Eye contact
7. Movement
8. Personal space
9. Touch

Upon encountering one another, we notice, make assessments, and make decisions about how to interact with that individual based on these nine factors. How we respond depends on many variables; among them are our assumptions and expectations. For example, an African-American encountering another African-American would undoubtedly have a different reaction and set of expectations than a Euro-American meeting that same person. A man responds differently to meeting another man than to meeting a woman. These reactions, based on split-second assessments of others, influence our relationships. It is as if each of us were a member of an exclusive club in which we were the only member. Each new acquaintance is analyzed to see if there is enough similarity, comfort, and affinity to permit inclusion—or hiring or promotion.

The first three items on the list—skin color, gender, and age—would fall into the primary dimensions of diversity. They are virtually unalterable and extremely powerful in determining our life situation from where we live and work to whom we marry and how much we earn. The last six on the list are culturally influenced. Whether we give a handshake or a hug, a direct stare or lowered eyes, a nod or a frown is determined by the culture in which we are raised and is influenced by both the primary and secondary dimensions of diversity.

Consider people with whom you work, both those with whom you feel an affinity and those with whom you do not. How many dimensions of diversity do you have in common with each group? No doubt there are more commonalities both in primary and secondary factors among those with whom you feel a connection.

Analyzing Your Organization's Work-Force Trends

Forewarned is forearmed. Understanding the demographic shift at a societal level is a preamble to taking a look at your own specific work-force trends. It has been said that to find out who your entry-level workers will be in five years, you need only to go to your local junior or senior high school. However, you may want to conduct a deeper analysis. Questions such as those in the box may help guide your investigation.

A number of resources can help you in your data gathering and investigation. Local governments and organizations such as the Southern California Association of Governments often compile statistics and provide demographic information about the population, as do most school districts. Local colleges and universities generally have sociologists and statisticians who monitor trends in the population. Finally, the U.S. Department of Labor, Bureau of Statistics, offers state-by-state breakdowns from census figures. In addition, profession- and industry-specific associations often chart relevant trends.

Analyzing Your Organization's Work-Force Trends

Population Demographics

1. What is the projected breakdown of the community's population in 5 and 10 years in such areas as age, ethnicity, gender, and native language?

2. What is the projected breakdown of the local work force in 5 and 10 years by age, ethnicity, and gender?

3. What are the statistics regarding education level of the work force in 5 and 10 years by gender and ethnicity?

4. What different needs will these workers bring? How will they impact the organization?

Organizational Skills Needs

1. What is the projected number of new workers needed by your organization in 5 and 10 years by skill level such as unskilled, semiskilled, managerial, professional, and/or by type of work such as assembly line, clerical, data entry, and so on?

2. What is the projected gain or loss of employees by your organization in 5 and 10 years by department or function such as manufacturing, accounting, data processing, personnel, sales, marketing, and customer relations?

3. What will be the skill requirements of employees in 5 and 10 years, for example, English literacy or computer literacy?

Training and Development Needs

1. What tools do we need to develop to assess individual skill levels and job requirements?

2. What basic and job-specific skills will need to be taught to employees?

3. What managerial skills will need to be taught to those in supervisory and management roles?

Within the organization, information can be obtained from both existing data such as human resource statistics and the company's strategic plan as well as from management staff who can give a bird's-eye perspective on expected changes. The end result of your analysis should tell you what your organization will need and how well the work force will be able to meet those needs. You will then be in a position to strategically plan ways to bring the two closer together.

Myths and Realities about Today's Multicultural Work Force

"It ain't the way it used to be" may be true, but today's reality may not present as dismal a picture as many would paint. Dispelling some of the alarming myths about the diverse work force may help you have more realistic expectations about our future.

1. *Myth:* Immigrants are illiterate and uneducated.

Reality: Immigrants come with varying skills, talents, and education levels. Some may be rural peasants with little or no education seeking economic advantage in the United States. Others may be highly educated professionals who have come for political freedom and who are working at jobs well below their education level because of limited English skills that prevent them from passing licensing exams in their professions. *Workforce 2000* reports that during the decade of the 70s, 22 percent of immigrants were college graduates, while only 16 percent of native Americans had completed college.[23]

2. *Myth:* Immigrants are a drain on the economy.

Reality: The fear may be worse than the reality. Los Angeles, where over 1 million immigrants settled in the 70s, is a case in point. During that period, job growth exceeded the national level, while unemployment was below that of the nation as a whole. Manufacturing wages dropped but the wages in the service industry, an area in which native-born Americans were concentrated, grew at a faster rate than the national average. New, young workers may draw industries that create jobs. *Workforce 2000* also reports that census data and other studies indicate that in 10 to 20 years, immigrants and their children will out-earn comparable native-born Americans. In addition, UCLA's David Hayer-Bautista, in his book *Burden of Support*, gives a fresh perspective about California's large and soon-to-be-majority Latino work force. He projects that this group of younger workers will be supporting a huge population of retired baby boomers through taxes.[20]

3. *Myth:* Immigrants take jobs away from native-born Americans.

Reality: This complaint about immigrants has been made about every successive group from the Irish and Germans of the 1800s to the Italians, Slavs, and Jews of the early 1900s. While experiences vary from area to area, one report gives another view. A statistical analysis of 247 urban areas determined that black unemployment did not increase in proportion to Mexican immigration in that labor market. Immigration in these cases was complementary rather than competitive with the existing minority work force.[23] However, recent news events have pointed to a rift between African-Americans and both Mexicans and Koreans who live and work in close proximity in many cities. In tough economic times, conflicts may increase between groups who see themselves in competition for diminishing resources.

Strategic Implications of Increasing Diversity: Challenges and Opportunities

Our demographic destiny presents organizations with both challenges and opportunities. The central issue in dealing with diversity has little to do with language, culture, or other differences; rather, it is about power sharing. Giving every group in society a stake in the system, every group in your organization a "piece of the action," is at the heart of the most significant challenge that diversity presents. Becoming open to differences and creating an inclusive environment means that new groups will need to be let into positions of decision making and influence. It is rare in human nature to find examples of those in power who willingly share it. Managing diversity in a meaningful way demands that organizations deal with this fundamental strategic issue.

Beyond opening the system, organizations will need to create strategies to help staff at all levels overcome their resistance to this demographic transformation and deal with one another in harmonious, cooperative ways. Companies will find it necessary to overcome barriers to communication and create strategic ways to foster synergistic teamwork, educate and retrain employees, and meet the varying needs of their increasingly multifaceted staffs.

Diversity will also present opportunities for work-force development, service enhancement, and new-business creation. The opportunities to capitalize on a new world of workers is endless. Organizations are finding rich new labor resources among older workers and the differently abled. Creative recruitment strategies can develop pools of talented entry-level workers among many previously untapped groups. Developing the internal pool of existing employees represents another undercultivated resource.

A diverse population also means different needs in the marketplace. The chance to enhance service and thereby capitalize on new markets is wide open. Understanding the needs and preferences of the changing consumer base and responding to it in more effective ways is an important area for growth. Automatic teller machines in different languages and the growth of foreign-language television programming are examples of this service enhancement. Finally, new business opportunities in the form of new products and services are waiting to be created. The last few years have witnessed the growth of check-cashing services for those who have no bank accounts, personal errand runners, and fast-food and take-out restaurants for working singles and dual-career couples. None of these would have been necessary in the America of 20 years ago.

Turning Diversity into a Corporate Asset

Effectively managing diversity and creating an organization in which differences are truly valued is more than just a good idea—it is good business. It is propelled by more than a moral imperative—it brings a strategic advantage. Those organizations that meet the challenges and capitalize on the opportunities presented by a diverse work force will show bottom-line results and a significant edge over the competition.

1. Better Return on the Investment in Human Capital

The management of human resources is often talked about as the "soft" side of business. Yet most organizations spend more on their human capital than on any other resource. Misuse and poor management of this asset costs organizations in obvious and not so obvious ways. In clearly bottom-line-connected ways, the stress claims, grievances, and EEO suits resulting from diversity-related problems cost organizations millions of dollars annually. But there are more subtle costs as well. Absenteeism and turnover are typical signs of the employee dissatisfaction and stress that can result when staff members are blocked from moving up or are forced to fit into an uncomfortable mold. In addition, employees who feel undervalued don't commit their energy, ideas, or full ability to produce top-quality results. On the other hand, when they feel the organization's commitment to them, they reciprocate by giving both their concentration and commitment.

2. Attracting the Best and the Brightest

As the labor force shrinks, the competition will be heated for top-notch talent. As that talent pool becomes more diverse, those organizations with a reputation for meeting the needs of diverse staff and offering the best opportunities to talented, capable individuals of any stripe will be the employer of choice.

3. Increased Creativity

Creativity has sometimes been defined as the act combining old elements in new ways. Yet it is habitual to stick to the tried and true. The influx of new and different people into an organization can bring an infusion of fresh blood. Newcomers, former outsiders, and those who are different from the norm have new perspectives that can be the source of ideas, suggestions, and methods that have not been previously considered. Men and women tend to think and communicate differently. People from other cultures see and solve problems differently. Employees from varied backgrounds bring knowledge and information about the needs of different groups. If tapped, this diversity of style, experience, and knowledge enhances the organization's ability to respond creatively.

4. Capitalizing on a Diverse Market

A diverse population translates into a diverse market for goods and services. Organizations whose work forces mirror the composition of the society at large will be in a better position to understand and reach out to this pluralistic marketplace. Through the sharing of a common language and culture, diverse employees often have the empathy and sensitivity not only to relate to consumers of different groups but also to anticipate needs and suggest ways to reach new market segments.

Chapter 12

Valuing Diversity Means More than Equal Employment Opportunity

This chapter will give you:

1. A brief history of EEO and affirmative action.
2. A chart that contrasts and defines affirmative action, valuing differences, and managing diversity in six dimensions.
3. An assessment tool to measure your organization's progress in affirmative action, valuing differences, and managing diversity.
4. Tips for getting staff buy-in for diversity.

If you want to put a match to a powder keg, just utter the letters *EEO* or the words *affirmative action* in most organizations and you are sure to see an explosion. By now the issues are so politically loaded and the views so polarized that it is often difficult to have a rational discussion or reach a clear understanding about these programs and policies. Valuing diversity often carries the baggage of its precursors, both EEO and affirmative action. To understand the concept of valuing diversity, it is helpful to take a step back and get a historical perspective in order to see this fairly recent concept in an evolutionary light.

EEO Requirements: What the Law Says and Why

At the height of the civil rights movement in the early 1960s, Congress began enacting legislation aimed at eliminating discrimination in the workplace. Recognizing the existence of a long history of exclusion, segregation, and inequality for minorities and women, lawmakers began creating a series of laws that laid the foundation for the EEO requirements and affirmative action programs that exist in most organizations today. The cornerstones of that foundation were the following acts:

- *Title VII of the Civil Rights Act of 1964*. This statute prohibited on-the-job discrimination on the basis of race, color, religion, sex, or national origin and created the Equal Employment Opportunity Commission to enforce this law.
- *The Age Discrimination in Employment Act of 1967*. This piece of legislation prohibits discrimination against employees or job seekers who are aged 40 to 70.
- *The Vietnam Era Veterans Readjustment Assistance Act of 1972*. This law requires companies with government contracts to take affirmative action to hire and promote qualified disabled and Vietnam era veterans.
- *The Rehabilitation Act of 1973*. This law requires companies with government contracts to accommodate the physical and mental needs of qualified handicapped employees and job seekers.
- *Pregnancy Disability Amendment to Title VII (1978)*. This addition to Title VII prohibits the disparate treatment of pregnant women.

All of these laws rest on the premises that society has neither accorded equal treatment nor provided equal opportunity to all and that inequities in employment continue. Therefore, legislation is required to change conditions that unfairly block certain groups. Their aim is to create a workplace where the only considerations for hiring or promotion are those that pertain to ability to do the job rather than attributes specific to a group (race, color, religion, etc.). The byword of this legislation is *nondiscrimination*.

Affirmative Action: An Answer to Past Discrimination

In the evolution of workplace equity, affirmative action goes a step further. Its premise is that the elimination of discrimination is not enough to create workplace equity. Because of a long history of discriminatory practices, employers need to make positive efforts to recruit, hire, train, and promote qualified employees of previously excluded groups. Emphasis is placed on reaching parity with local work-force demographics. Generally, organizations either voluntarily or under consent decrees formulate affirmative action plans that spell out hiring and promotion goals in terms of employee statistics and the method for achieving these objectives. This generally requires some method that gives the advantage to previously disadvantaged groups in order to rectify past inequities. Proportionately more women, African-American, or differently abled individuals, for example, will be moved in and up until parity goals are reached. Affirmative action institutes a temporary imbalance to reach a new balance.

Where Affirmative Action Stops Short

According to Pam Fomalont, former affirmative action administrator at a major Southern California aerospace firm, "Affirmative action is an imperfect system, but it is still the best method we have for getting diverse people into the pipeline. Without affirmative action, there would not be the kind of diverse employee base we have today." One of affirmative action's most often cited limits is that it gets people in but not up. Its programs are generally more successful in getting women and non-dominant-group members hired than in getting employees of these groups promoted into middle and upper management.

Another place where affirmative action stops short is in advocating for only a few of the many groups who may be facing discrimination in the workplace. Women and African-Americans have historically been the greatest beneficiaries, while Latinos, Asians, and recent immigrants have been less aided by affirmative action programs.

Why the Resistance to EEO and Affirmative Action?

Let's take a look at why there is resistance to EEO and affirmative action programs.

1.   Perceived Restrictions on Individual Freedom

The first and perhaps most powerful reason for resistance is the perception by managers that affirmative action program goals restrict the manager's freedom and limit his/her control in making decisions about whom to hire or promote. The manager may be antagonistic toward affirmative action because he/she perceives it as an infringement on an important managerial prerogative, the freedom to make hiring and promotional decisions. Managers often fear that affirmative action goals may force them to hire or promote someone who is not their first choice.

2.   Perceived Dichotomy between Diversity and Quality

In many organizations the complaint about affirmative action is that it leads to a lowering of standards, a loss in quality of staff, and hence a loss in quality of

Quality and Diversity: Not an Either-Or

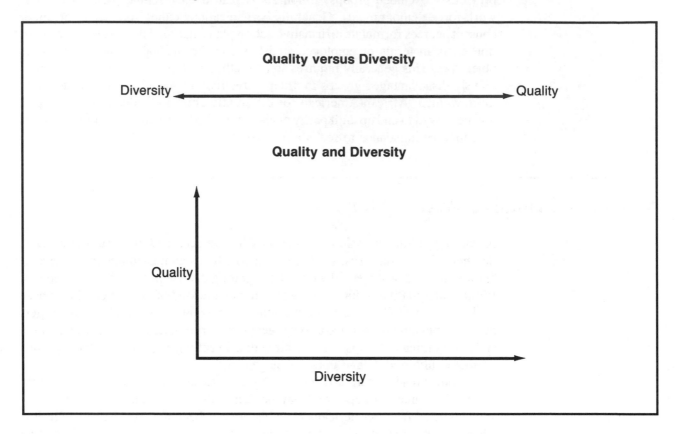

output. The underlying assumption is that quality and diversity are on opposite ends of a continuum, that one must be sacrificed for the other. According to this view, choosing the best employee means giving up on increasing the diversity of staff and, conversely, increasing diversity means that a less qualified person must be chosen. The choice is perceived to be between the most qualified candidate or a minority candidate. This perception leads to a polarization of views and an unwinnable debate over which is most important, a diverse staff or a competent and qualified one. A more helpful way to look at these dimensions is to consider them not as opposite ends of a continuum, but as two independent variables (see the diagram).

The organizational goal is to find, develop, hire, and promote individuals who are both high in quality and who increase the diversity of staff—those with the necessary skills, abilities, and experiences as well as diverse backgrounds that would enhance the organization.

3. Past Experience

Some employees and managers react negatively to affirmative action because of previous negative experiences with individuals whom they see as affirmative action appointments. If there have been less-than-qualified or undercompetent employees hired under affirmative action's banner, there may be a residue of mistrust and skepticism about future placements.

4. Supply Shortage

In many organizations the resistance is tied to the difficulty in finding qualified candidates from underrepresented groups. "I just can't find enough candidates," and "There aren't any minorities or women with the experience we need" are examples of the complaints heard.

5. Perception that They Are Being Made to Pay for Past Sins

Some resist because they feel that they are being inconvenienced by requirements and limited by guidelines that are designed to rectify a history of discrimination that they did not create. "It's not my fault. Why should I be the one to pay for it?" is their cry.

6. The Perception that It Solely Benefits Others

Another source of negative response to affirmative action is the sense that these programs and plans benefit only the targeted groups. In giving this advantage to others, managers as well as other employees may perceive they are putting themselves at a disadvantage. "It doesn't benefit me; it's for them" is sometimes heard.

Reverse Discrimination: A Real or Perceived Fear

The perception that affirmative action programs, in giving advantage to previously excluded groups, put others at a disadvantage is at the heart of reverse discrimination charges. Those who are passed over when women or non-dominant-group members are placed in positions often feel unfairly treated and discriminated against because of their race, gender, or color. Whether it is the cry of white male managers who have been passed over for promotions to executive ranks or qualified Asian students who are denied admission to universities, members of overrepresented groups who are "held back" to allow others admission often perceive their exclusion as reverse discrimination. However, the fear may be worse than the reality. In a *Los Angeles Times* poll about affirmative action (November 5, 1991), only 14 percent of whites, 16 percent of blacks, and 13 percent of Latinos responding reported they had experienced reverse discrimination.[4]

While there has always been hiring and promotion based on factors other than job qualifications (e.g., being the boss's son, a friend's son-in-law, or a cousin from the old country), there persists a deep American faith in meritocracy. We believe the most qualified person should get the job, and we feel betrayed when other factors are brought into the decision. It goes against the mainstream value placed on fairness and justice, basic philosophical underpinnings of American society. It is partially from this cultural emphasis on justice that both affirmative action and the charges of reverse discrimination result. Whether allegations of reverse discrimination are upheld or not in the courts is a moot point. What is more germane for today's organization is how to deal with this perceived reality, which creates resistance and undermines the commitment of some "old guard" employees who ought not to be discounted or alienated. In an environment that includes everyone, there is no room for those who perceive themselves to be losers, especially since losers can become powerful organizational saboteurs by withholding commitment and passively resisting.

In dealing with this backlash to affirmative action, organizations have developed some constructive responses. In the public sector, organizations such as school districts and county governments, for example, have instituted systems where promotional selections are made from groupings on a list rather than automatically taking the top ranking candidate. In this way, managers can choose from among an array of well-qualified candidates, the next five on the list or the top 20 percent of scorers on an exam, for instance. Within this grouping there are undoubtedly candidates from underrepresented groups, so the manager can choose for both quality and diversity.

Embracing Diversity Goes Far beyond EEO and Affirmative Action

Valuing diversity brings with it a paradigm shift, a new way of thinking about differences among people. Rather than arguing about how to cut up the pie and which group gets the largest slice, embracing diversity strives for a workplace where there are not only enough pies but also cakes, churros, and fortune cookies for all. Instead of pitting groups against one another, it works toward recognizing the uniqueness in everyone and valuing the contribution each can make. This concept aims at creating a workplace in which everyone and every group fits, feels accepted, has value, and contributes. Beyond changing numbers it aims at changing organizational cultures. It is right to remember that the intent of embracing diversity is not to replace affirmative action but to build on the critical foundation laid by workplace equity programs. Affirmative action, valuing differences, and managing diversity go hand in hand, each reinforcing the gains of the other.

Understanding the Difference between Affirmative Action, Valuing Differences, and Managing Diversity

While there is much overlap both in philosophy and practice, perhaps the easiest way to look at the differences is in the form of a few comparisons (see the table). In creating a truly diverse organization, all three of these stages of evolution play an integral part. Without affirmative action's commitment to hiring and promoting diverse employees, having the diversity of staff to reach a stage where differences are valued and diversity effectively managed rarely occurs. Once diverse staff are on board, the organization can focus on creating an inclusive environment where everyone's needs and values are taken into account, where no one is disadvantaged because of his/her differentness, and where organizational policies and management practices work for everyone.

Affirmative Action, Valuing Differences, and Managing Diversity Compared

Affirmative Action	Valuing Differences	Managing Diversity
Quantitative: Emphasizes achieving equality of opportunity in the work environment through the changing of organizational demographics. Monitored by statistical reports and analysis.	*Qualitative:* Emphasizes the appreciation of differences and creating an environment in which everyone feels valued and accepted. Monitored by organizational surveys focused on attitudes and perceptions.	*Behavioral:* Emphasizes the building of specific skills and creating policies which get the best from every employee. Monitored by progress toward achieving goals and objectives.
Legally driven: Written plans and statistical goals for specific group are utilized. Reports are mandated by EEO laws and consent decrees.	*Ethically driven:* Moral and ethical imperatives drive this culture change.	*Strategically driven:* Behaviors and policies are seen as contributing to organizational goals and objectives such as profit and productivity and are tied to reward and results.
Remedial: Specific target groups benefit as past wrongs are remedied. Previously excluded groups have an advantage.	*Idealistic:* Everyone benefits. Everyone feels valued and accepted in an inclusive environment.	*Pragmatic:* The organization benefits; morale, profit, and productivity increase.
Assimilation model: Assumes that groups brought into system will adapt to existing organizational norms.	*Diversity model:* Assumes that groups will retain their own characteristics and shape the organization as well as be shaped by it, creating a common set of values.	*Synergy model:* Assumes that diverse groups will create new ways of working together effectively in a pluralistic environment.
Opens doors in the organization: Affects hiring and promotion decisions.	*Opens attitudes, minds, and the culture:* Affects attitudes of employees.	*Opens the system:* Affects managerial practices and policies.
Resistance due to perceived limits to autonomy in decision making and perceived fears of reverse discrimination.	*Resistance due to* fear of change, discomfort with differences, and desire for return to "good old days."	*Resistance due to* denial of demographic realities, the need for alternative approaches, and/or benefits associated with change; and the difficulty in learning new skills, altering existing systems, and/or finding time to work toward synergistic solutions.

How Does Your Organization/Division/Department Measure Up?

To see how your organization is doing in each of the three areas—affirmative action, valuing differences, and managing diversity—respond to the assessment entitled *How Does Your Organization Measure Up?*

How Does Your Organization Measure Up?

Directions: Check off each statement on the list below that describes your organization or department.

Affirmative action is effective when:

_____ There is a good faith effort to recruit, hire, train, and promote qualified employees from underrepresented groups.

_____ There is a diverse staff at all levels.

_____ The composition of management staff reflects the composition of the work force in general.

_____ Internal networking surfaces qualified candidates who are from diverse groups.

_____ Mechanisms exist to identify and mentor diverse employees who show promotional potential.

_____ Managers recognize it as their responsibility to make progress in building teams that reflect the composition of the work force.

_____ There are few gripes about preferential treatment and reverse discrimination.

_____ Diverse individuals who are promoted are accepted in their new positions by the rest of staff.

_____ Managers' pay raises are tied to acheiving affirmative action goals.

Differences are valued when:

_____ Turnover among all groups is relatively proportionate.

_____ Employees form friendships across racial, cultural, life-style, and gender lines.

_____ Employees talk openly about differences in backgrounds, values, and needs.

_____ No group in the organization is the target of ridicule, jokes, or slurs.

_____ Individuals feel comfortable being themselves at work.

_____ It would not be surprising to employees if the next CEO is not a Euro-American, able-bodied man.

Diversity is being managed effectively when:

_____ Leave, absentee, and holiday policies are flexible enough to suit everyone.

_____ Cultural conflicts are resolved and not allowed to fester/escalate.

_____ Employees of all backgrounds feel free to give input and make requests to management.

_____ Diverse employees take advantage of career enhancement opportunities.

_____ Diverse teams work cooperatively and harmoniously.

_____ Productivity of diverse teams is high.

_____ Managers get commitment and cooperation from their diverse staffs.

_____ Organizational procedures such as performance review and career development have been restructured to suit the diverse needs of employees.

_____ There is diverse staff at all levels.

Suggestions for Using *How Does Your Organization Measure Up?*

Objectives:

- Assess your organization's effectiveness with regard to affirmative action, valuing differences, and managing diversity.
- Pinpoint diversity-related issues that need attention.
- Give feedback to executive management and human resource departments regarding aspects of diversity development.

Intended Audience:

- Managers, supervisors, and other staff members wanting to give feedback to human resource departments and executive management.
- Executives setting strategic planning goals.

Processing the Activity:

- Individuals respond by checking those statements that describe their organizations or departments.
- Responses are tabulated and data are presented to executive management and/or human resource professionals in charge of dealing with diversity issues.
- Executive and/or human resource staff analyze data and identify obstacles to capitalizing on diversity within the organization; they then plan ways to address these barriers.

Caveats and Considerations:

- These issues can provoke emotional and heated responses. This assessment activity can best be managed in small groups where venting can take place safely.
- Executives and/or human resource professionals on the receiving end of this feedback may react defensively. Help them to see the responses as valid perceptions of respondees so they can use it constructively.
- This assessment can also be used by affirmative action and human resource professionals in planning and training.

The more statements you have in each section, the greater your organization's effectiveness in that particular area. It is also important to look at those statements not checked. What obstacles are preventing these conditions from being the norm? What can you do about those obstacles?

A Stark Reality: The Pyramid Narrows at the Top for All

Even with all the predictions about the flattening of the structure in organizations, the typical American company is run in a hierarchical fashion, with an organizational chart in the shape of a pyramid. No matter how one cuts it, the number of positions decreases at each higher level. What this means for career plans and promotional aspirations is that competition for positions increases for everyone who aspires to move up the organizational ladder. When promotions are made in companies where there have historically been no minorities or women at upper levels, much attention is focused on who is selected. Previously excluded groups wait to see a sign that the organization is going to come through on its commitment to diversity, while white males who have traditionally been selected often feel they are quite likely to be overlooked.

In one civil service organization, all eyes were on the next promotion. Upper management was entirely white male, and there was a strong affirmative action mandate to increase the diversity within the department, especially at managerial and executive levels. Only one candidate was not a white male, an African-American veteran of the system with a strong background and ample qualifications who had filed an EEO suit against the department when he was not promoted previously. As you can imagine, the atmosphere was electrically charged in this environment, where resistance to affirmative action was the norm and where allegations of reverse discrimination were common. The department's decision to promote the African-American candidate, who brought both quality and diversity, was met with grudging acceptance by the other candidates for the position. While they understood the reasons, they weren't happy about not getting the promotion themselves.

When the pyramid narrows and there are fewer prizes up the organizational ladder, there will often be more losers than winners. For this reason, it is important to create alternative career paths that allow growth and advancement within a system that offers fewer positions at the top. One such solution is the creation of career ladders. These are promotional steps based on increased technical competence rather than managerial positional advances. Such systems work especially well in organizations with large professional staffs such as nurses, engineers, or accountants. An employee can advance within the organization, increasing salary and title—for example, engineer level I, II, III or nurse clinician I, II, III—without entering the ranks of management.

The Diverse Organization: A Model to Strive For

- A pregnant woman is told her position cannot be guaranteed when she returns from maternity leave.

- An Orthodox Jew can never take advantage of the informal mentoring from executive staff, which takes place Saturdays on the golf course.
- An architect who walks on crutches is not hired because it is believed he can't "walk a job" and properly oversee construction.
- A talented young lawyer doesn't take the desired month of parental leave when his first child is born because he's sure if he does he will be eliminated from the prospective partner list.

In each of these situations, both the organization and the individual are losers. When diversity is not capitalized on, the organization loses the full commitment, energy, and capability of the employee, while the individual loses both career opportunities and esteem. In addition, reduced productivity often results from the stress experienced by the employee grappling with these dilemmas.

No organization has a utopian environment where magical solutions appear. However, when an organization values differences and effectively manages its diverse work force, it meets these challenges in a constructive way. First, it sees these kinds of issues as normal challenges of organizational life, not as irritants caused by those who are different. Second, it recognizes the loss to the organization in not finding solutions. Proceeding from a kind of enlightened self-interest, the organization sees benefits in dealing constructively with the diverse needs of staff. Third, the organization responds with creative problem solving. Rather than complain about, blame, deny or resist the conflicts between employee needs and existing practices, the organization seeks new ways to satisfy both individual and organizational priorities. In such an organization, the scenarios above might be different.

- The pregnant woman and her boss sit down and discuss both the organization's requirements and the woman's personal and professional priorities. A flexible solution is arrived at that allows the employee various career options depending on when she chooses to return to work. During the leave she will remain in contact with her boss so they can discuss changes as they occur, both in the company and her life, and modify plans as needed. She may opt to work at home with a computer and modem or come back with a flextime schedule for a period.
- Executive staff spend time discussing the effectiveness of their informal mentoring and realize that it nets them a very homogeneous group of executives-in-training. As they examine the informal path to upward mobility in the company, they realize it generally excludes those who are not white males because of the arenas in which the relationships are built. The Saturday golf dates exclude not only Orthodox Jews but also many women and non-dominant-group members, who are not generally part of the country club set. Realizing this, executives strategize new mentoring methods that are truly inclusive.
- The interviewer feels comfortable enough with the issue of physical disabilities that he is able to "talk straight" with the applicant. He asks him about previous construction projects and inquires about the methods of supervision used. In this way, he gives the candidate a chance to explain how he oversees a project while on crutches. Convinced that the disability will not prevent the applicant from performing required job duties, the interviewer recommends the candidate for the position.
- The law firm spends time with each employee who is going through a major life change such as the birth of a child, marriage, divorce, or death of a spouse,

talking about the changes in life-style and priorities as well as needs the change may precipitate. The employee has a chance to talk about his/her preferences and discuss the career implications of each. However, because partners model the values the firm professes, the young lawyer knows that a few of the partners, both male and female, have taken parental leaves and were still made partners. It is clear that while there may be trade-offs, there are not sanctions. The lawyer makes a decision that means he won't have to cheat either of his roles— father or lawyer.

Getting Buy-In for Diversity: What's in It for Staff?

As long as managers and employees see the attention paid to dealing with, managing, and valuing diversity as something that benefits others, there will be resistance among all but the most altruistic. In order to get buy-in, the old WIFM formula— What's in It For Me?—needs to be applied. When all levels of staff see benefits for themselves, they will be more apt to commit wholeheartedly. Along those lines, organizations need to focus on the following.

1. Solicit and Pay Attention to the Needs and Priorities of All Employees

In a diverse organization, each employee is a minority of one, with unique preferences, desires, and needs. The most significant experts you need to consult are the employees themselves. Whether through employee surveys, discussions at staff meetings, or focus groups, find out the real issues for employees. You can't eliminate obstacles to employee commitment until you know what they are. You cannot reward appropriately unless you know what staff members want. It is difficult to increase morale if you aren't sure what diminishes job satisfaction for your employees. Ask. Then listen, without defensiveness or argument, to what they tell you.

2. Create Options and Alternatives

Once you have heard the variations in what employees want, formulate systems and policies that give them choices. By making policies flexible enough to suit different priorities, you can best meet everyone's (or almost everyone's) needs. Cafeteria plans for benefits, personal necessity leave days, flextime, insurance plan options, bonus alternatives, and individual discretion about the use of subsidies for child care or elder care are all examples of ways organizations respond to individual needs while making sure policies and benefits are equitable. The element of individual decision making is critical. A truism of human nature seems to be that people are more committed when they make the choice themselves. Allowing employees to select from an array of alternatives increases buy-in and sends the message that the organization is responding to employees' individual needs.

3. Focus on the Benefits to Individual Employees

In communicating any changes connected with diversity, emphasize the benefits to each employee. Hiring bilingual customer service representatives may mean less frustration for customer service staff in communicating with non-English-speaking clientele. Creating an on-site day-care center could lower the stress for employees with children, giving them convenient, accessible, safe, and affordable child care. For managers it may mean less absenteeism and turnover of staff. Make sure the benefits are brought down to the level of personal relevance for each employee. When these are adhered to, valuing diversity comes to mean paying attention to each person's unique situation and responding to it in a supportive way.

Chapter 13

Resources for Managing Diversity

This chapter will give you:
1. Annotated lists of general books about diversity as well as books about specific cultures and groups in the work force.
2. Information about journals, newsletters, and associations dealing with diversity.
3. Lists of training materials, including videos, experiential activities, and sources of learning activities for diversity training.
4. Information about diversity assessment tools.

While you may have found answers to many of your questions, solutions to some of your problems, and an increased understanding about issues you face in managing diversity, you may want or need more. Whether you would like additional information about diversity in general, knowledge about specific groups that make up your work force, learning activities or videos to use in training sessions, or assessment tools, you may find what you are looking for in the resources listed below.

- Books about diversity in the workplace.
- Books about specific groups within the work force.
- Training activities, structured experiences, and workbooks.
- Audiovisual resources.
- Assessment tools and instruments.
- Journals and newsletters.
- Associations.

Books about Diversity in the Workplace

Allport, Gordon W. *The Nature of Prejudice*. Reading, Mass.: Addison-Wesley, 1988. The classic study of the roots of discrimination, originally published in 1954, offers important information and insights for those training about or dealing with prejudice and stereotyping.

Asante, Melefi Kete, and William B. Gudykunst, eds. *Handbook of International and Intercultural Communications*. Newbury Park, Calif.: Sage, 1989. This collection of articles by noted experts deals with such topics as encounters in the interracial workplace and the cultural dimensions of nonverbal communication.

Fernandez, John P. *Managing a Diverse Workforce: Regaining the Competitive Edge*. Lexington, Mass.: Lexington Books, 1991. Based on a survey of over 50,000 managers and employees, the author documents the racism, sexism, and ethnocentrism present in organizations across the country. He goes on to highlight the problems and special concerns faced by each group, including white males, and offers steps both individuals and organizations can take to meet these challenges.

Gudykunst, William B. *Bridging Differences: Effective Intergroup Communication*. Newbury Park, Calif.: Sage, 1991. This book explains the process underlying communication between people of different groups and presents principles for building community with people from diverse backgrounds.

Gudykunst, William B.; Lea P. Stewart; and Stella Ting-Toomey, eds. *Communication, Culture, and Organizational Processes*. Newbury Park, Calif.: Sage, 1985. This collection of articles weaves theoretical issues with practical organizational concerns such as conflict, negotiation, and decision making.

Hacker, Andrew. *Two Nations: Black and White, Separate, Hostile, Unequal*. New York: Scribner's, 1992. A fresh and human analysis of race relations in America, diagnosing the problems but offering no prescription for solutions.

Hall, Edward T. *Beyond Culture*. New York: Anchor Books/Doubleday, 1989. This fundamental work on culture gives an in-depth analysis of the culturally determined yet unconscious attitudes that mold our thoughts, feelings, communications, and behavior. This continues from *The Silent Language* and *The*

Hidden Dimension to discuss the covert cultural influences that impact cross-cultural encounters.

Hall, Edward T. *The Hidden Dimension*. New York: Anchor Books/Doubleday, 1969. Written by a leading anthropologist, this book discusses proxemics, the ways humans use space in public and private. It provides insights about how this aspect of culture affects personal and business relations and cross-cultural interactions as well as architecture and urban planning.

Hall, Edward T. *The Silent Language*. New York: Anchor Books/Doubleday, 1973. Insights into the cultural aspects of communication are given in this fundamental work by a foremost anthropologist. The author explains how dimensions such as time and space communicate beyond words.

Harris, Philip R., and Robert T. Moran. *Managing Cultural Differences: High Performance Strategies for Today's Global Manager*. Houston, Tex.: Gulf, 1987. This business-oriented text on diversity gives a comprehensive treatment of cultural differences affecting business, focusing more on international than domestic intercultural issues. Includes questionnaires, surveys, and resources.

Hofstede, Geert. *Cultures and Organizations: Software of the Mind*. New York: McGraw-Hill, 1991. The author shows that effective intercultural cooperation is possible and explains under what circumstances and at what cost this can be done.

Hofstede, Geert. *Culture's Consequences: International Differences in Work-Related Values*. Newbury Park, Calif.: Sage, 1984. A foundation piece in the literature about culture, this research-based book discusses culturally based differences in values that impact the workplace. Aspects such as individualism, power distance, masculinity, and uncertainty avoidance are examined.

James, Muriel. *The Better Boss in Multi-Cultural Organizations: A Guide to Success Using Transactional Analysis*. Walnut Creek, Calif.: Marshall, 1991. This book aims at helping bosses value themselves and their own cultural diversity as well as that of others. It focuses on seven skills managers need and on how to use transactional analysis to increase effectiveness as a boss.

Jamieson, David, and Julie O'Mara. *Managing Workforce 2000: Gaining the Diversity Advantage*. San Francisco: Jossey-Bass, 1991. Built around the authors' six-step flex management model, this book offers practical strategies to help organizations attract, make the best use of, and retain employees of different groups in order to maintain a competitive advantage. Includes vignettes and case studies from over 80 organizations and lists of organizations with diversity programs as well as resources for dealing with diversity in organizations.

Johnston, William B., and Arnold E. Packer. *Workforce 2000: Work and Workers for the 21st Century*. Indianapolis, Ind.: Hudson Institute, 1987. Working from census figures and other demographic data, this report from the U.S. Department of Labor delineates work-force trends for the next decade and beyond. The report goes on to discuss the impact of these changes and the challenges they bring.

Knowles, Louis, and Kenneth Prewitt. *Institutional Racism in America*. Englewood Cliffs, N.J.: Prentice Hall, 1969. This book gives a comprehensive account of the pervasiveness of racism in institutions in this society.

Loden, Marilyn, and Judy B. Rosener, Ph.D. *Workforce America! Managing Employee Diversity as a Vital Resource*. Homewood, Ill.: Business One Irwin, 1991. This foundation piece in the literature about diversity makes a case for creating an organization that capitalizes on the richness in differences. It offers an insightful look at the issues as well as managerial and organizational strategies to deal with them.

Samovar, Larry A., and Richard E. Porter. *Intercultural Communication: A Reader*. Belmont, Calif.: Wadsworth, 1976. This anthology provides a series of 44 articles on culture in general as well as on specific cultures and aspects of intercultural communication. Both theoretical and practical information is given.

Thiederman, Sondra, Ph.D. *Bridging Cultural Barriers for Corporate Success: How to Manage the Multicultural Work Force*. Lexington, Mass.: Lexington Books, 1990. This handbook for cross-cultural communication gives managers and human resource professionals practical information about motivating, attracting, interviewing, retaining and training the multicultural workforce. This reader friendly book is full of applicable examples, how-to's and exercises for overcoming obstacles to intercultural communication.

Thiederman, Sondra, Ph.D. *Profiting in America's Multicultural Marketplace: How to Do Business Across Cultural Lines*. Lexington, Mass.: Lexington Books, 1991. In practical, readable terms, the author explains cultural effects on person-to-person behavior and how to communicate effectively with people of different backgrounds. This reader-friendly book gives anecdotes and tests for the reader that involve and teach.

Thomas, R. Roosevelt. *Beyond Race and Gender: Unleashing the Power of Your Total Work Force by Managing Diversity*. New York: Amacom, 1991. This book puts forth a plan for managing diversity coupled with practical examples of how organizations capitalize on their diverse staffs. It includes a strategy for a cultural audit as well as an action plan for change.

Ting-Toomey, Stella, and Felipe Korzenny, eds. *Cross-Cultural Interpersonal Communication*. Newbury Park, Calif.: Sage, 1991. This collection of articles is a source of information about current research and theories in cross-cultural communication.

Wurzel, Jaime B., ed. *Toward Multiculturalism: A Reader in Multicultural Education*. Yarmouth, Maine: Intercultural Press, 1988. The intent of this book is to help people develop a multicultural style of thinking, feeling, and self-awareness in order to cope better with change and conflict. The series of articles offers a combination of research studies and accounts of personal experiences with different cultures.

Books about Specific Groups within the Work Force

Althen, Gary. *American Ways: A Guide for Foreigners in the United States*. Yarmouth, Maine: Intercultural Press, 1988. This book is designed for those wanting to understand the behaviors and values of Americans. In easy-to-understand language and clear examples, the author describes the basic characteristics of American culture and offers suggestions for effective interactions with Americans.

Andres, Tomas. *Understanding Filipino Values: A Management Approach*. Quezon City, Metro Manila, Philippines: New Day, 1981. This book is a resource for understanding Filipino culture and values with an emphasis on management issues.

Astrachan, Anthony. *How Men Feel*. New York: Anchor, 1988. How men feel about women is the topic of this book, which contains a number of chapters focusing on work relationships.

Barker, Roger G. *Adjustment to Physical Handicap and Illness: A Survey of the Social Psychology of Physique and Disability*. New York: Social Science Research Council, 1953. This book combines a theoretical and a practical discussion of the social psychology of differently abled people. It also contains a chapter on employment.

Blumfeld, Warren J., and Deane Raymond. *Looking at Gay and Lesbian Life*. Boston: Beacon Press, 1988. Lesbian and gay life-styles in the United States are examined and discussed in this book.

Condon, John C. *Good Neighbors: Communication with the Mexicans*. Yarmouth, Maine: Intercultural Press, 1985. In this concise book, the author describes how the culture of the United States and Mexico differ, how Mexicans and North Americans misunderstand each other, and what can be done to bridge the gap. Vital information for those working with Mexicans is provided in a readable, interesting way.

Condon, John C. *With Respect to the Japanese: A Guide for Americans*. Yarmouth, Maine: Intercultural Press, 1984. In this handbook, the author discusses aspects of Japanese values and behavior that affect communications, business relations, and management styles. He goes on to make recommendations on how to deal with the Japanese during face-to-face encounters.

Davis, George, and Gregg Watson. *Black Life in Corporate America*. Garden City, N.Y.: Anchor Press/Doubleday, 1982. This book sheds light on the impact of American organizational culture on black employees.

Fernandez, John. *Racism and Sexism in Corporate Life*. Lexington, Mass.: Lexington Books, 1981. This book discusses the findings of a major study of black and white men and women in the workplace, focusing on how racism and sexism affect their work life.

Fieg, John Paul, and Elizabeth Mortlock. *A Common Core: Thais and Americans*. Yarmouth, Maine: Intercultural Press, 1989. Both commonalties and differences between Thai and American cultures are explained in this book. Authors go on to discuss the implication of the differences for those engaged in these cross-cultural encounters on and off the job.

Fisher, Glen. *International Negotiations: A Cross-Cultural Perspective*. Yarmouth, Maine: Intercultural Press, 1980. By comparing how Japanese, Mexicans, French, and Americans reach agreements, the author demonstrates how culture influences the negotiation process and suggests a useful line of questioning and analysis for intercultural negotiation.

Gardenswartz, Lee, and Anita Rowe. *What It Takes: Good News from 100 of America's Top Professional and Business Women*. New York: Doubleday, 1987. From interviews with 100 of America's top-achieving women, the authors distill five critical factors shared by all. This book dispels the myths about successful women and offers a guide for women wanting to create their own brand of success.

Gary, Lawrence. *Black Men*. Newbury Park, Calif.: Sage, 1981. This book discusses issues confronting black men in America today.

Gilligan, Carol. *In a Different Voice: Psychological Theory and Women's Development*. Cambridge, Mass.: Harvard University Press, 1962. This book presents a discussion of gender differences in moral/ethical developments and implications for the workplace.

Gochenour, Theodore. *Considering Filipinos*. Yarmouth, Maine: Intercultural

Press, 1990. This intercultural handbook contrasts the values and perspectives of Filipinos and Americans and offers guidelines for successful interaction between these two groups. It gives suggestions for bridging cultural differences in social and workplace settings as well as case studies showing cross-cultural dynamics in action.

Gutek, Barbara A. *Sex and the Work Place*. San Francisco, Calif.: Jossey-Bass, 1985. This book examines a critical aspect of male-female interaction on the job—the impact of sexual behavior and harassment on women, men, and organizations. The issue is looked at from managerial, legal, psychological, and social perspectives.

Kitano, Harry L., and Roger Daniels. *Asian Americans: Emerging Minorities*. Englewood Cliffs, N.J.: Prentice Hall, 1988. This book focuses on the various Asian ethnic groups, discussing their experiences in America.

Knouse, Stephen B., Paul Rosenfeld, and Amy Culbertson, eds. *Hispanics in the Workplace*. Newbury Park, Calif.: Sage, 1992. A comprehensive exploration of Hispanic employment factors, problems at work, support systems, and Hispanic women and work. Contributors deal with specific topics such as recruiting, training, and language barriers.

Kochman, Thomas. *Black and White Styles in Conflict*. Chicago, Ill.: University of Chicago Press, 1981. This classic study of black culture helps illuminate racial misunderstandings and explain the values and style differences that may be at the heart of problems in inter-ethnic communication. This book serves as a practical guide for crossing racial barriers in business and education.

Kras, Eva S. *Management in Two Cultures: Bridging the Gap between U.S. and Mexican Managers*. Yarmouth, Maine: Intercultural Press, 1989. This book pinpoints the principal differences between Mexican and U.S. cultures and management styles that cause misunderstandings and conflict. Concrete recommendations to both U.S. and Mexican managers for dealing more effectively with each other are given.

Lanier, Alison R. *Living in the USA*. Yarmouth, Maine: Intercultural Press, 1988. This book is designed to help foreigners and newcomers understand the United States. It provides a guide to customs, courtesies, and caveats and gives practical advice to anyone coming to the United States.

Lipman-Blumen, Jean. *Gender Roles and Power*. Englewood Cliffs, N.J.: Prentice Hall, 1984. This book explains the way in which the gender system is a foundation for all other power relationships.

Loden, Marilyn. *Feminine Leadership: Or How to Succeed in Business without Being One of the Boys*. New York: Times Books, 1985. This book delineates differences in male and female leadership styles, making implications for enhancing the workplace.

McLuhan, T. C. *Touch the Earth*. New York: Simon & Schuster, 1971. This book gives a recollection of the native American way of life and, in contrast, comments on mainstream American society and values.

Mead, Margaret. *Culture and Commitment: A Study of the Generation Gap*. Garden City, N.Y.: Doubleday, 1970. This anthropologist's look at the generation gap explains the differences in views and perspectives between the young and the old.

Milwid, Beth, Ph.D. *Working with Men: Professional Women Talk about Power, Sexuality, and Ethics*. Hillsboro, Ore.: Beyond Words, 1990. Interviews with 125 professional women provide a look at what it's like for women in the workplace. This book gives an insider's look at the pressures, problems, and hopes of women in the work world.

Miranda, Alfredo. *The Chicano Experience: An Alternative Perspective.* Notre Dame, Ind.: University of Notre Dame Press, 1985. The social and economic conditions facing Mexican-Americans are explained in this book.

Morrison, Ann M.; Randall P. White; and Ellen van Velson. *Breaking the Glass Ceiling.* Reading, Mass.: Addison-Wesley, 1987. Based on a study of executives, this book examines the factors that determine the success and failure of women in corporate America.

Nelson, Roberta. *Creating Acceptance for Handicapped People.* Springfield, Ill.: Charles C. Thomas, 1978. This handbook is designed to teach the community to be supportive and accepting of those with disabilities, both physical and mental.

Nydell, Margaret K. *Understanding Arabs: A Guide for Westerners.* Yarmouth, Maine: Intercultural Press, 1987. This readable cross-cultural handbook gives a concise and insightful look at Arab culture. It dispels common Western misconceptions regarding Arab behavior, and it explains the values, beliefs, and practices of Arabs particularly in terms of their impact on interactions with Europeans and North Americans.

Pearson, Judy C. *Gender and Communication.* Dubuque, Iowa: William C. Brown, 1985. This book focuses on the gender gap in interactions, discussing the difficulties and differences in communication between men and women.

Richmond, Yale. *From Nyet to Da: Understanding the Russians.* Yarmouth, Maine: Intercultural Press, 1992. This succinctly written book is a cross-cultural guide for dealing with Russians. The author outlines ways of responding most effectively to Russians on a personal level as well as in business.

Rodgers-Rose, LaFrances. *Black Women.* Newbury Park, Calif.: Sage, 1983. Issues and conditions confronting black women are discussed in this book.

Sagarin, Edward, ed. *The Other Minorities.* Waltham, Mass.: Xerox College, 1971. Nonethnic minorities, such as the differently abled, are the subjects in this collection of articles.

Sargent, Alice G. *Beyond Sex Roles.* St. Paul, Minn.: West, 1977. Through exercises and narrative explanations, the author and other contributors teach, raise awareness, and prod self-exploration about sex roles and change regarding those roles.

Secundy, Marian Gray, and Lois Lacivita Nixon. *Trials, Tribulations and Celebrations: African-American Perspectives on Health, Illness, Aging and Loss.* Yarmouth, Maine: Intercultural Press, 1992. This collection of short stories, narratives, and poems explores aspects of the life cycle from an African-American perspective. It is especially helpful for health-care providers as well as for those living and providing services in a multicultural society.

Stewart, Edward C. *American Cultural Patterns: A Cross-Cultural Perspective.* Yarmouth, Maine: Intercultural Press, 1972. Using the value orientation framework of Kluckholn and Strodtbeck, the author examines American patterns of thinking and behaving. He goes on to analyze the assumptions about human nature and the physical world that underlie these values, and to compare and contrast them with those of other cultures.

Tannen, Deborah. *You Just Don't Understand: Women and Men in Conversion.* New York: William Morrow, 1991. In a down-to-earth, reader-friendly style, the author explains gender differences in communication that produce obstacles. Recognizing and understanding these differences can be a help in avoiding barriers to clear communication between men and women.

Wenzhong, Hu, and Cornelius L. Grove. *Encountering the Chinese: A Guide for Americans*. Yarmouth, Maine: Intercultural Press, 1991. This useful book goes beyond description to explain Chinese behavior. It provides a cross-cultural analysis that can guide Westerners toward more effective relationships with the Chinese.

Work, John W. *Race, Economics and Corporate America*. Wilmington, Del.: Scholarly Resources, 1984. This book explores the socioeconomic factors and racism that impact the status of African-Americans.

Training Activities, Structured Experiences, and Workbooks

Bafa Bafa: Cross-Cultural Orientation. Gary R. Shirts, P.O. Box 910, Del Mar, CA 92014; (619) 755-0272. This experiential activity simulates the contact between two very different cultures, Alpha and Beta. The activity is structured so that participants learn through direct simulated experience and then apply that learning to real-life situations. (*Rafa Rafa*, a simplified version for elementary school children, grades 5-8, is also available.)

Barnga: A Simulation Game on Cultural Clashes. Thiagarajan, Sivasailam, Intercultural Press, Inc., P.O. Box 700, Yarmouth, ME 04096. Through playing a simple card game in small groups, participants experience the effect of simulated cultural differences on human interaction. This activity is easy to run in a relatively short time.

Basics of Intercultural Communication. Alexandria, Va.: American Society for Training and Development, ASTD Info-Line Series, 1990. This booklet explains the common stumbling blocks encountered and gives techniques to overcome barriers to intercultural communication. Designed as a tool for training and development professionals, it offers guidelines and practical tips.

Brislin, Richard W.; Kenneth Cushner; Craig Cherrie; and Maheulaini Yong. *Intercultural Interactions: A Practical Guide*. Newbury Park, Calif.: Sage, 1986. This book presents a set of training materials that can form the basis of cross-cultural orientation programs. Suggestions are made for use in training programs, college classes, and business programs.

Brocchi, Rosanne, and Shanthi Radcliffe. *A Shared Experience: Bridging Cultures. Resources for Cross-Cultural Training*. London Cross-Cultural Learning Centre, 533 Clarence Street, London, Ontario, Canada, N6A3N1. This manual provides guidance for facilitators in planning group sessions as well as activities and strategies for promoting cultural awareness through case studies, role playing, and simulation.

Complete Cultural Diversity Library. ODT, Inc., P.O. Box 134, Amherst, MA 01004. This collection of diversity awareness resources includes eight audiotapes, eight books, a diversity assessment tool, six booklets, and over 20 articles and tip sheets and four complete training modules. Best suited for training professionals, it gives both culture-general and culture-specific information.

How to Communicate Better with Clients, Customers, and Workers Whose English Is Limited. Los Angeles County Commission on Human Resources, 320 West Temple St., Suite 1184, Los Angeles, CA 90012. This small booklet gives tips for overcoming language barriers in communication. Gives basic dos and hints for customers and public service staff.

Kogod, S. Kanu. *A Workshop for Managing Diversity in the Workplace*. San Diego, Calif.: Pfeiffer & Company. This package presents a workshop designed for management training with 18 experiential activities as well as lecturettes for building awareness and knowledge. Design consists of three training modules and includes trainer's guide and handouts.

Pedersen, Paul. *A Handbook for Developing Multicultural Awareness*. Alexandria, Va.: American Association for Counseling and Development, 1988. This book is a practical guide for improving communication and cultural awareness among culturally different people. It outlines the three stages of multicultural development and offers techniques for counselors, trainers, and teachers.

Sherman, David A. *The Prejudice Book: Activities for the Classroom*. New York: Anti-Defamation League of B'nai B'rith, 1979. Anti-Defamation League of B'nai B'rith, 823 United Nations Plaza, New York, NY 10017. Experiential activities and involving learning tools for teaching about prejudice. While designed for the classroom, many activities can be adapted for an adult training environment.

Simons, George F. *Working Together: Managing Cultural Diversity*. Crisp Publications, 95 First Street, Los Altos, CA 94022-9803; (800) 442-7477. 1989. This practical handbook for managers gives how-tos for improving communication with employees from different backgrounds. It includes case studies and worksheets.

Simons, George F., and G. Deborah Weissman. *Men and Women: Partners at Work*. Los Altos, Calif.: Crisp Publications, 1990. The objective of this book is to help men and women approach each other openly, creatively, and with effective communication tools. Exercises and worksheets help readers identify and resolve gender issues that inhibit productivity and understanding.

Steps to Resolving Racial Conflict at the Workplace. Ontario Federation of Labor, 15 Gervais Drive, Suite 202, Don Mills, Ontario, Canada, M3C1Y8. This how-to guide for shop stewards and union personnel gives tips for resolving interracial disputes on the job.

Thomas, Barb, and Charles Novogrodsky. *Combating Racism in the Workplace: A Course for Workers*. Cross-Cultural Communications Centre, 965 Bloor Street West, Toronto, Ontario, Canada, M6H1R7. This guide is designed for practical application. It is labor-oriented, with written exercises, audiovisual aids, and readings designed to get workers to talk openly about racism.

Weeks, William H.; Paul Pedersen; and Richard W. Brislin, eds. *A Manual of Structured Experiences for Cross-Cultural Learning*. Yarmouth, Maine: Intercultural Press. This collection of exercises gives a series of activities that have proven successful in training programs. Designed to stimulate learning and interaction in multi-cultural groups, each exercise is accompanied by easy to follow instructions.

Work, John W., Ph.D. *Toward Affirmative Action and Racial/Ethnic Pluralism: How to Train in Organizations*. Arlington, Va.: Belvedere Press, 1989. This handbook is designed to help trainers design training and prepare materials for primarily non-dominant-group trainees in sessions about reducing the negative impacts of institutional racism. An outline and case studies are included.

Audiovisual Resources

Bill Cosby on Prejudice. Budget Films, 4590 Santa Monica Blvd., Los Angeles, CA 90029; (213) 660-0187. This film presents a monologue by Bill Cosby on prejudice.

Born Free. Educational Equity Act Publishing Center, 55 Chapel Street, Suite 231, Newton, MA 02160. These three half-hour videos feature panel discussions and interviews dealing with sex-role stereotyping.

Bridges: Skills for Managing a Diverse Workforce. BNA Communications, Inc., 9439 Key West Avenue, Rockville, MD 20850; (800) 253-6067. This eight-module video-based program is designed to train managers and supervisors in managing diverse workers. Both awareness about cultural/racial/gender differences and the skills to deal with them are given. The series includes manuals for trainees and participants.

Bridging Cultural Barriers: Managing Ethnic Diversity in the Workplace. Barr Films, 12801 Schabarum Ave., P.O. Box 7878, Irwindale, CA 91706-7878; (800) 234-7878. This half-hour film featuring Sondra Thiederman, Ph.D., teaches about the effective management of diverse workers through a simulated example of a manager resolving situations with two culturally different staff members. Vignettes are interspersed with lecturettes by Dr. Thiederman.

Faces. Salinger Films, 1635 12th Street, Santa Monica, CA 90404; (310) 450-1300. This one-minute, non-narrated video shows a kaleidoscope of human faces of different sexes, races, and ages merging and complementing each other to form an integrative whole. By showing the individual worth of each face as well as its contribution to the total picture, the video demonstrates that we are all unique, yet we share a common bond.

Living and Working in America. Via Press, Inc., 400 E. Evergreen Blvd., Suite 314, Vancouver, WA 98660; (800) 944-8421. A comprehensive three-volume audiovisual series for training non-native speakers of English in communication skills needed for supervisory/management positions in the multicultural workforce. Includes video scenes, textbook, audiotapes, and an instructors manual with experiential learning activities.

Managing Diversity. CRM Films, 2233 Faraday Avenue, Carlsbad, CA 92008; (800) 421-0833. This film combines dramatizations of information from experts in the field to focus on diversity issues such as stereotyping and communication as well as differences in perception regarding teamwork, power, and authority. It ends with a useful list of things people can do to improve communication in a diverse environment. A guide is included.

Managing a Multicultural Workforce: The Mosaic Workplace. Films for the Humanities and Sciences, P.O. Box 2053, Princeton, NJ 08543-2053; (800) 257-5126. This video training program consists of 10 videos addressing the issues of the diverse workplace. It covers topics such as understanding different cultural values and styles, men and women working together, and success strategies for minorities.

Partners in Change. American Association of Retired Persons (AARP), Program Resources Department, P.O. Box 51040, Washington, D.C. 22091. This 17-minute video demonstrates how a business can benefit from hiring the mature woman. It discusses the skills that displaced homemakers can transfer to a job as well as the commitment and stability they can bring to an organization.

Sandcastle: A Film about Teamwork and Diversity. Salinger Films, 1635 12th Street, Santa Monica, CA 90404; (310) 450-1300. Teamwork and the unique contribution of each diverse team member is illustrated in this Academy Award–winning, non-narrated 13-minute video. Unique story about the building of a sandcastle, the film demonstrates the value of diversity.

Serving the Diverse Customer. Salinger Films, 1635 12th Street, Santa Monica, CA 90404; (310) 450-1300. This video helps customer service staff understand the dynamics of cross-cultural communication and get beyond barriers to establishing positive relationships with diverse customers. Vignettes of typical customer/staff interactions are shown, and tips for providing top-notch service to a diverse population are given.

A Tale of "O." Goodmeasure, Inc., P.O. Box 3004, Cambridge, MA 02139. This film/video shows how a few O's learn to function in organizations made up of *X*'s.

Valuing Diversity. Copeland Griggs Productions, 302 23rd Avenue, San Francisco, CA 94121; (415) 668-4200. This seven-part film/video series for managers and other employees focuses on the advantages inherent in diversity. Segments deal with issues such as managing/supervising differences, upward mobility in a multicultural organization, and communicating across cultures. The series includes users' guides.

West Meets East in Japan. Pyramid Film and Video, Box 1048, Santa Monica, CA 90406; (800) 421-2304. This culture-specific video lets you experience Japanese culture from the point of view of an outsider learning the norms of Japanese etiquette. A study guide is included.

Working Together: Managing Cultural Diversity. Crisp Publications, 95 First Street, Los Altos, CA 94022-9803; (800) 442-7477. This video-book program teaches how to work productively in a multicultural environment. Users learn how to manage their attitudes and communication in interactions with people from other cultures. The kit includes a leader's guide.

Assessment Tools and Instruments

Grote, Karen. *Diversity Awareness Profile* and *Diversity Awareness Profile, Manager's Version*. Pfeiffer & Company, 8517 Production Avenue, San Diego, CA 92121; (619) 578-2042. A 40-item questionnaire that places the individuals in one of five categories on the "Diversity Awareness Spectrum." Suggests action steps and includes notes for trainers.

Halverson, Claire B., Ph.D. *Cultural Context Work Style Inventory*. School for International Training, Experiment in International Living, Brattleboro, VT; (802) 254-6098. This self-scored, 20-item questionnaire is designed for self-understanding based on the high-low context framework of Edward Hall. It includes background information, charts, and bibliography.

Kelley, Colleen, and Judith Meyers. *The Cross-Cultural Adaptability Inventory*. 2500 Torey Pines Road, La Jolla, CA 92037; (619) 453-8165. This self-scoring instrument is for those planning to work and live abroad. It measures four critical dimensions of cross-cultural adaptability. A trainee's manual is included.

Overseas Assignment Inventory (OAI). Moran, Stahl & Boyer, International Division, 900 28th Street, Boulder, CO 80303; (303) 449-8440. This self-response questionnaire measures 15 attitudes and attributes important to cross-cultural adjustment. Resulting in a profile of cross-cultural adaptability, this standardized and normed instrument can be applied in selection, placement, counseling, work force planning, career development, and self-selection.

The Questions of Diversity: Assessment Tools for Organizations and Individuals. George Simons (1990), ODT Incorporated, P.O. Box 134, Amherst, MA 01004; (413) 549-1293. This tool contains nine surveys that assess personal and organizational issues of diversity in the workplace. These instruments are intended as learning tools.

Journals and Newsletters

Asia Pacific Business Journal. Asia Pacific Business Journal, 2001 Sixth Ave., Suite 2328, Seattle, WA 98121; (206) 448-5622. This is a monthly publication reporting news and information relating to doing business with Asian countries. Information is provided on trade news, shows, opportunities, property development, protocol, finance, and travel, as well as political and cultural viewpoints.

Communique. SIETAR, 733 15th Street NW, Washington, D.C. 20009; (202) 737-5000. This bimonthly newsletter shares news in the field of intercultural relations, presents related information from the UN, and lists upcoming conferences in the field.

Cultural Diversity at Work. The GilDeane Group, 13751 Lake City Way NE, Suite 106, Seattle, WA 98125-3615; (206) 362-0336. This bimonthly newsletter focuses on helping diverse people work together and conduct business effectively. Issues include articles on pertinent topics as well as reviews of books and materials and interviews with experts in the field. The newsletter is supplemented by 11 monthly bulletins listing upcoming diversity meetings, seminars, and conferences. The publishers also offer a consultant listing and referral service.

Currents: Reading in Race Relations. Urban Alliance on Race Relations, 229 College Street, Toronto, Ontario, Canada M5T1R4. This quarterly journal focuses on contemporary issues in race relations.

Extend: Multicultural Magazine. Vista-Multi-Cultural Group, Inc., 3302 N. 7th St., Bldg. C, Suite 12, Phoenix, AZ 85012. This bimonthly magazine focuses on a variety of diversity issues and developments in business.

Intercultural News Network. PACIA, 16331 Underhill Lane, Huntington Beach, CA 92647; (213) 433-7231, (714) 840-3688. Published by the Pacific Area Communicator of Intercultural Affairs (FACIA), this bimonthly newsletter addresses cultural diversity in health, education, and public services. It serves as a clearinghouse for services, resources, materials, and events in and about the multicultural society on the West Coast of the United States.

International Journal for Intercultural Relations. SIETAR, 733 15th St. NW, Washington, D.C. 20009; (202) 737-5000. This quarterly journal presents scholarly articles and research in the field of intercultural relations.

Managing Diversity. Jamestown Area Labor Management Committee (JALMC), P.O. Box 819, Jamestown, NY 14702-0819; (800) 542-7869. This monthly newsletter is a source of information, ideas, and tips for managing diversity.

Each issue includes interviews with noted experts, articles on specific diversity issues, lists of resources, and book reviews.

Together. Communications Branch Multiculturalism and Citizenship Canada, Ottawa, Ontario, Canada K1A0M5. This quarterly newsletter features research updates, articles, and issues related to multiculturalism today.

Training. Lakewood Publications, 50 South Ninth, Minneapolis, MN 55402; (612) 333-0471. This monthly publication focusing on the ''human side of business'' offers frequent articles on diversity-related issues in the workplace as well reviews of books and other resources for training professionals.

Training and Development. ASTD, 1640 King Street, Box 1443, Alexandria, VA 22313-2043; (703) 683-8100. This monthly journal presents articles related to training America's work force, including frequent pieces on diversity by experts in the field.

Associations

American Association of Retired Persons (AARP). Business Partnerships Program, 1901 ''K'' Street NW, Washington, D.C. 20049; (202) 662-4888. This organization publishes booklets that assist organizations in attracting, managing, and training older workers. AARP also maintains a free database, the National Older Workers Information System (NOWIS), which catalogs programs concerning older workers.

American Society for Training and Development (ASTD). 1640 King Street, Box 1443, Alexandria, VA 22313-2043; (703) 683-8100. Association for T&D professionals holds annual national and regional conferences dealing with current workplace issues. Some local chapters have diversity special divisions which meet regularly to focus on T&D related to diversity.

International Communication Association. P.O. Box 9589, 100 Burnet Road, Austin, TX 78766. This professional organization publishes the *Journal of Communication* and *International and Intercultural Communication Annual*.

International Society for Intercultural Education, Training and Research (SIETAR). SIETAR/SASC, 8000 Westpark Drive, Suite 130, McLean, VA 22102; (703) 790-1745. This international association is aimed at increasing cross-cultural understanding and harmony. SIETAR holds conferences and publishes a journal.

Chapter 14

Making Diversity Work: Summing It Up

I am only one; but still I am one. I cannot do everything, but still I can do something;
I will not refuse to do the something I can do.

Helen Keller

Our goal in this book has been to help you get hands-on tools, strategies, ideas, and techniques that will enable you to lead productive work groups and organizations through the massive changes American business is undergoing. Specifically, we have discussed the following:

- Culture and its pervasive impact on behavior, norms, and values.
- Communication (or miscommunication) in a diverse environment, particularly as it relates to giving feedback and resolving culture clashes.
- How to build cohesive work teams in a cross-cultural environment.
- The ingredients to leading effective meetings and getting participation among diverse staff.
- How to conduct effective performance evaluations with employees of different backgrounds.
- How to create a corporate culture that is inclusive and welcoming to all people regardless of age, gender, race, ethnicity, sexual preference, religion, or physical ability.
- Considerations in determining what kind of audits to conduct and construct in order to assess your organization regarding diversity.
- What your organization can do to increase its chances of hiring, promoting, and retaining a pluralistic work force.
- How to open up the promotional systems to employees of all groups.
- The demographic changes that make diversity a critical bottom-line issue.
- The differences between EEO/affirmative action and managing diversity.
- Diversity-related resources.

A successful diversity effort rests on more than solid management techniques. It also requires a mind-set that helps you and your organization deal positively with this challenging phenomenon. The battle for effectiveness is waged on two fronts—the individual and the organizational.

The Individual: Ideas Central to a Diversity Mind-Set

1. "Diversity Is Not about 'Them'; It Is about Us."

When our colleague Terry Owens made the above statement, it had a ring of undeniable truth. First and foremost, diversity is about facing your own reactions to differentness and the discomfort it causes. While you do need to learn about the cultural norms, practices, and values of others, those pieces of information are not at the core of dealing with diversity. Rather, it involves taking a look at why holidays, practices, values, or languages different from yours trigger feelings of threat that build walls between us. Shirley MacLaine once said something pertinent to this issue: "The more I traveled, the more I realized that fear makes strangers of people who should be friends." Whether or not you choose friendship with those who are different from you, self-comfort is essential. People who accept themselves are not threatened by those who are different. Coming to terms with yourself literally and figuratively creates a world of difference.

2. Face the Fear of Change and the Perceived Losses

The greatest resistance to dealing with the changing work force comes when we see these changes as taking something away from us. Conscious and subconscious fears abound: ''Will my opportunities cease to exist?'' ''How much adapting will I have to do?'' ''When I hear co-workers speaking a foreign language, are they talking about me?'' Cries of ''It's so different since they came'' and ''I feel like a foreigner in my own community'' are common. In the face of these fears, it helps when we understand that all changes are two-sided coins. One eternal truth is that every change has both positives and negatives attached to it. Helping employees identify the positives is a good starting point. Then encouraging them to identify the perceived negatives and to problem-solve potential worst-case scenarios is essential to shrinking the losses down to manageable size. If employees don't get beyond the fear, they will never get beyond the resistance, and your diversity effort will continue to be sabotaged.

3. Create a More Fluid Power Structure

One concrete demonstration of a diverse organization is a multicolored management team. When that happens, the presumption of white male leadership will no longer be made. Imagine substituting some of the 14 white male senators who conducted the Clarence Thomas/Anita Hill hearings for a few women and people of color. At the very least, the sensitivities would have been different. Disparate viewpoints would have been heard. But societal changes of this magnitude evolve slowly, and alas, human nature seems to change even more slowly than organizations or society at large. We know that personal favoritism goes with the human territory and will never be eradicated. However, a more fluid power structure makes possible the time when society acknowledges that all people have a right to any job, regardless of background, age, gender, or life-style.

4. Shed the Predictable Habits and Learn New Behaviors

To be human is to be a creature of habit. All people have patterns of behavior that have become automatic over the years—sort of unconscious rituals. Coming face-to-face with diversity means shaking up these habits because many of the old behaviors no longer work in this new environment. Effective management is partially defined by a willingness to forgo the security of a world where everyone responds like clockwork to your tried-and-true techniques. Instead, you are asked to accumulate a repertoire of behaviors that offer responses to the eclectic etiquette and conduct you will continue to face on the job and in the marketplace.

5. Get beyond Ethnocentrism

Ethnocentrism need not be fatal. All of us see the world through our experiences; therefore, our own cultural milieu becomes the yardstick by which all other customs and norms are measured and evaluated. This practice, though common, can be destructive. Understanding that today's world is not only small and interconnected but also varied makes a strong case for developing tolerance. The recognition that there isn't a right way to greet people, or eat, or bathe, or treat elders—just a lot of different ways that feel comfortable to particular groups of people—goes a long way toward legitimizing variety and creating a positive experience among people of different backgrounds.

6.   Emphasize Common Experiences that Unify Rather than Differences that Divide

If we look at diversity through an anthropological human-behavior lens, what emerges is a picture of humankind that has shared the same basic experiences since time immemorial. While various cultural practices lead to different values, priorities, and behaviors, in truth there are only a few universal life events. Regardless of culture, period of history, race, religion, and a host of other factors, experiences such as birth, growth, marriage, death, the need to feel connected to others, and the desire to engage in meaningful work are shared by people the world over. Once you acknowledge that these milestones and needs are every person's common journey, it is easier to accept that we are more alike than different.

7.   Demonstrate Values through Actions, Not Words

It is easy to give lip-service commitment to diversity. While this movement has its share of detractors, it is also viewed as being "politically correct," timely, and pragmatic. Saying that you value diversity while maintaining the status quo won't cut it. Uttering the right words about inclusivity while conducting business in a static power structure will be self-defeating and will cost you the trust and commitment of employees.

8.   Remember that Diversity Includes Everyone

Much reference has been made throughout this book to the need for white males to change, because in most cases they do hold the reigns of power. However, some of the most open and generous people leading the way for change are white males. If we blame and rage against those who have held power, whatever their color, then we miss the point of the diversity movement. If we are to regain the competitive edge and create not only "kinder and gentler" but also more profitable and productive organizations, then it is time to share power. That means representing everyone in the decision-making process. Previously excluded groups who point their fingers and grind their axes move us backward, as do white males who cry reverse discrimination and resist any but token change. Any diversity effort that fails to extend empathy and understanding full circle will end up polarizing people and creating adversaries. We will all lose. Much is being asked of us, but much more will be given. A fuller utilization of all people's talents benefits you as an individual, the company for which you work, and all of us as a nation.

Individuals with open, pliable mind-sets are necessary for a vibrant organization, but unless the organizational systems are in place to support this change, consistency, productivity, and vibrancy won't happen. There are organizational imperatives that will help any willing organization manage a successful change effort. Before you start out on any diversity-related endeavor, consider these organizational "must haves." If they are conspicuous by their absence, do your best to make their presence felt. The success of your organization's venture depends on their full force.

Organizational Imperatives

The following 10 factors are indispensable to making diversity work in any organization.

1. Demonstrate Commitment at the Highest Levels

Without support from the president or CEO on down, any diversity program will always be sandbagged. It's not that individual managers dedicated to this issue couldn't do some good on their own. They can and should wherever possible. But to change the culture of an organization so that it offers genuine opportunity to all people requires not only support from the top but role modeling as well. A CEO who says he is committed to diversity but never expands the composition of the management team when there is an opening indicates lip service, not genuine commitment. At the highest levels, there has to be a willingness to hold people accountable and an unflinching readiness to invest scarce resources in this endeavor. There is nothing complicated about calibrating the commitment. It's either there or it isn't, and like Hansel and Gretel's crumbs, the clues are dropped all along the way in the choices made every day.

2. Seek Involvement and Commitment from the Bottom Up

Starting with entry-level employees, staff members need help in dealing with the frustrations they experience on a regular basis as they come face-to-face with customs foreign to them. Employees will benefit from training that helps create understanding about the impact of language differences, personal biases, cross-cultural norms, and the fears associated with change or feelings of loss. For an organization to prosper amid diversity, getting the involvement and commitment from those at the bottom ranks is just as critical as getting them from those at the top because it is in the day-in and day-out implementation of policy that irritations, prejudices, and lack of patience can sabotage productivity. A three-hour seminar won't do. Engaging in a long-term, reinforced, and sustained effort is the ticket to really changing organizational culture, up and down the line.

3. Teach a Wide Array of Management Techniques that Work Cross-Culturally

There is a prevailing belief that to be fair means treating all people the same. In truth, being an effective manager today means that you must treat all people with equal dignity, opportunity, and respect, but not necessarily the same. Treating people with equal respect may mean honoring different cultural norms. No managers reared in a homogeneous environment can be expected to adapt their style and techniques to concrete cultural differences without getting some retraining about what these disparities mean on the job. Enlarging the manager's bag of tricks is a worthy goal. Doing so will impact managerial functions such as performance reviews, interviewing, and building effective teams. Any company serious about having a competitive edge has to prepare its managers with the knowledge and information required to do the job. Teaching cross-cultural management tools is a must.

4.   Integrate Diversity into the Fabric of the Organization

As we said, there is a real place for training and education in ensuring a successful diversity venture. Both are necessary and helpful. But unless valuing diversity is built into the organizational bone marrow (i.e., the systems), it risks becoming another add-on or being viewed as a fad. If it remains separate from the operational structure, it will be relegated to a token attempt and conveniently ignored. Building diversity into existing systems and procedures in the areas of recruitment, career development, organizational communication, reward systems, and the like makes diversity an integral part of the organization. The backbone of competitive organizations is an adaptiveness to change. Altering old systems to suit a new work force indicates an earnest effort is afoot.

5.   Expect and Sustain a Long-Term Effort

Changing organizational culture so that it is more fluid, open, and responsive will take patience, perseverance, and vision. Living in a 30-second-sound-bite culture with a proliferation of fast-food chains, drive-in banks, and quarterly reports to stockholders makes it impossible to forget that we are used to instant gratification and results. A long-term change venture is counterculture, but it is also necessary. Clarify expectations at the beginning. Tell staff what's in it for them, and then be honest about the time commitment required. Set up benchmarks along the way so that progress can be duly noted and applauded, and then move right back to the fire—where you are holding those feet.

6.   Accept the New Demographic Reality

We saw the ultimate denial of the new demographic reality several years ago when a student in a doctoral program was so upset at the projected demographic changes that he walked out of the seminar. Most denial is handled in less overt ways but has just as much frustration attached. Accepting the changes in a world both close to home and far away is a significant first step. Our isolationist days are over. The world is too small and significantly intertwined. Beyond that acknowledgment, what's left is to see this change as offering both great opportunities and stimulating challenges. No one said creating harmony from such an amalgam would be easy, but then neither was crossing the continent, building a railroad, or going to the moon. Being the laboratory for this human experiment is our destiny, and the sooner we welcome that reality, the sooner we can make it work in our favor.

7.   Make Rapid Change the Constant

The cliché we grew up with was that the only constant is change, but that was in the 1950s and 60s. If you put that same thought on fast forward, you enter today's world where information explodes and change accelerates so rapidly that everything seems fluid. That's the good news. It also feels unstable, which is the bad news. A physiological verity is that human beings favor homeostasis. This desire for stability is equally true in the psychological arena. While there may be a wide variance in how much change people prefer, for the most part, there is a preference for the solid, secure, and predictable. Yet we find our world today in a state of hyperflux. The organization that is adaptable, flexible, and smart enough to find security in the predictability of change is the organization that will excel and remain healthy, productive, and vital in our swirling world.

8. Be Willing to Pierce the Power and Work through the Discomfort

Henri McClenney, who runs the Puget Sound Recruiting Network, counsels those who use his services that it is difficult to separate pain from change. Henri knows this because he helps employees from organizations around the Seattle area understand that diversity is about sharing power. It is a gritty, tough issue to deal with. Those who have power want to keep it, while those who don't want access to it. His viewpoint is that anger and frustration are a natural part of the process. He expects change but knows it will not come easily. He says with the assurance of his experience that there is no remedy where no one pays. Dialogue is the key to getting through the hard times. Shifting authority and making it more diffuse will not appeal to those who hold the reigns. In the short run, there may be some battle scars on both individuals and the organization alike. But in the long run, piercing the power structure is imperative. It is the most far-reaching way we have of fully investing all the players in our society.

9. Be Honest with Yourself and Others

The changes we are living through demand the best of us. They require stretching, growing, and adapting as we've never done before. In order to make these changes effective, a relentless honesty with the self is a critical starting point. Identifying areas of fear, threat, and discomfort is a must. We all have them. Once we acknowledge them, they are less potent and cease to be a knee-jerk reflex. Honesty can lead to tactful but clear interactions with others that ultimately make a company's diversity results much more positive.

10. Spread Goodwill toward All

As we finish writing this book, it is December of 1991. Chanukah has just ended and we look toward Christmas and the beginning of 1992. This time of year, more than any other, seems to evoke memories of that old-fashioned but essential concept, goodwill. Our lives would be more mean spirited and difficult without it. It is the mortar of the diversity movement, even of civilization itself. We think back to the many people we interviewed during the course of writing this book. We recall the countless examples described to us of human difference that could have led to irritating disruptions and painful conflict. What always saved the day, as clearly as any cape-flying Superman, was generosity of spirit. The bottom line? If you feel warmth and kindness toward people different from you, they will usually feel it and respond in kind. In fact, the Japanese have a proverb, "One kind word can warm three winter months." In the experiences recounted to us, no cultural norm was ever violated that left a harmful residue in the face of goodwill. However, it is not always easy to display respect and charity because it is not always easy to feel. Resources are in short supply, and organizational life can be stressful. But while the information we have written about in the prior pages can and should be extremely helpful, the ace you always have up your sleeve is a generous heart.

Goodwill alone cannot save us. We believe fervently that our competitive edge as a nation will be found in the advantage we gain from mastering the ability to work and live together in our mosaic-like communities. The change from relative homogeneity to extraordinary pluralism can be fraught with the pain of uncertainty. It can either immobilize us with fear and doubt, or we can work our way through it. Only when the latter occurs can we truly be a model for the rest of the world in the most fundamental and critical way. Humankind has no greater experiment at stake. The best of our collective human natures can rise to the challenge and meet it.

Bibliography

1. Adler, Nancy J. "Cultural Synergy: Managing the Impact of Cultural Diversity." *The 1986 Annual: Developing Human Resources*. San Diego: University Associates, 1986.

2. Adler, Nancy J., and Moses K. Kiggunder. "Awareness at the Crossroad: Designing Translator-Based Training Programs." In *Handbook of Intercultural Training*, Vol. II. Don Landes and Richard Breslin. New York: Pergamon, 1983.

3. Allport, Gordon W. *The Nature of Prejudice*. Reading, Mass.: Addison-Wesley, 1959.

4. Bearak, Barry, and David Lauter. "1991 Rights Bill a Return to Earlier Path of Bias Redress." *Los Angeles Times,* November 5, 1991, p. A1.

5. Bennet, Milton J. "Toward Ethnorelativism: A Development Model of Intercultural Sensitivity." In *Cross-Cultural Orientation: New Conceptualizations and Applications*, ed. Michael Paige. New York: University Press of America, 1986, p. 27.

6. Bernstein, Aaron. "Where the Jobs Are Is Where the Skills Aren't." *Business Week*, September 19, 1988, pp. 104–8.

7. Bridges, William. *Surviving Corporate Transition*. New York: Doubleday, 1988.

8. *How to Communicate Better with Clients, Customers, and Workers Whose English Is Limited.* Los Angeles County Commission on Human Relations.

9. "Classes, Those Who Teach Immigrants." *Los Angeles Times,* March 11, 1990, p. B6.

10. Condon, John C. *With Respect to the Japanese*. Yarmouth, Maine: Intercultural Press, 1984.

11. Cook, Mary. "The Workforce of the Year 2000." *Management Review,* August 1989, pp. 5, 34.

12. Dreyfuss, Joel. "Get Ready for the New Workforce." *Fortune,* April 23, 1990, pp. 165–81.

13. Elsea, Janet. *The 4 Minute Sell*. New York: Simon & Schuster, 1984.

14. Farb, Peter. "Man at the Mercy of Language." In *Toward Multiculturalism: A Reader in Multicultural Education*, ed. Jaime S. Wurzel. Yarmouth, Maine: Intercultural Press, 1988, p. 194.

15. "Federal Funds Help Boost Literacy in New Mexico." *California Hospitals,* July/August 1991, pp. 23–25.

16. Foster, Badi G.; Gerald Jackson; William E. Cross; and Rita Hardeman. "Workforce Diversity and Business." *Training and Development Journal,* April 1988, pp. 38–42.

17. Gibb, Jack R. *Trust: A New View of Personal and Organizational Development*. Los Angeles: The Guild of Tutors Press, 1978, pp. 16–17.

18. Hall, Edward T. *The Hidden Dimension*. New York: Doubleday, 1966, p. 49.

19. Harris, Philip R., and Robert T. Moran. *Managing Cultural Differences*. Houston, Tex.: Gulf, 1979, pp. 190–95.

20. Hayes-Bautista, David; Werner Schink; and Jorge Chapa. *Burden of Support: Young Latinos in an Aging Society*. Palo Alto, Calif.: Stanford University Press, 1988.

21. Hugh, Sinclair E., and Edward A. Quesada. "Back to Basics." *Personnel Journal,* October 1990, reprint #2127.

22. Jaffe, Dennis T., and Cynthia D. Scott. *Managing Organizational Change*. Los Altos, Calif.: Crisp Publications, 1989.

23. Johnston, William B., and Arnold E. Packer. *Workforce 2000: Work and Workers for the 21st Century.* Indianapolis, Ind.: Hudson Institute, 1987.

24. Josefowitz, Natasha. *Paths to Power.* Reading, Mass.: Addison-Wesley, 1980.

25. Konrad, Walecia. "Welcome to the Woman-Friendly Company." *Business Week,* August 6, 1990, p. 53.

26. Livingston, Abby. "12 Companies that Do the Right Thing." *Working Woman,* January 1991, p. 60.

27. London, Laura. "Understanding Female Diversity." A document for the Pepsi-Cola Company, November 1991, p. 14.

28. Loden, Marilyn, and Judy B. Rosener. *Workforce America! Managing Employee Diversity as a Vital Resource.* Homewood, Ill.: Business One Irwin, 1991.

29. Maier, Norman R. F. *Problem Solving and Creativity in Individuals and Groups.* Belmont, Calif.: Brooks/Cole, 1970.

30. Michaels, Antony J. "News/Trends: How to Beat Japan." *Fortune,* November 18, 1991, p. 13.

31. Milano, Carol. "Re-evaluating Recruitment to Better Target Top Minority Talent." *Management Review,* August 1989, pp. 30–32.

32. Morley, Eileen. "Management Integration." Paper presented at OD '80—A Conference on Current Theory and Practice in Organizational Development. San Diego: March 1980.

33. Peters, Tom. "Listen Up Guys: Women Fit the Profile of Execs of the Future." *Seattle Post-Intelligencer,* April 11, 1989, p. B6.

34. Romero, Estella. "Reaching Out to the Hispanic Immigrant Workforce." In *Interchange.* Los Angeles: Association of Training and Development, July 1989.

35. Rosener, Judy B. "The Valued Ways Men and Women Lead." *Human Resources,* June 1991, p. 149.

36. Rosener, Judy B. "Ways Women Lead." *Harvard Business Review,* November/December 1990, pp. 119–25.

37. Stowell, Steven J. "Coaching: A Commitment to Leadership." *Training and Development Journal,* June 1988, pp. 34–38.

38. Tannen, Deborah. *You Just Don't Understand: Women and Men in Conversation.* New York: Ballantine, 1990, p. 244.

39. Thiederman, Sondra. *Bridging Cultural Barriers for Corporate Success.* Lexington, Mass.: Lexington Books, 1990, p. 12.

40. Thomas, R. Roosevelt. "From Affirmative Action to Affirming Diversity." *Harvard Business Review,* March/April 1990, p. 108.

41. "Competing in a Seller's Market: Is Corporate America Prepared?" In *Workforce 2000.* Towers Perrin and Hudson Institute, 1990.

42. Watts, Patti. "Bias Busting: Diversity Training in the Workplace." *Management Review,* December 1987, pp. 51–54.

43. Willbur, Jerry. "Does Mentoring Breed Success?" *Training and Development Journal,* November 1987, p. 38.

44. Wolfe, Stephen M. "A New Perspective." *Vis á Vis,* June 1991, p. 12.

45. Woo, Elaine. "Evans School Is an Island of Refuge for Immigrants." *Los Angeles Times,* March 11, 1990, p. A1.

46. Zey, Michael G. "A Mentor for All Reasons." *Personnel Journal,* January 1988, pp. 46–51.

Index

MANAGING DIVERSITY
A Complete Desk Reference and Planning Guide

MANAGING DIVERSITY
A Complete Desk Reference and Planning Guide

Lee Gardenswartz

Anita Rowe

BUSINESS ONE IRWIN
Homewood, Illinois 60430

PFEIFFER & COMPANY
San Diego/Toronto/Amsterdam/Sydney

Copublished by BUSINESS ONE IRWIN/Pfeiffer & Company.

Editor-in-chief: Jeffrey A. Krames
Project editor: Jess Ann Ramirez
Production manager: Bette K. Ittersagen
Designer: Larry J. Cope
Compositor: Precision Typographers
Typeface: 11/13 Times Roman
Printer: Arcata Graphics/Kingsport

Library of Congress Cataloging-in-Publication Data

Gardenswartz, Lee.
    Managing diversity : a complete desk reference and planning guide
/ Lee Gardenswartz, Anita Rowe.
        p.   cm.
    Includes bibliographical references.
    ISBN 1-55623-639-5
    1. Personnel management.   2. Supervision of employees.
3. Minorities—Employment.   4. Psychology, Industrial.   I. Rowe.
Anita.   II. Title.
HF5549.5.M5G37   1993
658.3′041—dc20   92-26322

Printed in the United States of America
1 2 3 4 5 6 7 8 9 0 K 9 8 7 6 5 4 3 2